MEDIUM ÆVUM MONOGRAPHS

EDITORIAL COMMITTEE

K. P. CLARKE, A. J. LAPPIN, S. MOSSMAN

D. RUNDLE, P. RUSSELL, C. SAUNDERS

MEDIUM ÆVUM MONOGRAPHS
XLIII

DARK ARCHIVES
Volume I

Voyages into the Medieval Unread and Unreadable, 2019-2021

Edited By
STEPHEN PINK
&
ANTHONY JOHN LAPPIN

The Society for the Study of Medieval Languages and Literature
OXFORD MMXXII

THE SOCIETY FOR THE STUDY OF
MEDIEVAL LANGUAGES AND LITERATURE
OXFORD, 2022

https://aevum.space/monographs

© The Authors, 2022

British Library Cataloguing in Publication Data
A catalogue record for this book is available from
the British Library

ISBN-13:
978-1-911694-13-7 (hb)
978-1-911694-12-0 (pb)
978-1-911694-14-4 (pdf)

CONTENTS

Introduction. The Emergence of the Medieval Graphosphere: voyages into the unread and unreadable at the Dark Archives conferences, 2019-21.. 1
Stephen Pink and Anthony John Lappin

I. Mapping the Medieval Graphosphere
Loss Rates of Medieval English and Scottish Books 25
Eltjo Buringh

Survival and Loss: working with documents
from Medieval Scotland 61
Joanna Tucker

The Dark Sides of the Runes.. 97
John Hines

Dark Seals in Portuguese Archives.. 125
Maria do Rosário Barbosa Morujão

The Canon and Variants: boundaries and internal variation
in the corpus of Middle English *Pater noster* versifications 145
Monika Opalińska

L'Exploration des archives médiévales en France
avec Biblissima Project 169
Anastasia Shapovalova

II. Endless Deserts, Oceans & Mountains: The Metadata Crisis

Training Generic Models for Handwritten Text Recognition using Transkribus: opportunities & pitfalls 183
Achim Rabus

The Space Between: Jews, Christians & Muslims in Medieval Spain. MOOCS, citizen science, and digital manuscript collections 209
Roger L. Martínez-Dávila

Digital Archives and Damaged Texts: capturing, processing, and sharing multispectral image data 253
Alexander J. Zawacki & Helen Davies

Selva Oscura: in and out of a Dark Archive 269
Debra Taylor Cashion

III. The New Worlds of Medieval Scholarship

Corpus Philology, Big Dating and Bottom-up Periodisation 285
Mark Faulkner

Hidden in Plain Sight: the obfuscation of manuscript evidence in the modern critical edition 315
Michael G. Sargent

The Beautiful Glitch: human and machine in Luciano Floridi's philosophy of information 337
Lapo Lappin

Bibliography 348

The Emergence of the Medieval Graphosphere: Voyages into the Unread and Unreadable at the Dark Archives Conferences, 2019-21

> 'Nel suo profondo
> vidi che s'interna, legato
> con amore in un
> volume, cio che per
> 'l'universo si squaderna'
>
> 'In its depth I saw
> contained, bound with
> love in one volume, what
> is scattered as scraps
> through the universe'[1]
>
> Dante, *Paradiso*,
> XXXIII.85-88

Stephen Pink & Anthony John Lappin

---

[1] English translation indebted to many others, most recently Kirkpatrick 2007.

As we organised the first Dark Archives conference in 2019 on the praxis of digitisation and its impact on medieval studies worldwide, little did we think that we would be arranging its sequels during a worldwide pandemic, with medievalists struggling for access to archives and libraries, even those which had previously been anything but dark. And so this volume, born of the pre-coronal world, in gathering together articles from papers delivered at the first event, forms a composite with those that followed, which were celebrated virtually and have been published as an on-line record of papers delivered, discussions round-tabled, and blogs subsequently posted.[2] The development of Dark Archives into a hybrid, inseparably digital and physical, reflects the broader transformation of medieval studies and indeed our whole world: the digital substitutes which became necessary to living during the lockdowns of 2020 and 2021 have not only persisted afterwards but begun, in often unsettling ways, to blend with the old existence into something new (as in our part inhabitation of the now-omnipresent Zoom).[3] Clearly, we now dwell in a 'Metaverse' (as Neal Stephenson first termed it, and in the full intended sense of its latest proponents)[4] – an inseparably digital and

---

[2] See https://darkarchiv.es for the details of the successive events of 2019-21.

[3] As Elaine Treharne pointed out in her wide-ranging keynote on the relation between the material and the digital at Dark Archives 20 (Treharne 2020), one reason that prolonged Zoom use has felt so draining to many is that 'your eyes and ears take on … the entire responsibility of the in-person meeting'.

[4] Stephenson 1992, passim. Although the term is clearly a conflation of 'universe' and 'meta', the latter is susceptible to a range of interpretation: in OED, as 'beyond, above, at a higher level', certainly, but most relevant to the IT industry's current ambitions to create an indispensable hybrid reality for humanity, as 'denoting change, transformation, permutation, or substitution'. In 2021, reflecting such ambitions, Facebook Inc. renamed itself 'Meta'.

physical life with novel and still emergent properties, often as exotic as those of Jorge Luis Borges' *Orbis Tertius* or 'Third World'.[5]

As one journey therefore halted – the archives became inaccessible (literally dark, in most cases) in ways unknown since the birth of medieval studies – another began. Yet on reflection, this journey has been less one of actual praxis than of acknowledging an existing fact: a vast area of medieval studies has predominately been conducted within a Metaverse for more than a decade, the beneficiary (or victim, some would argue) of inexorable and massive increases in the digitised representations of physical sources, primary and secondary. The present time, *in annis coronae*, has therefore sharpened our awareness of the issues involved in the first Dark Archives conference rather than supplanted them. Our primary concerns, which structured the conference and the present volume, centred around our knowledge of the written heritage (subsumed under the heading of the 'Graphosphere'); its digital records ('metadata') alongside the huge challenge of harvesting, structuring and curating them; and the nature of the future scholarship that may resultantly emerge.

Mapping the medieval Graphosphere

The medieval 'Graphosphere', as we define it, is itself one such emergent Metaverse object – the totality of what was inked, traced, daubed, carved, and scratched in the medieval Old World, from (somewhat arbitrarily) the end of antiquity in the West to its gradual adoption of movable-type printing in the fifteenth century; and, further, the infinitesimal survival of those *scripta* into the present; (other names suggest themselves, such as Michael G. Sargent's

---

[5] The 'third world' is a new existence forged, in Borges' *ficción*, from the leakage into ours of the impossibly fantastic qualities of the world of Tlön; Jorge Luis Borges, 'Tlön, Uqbar, Orbis Tertius' (Borges 1940).

Pleroma (πλήρωμα or 'Fullness'), of the medieval written tradition).[6] Barely grazed by scholarship, to grasp this totality has for centuries been the province of ecstatic vision, theory, fantasy, and horror, but only in the last decade or two, of scientific quest.[7] Hugely lagging the parallel process for printed books, itself largely unaccomplished,[8] we feel ourselves at the equivalent stage of the Age of Discoveries, of multiple missions into the previously unknown, that broadly capped what we ourselves term the Medieval. The reference to the Portuguese expansion is not simply mad self-aggrandisement (brought on by Zoom over-exposure). It captures on the one hand how soaringly the Graphosphere dwarfs our existing working map in extent, and whose proper charting will, we suspect, marginalise the latter as far as the circumnavigators did the *Mappa Mundi*; on the other, the great energies we witnessed at Dark Archives being marshalled to this end. Examples included: the unprecedentedly large Polonsky Foundation-

---

[6] On πλήρωμα, see the debate in Trovato et al. 2021; on its theological connotations, see for example Jn. 1.16. We have drawn the general idea of a 'Graphosphere' from Simon Franklin's *The Russian Graphosphere, 1450-1850* (Franklin 2019), and less directly from Régis Debray's division of human signage into the 'logosphere', 'graphosphere' and 'videosphere' eras (see Debray 1995). Our consideration of the medieval Graphosphere broadly ends where Franklin's begins, chronologically at least, at the rise of movable-type printing in Europe; however, all boundary definitions commonly attaching to 'the medieval', itself hugely problematic, await reconsideration through a proper survey of the Graphosphere itself.

[7] For example Dante, *Paradiso*, XXXIII.85-88, quoted above; Karl Popper's 'Three Worlds' classification (e.g. Popper 1978, 144, 162-63); and Borges' 'Del rigor en la ciencia' (1946), following Lewis Carroll (1893, 169), in which human hubris creates a one-to-one scale map of the world, overlaid upon the world itself, with Babelian outcomes.

[8] In October 2019, Google Books reported that it had scanned more than 40 million printed volumes, in 400 languages, out of its earlier estimated total of c. 130mn (Haimin 2019; Taycher 2010).

The Emergence of the Medieval Graphosphere

funded scanning projects to digitally re-unite bodies of manuscripts dispersed since the medieval period, represented for us by the Polonsky Greek Manuscripts Project;[9] Sarah Savant's presentation on the KITAB digitisation project,[10] which had by around 2020 produced a database of 1.5 billion words of eighth- to fifteenth-century C.E. written Arabic; and the project of the Hill Museum and Manuscript Library to digitally preserve handwritten artefacts from across the globe.[11] Quantifying what is still extant in France's incredibly rich libraries and archives is the topic of Anastasia Shapovalova's paper, which describes the Biblissima project in which she is herself involved, as a tool for exploring this rich cultural reserve.

However, in seeking to even grasp the Graphosphere's vastness our terrestrial analogy falters (while cosmological ones beckon), for it must also encompass what has been lost – a body of 'dark matter', literally unreadable, itself in turn dwarfing the extant (read or unread).[12] The ambition to sketch and eventually restore this lacuna was highlighted at Dark Archives by Beyond2022, with its aim to

---

[9] Christopher Wright and Matteo di Franco spoke on the Polonsky Foundation Greek Manuscripts project, 'From isolation to integration: making Greek manuscripts readable' (DA19). One might point to the ambitious projects to digitize the manuscript holdings of the Herzog August Bibliothek Wolfenbüttel (Holscher & Mähler 2021, covering the Polonsky Foundation's project, 'Manuscripts from German-Speaking Lands') which has had subsequent knock-on effects such as the digitisation of the 127 manuscripts in the Staats- und Universitäts Bibliothek of Bremen between 2020-21, funded by the Deutsche Forschungsgemeinschaft.

[10] Sarah Savant, 'Finding Meaning in 1.5 Billion Words of Arabic: the KITAB project and its aims' (DA19).

[11] Stewart 2020.

[12] On 'dark matter', cosmic and written, see further Michael G. Sargent, 'Hidden in Plain Sight: the obfuscation of manuscript evidence in the modern critical edition', below, 315-35 (315).

reconstruct as fully as possible the centuries of material destroyed in the 1922 fire at Ireland's Public Record Office; Krista Murchison's similar efforts for manuscripts destroyed in the Second World War;[13] Joanna Tucker's presentation, 'Survival and Loss: working with documents from medieval Scotland', where monastic cartularies are excavated for information of lost documents, but disappeared monasteries are also queried for their lost cartularies; and our extended Dark Archives 20 round-table debate on 'Loss and Dispersal', chaired by Elizabeth Solopova.[14] Nor can one speak of the 'lost' as a constant, since it grew unevenly throughout the medieval period and continues to do so, if not at the past's calamitous rates.[15]

If one had to identify an inaugural journey of the Graphosphere era, it would be Eltjo Buringh's *Medieval Manuscript Production in the Latin West: Explorations with a Global Database* (2011).[16] By applying statistics to a small database of manuscript records, Buringh inferred outline numbers, with more detailed breakdowns, for the Latin West's total production from the sixth to the fifteenth centuries – c. 11mn whole manuscripts of which c. 0.75mn remain (albeit with major caveats to the definition of 'manuscript'), part of a more loosely estimated c. 3mn surviving manuscripts, produced as far afield as

---

[13] The project, 'Righting and Rewriting History: recovering and analyzing manuscript archives destroyed during World War II' (Murchison 2020a) will reach its completion in 2023. For her paper at Dark Archives 20/20, see Murchison 2020b.

[14] Solopova 2020.

[15] Further DA19 conference papers were given by Jo Story ('Insular Manuscripts: how many and what next?'; Ralph Cleminson ('Non leguntur: shedding light on Slavonic sources'; Adrien Quéret Podesta ('Textual Ghosts in the Oldest Central European historiography'); Daniel Sawyer ('At Knowledge's Edge: lost materials'), Gustavo Fernández Riva ('Network Analysis of Manuscripts').

[16] Buringh 2011.

The Emergence of the Medieval Graphosphere

Ethiopia and India, from the first to nineteenth centuries.[17] This was a marked development upon previous estimations[18] in its combined method, scale, and sheer ambition – an Erastothenes, Buringh longed to calculate the entirety of Old World medieval manuscript production, but was hampered by the time's limited techniques and (above all) data. Yet both the need and practicality of an interrogable, navigable model of the Graphosphere along these lines has become clearer with each annual flood of fresh data. Therefore we were delighted that Eltjo Buringh contributed the opening Keynote to the first Dark Archives conference, and the first chapter of this Proceedings, with a re-consideration of his methods in the context of lost codices in England and Scotland. It was remarkable to see the influence of his work in a range of other research presented at Dark Archives, including the flowering science of manuscript statistics.[19]

What has also become clearer is that any credible Graphosphere model must embrace not only all geographic areas of production, but all kinds of written artefact – from manuscript fragments (whose enormous scope for reconstructing the medieval was the subject of Lisa Fagin Davis' Dark Archives 20 keynote, and other presentations),[20] and writings neither on parchment nor paper such as graffiti,[21] to artefacts generally ignored as being 'written' at all (despite clearly possessing a laden semantic freight for their original

---

[17] Buringh 2011 (esp. 16-17, 99, 232, 259-63). For example, see the DA20 presentation on the 'elusive archives' of Livonia, whose independent existence ceased relatively early; Ropa & Rops 2020.

[18] See, for example, *Iter italicum* (Kristeller 1967-92; 2006) and the *Medieval Libraries of Great Britain* database (MLGB3, 2009-14).

[19] See also Kestemont & Karsdorp 2020a, 2020b, who adopt an 'unseen species model' used in calculating eco-diversity.

[20] See Fagin Davis 2020, Desmond 2020, Elis-Nilsson 2020.

[21] See Champion 2020 on the 'sea of lost words' carved into the fabric of English churches.

users). Two articles therefore explore the cast and the carved: Rosário Morujão describes the progress made in cataloguing, describing, analysing (from pictographic and chemical points of view) and preserving medieval Portuguese seals ('Dark Seals in Portuguese Archives');[22] and John Hines offers a discussion of the origin and importance of runic inscriptions throughout northern Europe, ending with a particularly illuminating case-study of a runic fragment and its attached object ('The Dark Sides of the Runes').[23] Materiality is here crucially important in the study of the written object, or the object with writing upon or within it.[24] The evident thing-ness of the wax seal, or bridle-bit runically inscribed, encourages us to consider it 'in the round', and so both description and photographic representation have been spurred to capture its 3D accents — such three-dimensional representations are already arriving for manuscripts, providing a depth to the otherwise flattened page and the physical volume of the codex. At the same time, excessive pursuit the perfect simulacrum (in the manner of the facsimiles produced with remarkable exactitude by Ediciones Siloé)[25] can draw us away from the inherent properties and possibilities of digitisation itself, not least that of simply preserving the physical aspects of manuscripts whose very existence, like both the libraries and the archivists that preserve them, is threatened.

[22] See below, 125-44. Seals were also the topic approached at DA19 by John McEwan, 'Reflectance Transformation Imaging and Medieval Seals'.
[23] See below, 97-124.
[24] Further engagement with materiality was found through the DA19 contributions of Henrike Lähnemann ('Nun's Dust'); David King ('The Corpus vitrearum medii aevi'), Ellie Pridgeon ('The Writing on the Wall: medieval painted inscriptions'), and Sarah Fiddyment ('Manuscript Palaeoproteomics').
[25] http://siloe.es. Most recently engaged by the Beinecke Library to produce a facsimile edition of the Voynich manuscript, which retails at around eight thousand euro.

We concluded our Mapping the Medieval Graphosphere session by turning to a third indispensable element of its dark matter, neither completely unknown nor destroyed: those things about which we know but which remain unread or unrated, dark in the archives because they remain unopened. Clearly, some of this neglect is due to difficulties of access, a point brought out by Paul Dryburgh – and sometimes that difficulty is purposeful (see the frustrations of Roger Martínez Davila in certain religious repositories in Spain, and Anna Dorofeeva's presentation on medieval ciphers);[26] but another aspect, as Monika Opalińska's article shows in its unpicking of vernacular English translations of the *Pater noster*, is due to unquestioning reliance on the assumptions of previous scholarship, and in the West a nineteenth- and twentieth-century system of values for the evaluation of its texts – religious texts have suffered particularly from this tendency to marginalize cultural production.[27] To that inheritance of distortions in western materials we must add its working archives of non-European writings, often the outcome of entirely arbitrary choices in the colonial era as to what should be sent home – a distortion which the Arcadia fund is correcting through its drive to digitally scan and preserve texts situated in areas from sub-Saharan Africa to East Asia.[28] We were also honoured to welcome the

[26] Paul Dryburgh, 'Peering into an Impenetrable Gloom and the "Tyranny" of Digital by Design: the future of medieval collections at The National Archives (UK)?' (DA19); Fagin Davis 2020; Dorofeeva 2020.

[27] See below, 145-67. Further DA19 papers on this theme were offered by Mathew Holford ('The Least Studied Manuscripts in the Bodleian') and David Rundle's characteristically provocative think-piece ('The Unbearable Lightness of the Archive').

[28] At DA20, Miri Rubin, Columba Stewart, Cornelis van Lit, and Maja Kominko engaged in an extended debate on 'Inaccessibility and Bias', chaired by Michael G. Sargent. (See Sargent 2020; also Vos 2020, McNutt 2020).

literary historian Yating Zhang, via Zoom, from Shaanxi, for an eye-opening history of the reception of medieval English texts in China, a perspective completely new to most scholars of medieval Europe who dwell on the continent itself or in North America.[29]

Liberation from the assumptions of our education (and that of our supervisors) may be the first great and necessary outcome of mapping the Graphosphere. By opening ever more doors and windows into the archive's darkness, allowing an ever fuller picture to be drawn, we expect so much of what went before (previously taken as the totality of the archive), to be confirmed as a somewhat arbitrary wandering through a fraction. Then we can truly grapple with what has survived and been lost, and fundamentally redraw mental maps of the Middle Ages whose shaky outlines were laid down in the late fifteenth century, or the Victorian age, or the period between the World Wars. Thus in one way, we stand like Henry the Navigator, the recipients of ever-increasing snippets of information that will supplement the metaphorical significance of the *Orbis terrarum* maps beloved of the illuminators of the Beatus manuscripts or the fillers-in of the *mappae mundi*; and in another, we peer like the seventeenth-century scientist Nicolaus Steno at a new historical geology, with the hope of now understanding its sediments and how they were laid down, in place of former explanations of self-serving etiologies.

See also the DA20 debate chaired by Suzanne Paul on 'The Future Archive' (Paul 2020).

[29] Zhang 2020.

Detail from *The Vision of St. Benedict* (Giovanni del Biondo, 14th Century).[30]

This depiction of Benedict's vision of 'the whole world ... as if gathered together' stands out in the tradition for accentuating the spherical aspect of the *Orbis terrarum*, and thus (somewhat contradictorily) that a portion is obscured from Benedict's as well as our direct view.[31]

Endless deserts, oceans & mountains: the Metadata Crisis

At both Dark Archives 19 and 20 we necessarily turned from the theoretical survey of the Graphosphere to the central practical challenge we must solve before we can even begin to own its territory – the 'Metadata Crisis', as our second keynote of Dark Archives 19, Will Noel, put it.[32] This crisis has been acutely one of scarcity of digital information, and the variable quality of much of what there is. Our physical written heritage remains overwhelmingly unscanned in a usable fashion, let alone described, most of all because of the prohibitive expense of doing so, limiting even the best-funded

---

[30] The original is in the Art Gallery of Ontario (https://ago.ca/collection/object/52/37).
[31] Gregory the Great, *Dialogi*, II, 35.
[32] Will Noel, 'Through a Screen Darkly: the Metadata Crisis and the authority of the digital image'. Further, at DA19, Toby Burrows ('Aggregating Provenance Metadata to Reveal the Histories of Medieval Manuscripts') showed how metadata can be used to good effect.

scanning initiatives to strategic selections of a few thousand folio pages.[33] We were pleased to welcome some of the major funders of these initiative for an insight into their motivations, represented by Marc Polonsky of the Polonsky Foundation, Maja Kominko and Simon Chaplin of Arcadia Fund, and Daniel Reid of the Whiting Foundation.[34] The 2019 Notre Dame fire reminded us of the pricelessness for their own sake of digital records of our vulnerable medieval heritage, quite besides that of data extraction – and until recently, indeed, one would have to question the latter motivation. By even an optimistic guess of numbers of people currently capable of reading a handwritten medieval text (and the rosiest forecasts for training more) it might take millennia to transcribe them all.[35]

To our initial rescue, *ex machina*, may come automated Optical Character Recognition (OCR), or for medieval manuscripts more precisely, Optical Handwriting Recognition (OHR). Previously a collection of techniques only achieving useful (if far from total) accuracy with uniform post-Gutenberg printed type, Achim Rabus' article demonstrates the huge progress, as well as limits, of the *Transkribus* project in machine reading the vastly greater complexity and variability of medieval handwriting.[36] Dark Archives was also privileged to hear Verónica Romero, from the Universidad Politécnica of Valencia, speaking on their own OHR successes;

---

[33] Marc Polonsky discussed the various strategies adopted by the Polonsky foundation in his address, 'Digitisation of Cultural Heritage: a funder's perspective' (DA19). Ben Kiessling, 'The Limits to Digitization' (DA19) sounded a warning note over some of these processes.

[34] 'Discussion: Funders' Perspectives', chaired by Peter Frankopan (Frankopan 2020).

[35] Thrope 2020 discussed the difficulties of balancing accessibility with the reading experience in making public the digitized Arabic manuscripts of the National Library of Israel.

[36] Achim Rabus, 'Training Generic Models of Handwritten Text Recognition using *Transkribus*: opportunities & pitfalls', below, 183-208.

Vincent Christlein who presented his own work on algorithm-driven identification of scribes, dating of hands and the recognition of document types, and Estelle Guéville and David Joseph Wrisley on advances in machine-reading manuscript abbreviations.[37] Roger Martínez Davila's article in this volume approaches the same problem with a truly impressive alternative: the harnessing of the general public, and its interest in its own heritage, to transcribe documents via Massive Online Open Courses (MOOCS) with high accuracy – in this case, the archives of multi-confessional medieval Iberia;[38] a similar approach but with more specific goals was the *La Sfera* transcription competition described for us by two of its organisers, Laura Morreale and Ben Albritton.[39] Effective not only in transcribing texts beyond the competence of current OHR, the results of such crowd-sourced endeavours can also be used in turn to train yet more accurate OHR models. Indeed, with the advent of ever more powerful forms of machine-learning, the latest of which teach themselves without human re-training, it seems only a matter of time before machines deliver a huge new archive of materials that medieval studies will then be obliged to incorporate within itself.[40]

However, exactly such progress in automation is hastening what we believe to be the crux of the Metadata Crisis: not the scarcity but the potential endlessness of information about a physical written

---

[37] Verónica Romero, 'Interactive-Predictive Transcription and Probabilistic Text Indexing for Handwritten Image Collections' (DA19); Vincent Christlein, 'Scribal Identification and Document Classification' (DA19); Guéville and Wrisley 2020.

[38] Roger L. Martínez-Dávila, 'The Space Between: Jews, Christians, and Muslims in Medieval Spain. *MOOCS*, citizen science, and digital manuscript collections', below, 209-51.

[39] Morreale & Albritton 2020

[40] See Hassabis 2019 on the ground-breaking AlphaGo Zero and 'The Power of Self-Learning Systems'; Mattingly 2021.

artefact that might be digitally captured and represented. Throughout *Dark Archives*, the related debates on what the digital can, cannot or can only capture of the physical have often seemed at root metaphysical (and emotively so, amplified by the unique stresses of the pandemic). At the Dark Archives 20 panel, 'The Whole Book?', chaired by Lisa Fagin Davis, and its associated papers there emerged on the one hand a palpable excitement that we now possessed a new object of study, inseparably material artefact and digital representation, generated by their constant interplay (see, for example, the presentation of Lena Vosding, Natascha Domeisen, Luise Morawetz, and Carolin Gluchowski).[41] On the other there was great discomfort at the huge potential damage of equating digitised information, no matter how plentiful, with the *ipsissima res* of each unique medieval manuscript. Indeed, it was argued, the futile quest for digital verisimilitude of the physical should be abandoned, so that the digital may be re-evaluated on its own terms.[42] Yet, before our eyes, such debates are fast being sidelined by the onrush of data now being generated, with manuscript folio images alone now numbering in the millions. Its sheer range and quantity was on display at Dark Archives, from Vincent Christlein and Daniel Stromer's digital unwrapping of fragile rolls of text using tomography, and Alexander J. Zawacki and Helen Davies' related recovery of palimpsested text via spectrography, to Sarah Fiddyment's capturing of the DNA and other biological markers left on codices – the very 'writing of life', of huge significance to a range of historical enquiries beyond codicology itself.[43]

It is this tsunami of unprocessed information that threatens to define our Metadata Crisis as one of 'superabundance', as Elaine

---

[41] Fagin Davis et al. 2020; Morawetz, Domeisen, Gluchowski & Vosding 2020. See further discussion of this phenomenon in Lapo Lappin, 'The Beautiful Glitch: human and machine in Luciano Floridi's philosophy of information', below, 337-55 (esp. 345-46).

[42] Brookes 2020; Treharne 2020.

[43] Fiddyment 2020.

Treharne termed it in her Dark Archives 20/20 keynote. In fact, this superabundance is welcomed by Treharne and others as a transforming catalyst to scholarship, premised upon automated machine-categorisation evolving to carve out navigable pathways for human scholarly explorers. The power of such algorithms to classify manuscript images was already on display in her collaborator Ben Albritton's presentation (in this case, by isolating illuminated initials); techniques promising to knit our digital records, regardless of the fragmentation of metadata and physical sources, into a massive, open and online 'Future Archive' (these issues and more explored in the eponymous panel chaired by Suzanne Paul).[44] We also saw how other medieval data scientists are working to lend such images at least a metadata skeleton, as witnessed by Andrew Hankinson's presentation on the crucial International Image Inter-operability Framework (IIIF) protocols in which major scanning initiatives are now encoded.[45] Likewise, Debra Cashion's article here presented ('Selva Oscura: in and out of a dark archive') demonstrated the great use to researchers of the attachment of provisional meta-data to digitised images.[46] Yet without rapid advances, *ex machina,* of the kind anticipated by Treharne to structure, interrogate, and interpret the data – a recurrent demand of our contributors – we are faced with what Zawacki and Davies term a 'new kind of dark archive … a "digital palimpsest"'.[47]

Moreover, as William Mattingly's Dark Archives 20/21 presentation at 'UnEdition' soberingly brings home, the very likelihood that independent self-teaching AI will complete the

---

[44] Treharne 2020, Albritton 2020, Paul 2020.
[45] Andrew Hankinson, 'Discovery through Data: how IIIF shines a light into the dark archive' (DA19); Albritton 2020.
[46] See below, 265-78.
[47] Alexander J. Zawacki and Helen Davies, 'Digital Archives and Damaged Texts: Capturing, Processing, and Sharing Multispectral Image Data', below, 253-67 (267).

scanning of our archive without human input threatens us not only with a vast further body of data, but one which we may not immediately, fully (or ever) comprehend, or trust.[48] As of 2022, such a scenario seems closer than ever with the astonishing progress and apparent creativity shown by machine interpretation of humanity's cultural heritage, along with indifference to our distinctions between 'truth' and 'fiction', as demonstrated by services such as *Dall-E* and *ChatGPT*.[49]

Thus, the lesson of our current struggle with metadata may be that setting out to know the medieval Graphosphere in any exhaustive, enumerative sense will achieve the very opposite, for its emerging territories and cruxes have the endlessness of a Mandelbrot fractal; as one kind of *Terra Incognita* disappears, a vaster one takes its place. We have (perhaps comfortingly) come full circle. Yet, what should our goals be, if that of complete discovery is futile?

New worlds of medieval scholarship

Among major grounds for optimism is that medievalists are already constructing the worlds of scholarship that a realised Graphosphere might make possible – moreover these are evolutions, not supersessions, of existing scholarly techniques. One such field was demonstrated by Mark Faulkner, whose 'Corpus Philology, Big Dating and Bottom-Up Periodisation' brings that most traditional of disciplines, philology, into fruitful commerce with the developments in corpus linguistics over the last decades. As the title suggests, he imagines the scope of a fully realised digital corpus of medieval textual materials to uncover vernacular linguistic features previously un-systematised, or even simply ignored, in older surveys on which we

---

[48] Mattingly 2021.
[49] *DALL E 2* 2022 (https://openai.com/dall-e-2/); *ChatGPT* 2022 (https://chat.Openai.com/).

have relied. We may thereby transform, from 'the bottom up', our placement of 'the composition of texts in time and space'.[50] This approach indicates how medieval 'Big Data' may rebuild the entire foundation of assumptions upon which current medieval scholarship rests, as was on display throughout Dark Archives and specifically debated at our Dark Archives 20 Round-Table debate, 'The Future of Scholarship', chaired by Peter Frankopan.[51]

Perhaps the most often articulated ambition in the Dark Archives events was to liberate the scholarly presentations of texts from the constraints of the static two-dimensional page and dominant single-manuscript edition. Thus William G. Sargent's article invokes William Gibson's three-dimensional 'Cyberspace' (an inspiration for the 'Metaverse'): a realm of free mental movement to be contrasted with the crabbed world of our physical existence. In Cyberspace, Sargent suggests, we might finally experience the fullness of manuscript traditions – each represented as an independent 'arcology' with its dizzyingly complex networks of variances, distributions, sequence of recensions, and links to other such arcologies. Thereby we might dispel the 'obfuscation' of fixed print snapshots.[52] We were able to follow up this vision of the future Edition – or of the 'UnEdition', as Laura Morreale and Ben Albritton termed it, at an eponymous Dark Archives 20/21 event chaired by Paolo Trovato.[53] Presentations ranged from that of Wouter Haverals and Mike Kestemont on 'UnEditing the Herne Corpus', via a massively 'hyperdiplomatic', rapidly updateable and interactive digital edition of that monastery's entire library, through to Anthony Bale's evocation of the breathtaking permutations of John Mandeville's

---

[50] See below, 280-308. See also Scott Bruce's presentation at DA20 (Bruce 2020).
[51] Frankopan 2020.
[52] See Sargent, 'Hidden in Plain Sight', below, 315-35.
[53] Trovato 2021.

Travels as its own manuscripts voyaged through Europe's vernaculars – its true tale (inaccessible to rescensionist quests for an originary exemplar) one of constant re-fashioning in its medieval audiences' imaginations.[54]

However, UnEdition also made clear that a truly useful representation of this complexity still belongs to a more advanced ludic future age (except, that is, via the royal road of narrative description demonstrated by Bale himself). One route ahead was signalled by the Digital Editions Live workshop co-hosted by Dark Archives in 2021 (with Oxford Medieval Studies, and OCTET, the Oxford Centre for Textual Editing and Theory), reflecting on the digital editions recently crafted by Oxford medievalist students, based upon the protocols of the Text Encoding Initiative (TEI).[55] Perhaps the event's greatest lesson in this regard was that scholarly discernment, including traditional rescensionist editing skills, will be more important than ever in crafting useful scholarship from the vast amounts of data now available. Another lesson was the pressing need (as in humanities *tout court*), for a proactive digital pedagogy to gradually incorporate these new skills, even as digital technology itself constantly evolves. Perhaps the most novel aspect of Digital Editions Live was the augmentation of each presentation with a 'live-feed' consultation, from the Bodleian, of the physical original, an art brought to perfection by Andrew Dunning (so dramatically present did the three-dimensional physical artefact feel that one convenor nearly shouted when a student's desktop cup of coffee appeared side-by-side with 'her' manuscript on the screen)!

Digital Editions Live is also the latest of our learning experiences in crafting the Dark Archives series itself, which now ranges from the workshops of 2019 (which covered skills from spectrography, and the scanning of seals on a budget, to crowdsourcing transcriptions) to the

---

[54] Haverals & Kestemont 2021; Bale 2021.
[55] *Digital Editions Live* 2021.

organising of subsequent events online in and after lockdown.[56] Freed from the constraints of physical space and (in many ways) time, and to involve a truly global audience, we arranged for Dark Archives 20 presentations to be entirely pre-recorded, pre-captioned (by computer, sometimes amusingly) and released several days ahead of the scheduled live panels, with all participants encouraged to digest them beforehand. This front-loaded approach allowed us to concentrate the live events themselves (also computer live-captioned) in the early afternoon to early evening GMT, maximising the active attendance of many hundreds from as far afield as the US West Coast and China. Alongside the Zoom events we ran a separate online text forum (on 'Discord') allowing discussion of themes at any time. Behind the scenes the event was kept going by shifts of unseen but vital online moderators, from Oxford Medieval Studies, the University of Fribourg, and the University of Colorado (Colorado Springs). This born-digital approach also greatly facilitated the creation of a comprehensive digital archive of the event's metadata (to fuel future discussion, events and scholarship (see https://darkarchiv.es). Yet among the most impressive achievements were those 'outreach' events that took place between the main sessions: the 'Blogging with Manuscripts' Presentations and Prize (also awarded via Zoom) associated with the #PolonskyGerman Project;[57] and, finally, 'Singing Together. Apart', an extraordinary Zoom Compline in the evening (GMT) of the second day, which

---

[56] All at DA19: Verónica Romero, 'Hands-on Workshop on Assistive Technologies to Access the Contents of Handwritten Text Manuscripts'; John McEwan, 'Imaging Seals on a Budget'; Roger Louis Martinez-Davila, 'Crowdsourcing Manuscript Transcriptions: opportunities and challenges using MOOCs, social media, and emerging platforms'; Alexander Zawacki and Helen Davies, 'Multispectral Imaging: technologies, techniques, and teaching'.

[57] Lähnemann et al. 2021.

united in perfect synchrony singers physically dispersed across many locations (from St Edmund Hall's crypt to the Church of St Barnabas Church in Jericho) together with all of the people who digitally attended from around the world.[58]

*

Throughout our discussions at Dark Archives has run a quandary, explicitly or in the background — what truly *is* a digital representation of a material thing; what truly *are* the two taken together? Far from being esoteric, in the last few years we have recognised it to be an existential issue, for it has convulsed all our lives, and as yet we have no answers. To explore it more broadly, we invited Luciano Floridi to present a Dark Archives keynote, to which he very graciously agreed.[59] However, his planned article became another casualty of the times, as he became wholly involved in advising on various privacy issues regarding the UK Government's 'worldbeating' COVID-19 app that would potentially allow an efficient track-and-trace operation to be launched, thereby saving countless lives. Professor Floridi's contribution to the philosophy of information has been so important that we sought another philosopher who might be able to give an overview of Floridi's thought and its implications for digital humanities – in particular Floridi's situating the historical archive at the heart of human life via the digital, as encapsulated in his conception of *hyperhistory* (our dependence upon the digital, and our incessant creation of digital traces).[60]

Whatever our future digital representation of the medieval world, already clear is that it will not be the nightmare of Borges' *Tlön*. Rather, it *is* the medieval world in ways that we have never before experienced it, part of its physical existence as inseparably and

[58] St. Edmund Hall Choir & friend 2020.
[59] Luciano Floridi, 'Semantic Capital: its nature and value' (DA19).
[60] Lappin, 'The Beautiful Glitch', below, 331-48.

magically as Dante's vision in *Paradiso* of the pages scattered throughout the universe, beheld re-bound 'in one simple light'.[61] Our manner of marvelling at this has taken the form of articles — such as those here — and blogs and presentations —such as those found on our website—followed by questions and the search for answers, the discussions of roundtables, all of which have deepened our knowledge of the written universe beyond us. We hope that the volume you hold in your hands, or your eyes scan on a screen, will mark the beginning of numerous exploratory paths for you into this newly revealed world.

Acknowledgements
We must thank everyone who has made the Dark Archives series thus far possible, including our presenters, panelists and chairs, and all those who kept things running behind the scenes: Pablo Acosta-García, Tuija Ainonen, Benjamin L. Albritton, Anthony Bale, Graham Barrett, Zoe Bartliff, Josephine Bewerunge, Elizabeth Biggs, Mary Boyle, Stewart J. Brookes, Scott Bruce, Eltjo Buringh, Toby Burrows, Daron Burrows, Debra Cashion, Matthew Champion, Simon Chaplin, Vincent Christlein, Sophie Clayton, Ralph Cleminson, Julia Craig-McFeely, Robin Darwall-Smith, Helen Davies, Karen Demond, Matteo di Franco, Maria do Rosário Morujão, Natascha Domeisen, Anna Dorofeeva, Sebastian Dows-Miller, Paul Dryburgh, Andrew Dunning, Sara Elis-Nilsson, Lisa Fagin Davis, Mark Faulkner, Gustavo Fernández Riva, Sarah Fiddyment, Chris Fletcher, Molly Ford, Alex Franklin, Peter Frankopan, Carolin Gluchowski, Emma Goodwin, Estelle Guéville, Andrew Hankinson, Wouter Haverals, Carrie Heusinkveld, Sam Heywood, John Hines, Matthew Holford, Kyle Ann Huskin, Folgert Karsdorp, Martin Kauffmann, Mike Kestemont, Ben Kiessling, Lynn Killgallon, David King, Maja Kominko, Pavlina Kulagina, Henrike Lähnemann, Franziska Lallinger, Andres Laubinger, Caroline

---

[61] Dante, Paradiso, XXXIII.85-90.

Lehnert, Molly Lewis, James Louis Smith, Roger Louis Martinez-Davila, William Mattingly, John McEwan, Genevieve McNutt, Luise Morawetz, Laura Morreale, Krista Murchison, Eva Neufeind, Mary Newman, Will Noel, Monika Opalińska, Richard Ovenden, Nigel F. Palmer, Suzanne Paul, Luca Polidoro, Marc Polonsky, Dot Porter, Ellie Pridgeon, Adrien Quéret-Podesta, Achim Rabus, Henry Ravenhall, Daniel Reid, Tom Revell, Shannon Ritchey, Jane Roberts, Natasha Romanova, Verónica Romero, Anastasija Ropa, Edgar Rops, Miri Rubin, David Rundle, Rebeca Sanmartin Bastida, Michael G. Sargent, Sarah Savant, Daniel Sawyer, Marlene Schilling, Carolin Schreiber, Anastasia Shapovalova, Elizabeth Solopova, Lesley Smith, Emma Stanford, Alyssa Steiner, Columba Stewart, Jo Story, Justin Stover, Daniel Stromer, Jane H.M. Taylor, Keri Thomas, Samuel Thrope, Elaine Treharne, Paolo Trovato, Joanna Tucker, Cornelis van Lit, Stacie Vos, Lena Vosding, Julia Walworth, Michelle R. Warren, Teresa Webber, Thomas White, Pip Willcox, Lois Williams, Damon Wischik, Christopher Wright, David Joseph Wrisley, Ulrike Wuttke, Alexander Zawacki, and Yating Zhang. Finally, we must thank our sponsors, *sine qua non*: Medium Ævum, Oxford Medieval Studies, the Bodleian Library, and the Oxford English Faculty which freely and graciously provided our venue for the first physical conference in 2019.

Stephen Pink
Anthony John Lappin

I. Mapping the Medieval Graphosphere

LOSS RATES OF MEDIEVAL ENGLISH AND SCOTTISH BOOKS

Eltjo Buringh[1]

Abstract

The new online beta-version of MLGB3 contains the titles of books and their survival from Medieval Libraries in Great Britain.[2] This data allows the calculation of loss rates in percent per century (essential for reconstructing medieval book production). The current – and substantially larger – data set of English and Scottish loss rates turns out to be rather similar to previously published values for the twelfth to sixteenth centuries. Regression analysis and a simulation model substantiate the previous default value (–25 %) of medieval manuscript losses per century and, therefore, the previous numerical reconstruction of medieval book production also still stands.

---

[1] The original text of my contribution to the 'Dark Archives' conference can be found in Buringh 2014. A shorter and more general version is Buringh & van Zanden 2009, while a more detailed version can be consulted in Buringh 2011. I would like to very much thank James Willoughby and Teresa Webber for reading and commenting on a previous version of this paper that arose as a result of the discussions during the 'Dark Archives' conference. Of course, I am solely responsible for the contents of this paper and all mistakes it contains are mine.

[2] MLGB3 2009-14.

Introduction

In the recent past a quantitative reconstruction of book production has shed light on the development of the European economy (Buringh & Van Zanden 2009). Books were thereby seen as a proxy for ideas, which are an important variable in the theory of economic growth. One of the essential elements in this reconstruction of medieval book production are the loss rates of manuscript books from libraries. The way that some of these have been estimated by Buringh 2011, 179, was questioned during the 2019 *Dark Archives* conference in Oxford.[3] Teresa Webber raised the point that Neil Ker, 1964, had excluded manuscripts still surviving at their original medieval colleges from his *Medieval Libraries of Great Britain*, which in the past has been the major source of British loss rates. The previously excluded data is currently being added to the online version of Medieval Libraries of Great Britain. Inclusion of these surviving manuscripts not mentioned in Ker (1964) substantially changes a number of previously estimated loss rates for Oxford and Cambridge colleges. This justifies a closer look at the newly available data and their overall influence on British loss rates, and thus possibly on the reconstruction of medieval book production as well.

In the first section of this paper I describe the wealth of data on medieval library records that has become available with the beta-version of MLGB3, and that allows a calculation of loss rates (of samples) from libraries or other collections of books. In the next section of this paper I report around hundred and eighty new estimates of loss rates for medieval book lists in England and Scotland based on MLGB3 and additionally nearly thirty loss-rate estimates based on previous research (not covered by MLGB3, but to be found in Annexes L and N from Buringh 2011). The total number of loss-rate estimates from the twelfth to sixteenth century inclusive has thereby nearly quadrupled compared to the previous exercise. Such

---

[3] DA 2019.

an increase was possible because of the great number of medieval lists from medieval English and Scottish libraries that have now become accessible online in MLGB3. The fourth section describes how this larger set of new loss rates (with of course somewhat different values) nevertheless turns out to be quite similar in nature to the older, smaller set. Finally, I will delve into the ins-and-outs of my approach and conclude that these new loss rate estimates do not really qualify the previous quantitative reconstruction of European book production.

The online version of MLGB3

Already at the turn of the twentieth century, M.R. James had begun editing medieval library catalogues from the British Isles. By the nineteen-forties it was the firm ambition of many scholars to produce editions of such documents, and in the eighties a project was started to collect and edit all extant medieval lists of books in institutional ownership from Britain, as a follow-up to the work of Neil Ker and others on medieval inventories of book holdings, borrowing lists, records of donations, etc. Early on, R.A.B. Mynors, Professor of Latin at Oxford, played a leading role in the project. His edition of the *Registrum Anglie* was published in 1991 (Rouse et al. 1991). The actual electronic resource, *Medieval Libraries of Great Britain* (MLGB3), was begun in 2009 with funding from the Andrew W. Mellon Foundation and from the Neil Ker Memorial Fund together with the institutional support of the Bodleian Library. MLGB3 is an electronic and enhanced version of Ker's *Medieval Libraries of Great Britain* (i.e. listing surviving books, not medieval records of book ownership), and therefore not strictly speaking an outcome of the project to edit the various British book lists (the Corpus of British Medieval Library Catalogues). Richard Sharpe and James Willoughby direct this online resource which has turned out to be a real treasure trove because of its inclusion of numerous medieval records. The version that was consulted when writing this paper was the beta-version of September/October 2019.

It is planned that MLGB3 will eventually encompass some 920 medieval book lists, catalogues, inventories, bequests, commissions, donations, and so on, from libraries in Great Britain.[4] It remains a work-in-progress because it requires meticulous, time-consuming labour. There are 215 lists that still have to be included online. However, not all of the currently available lists are usable by me to estimate loss rates of manuscripts because they do not contain information on enough medieval books. In order to minimize bias and to prevent substantial 'noise' in the estimates of loss rates, the main criterion for inclusion of a medieval library or list in the current paper was that it contained a minimum number of ten manuscript books. A second criterion was that the numbers of manuscripts had to be unambiguous. Some lists (all post 1450) had therefore to be left aside because the numbers of printed books could not be reliably estimated and then subtracted from the surviving manuscript books in which we are solely interested. These two criteria mean that 526 lists are not usable for our purposes (of these unusable lists, 175 only mentioned one or two handwritten books). Nevertheless, this still leaves us with the enormous number of 179 lists, containing ten or more manuscript books, that can be used for estimates of medieval loss rates from libraries (173 in England and 6 in Scotland). These new data considerably expand the previously available information on surviving medieval books from Britain.

The previously described two criteria, used to include a book list mentioned in MLGB3, imply that only those inventories, catalogues or bequests have been included that described ten or more manuscripts (the reason for excluding lists with fewer manuscripts being that these would introduce a bias and more uncertainty into the

---

[4] Not counting the lists of Henry de Kirkestede and the *Registrum Anglie*.

estimated loss rates)[5]. Additionally, later fifteenth-century lists have been omitted when there was no clear way of determining the fraction of printed books. All manuscripts marked in MLGB3 with an asterisk, or indicated in MLGB3 as belonging to one of the surviving books on the lists in a medieval library (and not being printed books) have been counted as a surviving manuscript. Possible survivals marked in MLGB3 (with 'perhaps ?' or '?') have all been assumed to be actual survivals.[6] When there were very large gaps in the numbering of the medieval lists, such missing numbers have not been counted as manuscripts so as not to overestimate loss rates.

The calculation of the uniform loss rates was similarly executed to what has been reported previously by Buringh 2011, 54.[7] The original number of manuscripts (b) as well as the surviving numbers (c) have been derived from MLGB3. For the date in the past (B), expressed in units of whole centuries, I have used the date indicated in MLGB3 of the medieval list or bequest, or its arithmetic average when a range of years was reported. For the current date of MLGB3 I used the year 2015, which results in 20.15 when expressed in whole centuries. The

---

[5] Of course the eventually surviving number of manuscript books can be substantially lower than ten. Even zero survival of a specific medieval list was used to calculate a loss rate, by assuming a surviving number of 0.4, see Buringh 2011, 55 where this approach is explained.

[6] One problem is that not all book lists contain sufficient information in their entries to identify with certainty an entry with a particular manuscript. This may lead to an underestimate of the surviving manuscripts of a specific medieval list, and therefore also all possible attributions have been counted as certain. These unidentifiable manuscripts are a rather fundamental problem of my approach. How this works out numerically in the actual loss rates will be discussed in more detail in the final discussion section.

[7] With a uniform loss-rate we mean that for every century starting with the original date B in the past up to 2015 a similar fraction (percentage) of the library in question is assumed to have been lost.

formula for calculating a uniform loss rate (L_i) in percent per century of a medieval book list at time i is then as follows:

$$L_i = -\,(\,1 - \exp\,(\,\ln\,(c/b)\,/\,(20.15 - B)\,)\,)\,*\,100\,\%$$

The values for the individual libraries and lists derived from MLGB3 are reported in Annex A, organised by year of the list, and complemented with 29 previously estimated loss rates (Annexes L and N from Buringh, 2011) from Great Britain that were not covered by MLGB3. As a matter of course, all sources have been referenced in Annex A.

Average loss rates in Great Britain

In total we now have 204 uniform loss rates from British book lists between the twelfth and sixteenth centuries, which is a considerable increase upon the mere 52 loss rates previously reported by Buringh 2011. Just as was done before, the geometric mean per century has been determined by the individual loss rates. We use this geometric average in order to minimize the influence of outliers. The results of the new exercise including the currently available information in the beta-version of MLGB3,[8] alongside the old estimates (still from before MLGB3), are reported in Table 1.

---

[8] The beta-version of MLGB3 was accessed in the months of September and October 2019.

Table 1

Old and new geometric mean loss rates in percent per century in medieval book lists from England and Scotland.

	12th	13th	14th	15th	16th
old- N =	4	6	15	21	6
old loss rates	-22 %	-28 %	-37 %	-39 %	-44 %
new- N =	16	20	47	80	41
new loss rates	-28 %	-32 %	-37 %	-38 %	-37 %

Sources: Annex A of this paper and annexes L and N and p. 194 in Buringh 2011.

Of course, the new inclusion of the surviving manuscripts from a number of colleges in Oxford and Cambridge, missed in the calculations done before 2011, has led to a lower individual loss rate than previously estimated for those specific institutions. For instance, when all *in situ* surviving medieval books are included for Peterhouse in Cambridge, the average medieval loss rate (based on a list of 1418) changes from −47 % previously to −13 % per century. And for Lincoln College (Oxford) it decreases from −44 % to −18 % per century, based on all surviving manuscript books on a 1474 list from this college. However, Table 1 shows that overall the geometric average values of the loss rates in the twelfth and thirteenth centuries seem to have gone up somewhat, and those later, in the sixteenth century, to have gone down. Each of these three centuries with their substantially changed loss rates had only six or fewer samples contributing to the old loss rate estimates.

The new calculations, with their higher number of samples, indicate that we have to take these new numerical values presented in Table 1 more seriously than those of the previous estimates because we now have considerably more data points. Especially when comparing the current and previous estimates for the fourteenth and fifteenth centuries we see that there is little change - for both estimates we had fifteen to twenty samples in the first attempt (without MLGB3) and more than triple that number in the last exercise with MLGB3. Based on statistical intuition such a higher number of samples should be more stable over time, which Table 1 confirms. The geometric mean of the 92 independently calculated loss rates for the *Registrum Anglie* (Rouse et al., 1991) comes to a loss rate of −37 % for the fourteenth century in England, (see Buringh 2011, 194 and annex M), comparing very well with the same value of −37 % found in Table 1. Please note that the loss rates derived from the *Registrum Anglie* are based on a very different sample of libraries in Great Britain. It is important to stress that the general pattern of the new loss rates shown in Table 1 (showing lower loss rates in the earlier centuries which become higher over time) is rather similar to that of the old loss rates. A possible explanation for this unexpected phenomenon of increasing uniform loss rates over time will be presented in the next section.

Just as with the old loss rates (Buringh 2011, 197) the new ones have no relationship with the original size of the book list or bequest. Figure 1 presents this (lack of) relationship for the ^{10}log of the various list sizes, expressed as numbers of books. Because of the criterion for inclusion, all lists contained ten or more manuscripts, which results in the list-size on the x-axis in Figure 1 starting at a value of 1, meaning 10^1, or ten manuscript books, etc. The value 2 on the x-axis in Figure 1 indicates 100 books (10^2), while 3 stands for 1,000 books (10^3). The ^{10}log has been used here to clarify what would otherwise have been a clustering around the low library sizes, which could have obfuscated the overall picture when looking at a data cloud on a linear scale. The R-square of zero in Figure 1 indicates that there is no relationship whatsoever between the medieval list sizes and the magnitude of the later book losses.

Figure 1

Medieval list size (^{10} log) on the x-axis and the new loss rates (in percent per century) on the y-axis.

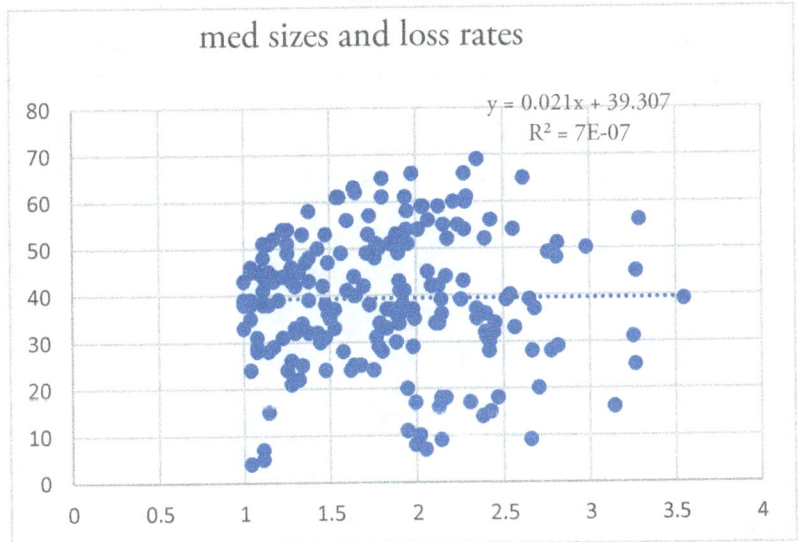

Source: Annex A of this paper.

Strictly speaking, when no manuscripts survive from a medieval list a loss rate cannot be calculated with the formula presented above (because taking a logarithm of zero is impossible). Therefore, in Buringh, 2011, 55, the loss rate for such a list with zero survivals was calculated by assuming 0.4 of a surviving manuscript instead of 0. Because we have varying numbers of surviving manuscripts in most of the lists, we can find out if such an approach can be corroborated by the loss rates that we determined from actual survivals. By classifying all British loss rates into a few broad classes of surviving numbers of manuscripts (based on the various powers of 2: [2^0 to 2^1] is the class with 1-3 surviving manuscripts; [2^2 to 2^3] is the class with

4-15 manuscripts, etc.) and calculating the geometric mean of these classes, we can produce Figure 2 from the data.

Figure 2

Geometric mean of the loss rates (in percent per century) (y-axis) for four size classes of surviving manuscripts (x-axis: 1= 1-3 mss; 2= 4-15 mss; 3= 16-63 mss; 4= 64 mss and over).

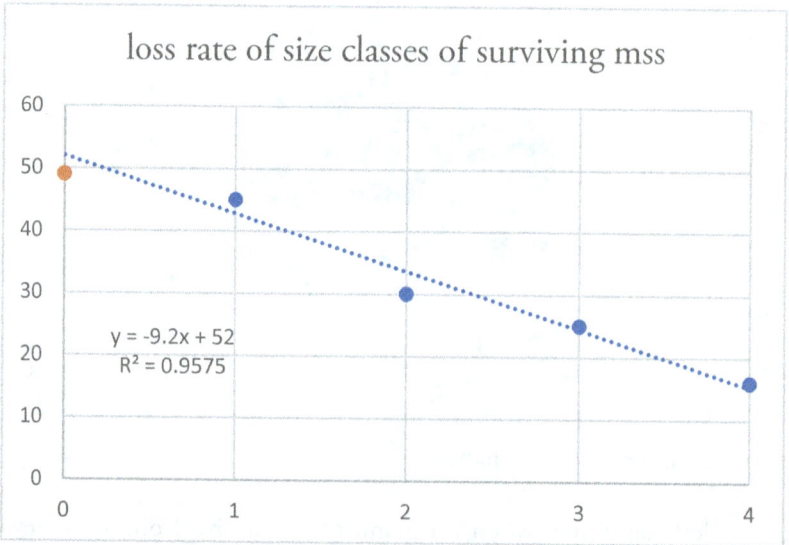

The geometric mean loss rates of the four size classes of surviving manuscripts show that a linear extrapolation (see Buringh, 2011, 225), with an R-square of 0.96, to the size class zero, would lead us to assume a loss rate of –52 % for this class. The approach followed (by assuming a survival of 0.4 manuscript) for these British lists with zero survival actually led to a geometric mean loss rate of –49 %, which is fairly close. The fact that the information contained in the lists with zero survival can also be used via this approach is an important extension of the ability to estimate loss rates. It is also essential because it also shows that neglecting this considerable class of lists would have led to an underestimate of the average British loss rates.

Explaining the observed loss rates

It is a trifle cheap to blame the high losses of manuscripts entirely on Henry VIII, who in the second quarter of the sixteenth century was responsible for the dissolution of the English monasteries and religious institutions as well as for the confiscation of all their revenues and possessions. Henry VIII did not actually confiscate the libraries – no mention was made of what should become of this category of possessions. Thus, the fate of books varied from institution to institution and could depend a great deal upon personal initiative (see e.g. James P. Carley, 2006). The introduction of the printing press to England at the end of the fifteenth century – already present in continental Europe for some decades before that – had brought down book prices considerably. Within a few decades this modern technology had generally made handwritten books old-fashioned and more expensive than printed books when produced to order. The advent of printing will undoubtedly have contributed to higher losses of manuscript books in the following century, nor was it the case that print manuscripts had an eternal life before that, being often in regular use. Such losses due to wear and tear, and sometimes inadequate storage conditions, must have been considerable in the libraries, churches and other religious institutions that all housed books during the Middle Ages. The newly constructed dataset of 204 uniform loss rates from between the twelfth and sixteenth century presents an opportunity to develop a simple multiple linear regression model (MLR), to quantitatively evaluate the influence of the various periods and events on the loss rates (L_y) in libraries in Great Britain. It is basically composed of a general loss rate (a) in percent points, with an additional specific century effect (b) in percent points for century x_i, and to which is added an effect with a value of (c) in percent points for the dissolution by Henry VIII (D_H), and of course random effects (ε) that are not modelled:

$$L_y = a + b*x_i + c*D_H + \varepsilon$$

The various values of the variables *a*, *b* and *c* can then be estimated with the MLR-model. That still leaves the modelling of the effect of Henry VIII's dissolution (D_H), however. A major part of the institutions in MLGB3 were in some way connected to the Church and so have been subjected to Henry's whims, but not all those 'dissolved' institutions were so gravely affected. Institutions that were already cathedrals but had previously been served by monastic cathedral chapters (Canterbury, Durham, Winchester, etc.), or in the instance of Carlisle by Augustinian canons, continued as cathedrals but with new secular chapters. The foundation of a number of new cathedrals also led to certain abbey churches, whose monastic communities had been dissolved, being re-founded as cathedrals with secular chapters (e.g. Peterborough, Gloucester and Oxford). Elsewhere, a number of priories and abbeys became the parish churches they still are. Colleges at Oxford and Cambridge were excluded from the provisions of the second Chantries Act of 1546 which closed all other collegiate churches in 1547. Eton and Winchester were also excluded, as sister colleges to colleges at Cambridge (King's) and Oxford (New). King's Hall (Cambridge) was demolished to make way for the king's new foundation of Trinity College. Durham and Canterbury Colleges were closed along with all other monastic colleges at the time of the dissolution of the monasteries. The real estate of many English abbeys, priories, monasteries and other ecclesiastical institutions was either given to Henry's favourites, and often turned into stately homes, or was gradually demolished as a source of building material, or fell into ruins through neglect.

Only those institutions that ceased to function after the dissolution have been classified in this paper as actually being impacted by Henry's decision to dissolve English Church institutions. For those institutions that ceased to function, the variable (D_H) gets the value 1 and in all other cases it becomes 0 (see Annex A). There still is one snag, however, which is that although book losses after the dissolution are post-medieval (and probably mainly sixteenth-century), quite a few lists (and consequently their loss rates) are from the preceding centuries. Therefore, for those earlier lists the loss rate attributed to D_H gets spread out over more centuries than when a loss rate is calculated for a sixteenth-century list. To take this into account, the value 1 for D_H in the sixteenth century is decreased to 0.68 for lists from fifteenth century, 0.56 for the fourteenth, and to 0.48 and 0.44 respectively for the thirteenth and twelfth. The value of the parameter c that finally emerges from the regression analysis is the contribution of Henry's dissolution (D_H) to the loss rates in the sixteenth century. For the other centuries, this value of c has to be multiplied by the fractions given above. The results are presented in Table 2. Please note that the overall R-square of the MLR-model is low: only 0.12. This implies that 88 % of the variance of loss rates has not been covered by the model, and that other unknown and chance effects have to a very large extent influenced the actual medieval loss rates in the various medieval libraries. Despite the low R-square, the also-low standard deviations of the estimated parameters a, b and c in Table 2 show that quite some values found in the MLR-analysis are significant (*) at $P<0.05$.

Table 2 shows that the basic uniform loss rate is −28 % point, to which a century effect has to be added. For the thirteenth and fourteenth century this is respectively a relatively modest: −3 % point and −7 % point, which are both not significant. However, for the fifteenth and sixteenth century the century effects on the loss rates of −11 % point and −9 % point respectively are significant. Also, the contribution of Henry VIII to the medieval loss rates of vanished or demolished institutions in the form of (D_H) comes out significantly from the analysis, and in the sixteenth century contributes an extra – 9 % point to the uniform loss rate of a dissolved medieval institution.

Table 2

Statistically modelled uniform English loss rates (and ± standard deviation) in percent point per century based on MLR-analysis of 204 loss rates between twelfth and sixteenth century indicating the influence of the dissolution ordered by Henry VIII.

MLR-analysis: loss rates	(a) Basic loss rate	(b) Extra century effect	(c) D_H	Still functioning institution	Disapp.rd Inst.tion
12th c.	28.4 (± 3.4)*	0.0	4.0 (1.2)*	–28 %	–32 %
13th c.	28.4 (± 3.4)*	3.3 (± 4.4)	4.4 (1.3)*	–32 %	–36 %
14th c.	28.4 (± 3.4)*	7.2 (± 3.8)	5.1 (1.5)*	–36 %	–41 %
15th c.	28.4 (± 3.4)*	10.9 (± 3.6)*	6.2 (1.8)*	–39 %	–46 %
16th c.	28.4 (± 3.4)*	8.7 (± 4.0)*	9.1 (2.7)*	–37 %	–46 %

Source: annex A

A completely different way of visualising the influence of the large sixteenth-century loss of manuscript books is by building a simulation model, and finding out whether such a model can corroborate the MLR-analysis above as well as quantitatively substantiate the overall findings of Table 1. The results of a very simple simulation model are shown in Table 3. This simulation model is specific to Britain because of its timing. In the simulation we do not use a uniform loss rate that does not change over the centuries, but instead we use a century specific loss rate. First of all, for the whole Middle Ages up to the fifteenth century a loss rate of –25 % per century is assumed (see

Buringh 2011, 227ff for the substantiation of this value), while for the modern period of the eighteenth to twentieth centuries, a very much lower value of –1 % per century seems more appropriate to describe the average loss rates of medieval manuscripts. The bulk of the British losses probably occurred during the sixteenth century, for which we will assume a general loss rate of –90 % per century. The loss rates of medieval manuscripts in the seventeenth century were probably somewhat higher still than in the modern period because at that time too England certainly knew periods of turmoil: say –5 % per century. With these hypothetical loss-rate values across the centuries we can simulate the losses from a medieval library of a certain size, and calculate how many books currently survive from those that were once present in a library or list from the twelfth to sixteenth centuries. Afterwards, we can calculate the uniform loss rate per century for books on the lists originating in those different centuries with simulated numbers of manuscripts surviving to the date of 2015, in a very similar way to how the loss rates in Annex A were calculated.

This is reported in Table 3. Hypothesis A is the one just described, with a loss rate of –90 % in the sixteenth century: in this period the more recent medieval manuscripts, dating from the fifteenth and possibly fourteenth centuries, might have undergone such a high loss rate because the then-modern printing press had caught up with the now (to a large-extent) obsolete process of copying by hand[9], and of course Henry VIII's dissolution of English monasteries contributed to this high rate. Hypothesis B is the very same simulation, with the sole difference that it uses a lower loss rate of –80 % in the sixteenth century. Such a slightly lower loss rate might have been appropriate

---

[9] The introduction of printing by movable type did not make copying by hand totally disappear overnight. For many kinds of material, production and circulation in manuscript form remained common in the sixteenth and seventeenth centuries.

for manuscripts that were already then antique and might therefore have been considered more special, dating from the twelfth or thirteenth centuries or even before.

Please note that with a loss rate of −80 % instead of −90 % the chances of a book surviving over a period of a century double. The numbers of surviving books presented in Table 3 have been based on a hypothetical library with 1,000 books in century i. Under hypothesis A, from a twelfth -century library only 29 manuscript books currently remain from the original 1,000. For a similar sized sixteenth-century library the simulated survival is 92 manuscripts, etc. With the surviving simulated numbers, the original size, and the medieval date, we can recalculate the uniform loss rate (L_i) in the same way as has been done for all British loss rates. The calculated uniform loss rate (L_i) is different, of course, from the century specific loss rates that were the input of the simulation model. In a uniform loss rate all the losses (medieval and post-medieval) are spread uniformly over the various centuries that have passed.

The results of table 3 make it plausible that a high post-medieval loss might explain the pattern observed in Table 1, with lower uniform loss rates for manuscripts in libraries from the twelfth century and gradually increasing uniform loss rates in later periods. Table 3 also corroborates the MLR-analysis reported in Table 2. In fact, the results of the calculations reported in Tables 1, 2 and 3 mean that a high post-medieval loss becomes spread out over more centuries as one looks further back in time. In this way, the uniform twelfth-century loss rates end up being lower than those of the fifteenth.

Hypothesis B indicates that a second factor may probably be playing a role too, with older manuscripts held in somewhat higher regard and therefore suffering slightly less than manuscripts that were relatively recent (and for a large part probably less than a century

Table 3
Simulation with hypothetical loss rates in Great Britain.

Century i:	12th	13th	14th	15th	16th	17th	18th	19th
Loss rate in simulation, hypothesis A (%)	-25	-25	-25	-25	-90	-5	-1	-1
Surviving mss from century i	29	39	52	69	92	921	970	980
Calcul. uniform loss rate L_i (%)	-34	-35	-37	-38	-41			
Loss rate in simulation, hypothesis B (%)	-25	-25	-25	-25	-80	-5	-1	-1
Surviving mss from century i	58	78	104	138	184	921	970	980
Calcul. uniform loss rate L_i (%)	-28	-29	-29	-30	-31			
Observed uniform loss rates (Table1) (%)	-28	-32	-37	-38	-37			

Source: see text.

old).[10] Hypothesis B gives a plausible explanation for the numerical value of the observed uniform loss rate for lists dating to the twelfth century.[11] For lists from the next century, a loss rate somewhere

---

[10] The fact that in the beginning of the sixteenth century Leland and others were travelling around the country looking for books in monastic libraries and noting that some were 'a rich storehouse of ancient manuscripts' (Carley, 2006, 267) shows that such an interpretation probably is not too far-fetched.

[11] These are manuscripts on twelfth-century lists, which implies they may be very well be older than the twelfth century, and quite a lot actually were. They most certainly are not only twelfth-century books!

between those of hypotheses A and B can present a plausible explanation. An alternative explanation for lower losses in older lists could be that the old manuscripts they contain had been in libraries longer than their later counterparts – which may have meant they have had a better chance of getting marked with an *ex libris* at some point in the Middle Ages, and therewith have become more visible in MLGB. Numerically there seems to be some difference between the simulated –41 % for the sixteenth century and the observed value of –37 % per century. However, if we consider the two sixteenth-century samples from Balliol College, Oxford (UO 21 and UO 22 in MLGB3/ Corpus of British Medieval Library Catalogues) to be outliers in our data set, these two samples had uniform loss rates of only –5 % and –7 % per century, which were by far the lowest loss rates to be observed from this period. The geometric mean loss rate in sixteenth-century Great Britain becomes –41 % (N = 39). This brings it perfectly in line with the simulated value.

Discussion and conclusions

A plus point of the approach in this paper is that changes in medieval (or later) ownership, or the actual contents of the books in question (e.g. bibles, patristic or liturgical works, etc.) are not important for the obtained results. We only look at the year of the medieval list that contains a sample mentioning then-existing manuscripts, and whether the books mentioned on that specific list currently still survive. By taking into consideration various and often quite different medieval book lists (e.g. bequests, donations, library holdings, and church inventories) of a certain minimal size, we get a very broad general picture of the loss rates of medieval books for the period when the list was drawn up, and for the current date. One must also be aware of the fact that the year of the book list implies that all books on that list are from before that date, and also, more importantly, that some may even be considerable older. Therefore, a twelfth-century list does not by definition mean that it only contains books from that specific century! Only that the list itself is drawn up in the twelfth century.

A first point for discussion is the large variation in survival. Taken together, the dissolution of the monasteries by Henry VIII and century-specific effects could only explain 12 % of the variation in the loss rates of manuscripts between individual institutions. The simple regression model for the 204 British loss rates from the twelfth to sixteenth century used in this paper therefore still leaves a high variance unexplained – some 88 %. This means that the actual values of most individual loss rates of libraries or bequests are largely due to other unmodelled factors, and to chance. The data themselves also substantiate this point. For the fifteenth century (N = 80), the uniform loss rates of the various individual institutions vary between –4 % and –69 % per century. Because these are uniform loss rates, one must be aware that for every institution this same numerical value subsequently applies to its manuscript losses in each consecutive century from the fifteenth onwards. Therefore a uniform loss rate of –69 % per century, for example, was not a one-off, but this fraction of loss occurred in each century right up to the current date for that specific library. And for the sixteenth century, the range of loss rates stretches from –5 % to –66 % (N= 41). Such numerically contrasting values within the very same century imply that in a number of medieval libraries meticulous care was taken over centuries of the various manuscripts in their possession, while in others their liquidation (or maybe some other mishap) has led to a virtual disappearance of their medieval contents. There is of course always danger in using the surviving evidence from large individual communities (such as Christ Church or St Augustine's, both in Canterbury) to infer patterns for other communities, since their histories of institutional book ownership may have been very different. The other complicating factor is the large variation in book survival rates between different types of institutions (such as the very low survival levels in female houses or among the friars), as well as the substantial geographical variation (for example, between the east and west Midlands) in the survival rates of different types of book. One might, for example, contrast the rate of identified survival from the abbey of Leicester – for which we have an unusually full record of its medieval holdings of more than one thousand books, of which fewer than twenty can be shown to survive – with very much higher rates of survival demonstrable for St Augustine's, Canterbury. The reasons for this difference are to be sought in the different historical circumstances of each, which make it impossible to extrapolate from both or either, and so to draw general conclusions. Therefore, the solution has to be sought in increasing the numbers of loss rates. The substantial extension of the numbers of samples through the online availability of the beta-version of MLGB3 helps in arriving at new and better estimates of the uniform loss rates in the various centuries. Leaving the dissolution of monasteries by Henry VIII (D_H) out of the MLR-analysis leads to an explained variance of only 7%. This suggests that the specific contingency caused by Henry VIII was significance for the survival of English medieval books (or maybe it would be better to say the lack of their survival).

A second element for discussion is the inclusion criterion of ten manuscripts on a list. When using lower numbers as an inclusion criterion, on the one hand the calculated loss rates will vary more (a basic characteristic of smaller sample sizes), leading to a higher noise in the results, and on the other hand a lower number of manuscripts in a sample will also lead to a selective downward bias in the results. A numerical example can illustrate this last point. Let us assume that there is a twelfth-century list with just one manuscript, that has not survived. With the method followed in this paper a loss rate of only −10 % per century is estimated for this library possessing just one non-surviving book. This loss rate will be the same for all other twelfth-century libraries with only one non-surviving book and can never become any higher, because we have assumed 0.4 manuscripts to survive, so as to avoid a natural logarithm of zero, when calculating a uniform loss rate. If on the other hand this one manuscript had by chance indeed survived, then we would have found an even lower loss rate of –0 %. In both cases these two lower loss rates differ substantially from the geometric average obtained in Figure 2, which is –52 % based on extrapolation and –49 % based on the geometrical average of the actual lists.[12] By close inspection of Figure 1 this bias effect is even to some extent visible. Figure 1 shows something of an 'empty shoulder' in the higher values of loss rates for small list sizes. Because there is no relationship between the medieval list size and loss rates, we would expect as many loss rates above the average as below. However, the higher loss rates fail to show up above the actual data in Figure 1 for smaller list sizes, leading to such an 'empty shoulder' – that the latter may occur in practice can easily be calculated. For a medieval list from 1215 describing ten manuscripts of which none has survived, we can calculate a uniform loss rate of –33 %. A similar list from 1515 yields a uniform loss rate of –47 %.[13] This indicates that there can be no occurrences above these calculated maximal loss rates with a sample of ten books, and that with one or more surviving books the uniform loss rates will turn out even lower for such a small sample. Statistically higher loss rates than average would nevertheless have been expected with those small lists of ten or slightly more manuscript books. Therefore, even an inclusion criterion of ten manuscripts is by itself somewhat of a tradeoff, leading to a slight downward bias.

Third, in our discussion we should mention the current date relative to which the loss rates are calculated. In the previous exercise, working with Neil Ker's book from 1964, this was 19.64 in whole centuries. Now, we have taken a middle date in the development of

---

[12] Observing a uniform loss rate of –0% would even preclude calculating a geometric mean.

[13] Both values for a sample of ten books are lower than the observed geometric mean of –49 % when no medieval books survive.

the beta-version of MLGB3, and chosen 20.15 as our reference date for the calculations. This means that all loss rates have been recalculated by dividing the natural logarithm of (c/b) by a ΔT that is in fact 0.51 higher than previously. This quotient with a larger divisor will therefore produce a somewhat lower value of the estimated loss rate in this paper compared to the previous estimates using 1964 as a reference date.

A fourth point for discussion is the undeniable fact that fly-leaves with notations or other marks of medieval ownership sometimes get lost from a manuscript over time. This naturally complicates ascription of a certain book to a specific medieval list or institution. However, there are other ways than such obvious marks of medieval ownership to prove that a manuscript has come from a specific medieval library. Sometimes medieval lists contain the first few words of the second folio of a manuscript, which in the Middle Ages was a unique and distinctive way to discriminate between different handwritten books. This, too, is often a useful means to ascribe the provenance of a manuscript. Additionally, other codicological data may sometimes be used to ascribe a book to a medieval library or list. To err on the safe side, as we did not want to have missed any manuscripts, all possible attributions mentioned in MLGB3 have been considered to be certain attributions. However, we can never be certain that all ascriptions will have been completely finalised to the complete satisfaction of the last codicologist. Moreover, MLGB3 itself remains a work in progress because a substantial number of medieval lists still have to be added, which will generate new data. Therefore, the results presented in this paper will likewise certainly not be definitive, and remain a work in progress.

The final point of the discussion – and this is a very fundamental one – is the objection sometimes raised that the whole approach of this paper must be flawed because some still surviving manuscripts, that were once mentioned on a medieval list, will not be identifiable, as they might have lost their marks of medieval ownership or maybe even never had such a mark. This objection would make the whole idea of calculating a loss rate for a certain library by using survival rates unknowable in principle. Of course, this argument cannot be refuted. It is clear that we will always have missed a number of manuscripts, no matter how hard we will have tried to be complete. (Nevertheless virtually all codicologists agree that survival rates of the individual medieval British libraries are actually very different, varying between near-complete survival of the contents for some libraries to near-complete disappearance for others).[14] The question is, however, one of the numerical importance of neglecting such unidentified but still surviving manuscripts for this paper's calculated average loss rates. When certain surviving manuscripts from a list are not recognised as such, as undoubtedly will have been the case a number of times here, it will result in an overestimate of the calculated loss rate. To compensate to some degree for this, the various uncertain or questionable ascriptions of survival have all been counted as certain. Also, the 'empty shoulder' in Figure 1, which has arisen through using ten manuscripts as an inclusion criterion, suggests that for lower list sizes loss rates are to some extent underestimated by the approach followed in this paper. Both approaches in this paper will therefore partially meet this objection over missed survivors, but because the exact magnitude of non-identifiable manuscripts is unknowable it is impossible to give a direct numerical answer.

What we do know, however, is that there also are other and fundamentally different methods of calculating or estimating loss rates (or other factors which are in fact similar to loss rates, because they are complementary, such as the survival factors of manuscripts). Uwe Neddermeyer, 1998, has used losses of incunabula to estimate the medieval loss rates for contemporary manuscripts. Buringh (2011,

---

[14] If the objection in this final point of discussion would have been taken literary by these objectors it would also imply that such statements concerning British libraries cannot be made because these too are unknowable.

232ff) indicates that Neddermeyer's survival factor of 15.0 for the fifteenth century is identical to the one found by using the approach described in this paper. As a way to check his results Buringh (2011, 227ff) also calculated loss rates in a very different way by looking at the survival of actual texts of early Christian authors from around 400 to 500 CE, and found similar numerical results in percent per century to those obtained with the loss rates calculated from high-medieval lists. Also, a comparison with the dating of palimpsests gave similar results for average medieval loss rates (see Buringh 2011, 238ff). Therefore, our conclusion from all these very different exercises, which obtained their results independently of the unidentifiable surviving manuscripts that currently haunt us, is that the influence of such manuscripts is probably not very large. The results of this paper and of a number of totally different and independent methods arrive at virtually the same outcomes. Because this paper contains nearly four times as many loss rates as previously, we can also be more certain of the numerical values here presented, and for the time being regard them as the most robust estimate of British loss rates available.

The final (and possible most important) conclusion is that the numerical values of the 204 loss rates that were obtained from MLGB3 and other sources, and those that were used in the simulation, match very well across the various centuries. They thereby substantiate the plausibility of a medieval loss rate with a default value of −25 % per century as suggested by Buringh (2011, 220ff), for the purposes of calculating book production. This agreement also implies that the numerical values of the various survival factors that were originally used to estimate medieval book production can remain as they are, and that the previously obtained numerical medieval production rates in manuscripts per century therefore still stand.

Annex A

More information on the various libraries, lists, institutions, and so on can be found by their identification mark in MLGB3 or in Annexes L or N in Buringh (2011).

In this annex the loss rates have been ordered by the year in which the list was drawn up. Surviving # and medieval # are in numbers of manuscripts. The uniform loss rates are in percent per century (up to 2015) and have to be given a minus sign. For D_H, see the explanation in the text on the dissolution of monasteries by Henry VIII. (0 = institution not affected by the dissolution).

Notes to table [see relevant superscript number in first column].

[1] not in MLR-analysis [2] indicated in Kren as a cell of reading
[3] Kren (1964, 81) gives 1 ms on Marlborough list
[4] cell of thorney [5] according to Ker 94 mss
[6] according to Ker 75 mss on cartulary
[7] cannot be printed books, which MLGB3 claims, too early!
[8] UO 52 goes to 148 but in the medieval library of Merton College a number 149 seems to be mentioned
[9] 678 original mss as indicated in MLGB3 seems in error
[10] 250 original mss as indicated in MLGB3 seems in error
[11] result is corrected from annex L
[12] after 1451 [13] Ker indicates 18 mss
[14] estimated by subtracting fraction of printed books
[15] 165 original mss as indicated in MLGB3 seems in error
[16] or is it 79 original medieval mss?

Place	List	Source	Year	Surviving #	Medieval #	loss rate	D_H
Peterborough[1]	Donation: Aethelwold	BP 1	984	0	20	32	-
Abingdon	Books commissioned by Faricius	B 2	1110	0	12	31	0.44
Worcester	school books	B 115	1120	0	50	42	0.44
Peterborough	Catalogue	BP 2	1120	3	61	29	0
Rochester	Catalogue	B 77	1123	49	99	8	0
Glastonbury	Copied for Henry of Blois	B 37	1149	0	40	41	0.44
Lincoln	Old Cat.	annex L	1150	33	89	11	0.44
Bury	Cat. Rom.	annex L	1150	28	139	18	0.44
Canterbury	Old Cat.	annex L	1150	7	251	36	0.44
St Albans	Bale's excerpts	B 85	1180	1	81	41	0
Whitby	Catalogue	B 109	1180	1	86	41	0
Canterbury	School books	BC 1	1180	5	223	37	0
Welbeck	Catalogue	P 9	1180	2	81	36	0.44
Peterborough	Copied for Abbot Benedict	BP 3	1185	1	54	38	0
Reading	Catalogue	B 71	1192	43	204	17	0.44
Leominster[2]	Catalogue	B 75	1192	4	77	30	0
Rievaulx	Catalogue	Z 19	1195	9	284	34	0.44
Bury	Cat. Arab.	annex L	1201	24	268	15	0.48
Rochester	Catalogue	B 79	1202	73	241	14	0
Waltham	Catalogue	A 38	1220	5	130	34	0
Bridlington	List of Books	A 4	1220	1	117	45	0

Evesham[3]	Acquired by Thomas Marlborough	B 29	1220	1	32	35	0.48
Rochester	Acquired by Alexander	B 80	1220	1	15	29	0
Flaxley	Catalogue	Z 7	1220	0	79	49	0.48
Crediton	Bequest: Barthelemew St David	SC 220	1225	0	10	33	0
Peterborough	Donation: Walter of St Edmund	BP 7	1239	0	11	35	0
Coventry	Written by John de Bruges	B 23	1240	0	29	42	0
Bury	Refectory	B 14	1250	1	17	31	0.48
Gloucester	Books owned by Robert of Aldsworth	B 47	1250	1	34	37	0
Ramsey	borrowed by John de Haliwell	B 69	1250	1	12	28	0.48
Reading	Copied by William of Wycumbe	B 76	1250	4	14	15	0.48
Peterborough	List in Refectory	BP 20	1250	2	68	37	0
England	Bestiaries	annex N	1250	50	657	29	0.48
Peterborough	Donation: Robert of Sutton	BP 10	1269	0	14	38	0
Bradsole	Catalogue	P 2	1280	0	144	55	0.48

Glastonbury	Bequest: John Taunton	B 40	1291	0	24	43	0.48
Peterborough	Donation: William of Woodford	BP 13	1297	1	12	29	0
Anglesey	List of Books	A 1	1314	1	30	38	0.56
Oxford	Catalogue	annex L	1315	1	44	44	0.56
Crowland	Select List	B 24	1320	9	96	29	0
Thorney	Borrowers List	B 100	1320	0	118	56	0.56
Oxford	Philosophy Books Catalogue	UO 46	1320	3	84	38	0
Canterbury	Catalogue	annex L	1320	164	1803	31	0.56
Peterborough	Donation: Adam of Boothby	BP 15	1330	0	11	38	0
Canterbury	H. Eastry	annex L	1331	6	80	34	0.56
Hinton	Loan to another charterhouse	C 1	1343	0	19	44	0.56
Peterborough	Donation: Henry of Morcott	BP 16	1346	0	11	39	0
Chester	Will Richard of Chester	B 21	1347	0	21	45	0.56
Norwich	Books owned by Simon Bozoun	B 58	1350	5	30	24	0
Ramsey	Fragm. Catalogue	B 67	1350	0	196	61	0.56
Reading	Books in Dormitory	B 74	1350	4	21	22	0.56

Loss Rates of Medieval English & Scottish Books 53

Deeping[4]	Inventory	B 102	1350	0	18	44	0
Ipswich	Donor list	F 17	1350	0	13	41	0.56
Waltham	Press marks	annex L	1350	18	279	32	0.56
Cambridge	Grant founder	UC 57	1352	2	80	43	0
Oxford	Theology books Catalogue	UO 47	1355	30	263	28	0
Oxford	Bequest Stephen Kettelbegh	UO 80	1359	6	98	35	0
Lanthony	Leche bequest	A 17	1361	9	57	24	0.56
Cambridge	Inventory	UC 31	1361	0	17	44	0.56
Cambridge	Donation Edward III	UC 32	1368	0	10	39	0.56
Oxford	Electio list	UO 48	1372	8	141	36	0
Oxford	Donation: William Read	UO 34	1374	2	24	32	0
Oxford	Donation William Reed	UO 49	1374	29	99	17	0
Glastonbury	Acquisition by Walter of Monnington	B 43	1375	5	96	37	0.56
Westminster[5]	Bequest Langham	B 105	1376	1	90	51	0.56
Cambridge	Inventory	UC 18	1376	0	53	53	0
Oxford	Books returned to college	UO 82	1378	1	24	39	0
Lanthony	Catalogue	A 16	1380	124	508	20	0.56
Ramsey	Roll Catalogue	B 68	1380	8	575	49	0.56
Peterborough	Catalogue	BP 21	1380	14	348	40	0
Aylesford[6]	Part of a catalogue	F 1	1381	0	14	43	0.56

King's Lynn	Bequest: Thom Lexham	F 19	1382	8	64	28	0.56
York	Catalogue	FA 8	1382	10	646	48	0.56
Oxford	Inventory	UO 70	1386	60	465	28	0
Westminster	Service Books Inventory	annex L	1388	2	30	38	0.56
Dover	John Whitfield Catalogue	BM 1	1389	21	449	39	0.56
Cambridge	Catalogue	UC 36	1391	0	110	59	0.56
Evesham	Bequest: Prior Nicholas	B 30	1392	0	108	59	0.56
Durham	Catalogue	annex N	1395	320	1395	16	0.56
Westminster	Bequest Richard Exeter	B 107	1396	0	15	44	0.56
Meaux	Inventory	Z 14	1396	3	361	54	0.56
Cobham	Inventory	SC 217	1397	0	24	48	0.56
Titchfield	Catalogue	P 6	1400	16	224	35	0.56
Oxford	Donation: William Read	UO 35	1400	2	45	40	0
Oxford	Donation: John Campeden	UO 71	1401	3	34	33	0
Winchester	Inventory	SC 330	1405	2	31	36	0
Oxford	Donation: Nicholas Wykeham	UO 72	1407	0	27	50	0
Cambridge	List borrowed books	UC 26	1408	30	264	30	0
Oxford	Electio list	UO 51	1409	9	182	39	0
Canterbury	Bequest: Thomas Chillenden	annex L	1411	4	28	30	0.68

Oxford	Donation: John Elme	UO 73	1412	2	14	28	0
Winchester	Purchase of books	SC 332	1413	0	13	44	0
Cambridge	Catalogue	UC 48	1418	254	456	9	0
Oxford[7]	Noted by Thomas Gascoigne	F 37	1420	0	14	45	0.68
Winchester	Inventory	SC 334	1422	1	76	52	0
Oxford[8]	Warden's collection	UO 52	1423	5	149	44	0
St Albans	Borrowers list	B 87	1429	1	61	50	0
Winchester	Inventory	SC 335	1429	5	125	42	0
St Albans	Whethamstede's accounts	B 88	1430	9	48	25	0
Cambridge	Benefactors	UC 2	1432	5	123	42	0
Glasgow	Inventory	S 12	1433	2	152	52	0
Winchester	Inventory	SC 338	1433	2	190	54	0
Aberdeen	Catalogue	S 1	1436	1	193	60	0
Cambridge[9]	Bequest: Thomas Markaunt	UC 19	1439	5	72	37	0
Oxford	Donation: Humphrey Duke of Gloucester	UO 1	1439	6	135	42	0
Cambridge	Inventory	UC 11	1440	0	87	61	0
Cambridge	List benefactors	UC 12	1440	0	54	57	0

Cambridge	Donation: Henry VI	UC 39	1440	1	77	53	0.68
Oxford	Donation: Henry VI	UO 5	1440	3	27	32	0
Oxford	Donation: Humphrey Duke of Gloucester	UO 2	1441	0	10	43	0
Oxford	Inventory	UO 6	1443	36	369	33	0
Oxford	Inventory	UO 7	1443	34	480	37	0
Oxford[10]	Donation: Humphrey Duke of Gloucester	UO 3	1444	13	136	34	0
Fotheringhay	Inventory	SC 244	1445	0	190	66	0.68
Oxford	Electio books Henry Scayfe	UO 83	1445	1	10	33	0
Sudbury	Bequest: Geoffr Bryce	SC 304	1446	0	18	49	0.68
London	Inventory	SH 33	1448	1	59	51	0.68
Bury	Benefactors	B 15	1450	1	16	39	0.68
Worcester	Books at Oxford	B 116	1450	0	30	53	0.68
York	Index Catalogue	B 120	1450	12	653	51	0.68
Canterbury	Catalogue	BA 1	1450	351	1849	25	0.68
Cambridge	Books in accounts	UC 40	1450	0	40	56	0.68
Oxford	Inventory	UO 8	1450	31	254	31	0
Battle[11]	Press marks	annex L	1450	10	188	43	0.68
Lincoln	Catalogue	annex L	1450	84	139	9	0.68

Bury	Press marks	annex L	1450	274	3563	39	0.68
York	Press marks	annex L	1450	11	140	39	0.68
Fountains	Press marks	annex L	1450	6	249	52	0.68
Leicester	Catalogue	A 20	1450	18	1957	56	0.68
Norwich	Press marks	annex L	1450	85	1866	45	0.68
Oxford	Electio list	UO 54	1452	1	165	60	0
St Albans	Whethamstede books after 1452	B 89	1454	6	62	34	0
Cambridge[12]	Godshouse Inventory	UC 9	1454	0	12	45	0
Cambridge	Inventory	UC 29	1457	2	175	55	0
Cambridge	Bequest: John Titlehall	UC 20	1458	0	11	45	0
London	Catalogue	annex L	1458	8	77	36	0.68
Aberdeen	Catalogue	S 2	1465	1	135	59	0
Eton	Inventory	SC 229	1465	9	44	25	0
Warwick	Inventory	SC 319	1465	1	20	42	0.68
London	List books	SH 47	1470	9	13	7	0.68
Cambridge	Inventory	UC 50	1472	0	226	69	0
Arbroath	Bequest: Richard Guthrie	S 6	1473	1	31	47	0
Cambridge	Register	UC 3	1473	22	330	39	0
Witham	Donation: John Blacman	C 8	1474	8	68	33	0
Glasgow	Donation Duncan Bunch	S 13	1474	0	11	46	0
Cambridge	Book donations acta 1448-1505	UC 13	1474	0	18	51	0

Oxford	Inventory	UO 38	1474	52	135	16	0
Oxford[13]	Donation: William Aspylon	UO 85	1474	4	18	24	0
Oxford	Electio list	UO 39	1476	1	37	49	0
Glasgow	Donation: John Brown	S 15	1480	0	13	48	0
Oxford	Chained books library	UO 12	1480	8	59	31	0
Canterbury	Bibles	annex L	1480	8	38	28	0.68
Oxford	Warden's study	UO 55	1483	0	64	61	0
Oxford	Donation: John Gygour	UO 56	1486	4	19	26	0
London	Catalogue	annex L	1486	2	52	49	0.68
Darlington	Inventory	SC 222	1487	1	13	38	0.68
Oxford	Donation: John Neele	UO 44	1489	1	19	43	0
Oxford	List: Scholar's study	UO 75	1489	0	22	53	0
Cambridge	Benefactors	UC 43	1490	53	148	18	0
Oxford	Donation: William Romsey a. o.	UO 59	1494	9	11	4	0
Oxford	Inventory	UO 13	1495	33	250	32	0
Cambridge	Unbound books	UC 14	1496	1	89	58	0
Rotherham	Bequest: archbishop	SC 288	1500	2	58	48	0.68
Leicester	Libraria	annex L	1500	5	269	56	0.68

Oxford	Donation: William Dennis + Richard Sater	UO 11	1501	5	22	25	0
Oxford	Catalogue	annex L	1501	3	414	65	1
Arundel	Inventory	SC 204	1505	2	103	54	1
Canterbury	Ingram	annex L	1508	121	295	18	1
Syon[14]	Library	SS 1	1512	28	962	50	1
Cambridge	Benefactors	UC 53	1513	0	95	66	0
Winchester	Reginensis	B 113	1520	2	71	51	1
London	Carmelite, Reginensis	F 26	1520	0	15	52	1
London	Franciscan, Reginensis	F 31	1520	0	13	51	1
Oxford	Dominican, Reginensis	F 39	1520	0	14	51	1
Oxford	List: Italian Visitor	UO 21	1520	10	13	5	0
Oxford	List: Italian Visitor	UO 76	1520	0	14	51	0
Oxford	List: Italian Visitor	UO 4	1520	0	18	54	0
Boston	Linc.shire list	F2, F 3, 4, F 5	1528	1	23	47	1
Grimsby	Linc.shire list	F 12, F 1	1528	0	45	62	1
Lincoln	Linc.shire list	F 21	1528	0	13	51	1
Lincoln	Linc.shire list	F 22	1528	0	17	54	1
Pleshey	Inventory	SC 283	1528	2	88	54	1
Exeter	Leland	F 10	1535	0	64	65	1
Richmond Palace	Books of Henry VIII	H 1	1535	65	105	10	0

Oxford	Leland	UO 22	1535	81	113	7	0
Oxford	Leland	UO 5	1535	0	35	61	0
Cambridge	Leland	UC 6	1535	3	11	24	0
Rochester		annex N	1535	135	600	28	1
Oxford	Leland	UO 77	1536	11	42	24	0
Glastonbury	Leland	B 44	1538	4	44	40	1
Gloucester	Leland	B 49	1538	3	20	33	0
Sherborne	Leland	B 94	1538	1	10	38	0
Westminster	Leland	B 108	1538	1	15	43	1
Peterborough	Leland	BP 23	1538	3	15	29	0
Cambridge	Leland	F 6, F 7, F 8	1538	0	24	58	1
London	Leland	F 24	1538	0	44	63	1
Oxford	Carmelite, Leland	F 36	1538	0	36	61	1
Rievaulx	Leland	Z 21	1538	3	22	34	1
Warden	Leland	Z 26	1538	1	19	46	1
Cambridge	Leland	UC 15	1538	5	30	31	0
Cambridge[15]	Leland	UC 27	1538	6	19	21	0
Cambridge	Leland	UC 49	1538	31	89	20	0
Cambridge[16]	Leland	UC 52	1538	0	44	63	0
Westminster	Service books Inventory	annex L	1540	3	26	40	1
St Albans	Bale's excerpts	B 90	1550	3	17	31	0
Lichfield[1]	Catalogue	annex L	1622	1	79	69	-
Worcester[1]	Catalogue	annex L	1622	266	343	7	-
London[1]	Fire	annex N	1731	738	958	8	-

SURVIVAL AND LOSS: WORKING WITH DOCUMENTS FROM MEDIEVAL SCOTLAND

Joanna Tucker[1]

When we think of losses of medieval documents, our minds naturally turn to the more notorious examples. Scotland has had its fair share of these. Glasgow Cathedral's medieval muniments, for example, were taken to Paris during the Reformation of 1560 for safekeeping where subsequently most of the original documents were destroyed during the French Revolution.[2] At Scone Abbey, a disastrous fire in the mid-twelfth century consumed whatever existed of its archive at that time.[3] The earliest Scottish royal archive, comprising those records accumulated during the twelfth and thirteenth centuries, has also been lost, with only a handful of derivative summaries and copies remaining that offer a tormenting glimpse into its original contents. An inventory of the archive produced in 1292, for example, describes a single basket as containing a 'sealed protest of Robert de Brus', a 'calendar of royal charters', 'another similar roll of memoranda of

---

[1] I am grateful to the organisers of the Dark Archives conference for inviting me to participate in the event. I am also very grateful to Dauvit Broun, Matthew Hammond and Alice Taylor for providing some critical feedback on drafts of this chapter. All remaining errors or oversights are my own.

[2] McRoberts 1977, 61–68 and 87–94.

[3] This prompted a royal confirmation of Scone's possessions and privileges in 1163 or 1164: Barrow 1960, no. 243; Broun 2005, 171.

charters', 'four rolls of transcripts of charters, letters and bulls', 'one roll of statutes of King Malcolm', and 'seven rolls of memoranda and transcripts of agreements, treaties, expenses, and various other things'.[4] A series of conquests, fires and a sinking ship in the seventeenth century have ensured that historians today are unable to access the exact content of these rich materials.[5] In very many other cases, entire collections of medieval documents, along with any later copies of them, have quietly disappeared from view.

Instead of focusing on some or all of these infamous cases, this chapter will attempt to place them in a wider context. Scotland's medieval documents are particularly well served by a long history of scholarship aimed at making the texts more accessible. Not only has most of what survives been published, there are also a number of digital resources now available for using these texts for research. Collectively, these resources provide an opportunity to look more holistically at what survives from the medieval kingdom, to an extent that may not be so readily achievable elsewhere. Such a wealth of resources also, however, presents its own issues. Rather than simply shedding a brighter light on survival and loss than might be possible elsewhere, these resources allow us to appreciate more fully the ways in which printed texts and digital resources can in fact obscure critical aspects of the corpus and its survival patterns. This exposes other dimensions to the 'dark archive' beyond the loss or inaccessibility of material from the past.

This chapter will survey the surviving corpus of Scottish documents from the central Middle Ages as seen through lens of our current scholarly resources. First, it will look at the printed editions

---

[4] Thomson & Innes 1844, 113–17 (no. vi, at 116–17). The original document is Edinburgh, NRS SP13/1.

[5] Someone who has managed to use these derivative sources to paint a compelling picture of Scottish royal government before 1290 is Alice Taylor: Taylor 2015, and esp. Taylor 2016.

and digital tools available for studying Scotland's documents. It will then examine the nature of the surviving corpus itself, from both quantitative and qualitative perspectives. It will become apparent that the manuscript context, as well as the broader archival setting for each text, can be difficult to ascertain for the corpus as a whole through the existing resources, which have tended to be interested in the 'texts' rather than the textual artefacts. An attempt will be made in the final section to examine the survival of documents by individual medieval archive, based on the existing infrastructure of catalogues, editions and databases. This will point towards work that remains to be done and provide a springboard for further research.

Before setting out, some terminology should be confronted. In a Scottish context at least, the form of the single-sheet document in question is often broadly referred to as a 'charter'; however, the same term has also come to be used to describe a particular type of text recorded on one of these sheets (a dispositive instrument with an address clause, witness list, and effecting an action such as a grant of privileges or gift of properties).[6] Single-sheet, sealed documents might equally host other kinds of texts, such as agreements, instructions and letters. 'Charter' can, therefore, have a broad sense (as a single-sheet document) and a narrow sense (as a particular type of text). The 'archive', on the other hand, usually describes a collection of single-sheet documents (sometimes also referred to as the 'muniments'). Derivative copies of the 'original' documents (such as in manuscript books or rolls) are related to, but are not necessarily considered part of, the 'archive'.

---

[6] *People of Medieval Scotland* [PoMS] 2018, Glossary of terms: 'charter'.

Publishing Scotland's surviving document texts

One advantage of working with Scotland's document texts is that most have been published in some form. This is largely due to the work of nineteenth- and early twentieth-century antiquarian clubs and societies who were especially thorough in their production of volumes based on the archives of various ecclesiastical institutions as well as of some lay families.[7] Each volume contains an extensive historical introduction to the subject in question followed by a sequence of charter texts, often arranged chronologically by the editor. It is probably fair to say that the editors were generally less interested in 'editing manuscripts' and more concerned with gathering together the document texts derived from a single medieval archive. To do this, they would use whatever manuscript sources were known to them in order to present as full a picture as possible of that particular medieval archive. As a result, these volumes collectively present a seemingly homogeneous corpus of document texts which can belie the complexities of the manuscripts beneath.[8]

As editorial practices have developed, Scotland's charter texts have continued to be published. A notable effort has been the longstanding project *Regesta regum scottorum* ('Registers of the Kings of Scots'), which began in the 1950s and comprises seven volumes (five of which have been published).[9] In contrast to the antiquarian club public-

---

[7] Tucker 2019, 140–43.

[8] For critiques of the antiquarian approach to editing (especially where cartularies are involved), see Geary 1994, 81–114, and Ross 2006, esp. 207–24.

[9] The volumes cover the reigns of Malcolm IV (*RRS*, i), William I (*RRS*, ii), Alexander II (*RRS*, iii, forthcoming), Alexander III (*RRS*, iv, part 1), the Guardians of Scotland and King John Balliol (*RRS*, iv, part 2, in progress), Robert I (*RRS*, v), and David II (*RRS*, vi). (The charters of David I were published separately: Barrow 1999.) For full bibliographical details, see the PoMS bibliography.

ations (which focused on beneficiary archives), the *Regesta regum scottorum* series provides a 'donor' view of the corpus, assembling the written documents or 'acts' in the name of each king. The texts themselves are arranged and numbered in a roughly chronological order, providing a broad impression of the progression of the reign.[10] The original rationale of the series was essentially about filling a gap in the publication of Scotland's royal *acta* between 1153 and 1371.[11] The success of the *Regesta regum scottorum* series and its editors (especially G. W. S. Barrow) led David Bates to note that, in relation to the twelfth-century royal charters of Britain and Ireland, 'Scottish charter scholarship is well in the lead'.[12]

One way in which the *Regesta regum scottorum* volumes go beyond the antiquarian editions is in the inclusion of lost documents of kings of Scots. These are usually listed at the end of the main sequence of edited texts. Care is required when interpreting these references, especially those 'lost acts' from the twelfth century, since not all explicitly mention a document as such but are rather references within an extant document to a previous action by the king (such as an earlier donation or renewal).[13] The presence of the lost acts serves as an

[10] By contrast, some editions of English royal charters have arranged the texts by beneficiary archive, rather than in a single chronological series: see Bates 1998 (for the acts of William I), and Sharpe with Carpenter (for the acts of William II and Henry I).

[11] These limits were taken from A. C. Lawrie's *Early Scottish Charters Prior to 1153* (published in 1905) and the *Register of the Great Seal* (Thomson et al. 1882–1914).

[12] Bates 2005, 6.

[13] Barrow (1960; 1971; 1999) used an asterisk to distinguish those cases where a document is explicitly mentioned. The proportions of 'lost acts' that include a reference to a lost document are as follows: for the acts of David I and Earl Henry only 30% of lost acts explicitly mention a document (19 out of 64); for the acts of Malcolm IV it is 42% (22 out of 52); for the acts of William I it is 51% (37 out of 73).

important reminder of the significant losses of royal charters that have occurred. The fact that the lost acts are numbered as a continuation of the main sequence of charter texts might seem misleading, especially since not all were certainly 'documents'. This approach agrees, however, with the subject of the series: the 'acts' of the kings of Scots. This exposes the dual meaning of the term 'acts' which can naturally be used by scholars for both the documents and their content (the 'action' recorded in the text).

In the twenty-first century, Scottish charter studies took a turn towards the digital with the publication of the resource, *People of Medieval Scotland* (https://www.poms.ac.uk). PoMS is a searchable database of information from all document texts (broadly defined) produced in, or relating to, Scotland between 1093 and 1314, and now expanded to include the royal charters up to 1371. It resulted from a series of collaborative projects that have run almost continuously from 2007 to 2020, involving historians and digital humanities specialists from a large number of institutions across the UK.[14] In the most recent version (PoMS 2018) the interface was redesigned to improve the search facility by integrating the 'search' and 'browse' features. It is important to point out that PoMS is not a database of transcribed texts; it contains information (or 'factoids') extracted from the texts that has in turn been structured into a searchable database (the names of the people and places mentioned, the type of action the texts record, any terms of tenure, stated relationships, spiritual benefits, and so on).[15] PoMS's corpus embraces a wide variety of 'text types' including, for example, charters, inquests, settlements, petitions, letters and brieves, as well as a collection of material relating to Scotland kept by the English royal

---

[14] A full list of the many individuals who have been involved in these projects can be found at https://www.poms.ac.uk/about/project-team/ [accessed 20 February 2020].

[15] Bradley & Pasin 2013.

administration from the 1290s.[16] As the name suggests, this breadth reflects the fact that PoMS is interested primarily in the *people* of medieval Scotland and their interactions and roles in a range of documentary contexts.[17] To fully understand what is possible through PoMS, it is important to understand that its raw 'data' has been extracted from the most recent printed edition of each text (only occasionally from an unpublished manuscript).[18] In many cases the most recent edition is still the antiquarian club publications; in other cases there are more recent editions (such as *Regesta regum scottorum* for the kings of Scots, or Norman Shead's edition of the acts of twelfth-century Scottish bishops, or Keith Stringer's edition of the acts of David, earl of Huntingdon).[19]

Most recently, a successor project to PoMS that ran between 2014 and 2017 has resulted in the creation of another digital resource, this time relating to original documents. *Models of Authority: Scottish Charters and the Emergence of Government, 1100–1250* (www.models ofauthority.ac.uk), presents digital images, Latin transcriptions and English translations of charters derived from a few medieval archives across Scotland between 1100 and 1250. Particular attention has been paid to the palaeography and diplomatic of these texts. *Models of Authority* is directly linked to the PoMS database, drawing much of its information from PoMS such as the dating of the texts and their bibliographical references.

[16] For the full range of text types in PoMS 2018, see 'Document type' under the 'Sources' facet. For an important discussion of the terminology used to describe transaction types in PoMS (especially in terms of how this relates to the 'dispositive language' used in the Latin texts themselves), see Davies 2011.

[17] Hammond 2013, esp. 3–13.

[18] An example of a manuscript used as a direct source for PoMS is London, BL Add. MS 33245 (a sixteenth-century cartulary from Arbroath Abbey).

[19] For full references to these and other editions, see the PoMS bibliography https://www.poms.ac.uk/information/reference-information/bibliography/ [accessed 20 February 2020].

Behind many of these editions and digital tools lie a number of other resources (some published, some unpublished), produced as part of the essential groundwork for these projects. The *Regesta regum scottorum* project initially involved the production of 'handlists' of royal charters that formed the basis of each edition.[20] In preparation for PoMS, Matthew Hammond and others compiled 'calendars' which identified the corpus and then applied a three-part numbering system to every text (known as 'Hammond numbers').[21] These calendars therefore represent a significant effort to conceptualise and rationalise the corpus as a single 'whole'. Running in parallel to the *Regesta regum scottorum* project has also been the *Syllabus of Scottish Cartularies*.[22] Each syllabus is based on a particular printed publication relating to an ecclesiastical institution or lay family. They provide a summary, dates or date ranges, and other information for each text in the publications. These various compilations have therefore been an integral part of the infrastructure for making Scotland's charter texts more readily available.

Combined, this intertwined web of printed editions, calendars, handlists, syllabuses and digital tools represents a wealth of resources for accessing and studying Scotland's corpus of charter texts. The breadth of resources means that Scotland's charters are relatively uniquely placed for interrogating patterns of survival in the context of medieval documents.

[20] The handlists exist only as typescripts, originally circulated to members of the Scottish Medievalists and a few libraries.

[21] For an explanation of the 'H-numbers', see https://www.poms.ac.uk/information/numbering-system-for-documents/.

[22] Cunningham 1995. Like *Regesta regum scottorum*, this project was initiated by the Scottish Medievalists and has continued to bear fruit until the present. A list of the syllabuses can currently be found at *Scottish Medieval Charters* (https://scottishmedievalcharters.wordpress.com/scottish-cartularies/).
Matthew Hammond has also been active in extending this project in recent years.

The survival of Scotland's document texts

A key virtue of PoMS is that it embraces the totality of the known corpus of Scottish documents. It can therefore provide a quantitative starting point for investigating survival and loss. Currently, the total number of texts in PoMS is 10,031. Of these, just over half (5,426) are categorised as 'charter texts'.[23] To reiterate, this is the number of surviving charter texts up to 1314 plus royal charters up to 1371. The total figure for 'charter texts' up to 1314 is 4,238. In a British and Irish context, this falls well below the figures for charter texts from England, but sits well above contemporary equivalents for Ireland or Wales.[24]

Let us take a closer look at this raw total of 5,426 charter texts. Only a proportion of these survive as a 'contemporary original', that is, a single-sheet document produced at the time (or soon after) the transaction it recorded: the number according to PoMS is 1,615 (29% of the total).[25] Less than one third of Scotland's charter texts therefore currently survive in their original form. The remaining 71% can be found in later copies, including a variety of medieval and early modern transcripts and summaries. The majority of copies survive in one particular kind of source: manuscript books known as 'cartularies'. These were generally produced by the holders of the original charters, who might copy documents from their archive into a codex. In Scotland, cartularies were produced from the early thirteenth century onwards, especially by major ecclesiastical

---

[23] PoMS 2018. The figures can be found when searching by 'Sources' and looking at 'Document type: Charter' under the 'Sources' facet. All figures quoted here from PoMS 2018 were accessed on 15 February 2020.

[24] Bates 2005, 7.

[25] To filter by 'Originals (contemporary)', see under the 'Source features' facet. If the date range is reduced to 1314 (to exclude the royal charters up to 1371), the proportion is almost identical: 1,184 'Originals (contemporary)' out of 4,238 charter texts (28%).

institutions with growing archives of documents.[26] While PoMS does not allow users to refine the manuscript source to this level of detail, it is probably fair to say that the majority of the charter texts that survive as a copy do so in a medieval cartulary of some sort.[27] What these bald figures reveal (29% originals versus 71% copies), therefore, is just how far copies bulk out the surviving corpus of charter texts from Scotland in this period. Clearly, our view of the kingdom and its inhabitants from the eleventh to fourteenth centuries would be quite reduced (and even more unevenly so) had charters not been copied into cartularies and other later manuscripts.

PoMS is therefore a powerful tool for counting texts that survive in any physical form. What cannot be so readily discovered through PoMS, however, is the precise form in which each text currently exists, beyond the basic question of whether it is an 'original' or not.[28] It is not possible to view the corpus from a 'manuscript' perspective. This is primarily a result of the database resting on the printed editions. Such a manuscript perspective was not the aim of PoMS, and frankly would have been an insurmountable task given the

---

[26] Another context for copies apart from cartularies is in charter rolls. In England royal charter rolls survive from the 1190s. Any royal charter rolls that once existed in twelfth- and thirteenth-century Scotland were lost with the rest of the early royal archive. Only fragments of those compiled in the fourteenth century survive. For a deft summary of the complex survival of King Robert I's charters (including some in rolls), see Hammond [2020].

[27] This situation is not unique to Scotland: cartularies are a major source for charter texts across Europe, though it is not generally possible to be as precise about the proportions of survival. For an online database of cartularies from French-speaking regions, see *CartulR: Répertoire des cartulaires médievaux et modernes* (http://www.cn-telma.fr/cartulR/index/).

[28] Under the 'Source features' facet, the full range of options are: Chirograph, Duplicate original (contemporary), Duplicate original (non-contemporary), Letter patent, Original (contemporary), and Original (non-contemporary).

complexity of the situation. Many texts in PoMS, for example, appear in multiple manuscript copies.

The manuscript context is, however, extremely significant for charter texts, especially for their transmission and preservation. A cartulary copy is very different from the original document: it is not just the seal that is lost but also other features such as the handwriting, the size of the document, its folding patterns, endorsements and the original spellings. While cartularies have always been treated with a level of caution as a source for originals by charter scholars, the manuscripts themselves are more dynamic than has always been appreciated, in ways that can have significant implications for the preservation of charter texts. Since the 1990s in particular, a new body of scholarship has emphasised that whereas previously the cartulary had been viewed as essentially a copy of an archive of charters, produced as a back-up in case of losses, in fact cartularies can often be shown to be selective in their contents.[29] The scribes, in other words, were making creative decisions about what they copied from the archive, and in what order. They may also contain unexplained 'duplicates' of texts. The cartulary is not, therefore, a mirror image of the contents or organisation of the archive.[30] At a deeper level, however, the cartulary manuscripts themselves are often dynamic sources in terms of their construction and use. Many contain 'multi-scribe', piecemeal additions which reveal—in their particular nature—that these manuscripts were read and extended by their communities, in a sense as 'active' manuscripts that 'lived' alongside the archive.[31] In these cases, the choice of which texts to copy was often more about individuals actively responding to the cartulary's

---

[29] For example, see the various essays in Guyotjeannin, Morelle & Parisse 1993.
[30] Some cartularies are explicitly related to an archive, noting, for example, the location of the document in the archive. A good example of this is Byland Abbey's early fifteenth-century cartulary: see Burton 2004.
[31] Tucker 2020.

form and contents than it was a pre-planned campaign of what to include or omit. The result is that the cartulary's overall contents, and which charter texts it ended up preserving, is essentially unpredictable and down to the work of individual scribes.

For the question of survival, it is therefore imperative to move beyond the simple binary of 'originals' versus 'copies', and not to group all 'copies' into the same category. This is especially important when using a resource like PoMS which encompasses charter texts found in medieval cartularies but also in antiquarian transcripts and later judicial records. Even for the category of 'originals' there are grey areas of whether they are contemporary or later productions.[32] In order to discover this level of detail, users typically have to leave PoMS and return to the editions.

How are the manuscript sources for each text to be identified? Shelf-marks of original charters are sometimes noted in PoMS (under 'notes' in the document's profile page), but PoMS's main references are to the printed editions. These references in isolation do not usually reveal the manuscripts in question.[33] In the more modern printed editions, such as the *Regesta regum scottorum* volumes, the manuscript sources themselves are of course given in the notes under each text. These provide the manuscript shelf-mark but usually do not include a description or title for the manuscript (such as whether it is a cartulary). A certain amount of familiarity with the conventions is

---

[32] For a useful discussion of charter 'authenticity', see Mortimer 1990. See also the category of text in PoMS described as 'Original (non-contemporary)' under 'Source features'. These are single-sheet documents which appear to have been written long after the transaction they record but not always in the context of forgery.

[33] Some printed publications are based on a single manuscript, in which case the manuscript can be ascertained from the bibliographical reference alone (at least by those users equipped with this knowledge). An example is Dowden 1903 (an edition of a cartulary manuscript from Lindores Abbey discovered in Caprington Castle).

therefore required to interpret these references. Some 'physical description' is usually provided beyond the shelf-mark: for originals there are notes on the sealing and endorsements, and for copies in books the editor might note the date of the manuscript and any rubrics or significant marginalia. Readers might also discover that the editorial approach in the *Regesta regum scottorum* volumes generally differs depending on whether the source is an original, an early copy, or a later copy. Punctuation, for example, might be retained for originals and certain 'early' copies, but be editorial for later copies.[34] A natural hierarchy also exists whereby originals were generally not collated against later copies since it was the original texts that were the main subject of interest.

When using PoMS or the editions of royal acts, it is easy to lose sight of the archival and manuscript context, and the nuances of how and where each text survives. Much of this context requires codicological and palaeographical descriptions that such printed editions or digital resources could not possibly have offered for each of its sources within the scope of their projects. It is therefore up to the users of these publications to be aware of the effect they have in 'flattening' the corpus of charter texts.

It could be argued that PoMS provides an extensive quantitative view but a limited qualitative view of the surviving corpus. It should be said that these limitations largely reflect a new direction of travel for charter scholarship since 2007, one in which PoMS itself has been an important engine powering new lines of questioning and opening up alternative routes of investigation. Scholars have become more interested, for example, in the 'physical context' of the text and not

---

[34] This was Barrow's general principle, with 'early' meaning pre-fifteenth-century manuscripts (Barrow 1960, 128; Barrow 1971, 115). Duncan (1988, 271), on the other hand, used editorial punctuation for all texts, even originals.

solely its content.³⁵ This is partly reflected in the development of *Models of Authority*, which is furnished with images of the documents that allow the texts to be viewed immediately in their 'manuscript context'. In order to begin exploring new avenues such as these through PoMS, however, it is imperative to travel with an appreciation for the archival setting in which charter texts from Scotland have survived or perished. Charter scholars are well aware of the significance of the 'archival perspective', especially for patterns of survival.³⁶ What is missing from the current scholarly infrastructure for Scotland's charters is a detailed survey of survival by medieval archive. The final section offers an attempt to address this question.

Mapping the survival and loss of Scotland's medieval ecclesiastical archives

It is fair to say that no archive of original charters from Scotland has survived completely intact, nor does any collection of documents remain in its original medieval location. Many collections have been dispersed or lost as a result of changing of hands, especially after the Reformation. Most of Scotland's original charters and copies of charter texts reside today in a variety of repositories, especially the National Library of Scotland (NLS), the British Library (BL), the National Records of Scotland (NRS), The National Archives (TNA),

---

[35] This interest was set in motion before the conception of PoMS: Broun 2001, 206–07. Broun compares the early editions of kings of Scots' charters to G.W.S. Barrow's 1999 edition of David I's *acta*, noting a change in perspective from seeing charters as 'quarries of information about people and places' to seeing them 'not only as texts, but (in the case of extant contemporary single sheets) as physical objects'.

[36] For example, Broun 2005, 168–79; Vincent 2005, 72–75; Pryce 2005, 186–87; Broun 2001, 211; Hammond 2013, 22–30.

and Durham University Library.[37] Our awareness of the existence of these documents is dependent on printed editions or modern catalogues produced by these repositories. In some cases, a substantial proportion of original documents from a medieval archive survive; in other cases, only a handful remain; for many institutions, there is no trace of any original medieval documents, even as copies. It is difficult to be precise about figures here since, despite all of the editions, calendars and digital resources, there is as yet no single catalogue of original charters from Scotland. This would be extremely useful as a future project.[38] Medieval cartularies are easier to identify because there is a single catalogue in this case compiled by G. R. C. Davis in 1958 and then revised and expanded in 2010.[39] 'Cartulary' as a term, however, can include a wide variety of manuscripts.[40]

The map here presents the information about the survival of charter texts from medieval ecclesiastical archives in Scotland as far as is currently known through the available resources.[41] The map is at best a single snapshot; more information will undoubtedly come to light in future. A few further dimensions should be noted. The survey asks what survives from that particular institution, whether a

[37] Coldingham Priory's archive perhaps suffered the least disruption, probably being kept at Durham Cathedral in its medieval lifetime (Coldingham being a cell of Durham) and being moved more recently to the University Library in 1948.
[38] The closest thing to a catalogue of pre-1250 originals at the moment is the resource, and associated documentation, for *Models of Authority* 2019, though this only relates to a few medieval archives. Matthew Hammond's work on the calendars of Scottish charters up to 1286 is also bringing to light many collections and individual documents.
[39] Davis 1958; Davis 2010.
[40] For the issues surrounding the definition of the cartulary, and for understanding the Davis catalogues, see Tucker 2019, 149–56.
[41] I am very grateful to Matthew Hammond for sharing his notes on collections of original charters for this article.

collection of originals, a cartulary (or more than one cartulary), both of these, or neither of these. For consistency with PoMS, 1314 has been taken as the temporal limit of this survey (PoMS deals only with extant royal charters for the period 1314–1371). The map therefore only considers the survival of charter texts datable before 1314, and therefore also only plots the major ecclesiastical institutions that existed by then.[42] The geographical bounds of PoMS have also been adopted for the survey, meaning the map includes Berwick and the Isle of Man but excludes the Northern Isles (Orkney and Shetland).[43] For the sake of space, the map has restricted the types of communities to essentially monasteries (monks and canons), monastic cells, and cathedrals. A full list is provided in Appendix 1.[44] Since 'lay' archives are harder to plot, these have been excluded. It should be noted, however, that had they been included they would add substantially to

---

[42] The relevant institutions have been identified using Ian B. Cowan and David E. Easson's *Medieval Religious Houses Scotland*, 2nd edition (Cowan & Eason 1976), which lists the religious houses in Scotland up to the Reformation in 1560. Any communities which had dissolved already by 1314 are not included, such as the foundation of Gilbertines at Dalmiling, Ayr. In practice, the latest foundations in the survey are late-thirteenth century: Fogo Priory (fd. 1253 × 1297), Fyvie Priory (fd. 1285), Sweetheart Abbey (fd. 1273) and Abernethy Priory (fd. 1272 or 1273).

[43] PoMS's boundaries reflect the extent of the kingdom at the death of King Alexander III on 19 March 1286. The Northern Isles did not become part of the kingdom until the fifteenth century.

[44] Those communities excluded from the maps (but included in Cowan & Easson 1976) are: the Blackfriars, Franciscans, Carmelites, Augustinian friars, Friars of the sack, Knights Templars, Knights Hospitallers, Hospitals, Secular colleges, and Trinitarians. (Other communities are automatically excluded, such as the Carthusians or secular academic colleges, because none existed before 1314.) Those communities included on the maps are, therefore: Augustinians, Benedictines, Cistercians, Cluniacs, Premonstratensians, Tironensians, Valliscaulians, and cathedrals chapters.

the picture of loss given that little survives from Scottish lay archives from the period before 1314.[45] Another factor to bear in mind is that PoMS itself also depends significantly on the collections of charter texts from institutions based outside of Scotland where these related to lands in Scotland (notably Durham Cathedral Priory and Holm Cultram Abbey).

Out of the 72 institutions plotted on the map, only nine have a 'substantial' number of originals (13%), and only 18 have an extant medieval cartulary (25%). This is in stark contrast to those 48 institutions with no surviving collections of charter texts (67%). Let us first consider the various surviving corpora, in all their forms, before turning to the total losses.

In terms of original documents, the map distinguishes between 'substantial' and 'small' numbers. The full details of these collections (as they are currently understood) have been laid out in Appendix 2. The category of 'substantial' conceals a broad spectrum. The largest collections comprise hundreds of pre-1314 documents, such as those for Coldingham Priory (about 428 originals) or Melrose Abbey (about 258 originals); the smallest in this group are in the dozens, such as those for Newbattle Abbey (at least 42) or North Berwick Priory (24 originals). However, scale is not necessarily an indicator of survival success here: North Berwick's may be a modest number of originals, but as a small nunnery this may in fact represent a larger proportion of its original pre-1314 archive than for some of the other institutions. The 'small' category represents those for which

---

[45] Hammond 2013, 27–9; Hammond 2014, 114–15. Notable exceptions are charters derived from the archive of the Bruces of Annandale (TNA, Duchy of Lancaster collection), and the cartularies of the earls of Douglas (NLS 72, fourteenth century) and the earls of Lennox (NRS GD220/2/202, fifteenth century).

Map: Survival by archive of document texts (datable before 1314) from monastic and cathedral communities founded by 1314

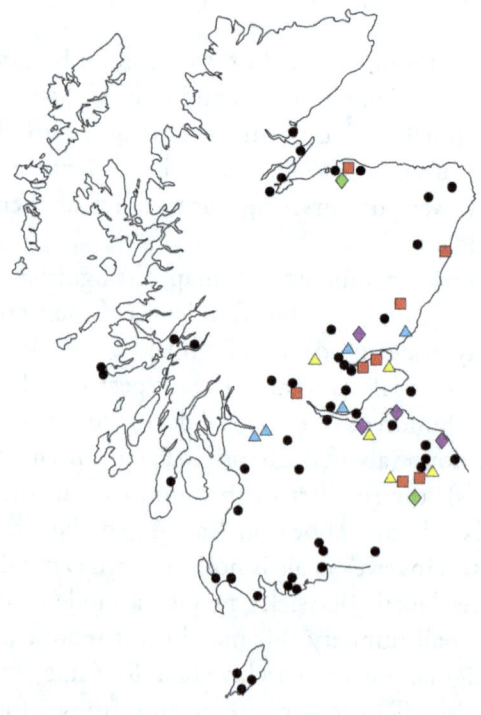

Key

△ Cartulary/cartularies plus substantial number of pre-1314 originals (total 5)
△ Cartulary/cartularies plus small number of pre-1314 originals (total 5)
■ Cartulary/cartularies (sometimes with one or two pre-1314 originals) (total 8)
◆ Substantial number of pre-1314 originals (total 4)
◆ Small number of pre-1314 originals (total 2)
● No cartulary or collection of originals (sometimes one pre-1314 original) (total 48)

only a handful of originals have been identified which mainly survive together. Scone has the largest with at least 13; the others all have between four and six known documents (the abbeys of Paisley, Arbroath, Jedburgh and Dunfermline, Pluscarden Priory, and Glasgow Cathedral). Another group of institutions are those which have a cartulary and sometimes one or two originals. Examples include Kelso Abbey and Aberdeen Cathedral.[46] It is likely that many more stray survivals exist and will be brought to light in future, and that as a result some institutions might be re-categorised on the map.

As for medieval cartularies, the map represents the conventional view of the corpus as originally established by G.R.C. Davis in 1958, excluding what he described as 'other registers'.[47] It must be remembered, however, that there are a range of sources for copies of charters texts not included here, including early modern or antiquarian transcripts.[48] It is also important to remember that the map presents survival and loss by archive, not in general. There are cases where documents from one archive have found their way into the manuscripts from another institution (such as being copied into

---

[46] For Kelso, there is a charter of King Malcolm IV in the NLS (Dep. 255; Barrow 1960, no. 131; deposited since 1924 by the Duke of Roxburghe) and a charter of King William in the Yule Collection in NRS (GD90/1/8; Barrow 1971, no. 367). For Aberdeen, there is one pre-1314 original in the NLS (Adv. MS 15.1.18, no. 84).

[47] The only exception is St Andrews Cathedral Priory's thirteenth-century cartulary (NRS GD45/27/8) which has been included on the map despite not being in Davis 1958 (it was only 'rediscovered' in the 1960s). On Davis' system of categorisation, see Tucker 2019, 149–56.

[48] For example, the charters of Beauly Priory have been published from an eighteenth-century transcript by Walter MacFarlane (NLS Adv. MS 35.2.4): Batten 1877. For Coupar Angus Abbey, as well as its collection of original charters (published as Easson 1947) there is also Sir James Balfour of Denmilne's seventeenth-century transcript of a lost register (NLS Adv. MS 33.2.9): Rogers 1879–80.

their mother house's cartulary), but these do not count on the map as an example of 'survival'.[49] Seven of the institutions on the map have more than one medieval cartulary (the abbeys of Scone, Melrose, Lindores and Arbroath, and the cathedrals of Elgin, Glasgow and Aberdeen). As already mentioned, medieval cartularies were not usually an exact 'file copy' of an entire archive but instead can be shown to be selective in what the scribes chose to copy. This selectivity is one reason which puts to bed the idea that cartularies were compiled for the sake of the 'preservation' of the archive.[50] Cartularies therefore represent a fundamentally different form of 'survival' from collections of originals. Those institutions for which 'only cartularies' survive should be read as collections of texts that could often have been shaped by fundamentally individual, responsive and sometimes unpredictable conditions.

From the proportions alone, it appears that cartularies were more likely to survive than collections of original charters. It is not hard to imagine why this might be, given the general portability of a manuscript book over a stack of fragile parchment sheets. However, any pattern that may exist is not a general rule. Coupar Angus Abbey is an example where many original charters survive but the medieval cartulary, which is known to have existed into the seventeenth century, is lost.[51] For some other institutions with only a collection of originals, it is not clear that there ever was a cartulary (including North Berwick Priory, Holyrood Abbey, Coldingham Priory,

---

[49] The thirteenth-century cartulary from St Andrews Cathedral Priory, for example, contains sections of documents for Loch Leven Priory, Monymusk Priory, and the Isle of May Priory. See, respectively, Thomson 1840, 113–18, 362–76 and 379–97.

[50] For a critique of the general idea of cartularies as a means of 'preservation', see Tucker 2020, 20, 191 and 226–27.

[51] See n. 48.

Pluscarden Priory and Jedburgh Abbey).[52] Losses of medieval cartularies have certainly been significant. A notable example is the *Magnum registrum* of St Andrews Cathedral Priory which is known to have contained some copies of charters to the priory (though a thirteenth-century cartulary does survive).[53] In some cases, such as Glenluce, Kilwinning and Crossraguel (all monasteries in south-west Scotland), the cartulary manuscripts appear to have existed as late as the eighteenth century but have now disappeared from view.[54] It is not impossible that cartularies might resurface in future: the most recent 'rediscovery' was St Andrews Cathedral Priory's thirteenth-century cartulary which was deposited in the Scottish Record Office (now NRS) in the 1960s.[55] The extant corpus of cartularies is therefore infused with a certain level of unpredictability and chance, both in terms of which manuscripts survive as well as what they each contain.

Each archive has therefore experienced its own individual journey. This is reflected in the fact that often the manuscripts from a single institution exist in different repositories today. A striking example is the charters and cartularies of Melrose Abbey. The documents mostly reside in a single collection in the NRS (GD55); a few ended up in the Cotton collection and are now in the BL (principally in Cotton Chrs xviii); the earlier cartulary, now in the NLS (Adv. MS 34.4.11), was donated by Henry Malcolm, minister of Ballingry, to what was then the Faculty of Advocates Library in 1708;[56] and the later cartulary, now in the BL (Harley 3960), passed through various hands

---

[52] Davis 2010 lists manuscripts associated with Holyrood, Coldingham and Jedburgh, but these are what he described in his 1958 catalogue as 'other registers'.

[53] For the lost register, see Davis 2010, no. 1176, and Anderson 1980, 55.

[54] Durkan 1971; Hammond 2013, 23.

[55] The manuscript was listed as 'untraced' in Davis 1958 (no. 1175) but in Davis 2010 it is present with its shelf-mark (GD45/27/8).

[56] Cunningham 1989, 125.

before ending up in Robert Harley's collection and then being purchased by the British Museum. Ultimately, every individual collection of charters has been shaped and re-shaped by a range of factors, choices and events, both accidental and deliberate, across its medieval, early modern and modern lifetime. The map is necessarily a simplification of this situation.

Turning now to the abundance of black dots on the map, the contours of survival become even more vivid. Each of these represents a case where, whether original documents or cartularies once existed or not, they have now disappeared. It is immediately apparent that the geographical distribution of Scotland's extant corpus of charter texts is very uneven. Now, to be clear, the points on the map simply represent institutions and their respective collections of charter texts. It is important to note, therefore, that while the institutions in, for example, Galloway in south-west Scotland have essentially suffered a total wipe-out, there are surviving texts which relate to that region since other churches with surviving charter collections did have dealings there (notably the abbeys of Holyrood, Kelso and Holm Cultram).[57] Equally, the institution or its properties might make an appearance in agreements or other documents preserved in another archive or cartulary.[58] Furthermore, the map does not reveal Scotland's topography which can explain some of the white space (notably in the central highlands, for example, where no monasteries

---

[57] Stringer 2000, 212–34. The losses for Galloway are exemplified in *Wigtownshire Charters* (Reid 1960), which is a compilation of documents drawn from various sources relating to Whithorn, Glenluce, Soulseat, Wigtown and Cruggleton.

[58] This is where PoMS is indispensable. It allows us to scour the corpus of documents for mentions of any people or institutions involved in a transaction. For example, Whithorn Cathedral Priory has 48 'transaction factoids' associated with it in PoMS; Dundrennan Abbey has twelve; Sweetheart Abbey has fourteen; and Glenluce Abbey has one. There are three abbots of Tongland in PoMS, and one prioress of Lincluden.

were founded). Nevertheless, the geographical concentration is stark. In western Scotland and the very north, there are far fewer relevant institutions, and nearly no charters record gifts of lands in these areas. Fife, on the other hand, in eastern Scotland, is relatively rich with surviving document texts, owing to the archives and cartularies of the many monasteries of the new orders founded here in the twelfth and thirteenth centuries, each endowed with substantial grants of property in the surrounding area.

One example of where this disparity has had a significant impact is in placename studies. Surviving collections of charter texts have allowed the medieval forms of names and their development to be traced in great detail for Fife in five volumes produced by Simon Taylor with Gilbert Márkus.[59] Similar work has recently been undertaken by Simon Taylor, Eila Williamson and Carole Hough (with others) for the placenames of Berwickshire in south-east Scotland, which is also well served by monasteries and their charter collections from the central Middle Ages.[60] The distribution of surviving corpora of medieval charter texts has therefore played, and continues to play, a significant role in steering the research of early placenames.

The archival context of survival therefore puts the extant corpus of charter texts, as amassed in PoMS, in a new light. Its geographical limitations become immediately apparent, and the distinction between collections of originals and collections of copies in cartularies also comes to the fore as a key part of the corpus's character. Those of us who regularly use charters in our research may be generally aware of the issue of losses and the uneven spread of the surviving corpus, and we may also be intensely aware of the significance of an original versus a cartulary copy or an antiquarian transcript. The challenge, however, is to hold these issues in the foreground at all times, even

---

[59] Taylor with Márkus 2006–12.
[60] *The Berwickshire Place-Name Resource* (Hough et al. 2019).

when the editions or digital representations do not emphasise these dimensions or 'flatten' the corpus and its texts. The question of how a text has survived is not, therefore, simply background information; it is the primary lens through which we must conceptualise and read the corpus of extant charter texts.

Conclusion

It is not straightforward to establish how many manuscripts or archives of documents survive from medieval Scotland. Much depends on what is being counted. Nevertheless, it is possible to paint a relatively detailed picture of the current state of our knowledge. It is obvious, especially when looking through an archival lens, that this corpus has suffered many losses, both of originals and of medieval cartularies. This can have serious implications for our research. It is natural for historians to fix their gaze on extant texts. For charters, however, it is important to be aware of the unpredictability of survival patterns, especially where cartularies are concerned. It is equally important to be continuously mindful of how we access those texts that do survive, and how this can implicitly shape our perspective by accentuating some aspects of the corpus but minimising others, such as the manuscript context.

The extent to which the picture presented here is reliant on the available scholarly infrastructure cannot be overstated. A wealth of resources is now available for investigating the survival and loss of documents from medieval Scotland. As such, Scotland is one of the few examples in western Europe where such information can be readily assembled and presented for the entire kingdom. At the same time, it is perhaps precisely because of this abundance of resources that charter scholarship relating to Scotland is able to be more critical of our own approaches to the corpus as a whole. This chapter has attempted to survey some of these resources and assess their distinct virtues, whilst also appreciating their unique scope and limitations. Each has its own emphasis, which has changed and grown with the scholarly community's research interests. Many of these resources are intertwined, and as such they enrich one another when used in combination.

The long tradition of printed editions of charters since the second quarter of the nineteenth century has significantly enhanced our work today, especially in identifying manuscripts, ascertaining their provenance, as well as in reading their Latin texts. The enormous scope offered by PoMS has changed the way Scottish charter scholarship can be conducted in the twenty-first century. While this is manifestly an asset, there are also hidden hazards in accessing such a sweep of information through a structured digital database. Most notably, it is not possible to look at the data from a manuscript perspective. Questions relating to the manuscripts can be pursued through the printed editions, which usually provide much of the necessary detail, but only to an extent. The edited texts can still be 'removed' from their manuscript context in significant ways. A text in a cartulary, for example, can benefit from being read in its 'physical' context, especially in relation to the arrangement of the documents and the scribes that copied it. Such contextual reading can offer a deeper insight into the patterns of charter text survival, and how contingent this might be on the activities of individual scribes. A map such as that included here can provide another perspective on the corpus as it stands today. Such a broad-brush approach can also, however, make the data appear two-dimensional, concealing the individual characteristics of each archival environment, its losses and historical development. In future, it is hoped that this archival picture of survival might be sharpened in order to act as a complement to the existing suite of resources. Such future work should seek not to replace what exists but to add fresh perspectives onto what is already available. Charter scholarship is, after all, most effective when it combines resources, methods and perspectives.

The 'darkness' in our archives might be understood, therefore, as not just the losses and gaps in the historical record. It can also be present in how we conceptualise, represent, and interact with those materials that do survive in any given context. Charters from Scotland are increasingly moving into a digital world, not just via digital databases but also with the digitisation of older printed editions as well as the mass digitisation of charters and cartularies, all freely available online.[61] Faster, more powerful, more wide-ranging digital resources can certainly shine a new light on our sources, but they cannot capture all of their key dimensions. They depend inevitably on choices and priorities that can obscure as well as reveal aspects of the source material itself, such as the manuscript context or archival setting, both key features of the broader context of survival. The movement towards the digital therefore calls for an even greater critical awareness of the manuscripts from which they are derived, and the archival settings which preserved them or copies of them.

---

[61] The digitisation of Scottish charters has been brought to a new level via *Models of Authority*. The NLS is currently digitising its collection of 27 cartulary manuscripts, which are due to be put online by the end of 2021 and will be available according to the International Image Interoperability Framework (IIIF) standards.

Appendix 1
A list of the communities included on the maps

Pre-1975 county[62]	Religious house	Community status	Archival status for pre-1314 charter texts
ABD	Aberdeen Cathedral	Cathedral, secular chapter	Cartularies only
	Deer Abbey	Cistercian	Neither
	Fyvie Priory	Tironensian	Neither
	Monymusk Priory	Augustinian	Neither
ANG	Arbroath Abbey	Tironensian	Cartularies plus small no. of originals
	Brechin Cathedral	Cathedral, secular chapter	Cartulary only
	Restenneth Priory	Augustinian	Neither
ARG	Ardchattan Priory	Valliscaulian	Neither
	Iona Abbey	Benedictine	Neither
	Iona Priory	Augustinian	Neither
	Lismore Cathedral	Cathedral, secular chapter	Neither
	Saddell Abbey	Cistercian	Neither
AYR	Crossraguel Abbey	Cluniac	Neither
	Kilwinning Priory	Tironensian	Neither
BWK	Berwick Priory	Cistercian	Neither

[62] These county abbreviations are explained in PoMS 2019, https://www.poms.ac.uk/information/county-abbreviations-list/ (accessed 17 February 2020).

	Coldingham Priory	Benedictine	Substantial no. of originals only
	Coldstream Priory	Cistercian	Cartulary plus substantial no. of originals
	Dryburgh Abbey	Premonstratensian	Cartulary only
	Eccles Priory	Cistercian	Neither
	St Bothan's Priory	Cistercian	Neither
DMF	Canonbie Priory	Augustinian	Neither
	Dercongal Abbey	Premonstratensian	Neither
	Lincluden Priory[63]	Benedictine	Neither
ELO	Haddington Priory	Cistercian	Neither
	North Berwick Priory	Cistercian	Substantial no. of originals only
FIF	Balmerino Abbey	Cistercian	Cartulary only
	Culross Abbey	Cistercian	Neither
	Dunfermline Abbey	Benedictine	Cartulary plus small no. of originals
	Inchcolm Abbey	Augustinian	Neither
	Lindores Abbey	Tironensian	Cartularies only
	May Priory /Pittenweem[64]	Benedictine	Neither
	St Andrews Cathedral Priory	Augustinian	Cartulary plus substantial no. of originals

[63] Cowan & Easson 1976, 143, list the Benedictine nunnery of Lincluden in Kirkcudbrightshire, but in fact it falls just within what was Dumfriesshire.

[64] For the complex history of this community (which was originally a cell of Reading Abbey but, by 1318, had been transferred to St Andrews Cathedral Priory, thus becoming Augustinian), see Cowan & Easson 1976, 59–60 and 94–95.

INV	Beauly Priory	Valliscaulian	Neither
Isle Man/INV	Peel Cathedral/ Snizort (bishop of the Isles)[65]	Cathedral, chapter status unknown	Neither
Isle of Man	Douglas Priory	Cistercian	Neither
	Rushen Abbey	Cistercian	Neither
KCB	Dundrennan Abbey	Cistercian	Neither
	St Mary's Isle Priory	Augustinian	Neither
	Sweetheart Abbey	Cistercian	Neither
	Tongland Abbey	Premonstratensian	Neither
KNR	Lochleven Priory	Augustinian	Neither
LAN	Blantyre Priory	Augustinian	Neither
	Glasgow Cathedral	Cathedral, secular chapter	Cartularies plus small no. of originals
	Lesmahagow Priory	Tironensian	Neither
MLO	Holyrood Abbey	Augustinian	Substantial number of originals only
	Newbattle Abbey	Cistercian	Cartulary plus substantial no. of originals
MOR	Elgin Cathedral	Cathedral, secular chapter	Cartularies only
	Kinloss Abbey	Cistercian	Neither

[65] This seat is plotted at Peel (Isle of Man) on the map. Also known as the diocese of 'Sodor', two separate bishops (one for the Isle of Man, one for the Western Isles) only emerged after the Great Schism of 1378: Cowan & Easson 1976, 209. There may have been an attempt in the early 1330s to move the seat from Peel to Snizort on the isle of Skye: Thomas 2009, 155–56.

	Pluscarden Priory	Valliscaulian	Small number of originals only
	Urquhart Priory	Benedictine	Neither
PER	Abernethy Priory	Augustinian	Neither
	Coupar Angus Abbey	Cistercian	Substantial no. of originals only
	Dunblane Cathedral	Cathedral, secular chapter	Neither
	Dunkeld Cathedral	Cathedral, secular chapter	Neither
	Elcho Priory	Cistercian	Neither
	Inchaffray Abbey	Augustinian	Cartulary plus substantial no. of originals
	Inchmahome Priory	Augustinian	Neither
	Perth Priory (St Leonard's)	Augustinian	Neither
	Scone Abbey	Augustinian	Cartulary plus small no. of originals
RNF	Paisley Abbey	Cluniac	Cartulary plus small no. of originals
ROS	Fearn Abbey	Premonstratensian	Neither
	Fortrose Cathedral	Cathedral, secular chapter	Neither
ROX	Fogo Priory	Tironensian	Neither
	Jedburgh Abbey	Augustinian	Small no. of originals only
	Kelso Abbey	Tironensian	Cartulary only

	Melrose Abbey	Cistercian	Cartularies plus substantial no. of originals
STL	Cambuskenneth Abbey	Augustinian	Cartulary only
SUT	Dornoch Cathedral	Cathedral, secular chapter	Neither
WIG	Glenluce Abbey	Cistercian	Neither
	Soulseat Abbey	Premonstratensian	Neither
	Whithorn Cathedral Priory	Premonstratensian	Neither
WLO	Manuel Priory	Cistercian	Neither

Appendix 2
A summary of the collections of originals on the map

The information presented here will certainly change as our knowledge of the extant corpus grows and becomes more defined. The figures relate to original documents of all kinds (not just 'charter texts' narrowly defined) definitely datable before 1314. I am grateful to Matthew Hammond for sharing his notes with me to update my own knowledge of the surviving collections. The tables below reflect much of his ongoing research (though any oversights or inaccuracies are my own). I am also grateful to Alan Borthwick and Alison Rosie for providing some points of clarification on some of the NRS collections.

Table 1

Those institutions on the map with a 'substantial number of pre-1314 originals'

Religious house		Centre column: No. of pre-1314 originals Right column: Notes
Coldingham Priory	c. 428	The current location of these originals is Durham, DCA Misc. Chrs. For the dates and shelf-marks, see Scott and Hammond [n.d.]. The figure of 428 has been extracted manually from the *Syllabus*.
Melrose Abbey	c. 258	See Innes 1837 (volume 1 lists 252 originals; volume 2 lists six pre-1314 originals, nos. 376–80 and 383). The bulk of Melrose charters are in NRS GD55 ('Charters of the Abbey of Melrose', deposited by the Duke of Buccleuch in 1952). There are also some in London, BL Cotton Chrs xviii. For Melrose's pre-1250 charters, see *Models of Authority* (which also includes two charters in other BL collections in which Melrose is the beneficiary: Add. Ch. 76747 and L.F.C. Ch. xxx.7).
Inchaffray Abbey	120	See Lindsay, Dowden and Thomson 1908, nos. 1–120. (Note that the editors also include charters in the Appendix but not all are originals or related to Inchaffray.) The charters are part of the earl of Kinnoull's muniments, and were previously held at Dupplin Castle. They were damaged in a flood while in Perth in 1993, and now reside in the NRS.
Holyrood Abbey	84	See Innes 1847b, nos. 1–84. For the precise dates, see Cunningham 2001. The bulk of the

		Holyrood charters are in NRS GD45/13 ('Papers of the Maule Family, Earls of Dalhousie'). There are also four in the 'Yule Collection' (NRS GD90/1/3, 10, 11 and 16). For Holyrood's pre-1250 charters, see *Models of Authority*. Some originals printed in the 1847 edition have since disappeared: see Broun 2005, 167.
Coupar Angus Abbey	at least 78	See Easson 1947, see nos. 1–96. Of these, the originals definitely pre-1314 (identified in combination with PoMS's more accurate dating) are nos. 1–66, 69–70, 72–73, 75, 80–81, 83–85, 87 and 96 (78 in total). The other eighteen have been excluded either because they are post-1314 (nos. 67–68 and 94–95), because they span the 1314 boundary (nos. 71 and 88–93), or because they can only be roughly dated 'circa' the years between 1302 and 1306 (nos. 74, 76–79, 82 and 86). The charters are currently in the earl of Moray's muniments at Darnaway Castle.
St Andrews Cathedral Priory	at least 53	The bulk of the priory's charters (pasted into volumes by James Balfour of Denmilne, d. 1657) are in NLS Adv. MSS 15.1.18 (charters) and 15.1.19 (papal bulls). There are 47 pre-1314 charters in 15.1.18 (for those that are pre-1250, see *Models of Authority*). For the papal bulls, the NLS's online catalogue states that 17 relate to St Andrews (nos. 1–2, 4–7, 11–13, 17–23 and 25), though it is not clear how many of these are pre-1314; four certainly are since they are in PoMS (nos. 13, 19, 21 and 22). Additionally, there are two in the 'Yule

		Collection' (NRS GD90/1/2 and 5). There may also be some charters for the priory in St Andrews University Library.
Newbattle Abbey	at least 42	The bulk of Newbattle's charters are in NRS GD40/1 ('Papers of the Kerr Family, Marquises of Lothian'). The first 32 are pre-1314; there are also nine pre-1314 papal bulls (GD40/1/85–93). See the NRS's online catalogue for full details. Additionally, there is one Newbattle charter in the 'Yule Collection' (NRS GD90/1/6). Innes 1849 (which prints the cartulary) refers to some of these charters in the *Tabula* and in the Appendix.
Coldstream Priory	at least 35	Matthew Hammond has identified 31, pre-1314 Coldstream charters in NRS GD212 ('J. Maitland Thomson collection') and at least four in RH6 ('Register House charters, 1st series').
North Berwick Priory	24	See Innes 1847a, nos. 1–24. The *Tabula* identifies various locations and owners of the charters, most of which can now be tracked: those 'at Panmure' are in NRS GD45/13 ('Papers of the Maule Family, Earls of Dalhousie'); those 'at Marchmont' are probably in the collection of the Rt Hon Lord Polwarth (NRAS 245); those with Mr C. Innes and one of those with Mr. A. MacDonald are in NRS RH6 ('Register House charters, 1st series'); the other with Mr. A. MacDonald is NRS GD90/1/14; the one with Mr Joseph Paton is NLS Ch. 670; and the one in General Register House is NRS CH7/14.

Table 2

Those institutions on the map with a 'small number of pre-1314 originals'

Religious house	No. pre-1314 originals	Notes
Scone Abbey	at least 13	Matthew Hammond has identified thirteen pre-1286 charters for Scone in NRS RH6 ('Register House charters, 1st series'). The online catalogue for RH6 currently only covers those from 1408.
Glasgow Cathedral	at least 6	See Duncan 1998, who came across these six in Paris (BnF MSS Français 26286 and 26237). Five of these relate to the Murrays of Bothwell; one is a charter of King Robert I (1309).
Arbroath Abbey	at least 6	There are at least six pre-1314 royal charters for Arbroath in NRS RH6 ('Register House charters, 1st series', RH6/25, 72A, 73, 74, 75 and 75A).
Paisley Abbey	6	Four of these are in Belfast, PRONI D623 (Abercorn papers). The online catalogue states that there are 14 charters relating to Paisley, four of which are papal bulls between 1219–1265. This matches a statement in Innes 1832 (p. xxiv n. z) where the editor notes that he has examined an inventory of the charter chest of the Marquis of Abercorn but not the originals, and his summary of the inventory includes four bulls of Popes Honorius III, Gregory IX and two of Clement IV. There is also a

		charter in the NRS (GD90/1/17, 'Yule Collection') and a bull of Clement IV in Paisley Museum.
Jedburgh Abbey	5	These five are in NRS AD1/1–5 ('Crown Office Writs, 1147–1889'). See the NRS's online catalogue for AD1. Four of these five relate to Ranulf Soulis. There are three other pre-1314 charters in this collection (nos. 6–8) which do not seem to relate to Jedburgh.
Dunfermline Abbey	at least 5	There are a few Dunfermline charters in the collection of James Balfour of Denmilne (d. 1657): NLS Adv. MSS 15.1.18 (charters) and 15.1.19 (papal bulls). There are five pre-1314 charters in 15.1.18 (nos. 29, 63, 71 and 81–82). For some of these, see *Models of Authority*. For the papal bulls, the NLS's online catalogue states that four relate to Dunfermline (nos. 3, 8, 10 and 14), though it is not clear how many (if any) are pre-1314.
Pluscarden Priory	4	The John Rylands Library, University of Manchester, has a collection of fourteen documents from Pluscarden, the first four of which are pre-1314 (GB 133 PLU nos. 1–4). See the Library's online catalogue for further details.

THE DARK SIDES OF THE RUNES

John Hines

The runic script is an alphabetic writing system: i.e. one which uses graphs to represent individual consonants and vowels of the spoken language. In that respect it has an important degree of homology with the 'roman' (Latin) script that has been standard for English and in western Europe, effectively from time immemorial, and has a global contemporary range. Runic writing was developed within the Germanic-language zone of the Continent and Scandinavia, and the known corpus of runic texts predominantly represents varieties of vernacular Germanic language; there are also, though, significant and interesting examples of Latin — usually ecclesiastical or liturgical texts — being written in runes as well (for reliable overviews of the whole runic material, see Düwel 2008 and Barnes 2012).

The earliest securely identified and dated examples of runic script are from the second half of the second century AD, and from Denmark in southern Scandinavia. There is a small number of other finds which tantalisingly *might* represent even earlier examples, if not some embryonic stage in the development of the script, such as the Meldorf 'fibula' from Schleswig-Holstein dated to the first century AD (Düwel 2007 and refs). Except, however, for the case of a possible inscription of some sort on a sherd of pottery from Dziedzice in the south of Poland (Krause 1934; Arntz and Zeiss 1939, 97–105; Krawczuk 2013), these do not significantly redirect the focus of attention in respect of where we can look in order to see runic script emerging either geographically or chronologically. Many different theories of the derivation of the runic alphabet have been proposed and debated, and no consensus has ever been achieved; however, it is probably correct that a majority of scholars now believes both the formal properties of the runic script, and the known archaeological and historical circumstances in which it first becomes apparent, to favour the proposition of its being a Germanic adaptation of Roman Latin literacy — rather than being based upon the Greek script, adopted for writing Gothic in the fourth century AD, or on earlier Continental derivatives of the Phoenician consonantal script such as Venetic Etruscan (Barnes 2012, 9–15; Düwel 2008, 175–81; Odenstedt 1990; Looijenga 2003, esp. 78–104).

These issues are particularly significant in the present context, because in terms of the digitised storage and handling of runic data, the close relationship between the runic graphic system and the roman alphabet is helpful in some respects and a source of significant problems in others. The geographical range of the Germanic language family expanded dramatically during the first millennium AD — by no means always permanently — with the 'Anglo-Saxon' settlement in Britain, and other expansion and conquests of the Migration Period reaching across the Continent to the Mediterranean and into North Africa in the south and to the Crimea in the south-east; and later the Scandinavian 'Viking' expansions again spreading down the major Russian rivers in the east, and across the North Atlantic to Iceland, Greenland and even (temporarily) Newfoundland to the west. In some, admittedly marginal, areas, the runic script remained in regular use to the end of the Middle Ages in the fifteenth century; a few antiquarian or fossil practices mean that the runic script has never quite died out (Barnes 2012, 99–143).

What the above inevitably means is that the runic script — which can be postulated to have represented a unitary 'Common Germanic' with a close phonemic fit in the second century AD (see, e.g., Derolez 1998) — continued to be used in changing and diverging linguistic contexts. These gave rise to what is ultimately massive diversity in the forms of the graphs, and how the script was used to represent natural

Table 1

A summary conspectus of the principal regional and historical variant systems of the runic tradition.

	Original **fuþark** (by mid-C2 AD)	
Older **fuþark** (C2–C7 AD)	Older **fuþark** East Europe (C3–C5 AD) West Europe (with minor variance C5–C7 AD)	
		Anglo-Frisian **fuþorc** (C5–C11 AD) A closely related but not completely unitary branch, apparently surviving longer in England.
Younger **fuþąrk** (C8–C11 AD)	No true runic tradition	
Medieval runic alphabet (C11–C15 AD)		
SCANDINAVIA & NORTH ATLANTIC	**CONTINENT**	**ENGLAND & FRISIA**

language. Realistically, specialists in the early Germanic languages and philology who are also concerned with runology can map out an overall history of runography based upon a set of primary regional and historical varieties of the runic writing system (Table 1). The runic 'alphabet' itself is usually referred to by a name produced by the first six graphs of the 'rune row' in its consistent and standardised order. The earliest form of the system, and clearly the structure that is ancestral to the whole known tradition, is consequently known as the *Older futhark* (runic **fuþark**). This system appears to have been preserved in a secure form in Scandinavia from the second century AD to the seventh. It is also attested over a wide area of the Continent, albeit sparsely in most areas and for most of this period, as far east as the Ukraine; a relatively substantial number of 'South Germanic' inscriptions in the Alemannic area of western Germany of the fifth to seventh centuries use essentially the same graphemic system, although the development of a distinct double-barred form of **h** (Fig. 1, esp. 1b) — in the overall view, merely an allographic variant — is of considerable historic and practical importance as it was subsequently adopted in Anglo-Saxon England from the late seventh century onwards (Düwel 2008, 57; Looijenga 2003, 135–8; Parsons 1999, 81–2).

Runes are attested in England from as early in the transition from Roman Britain to Anglo-Saxon England in the second quarter of the fifth century (for the most recent overview: Hines 2019a, 57–59), and it was here — possibly under some substrate influence from indigenous language shifters (Schrijver 2014) — that a West Germanic language variety first underwent a dramatic process of change: most of which we can follow systematically in the form of reconstructable sound-changes, albeit with implications for morphology, and with processes of change being apparent in aspects of lexis too. Already before the end of the fifth century we have clear evidence of the development of a new rune-form — and most significantly a new graphemic distinction, between /ã:/ and /a:/, /a/

— representing a sound change (/a/ [before a sequence of nasal + spirant consonants] > /ã:/ > /o:/ [+ spirant consonant]) that is regular in Old English and Old Frisian and of which there are also some traces in Old Saxon (Nielsen 1995). The solitary nasalised vowel in

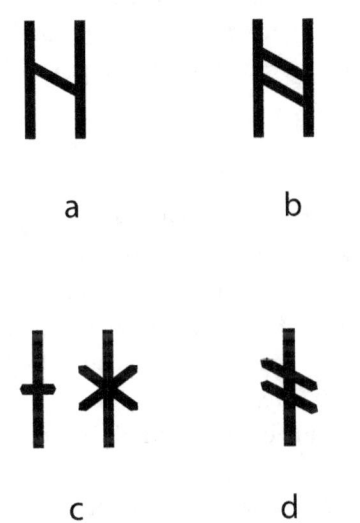

Figure 1
Principal variants of the **h** (*hægel*) rune. a: single-barred, *Older futhark*; b: double-barred, Continental (from the 5th century AD), Anglo-Saxon (from the later 7th century AD); c: single-stave variants of the *Younger futhark*, of which the 'star-rune' to the right is the most regular; d: single-stave variant of the Late Anglo-Saxon runic tradition.

the phonological system /ã:/ seems soon to have developed further to /o:/ (written *ō* in standardised Old English and Old Frisian), and by the first half of the seventh century a tripartite graphemic innovation based on the old a rune (Fig. 2) was becoming established in England and Frisia to represent the vowel phonemes /æ(:)/, /a(:)/ and /o(:)/ respectively.[1] Although phonemically crucial throughout the Germanic languages, the runic script itself never encodes vowel length, although orthographically long vowels are occasionally

---

[1] In accordance with standard IPA practice, slashes /-/ are used here to denote phonemic values and square brackets [-] phonetic values.

written double. Consistent with this shift in rune-forms and their sound-values, the Old English and Old Frisian runic alphabet is usually referred to as the *futhorc*. Simultaneously, the original **o** rune came to be used to represent an umlauted (i.e. fronted) rounded vowel [œ(:)], initially with allophonic status but also phonemicised by the mid-seventh century (Waxenberger 2017). These are only the first of several innovations in the *futhorc*, reflecting identifiable changes in both the vowel and consonant systems of the language.

Figure 2

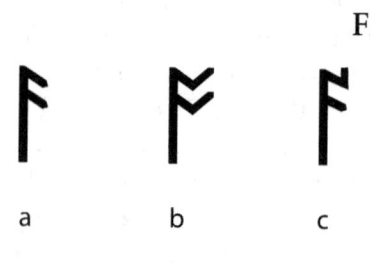

a   b   c

The three Anglo-Saxon/Anglo-Frisian variants of the original a rune. a: æ (*æsc*); b: ā later o (*ōs*); c: a (*āc*). The *ōs* and *āc* runes are shown as the 'obtuse angle' and 'acute angle' variants respectively: both may appear in either variant of design.

Although the ninth century appears to have seen a major shift away from widespread vernacular runic literacy in England, the Anglo-Saxon tradition continued in a more restricted — primarily ecclesiastical — range through into the eleventh century (Hines 2019a); the Frisian tradition appears to have ended by the close of the ninth century (Looijenga 1996; Hines and IJssennagger-van der Pluijm, eds 2021, 375-400). A massive shift in Scandinavian practice seems to have taken place around the late seventh century (there is little direct evidence to illustrate it in progress) which saw the *futhark* rune row reduced to just sixteen graphs, abandoning certain phonemic distinctions — for instance between voiced and voiceless consonants — and representing only three vocalic points of articulation, **i** (high front), **u** (high back) and **a/ã** (low: remarkably, here a distinction between a non-nasal and a nasal vowel can still be expressed) (Barnes 2012, 54–65; Spurkland 2005, 54–85). This alphabetic inventory is known as the *Younger futhark*:[2] orthographically it has variants known as long-twig and short-twig ranges (plus other minor, often highly localised, variants). By the early eleventh century, as Scandinavia was increasingly accommodating itself to the culture and practices of the Continent and Britain, a process of assimilation to the Latin roman alphabet was underway, the end result of which is to have a graphemic system that essentially matches the former letter for letter, although it also includes additional graphs such as þ and some rounded vowels appropriate to the phonology of the languages. Many of the supplementary graphs were produced by diacritic dotting of younger *futhark* runes (Fig. 3).

Figure 3

Examples of the generation of new graphemic distinctions in the Scandinavian medieval runic alphabet by dotting runes of the *Younger futhark*. a: **b** and **p**; b: **i** and **e**; c: **t** and **d**.

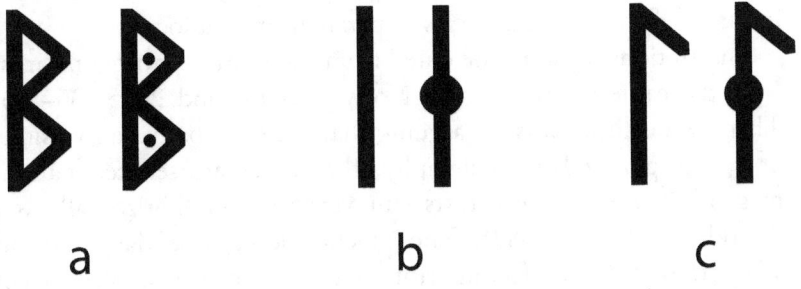

a   b   c

---

[2] With a high degree of correctness, some scholars now prefer to mark the fact that the fourth rune in this row is the nasalized /ã/, and write the term *futhąrk* (or *fuþąrk*).

Taking a similarly broad-brush perspective, an overview of the media — i.e. the primary physical contexts — of the runic inscriptions sheds clear light on significant features and contours of the changing role of literacy in the Roman-period, early-, and later-medieval Germanic-speaking societies that maintained this script. Unusually, we may start with a significant negative: namely that, until we reach the urban communities of High-medieval Scandinavia, we do *not* find evidence of the runic script having been used for bureaucratic record-keeping or accounting, or for straightforward communication in the form of writing notes or letters such as is abundantly in evidence in, say, the Vindolanda tablets (cf. Hines 1997). The earliest known runic inscriptions are mostly very short texts added to artefacts that were not just of practical but also of symbolic importance to the populations amongst whom they circulated: e.g. dress-accessories, primarily but not exclusively in the female sphere, and weaponry in the male sphere. Whatever the texts say — and interpretation is often highly doubtful and conjectural: some appear to be names, either of possessors or of the items themselves — those texts are *bound* to the artefactual context as an additional attribute to it; and therefore, unlike a short letter for instance, effectively meaningless separate from that locus.

Inscriptions on stone are dated from the fourth century onwards, with the earliest specimens in Norway (Spurkland 2005, 35–53). There seems little basis for arguing that these are barbarian versions of contemporary Latin epigraphy: the stones are selected natural megaliths, and the early texts run vertically not horizontally (cf. Spurkland 2010, 78–82). The practice looks essentially like an adaptation of the 'artefact inscription' to the use of rock to construct funerary monuments, which in itself makes and expresses a meaningful connection between the deceased, the deceased's kin or community, and the land. It appears also to be inappropriate at this stage to suggest that these texts function as no more than a decorative attribute to the objects they are placed upon: they are texts that say something — *somehow*, we must often ruefully admit. On the Scandinavian gold bracteates, the runic texts are quite regularly neatly organised in arcs around the edge of the central pressed design, but remain quite distinct from the iconographic motif and from the purely decorative punched borders that some of these discoid pendants have (Düwel 1992; Heizmann and Axboe eds. 2011; Wicker and Williams 2013). Acknowledging some comparanda on the Continent, it is largely in the post-Conversion and radically altered literary context of Middle Anglo-Saxon England (from the mid- to late seventh century onwards) that we see runic texts becoming assimilated into art: not just as quotations, but as *tituli* and other complementary components, for instance on the Franks Casket and Ruthwell Cross of the eighth century (Hines 2019a, 31–4). Here too we start to see *regular* sentence structure for the first time, with texts that are still profoundly inter-related with their physical contexts and yet are fully parsable and interpretable separated from those contexts. Concurrently, runic lettering starts to appear regularly on coins in England and Frisia as an alternative to roman capitals, apparently consistently preferred in some regions or for specific coin-types (Blackburn 1991; Page 1999, 117–29, 213–16). It proves to be a slow and gradual process to get to the point where we have evidence of the use of bone tablets to be filled with wax for writing, thin sheets of wood or soft lead plaques with inscriptions, which are solely utilitarian writing media, in a context where in the text itself and what it says has achieved near-exclusive significance and the material written upon is insignificant and dispensable (Hines 2019a; Spurkland 2005, 173–201; Düwel 2008, 153–71).

It is probably no coincidence, although not simply part of the same process, that it is around the same time that runes begin to appear to regularly in manuscripts, on parchment (Derolez 1954; Page 1999, 60–79, 186–99). Some of these are in fact 'dry-point' inscriptions, and thus not so different in terms of execution from carved or cut runes. From the later eighth century onwards, we find the runic graphs known as *thorn* and *wynn* (the former representing a pair of allophones in unvoiced [θ] and its voiced counterpart [ð]; the latter /w/) used with increasingly regularity in Anglo-Saxon manuscripts to represent sounds either not or imperfectly provided for in roman script. The writing of short codas or signatures in the runic script recurs quite interestingly in both Continental and English manuscripts from the ninth century, while there are also cases in England of runic graphs being used in lines of verse as logographs to represent the name given to the rune, a name which normally identifies the rune's sound-value on the acrophonic principle.

From this survey, we may attempt to summarise what the key variables in the runic corpus are and thus the key considerations for scholarly interpretation of any runic inscription or set of inscriptions which in turn will be fundamental to the digitised storage and dissemination of the data. The script is graphemically highly diverse. Fundamentally and thus always, it is related or at least relatable to the familiar roman/Latin alphabet, but it is never perfectly homologous with that script. This manifestly poses problems for the digitisation of runic texts other than purely as images. There are digital runic fonts available, but none is universal and none is comprehensive, particularly at the allographic level.

It is in fact quite illuminating how, some twenty years ago, before the flexibility of word-processed text and digital images improved greatly, critical evaluation of 'transliteration' as a rule-bound and disciplined process came to command a central place in runological discussions (Page 1984; Barnes 1994). These practices essentially hark back to the practicalities of the typewriter age. The hope, or even belief, appeared to be that, with sufficient care and commitment, a roman-script transliteration could adequately and scientifically represent what was in any given inscription. Without dismissing the practical necessity of transliteration for publishing and discussing runic texts, and importance of clarity and consistency in practice, that ambition does appear to have been gradually de-emphasised over the past twenty-five years. Robert Nedoma in particular has been highly consistent in using what he calls a *nichtinterpretatives Transliterationssystem*, but that is necessarily a complicated code, both to generate and to read. It must be open to constant updating, and I am not sure that a general, comprehensive key is to be found anywhere (Nedoma 2004, 21–2; 2016, esp. 3–4).

All of the variables reviewed above constitute complications enough, but it must then be recognised that even attempts to identify individual graphemes in runic inscriptions can give rise to competing reasonable readings, while the subsequent interpretation of the texts in terms of morphemes and lexemes is even more likely to involve a multiplicity of well-argued alternatives. If texts were carved on to objects many centuries ago, it is hardly surprising if the surfaces have deteriorated and the objects themselves have become fragmented. We are constantly faced with obscured and partial runic texts — and while strictly objective attempts to determine precisely what was incised must always be primary, any textual and epigraphic scholar would surely acknowledge that a thorough understanding of the language, and familiarity with its idioms and formulae, will be irrepressible and will very often assist in pointing the way to the most plausible identifications of imperfect inscribed evidence. At the same time, the proper recording and dissemination of the evidence must be able to accommodate alternative possibilities.

Finally, as noted, context is crucial: this means not only the material and the specific object into which the inscription has been carved, but also the whole material cultural milieu it belongs to: its archaeological fit. It will surprise many philologists, but from a historical point of view this may be considered equally vital to the most thorough possible grasp of the language for one truly to understand the inscription as a whole. Sometimes a fragment may be so reduced that it is near impossible to judge what type of artefact it has come from, and there are cases where one has simply to record the material and whatever is observable of its form — e.g., 'a cut sheet copper-alloy fragment'. In terms of archaeological identification and classification, meanwhile, it is essential to be aware that archaeological opinions on the date and provenance of an inscribed item *may* vary as significantly as philological points of debate. It is not disputed, for instance, that the earliest object which displays the *ōs* rune that in turn is the earliest dated evidence of a distinct pre-Old English/Old Frisian sound-change is a Class A gold bracteate reportedly found at Undley in Suffolk some forty years ago and datable to the second half of the fifth century (Hines and Odenstedt 1987). Archaeologically, however, the present author has always maintained that, despite its find-spot, there is a valid case to be made that the object was manufactured on the northern Continent, quite plausibly in the Anglian homeland in Schleswig-Holstein, and is an import to early East Anglia. The discovery of a hoard of two sets of three inscribed bracteates (of Classes A and B) at Binham in Norfolk with some definite detailed similarities to the Undley bracteates adds crucial additional evidence but does not — in my view — essentially alter the validity of that proposition (Behr & Pestell 2014: more of this hoard, now in the Castle Museum, Norwich, has been recovered through metal-detecting subsequent to that interim publication and assessment of the find; it is believed now to have been fully recovered). Yet mine is certainly an argument based on slender inference, and others find it either unnecessary or unconvincing (Hills 1991; cf. Suzuki 2006). It cannot be any more than an arguable hypothesis in respect of its implications for the dissemination of runic literacy in the fifth century AD, and indeed the location and extent of particular developments within the West Germanic language group.

Runic finds and runic databases

New runic finds are in fact being made at a steady rate. The access of new and genuinely interesting material from England is particularly high, due primarily to the popularity of hobby metal-detecting and the extent of contract archaeological excavation in advance of development on the one hand, and to the effectiveness of the system for reporting archaeological finds through area Finds Liaison Officers under the Portable Antiquities Scheme and the Treasure Act of 1996 on the other. The latter, with its online website ('Portable Antiquities Scheme': https://finds.org.uk), provides a forum for collating information on new finds and disseminating knowledge of them. This paper concludes with a case study of a recent find (January 2019) which is designed to illustrate and evaluate good practice but simultaneously to identify problems and opportunities for improvement. It is concurrently the case, unfortunately, that irresponsible treasure hunting also produces additional finds, of which glimpses may be caught, but reported information is normally untrustworthy. That can, of course, happen anywhere; especially saddening, however, are reported cases from the already poorly illuminated eastern range of the runic zone, for instance in Ukraine (Levada and Looijenga 2019).

What should be the most comprehensive on-line database of the runic corpus at present counts just over 8,000 runic 'finds' (*RuneS: Runische Schriftlichkeit*, www.runesdb.eu: total number of finds 8,097 on 27 May 2020) of which more than a thousand are examples of runes in manuscript contexts and slightly more than 7,000 are what we might call inscribed archaeological objects. Through relatively simple searches in this database one can get a good idea of variant weightings within the whole corpus. The database provides information on the provenance of the finds in terms of the modern nation they have come from — which is reasonable enough, although in key respects it creates divisions which differ markedly from the cultural and political zones of the historical period of relevance. The great majority of the individually recorded finds, 82.5%, are from mainland Scandinavia (Denmark, Norway and Sweden). The next most populous zone is the Viking-period and medieval Scandinavian sphere in the North Atlantic — Iceland, Greenland and the Faroes — with 732 finds (9% of the corpus). Britain and Ireland, including the Isle of Man, have 364 finds in the database; those however, we may note, include only two coins — both of which may in fact be Continental issues — and the scores of specimens of definitely Anglo-Saxon issues with runic legends of the seventh and eighth centuries are omitted. Germany has 173 finds, but at least a third of those are from the formerly Danish and Viking-period/medieval Scandinavian territory of Schleswig. The Scandinavian *Younger futhark* script accounts for more than 76% of the whole corpus.

While work on Anglo-Saxon, Frisian and Continental/ *Südgermanisch* runic material is anything but neglected or under-developed, it can be no surprise in light of the figures given above that 'Norse'-focused studies concerned with Scandinavia, especially from c. AD 700 through to the Late Middle Ages, figure very large in the overall range of runic scholarship. Accordingly, that is a field within runic studies (one can hardly call a field concerned with such a high proportion of the overall evidence a 'sub-field', although it is certainly a 'sub-division') where pioneering databases are to be noted, now complementary to the *RuneS* database just noted. The *Samnordisk runtextdatabas* (www.nordiska.uu.se/forskn/samnord.htm/ : the English name is the 'Scandinavian Runic-text Database') has been in existence since January 1993. In its very earliest manifestation it was effectively no more than a flat-field searchable table, identifying individual inscriptions by a code which identified them to region (within Sweden) or otherwise largely to nation, and numbered them, while also providing a transliteration of the inscription into roman script plus edited transcriptions into standardised Old Norse / Icelandic and appropriate regional variants (Old Danish, Old Norwegian, Old Swedish etc.). Other data lists had to be consulted to identify individual entries and to find out more about the inscribed objects, the circumstances of discovery, and so on. The facility was rapidly searchable for graphemic strings and linguistic interpretations, a situation which points to the practical philological interests that lay behind the original conception of the database. Meanwhile the influence of a 'Viking world' perspective is manifest in the fact that in the British Isles, England, Ireland, Scotland, Man, Orkney and Shetland are presented separately as geographical entities.

As one would anticipate, the *Samnordisk runtextdatabas* has been constantly updated, and indeed any such project should endlessly be a work in progress. The most significant new issue dates from 2014, which can be downloaded and installed as a database with a self-opening archive. From the current home page of the website it is possible, for instance, to download a substantial pdf file which records (in Swedish) adjustments to all of the entries from the period 2008–14. The downloadable database files include the basic list of inscription texts exactly as in the original issue but now with buttons and other links enabling the user to access information on the find place, suggested dating of the inscription, information on the material of the object, bibliography, and also links to images if any such exist on-line.[3]

For Denmark, the National Museum in collaboration with the Department of Scandinavian Languages at Copenhagen University produced a database of *Danmarks Runeindskrifter* in the period 2003–9 (www.runer.ku.dk), inevitably far superseding an earlier printed and numbered catalogue by Lis Jacobsen and Erik Moltke, published in two volumes in 1941–2. New finds are still being added to this on-line database, although it is kept up voluntarily by virtue of the commitment of a small number of Danish scholars. Per individual inscription, one may argue that this website has perhaps the most attractive and immediately informative layout (Fig. 4). Within the specialist field of runic studies it is not a great constraint, but the fact that it is only in Danish is surprising. The database as a whole offers summary but useful introductory information on, for instance, the

---

[3] In December 2020, access to this database moved to a new 'interface', *Runor*, maintained by Sweden's national *Riksantikvarieämbetet* (https://www.raa.se/hitta-information/runor).

three key stages of the runic script found in Denmark (including Skåne, part of Sweden since the sixteenth century, and Schleswig, annexed by Germany in the nineteenth century); in Danish archaeological and historical periodisation those are associated with the later phases of the Iron Age (to c. AD 800), the Viking Period (c. AD 800–1000) and the (post-Conversion) Middle Ages. The individual entries include relatively good although often single images, a transliteration of the inscription consistent with the *Samnordisk runtextdatabas*, an edited version in normalised Old Danish, and a modern Danish translation. The archaeological information provided on the material details, condition, and known history of the object is commendably comprehensive.

Figure 4

The webpage of the *Danmarks Runeindskrifter* website for the earliest known runic inscription, on a comb from the weapon hoard at Vimose on Fyn. Layout adjusted slightly for reproduction in this format; reproduced by kind permission.

Opslag – Enkelt genstand

Runedatabasens informationer for denne genstand:
(genstandid: 919)(indskriftid: 919)

Thumbnails af billeder:

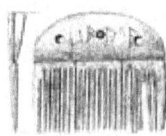

The Dark Sides of the Runes

Stamdata:

Titel: Vimose-kam	**Datering:** 150-160
Fundomstændigheder: Arkæologisk udgravning, Engelhardt m. fl.	**Dateringssikkerhed:** Nogenlunde Sikker.
Opbevaringssted: Nationalmuseet, Danmarks Oldtid.	**Dateringskommentar:** Arkæologisk datering. Kammen hører formentlig til nedlægningen Vimose 2.
Genstandstype: Kam.	**Fundsted:** Odense (Amt), Lunde (Herred), Allese (Sogn). Nr.: 080301
Genstandstypekommentar: Genstanden er en tolagskam, som typemæssigt er udbredt ® det fynske og sydjyske område i årtierne omkring overgangen fra ældre til yngre romersk jernalder.	**Fundstedssikkerhed:** Sikker.
	Fundår: 1865
Ejerinstitution: Nationalmuseet Frederiksholms Kanal 12 1220 København K. Danmark	**Arkæologisk periode:** Overgangen ældre/yngre romersk jernalder.
Inventarnr.: 22657	**Overordnet materiale:** Andet.
Sb-nr.: 1	**Underordnet materiale:** Tak.
	Dimensioner: 5,6 cm
	Bredde: 4,9 cm
	Tilstand: God.

Litteraturhenvisning(er):

Stoklund, Marie 1995 Ulla Lund Hansen et alii: (1995): *Die Runen der römischen Kaiserzeit Himlingøje— Seeland— Europa Nordiske Fortidsminder Serie B 13* p. 329-30/ 317-346. Det Kongelige Nordiske Oldskriftselskab, København

Henriksen, Mogens Bo 1996 (1996): *Harja-kammen fra Vimose-fundet Fynske Minder 1996* p. 48-54, 57. Odense Bys Museer, Odense

Stoklund, Marie 2006 (2006): *Vimose. Runologisch. Reallexikon der Germanischen Altertumskunde. Zweite Auflage 32* p. 410f./410-414. Walter de Gruyter, Berlin

Seebold, Elmar Klaus Düwel, (1994): *Die sprachliche Deutung und Einordnung der archaischen Runeninschriften Runische Schriftkultur in kontinental-skandinavischer und -angelsächsischer Wechselbeziehung. ERG 10* p. 56-94. de Gruyter, Berlin

Indskrift(er):

DK nr.: Fyn 19	**Tolkningskommentar:** Mandsnavn
Dansk oversættelse: Harja	**Runetypologi:** Urnordisk (U).
English translation: Harja	**Runetypologisikkerhed:** Sikker.
Transskription: harja	**Sprogtyp®):** Urnordisk.
Translitteration: harja	**Runehøjde:** Ca. 1,3 cm
Ornamenteret: Nej.	**Skilletegns®e(r):** Ingen skilletegn.
Oversættelses- og sagkommentar: Tolkes som runeristerens eller ejerens navn. Et alternativt forslag er, at harja kan oversættes med "ka" (Seebold 1994,71).	**Skriftordning:** Højrevendt.
	Indskriftplacering: På kammens ene side.
	Autenticitet: Ægte.
	DR-nr.: 207

The *RuneS* database entries (www.runesdb.eu) are thoroughly sound in attempting to provide summary information on the inscribed objects in archaeological terms as well as transliterations of the texts with translations into modern English and German. That is a very ambitious initiative, and it will clearly take a long time to populate the data resource to its full potential. At present, it is probably fair to opine that this database is most useful for comparative assessments of the whole corpus of runic evidence than for details of individual finds. Britain (including the Northern Isles and Man) is in a relatively unusual position — to some degree shared with Germany, as noted above — in that the earlier Anglo-Saxon runic tradition and the later Scandinavian one are really very distinct, and are studied for the most part by different scholars in different contexts and even for different purposes. A digital corpus for England has long been aspired to, but at present it is rational to take the view that the *RuneS* platform offers the only realistic prospect of achieving that. For overviews of the British material as a whole, we have been able to rely on a number of general monograph reviews (Page 1999, which was the substantially revised and expanded second edition of a monograph first published in 1973; Barnes 2019; Parson 1999 is consistently useful for reference too). New finds will not necessarily appear on the *Portable Antiquities Scheme* database (www.finds.org.uk, covering England and Wales), although one may search that using 'rune' or 'runic inscription' as a search term, and there is no regular process or outlet for publishing new finds. Dissemination of information within the interested field therefore relies primarily on goodwill and making an effort to share news when it comes in.

Constructively, therefore, we can reflect on a relative wealth of complementary experience, and use that to identify the key desiderata for further developments. It should go without saying that the ideal relational database will have multiple fields that allow one burrow down into details — graphically, linguistically, and contextually — and so to explore combinations of variables which in themselves no database design could ever exhaustively anticipate in terms of pre-set queries. In terms of the study of the script, it would ideally support work down to the allographic level; linguistically, a perfect database would recognise and cater for all levels of grammar from phonetics to lexis and syntax. Even with the intrinsically philological objectives that have lain behind the development of runic databases over the last three decades, these are palpably propositions that go far beyond anything *structurally* embedded in the sources' design as yet.

In representing the inscriptions themselves, it is surprising that to date imaging is not a field that has been especially determinedly addressed. Such is the nature of the primary evidence that ultimately no standardised approach to photography (or, in the future, scanning) can be expected to be able to represent the inscriptions perfectly any more than transliteration can. Interpretation and judgement will always be essential. The case study to be presented immediately below deals with an essentially clear text inscribed on two plane surfaces, and even here the need for specialist imaging technology to be applied and informed analysis to be exercised is critical. Besides emphasising the archaeological variables — and the expert variability — already noted, a general critique that seems to be called for is the fact that the interface between runic text and the artistic/art-historical elements of the artefact is as yet peripheral at best to the structure of the databases. Those aspects may indeed be relevant in a minority of cases — but that, of course, makes them no less fundamental to the adequate scholarly understanding not only of outstanding works of art such as the Franks and Gandersheim Caskets and the Ruthwell and Bewcastle Crosses, but also to more regularly reproduced runic media: the humbler sculpture of the Anglo-Saxon tradition, bracteates and coinage, and the many Swedish runestones, for instance.

A case study: an inscribed strap-end from near Winchester, Hampshire

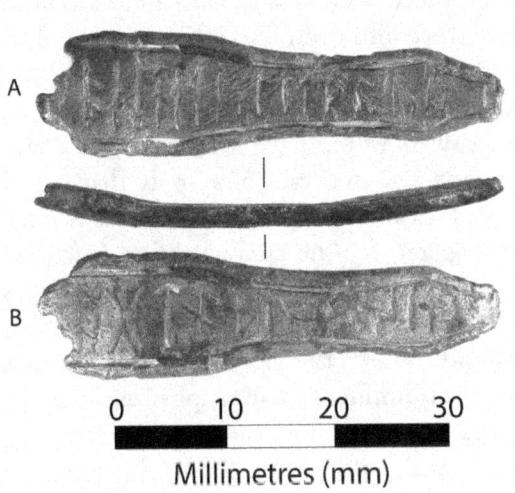

Figure 5

An inscribed silver strap-end, Portable Antiquities Scheme SUR-4A9C55. Scale 3:1. Photograph: Simon Maslin – layout adjusted by the author.

In January 2019, a silver strap-end measuring 41.2 x 10.5 mm found at an as yet undisclosed site in the vicinity of Winchester, Hampshire, was delivered to Simon Maslin, Finds Liaison Officer for Surrey and Hampshire (Fig. 5). The precious metal material meant that this object falls under the provisions of the Treasure Act (Treasure Case reference 2019T10). That it is inscribed with a row of runes on either side was obvious from the outset — often, inevitably, finders and Finds Liaison Officers are uncertain if marks are to be identified as runes or not. The present author was then approached to comment on and provide any further information on the inscription.

Strap-ends are common 'stray finds' of the later Anglo-Saxon period from the eighth to the eleventh century AD. They may come from straps of harness or unbuckled objects, but were also worn as belt/girdle terminals by both men and women. The authoritative comprehensive study is a regrettably unpublished PhD thesis by Gabor Thomas (2000). This specimen is in fact relatively unusual in shape, and also in its design insofar as it appears to have been produced only to carry the runes rather than any other cast or incised decoration on the faces of the object. The runes stand between framing lines which follow the contour outline of the faces, and in some areas these are still filled with black niello.

The split end of the strap-end has been broken, across the perforations through which rivets would have held it on to a strap. The part outlines of three non-symmetrical holes imply that it had been broken and repaired at least once in antiquity. There is parallel evidence from south-east England for the curation of an inscribed strap-end after it had become non-functional through damage (Hines 2019b, 297–8). We appear to have the complete inscription, which runs from the attachment end towards the narrowed terminal point on both sides, with some slight diminuendo in graph-size along the row. The shape of the runes unambiguously shows the direction of reading, although not at which side what should begin. Quite commonly, in fact, the beginning of a text will be marked with a cross, but not in this case.

It initially appears (but see further below) that we have 11 runes on one side and 12 on the other. Two runes, which in fact are positioned back-to-back, are obscured by corrosion, one of them seriously so, in fact almost totally. Personal examination of the object is almost always desirable to check and confirm readings from photographs, although in this case the high-quality photographs initially supplied allowed a great deal to be read. On these bases, an initial reading was:[4]

---

[4] Italicised letters represent less certain suggestions in the reading at this stage, and the point in Side B the place where the one rune is completely obscured (cf. Page 1984). The sides are labelled Sides A and B according to what can be inferred as the correct order of reading, as explained *infra*. The runes are referred to by number from left to right in the two rows.

Side A: æ i e r e l e w o r o

Side B: o g t æ þ i s . æ s i l

— Side A: (rune) 4 is a conjectural reading (Fig. 6a). A crudely executed **r** (which therefore differs in execution from A:10) makes best sense of the continuous lines observed through microscopic examination, but an additional by-stave in the top right-hand corner makes this resemble the **m** rune (Fig. 6b), which indeed is the impression it gives first to the naked eye. The **m** rune, however, should have a full diagonal cross between the vertical staves, and there is no such thing here.

— A:8 is a rune formed of an upright stave with a chevron 'pocket' to the right. This could be either **þ** or **w**: the former would have the pockets at mid-stave height, the latter at the top. How far the vertical stave extends upwards, and therefore where the pocket is located in relation to it, is, however, obscured by corrosion.

— B:7 and B:10 are unambiguously examples of the **s** rune, but are remarkable in form for being reversed from the direction we would expect (Fig. 6c–d).

— B:8 is completely obscured by corrosion.

— We may also note the clear inconsistency in the formation of the apparent **æ** rune at A:1, where the by-staves join the main stave around the middle and B:4, where they join it at the top as we would expect; B:9, meanwhile, is uncertain in these respects because the top may be lost to corrosion.

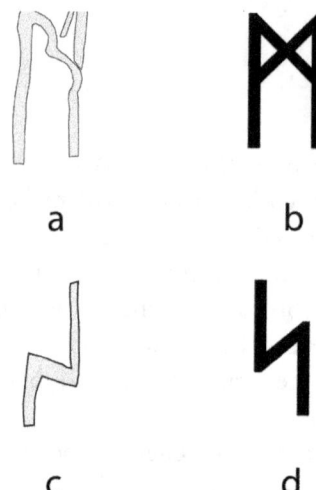

Figure 6

a: A drawing of rune A:4 (2:1); b, the standard **m** (*mann*) rune; c: a drawing of the **s** rune as formed on the strap-end, B:7 and B:10; d: the standard **s** (*sigel*) rune.

Guided by familiarity with the language and its formulae, as noted above, it was in practical terms immediately apparent that if A:8 is **w**, the sequence **woro/ogtæþis** is readily identified as Standard Old English *wrohte þis*, 'wrought/made this'. The peculiarities of spelling are explicable in terms of a 'parasite' vowel being introduced in the initial consonant cluster *wr-*, which is very common; dittography of the root vowel *o* where the word is broken over the line end — which could either be a scribal error or deliberate; while the final *-æ* of the verb ending preserves a regular early form that suggests that the inscription will not be much later in date than c. AD 800 — evidence which is consistent with an archaeological fit for the strap-end itself (Waxenberger 2006). The use of **g**, which may represent a voiced velar spirant, for the unvoiced velar spirant [χ], usually written *h*, is quite familiar (Campbell 1959, §57.4).

That is a sufficiently reliable foundation to proceed directly to its implications for the reading of the remainder of the inscription: that the opening sequence of line A should identify the subject of the verb *worohtæ*, probably with a personal name although possibly with a title, while the as yet partly legible sequence following *þis* probably gives us the Old English name for a strap-end. Both of these lead to genuinely interesting further lines of analysis and insights. We have a considerable stock of recorded personal names from Anglo-Saxon England and the contemporary Germanic Continent (*Prosopography of Anglo-Saxon England*; Searle 1897; Redin 1919; Okasha 2011; Förstemann 1900; Kaufmann 1968; Nedoma 2004), none of which can be identified with *Æierele* other than through highly contrived interpretations. There is, however, a well-recorded name *Hemele* (Old High German *Hemilo*: Redin 1919, 149; Förstemann 1900, col. 744; Kaufmann 1968, 170–1), and it is a relatively practical matter to explain and validate such a reading in this inscription. What appear to be runes A:1 and A:2 can be postulated as an inaccurate and misleading copying of an exemplar for **h** (Fig. 7), which in turn implies that our Hemele was not in fact runically literate. That can also explain the bungled rendition of A:4, which should have been **m** — and does at least *look* sufficiently like what it was supposed to be at first glance.

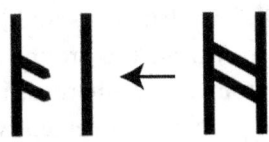

Figure 7

æi from **h**: a schematic representation of the miscopying of an exemplar by Hemele.

To read the end of the inscription in full, the object noun phrase to *worohtæ*, we need to find some way of removing or looking through the corrosion — hoping that the decay has not passed right through the body of the strap-end and removed all the detail. The demonstrative article in the accusative case could be either *þis* (neuter) or *þisnæ* (masculine), and from what can be seen from the surface the latter is possible. The final three graphs, however, **sil**, seem very likely to represent the Latin loanword *sigillum*, which has a rather complex history across the early Germanic languages (Hines 2020, 82–5), but is at least well attested in the sense of 'dress-accessory', 'costume-fastener', 'item of jewellery'. This appears in both feminine and neuter declensions in Old English but has not hitherto been seen declined as a masculine noun.

Professional cleaning of the object could remove the corrosion and so might reveal the surface; however it might remove material with there being nothing underneath to see, and this would not normally be considered proper handling of such a find without firm evidence that it would produce a justifiable result. The internal condition of the object could be assessed non-intrusively by X-radiography, and it is indeed possible that that process would itself be able to reveal the original graph through the corrosion producing the information desired for a full reading of itself. But here, however, we ran into practical obstacles. The object was held by the Surrey and Hampshire Finds Liaison Officer who did not have X-ray facilities, nor did he have the authority to release the object to myself for the procedure to be carried out at Cardiff University. The standard process for a 'Treasure find' is for the object to be transferred temporarily to the British Museum for assessment, but that process does not include X-radiography. A report was submitted suggesting that this should be done, but the *de facto* request was turned down on the grounds of pressure on the facilities. With goodwill from many quarters, and equally a commitment to try to resolve the problem, agreement was reached within a few weeks that the object could be released from the British Museum to Cardiff for this analysis to be carried out, although the transfer had to be made in the hands of a qualified curator, and so it had to await one of the regular but not frequent visits of the administrator of the Treasure Act in Wales to deliver and collect objects. It was consequently October of 2019 before the object came to Cardiff, and the technologically aided examination could be undertaken.

This was carried out by MSc Conservation student Madeline McLeod as a project under the supervision of Phil Parkes, Reader in

Conservation, and in consultation with myself. X-radiography swiftly revealed that the body of the strap-end is in fact largely sound, but disentangling the obscured areas of the runic inscription remained hard, not least because in fact this method superimposed the two lines of text on one another. Cleaning would have been justified in conservation terms, but that would have involved seeking further permissions with limited likelihood of success. In the event repeated X-ray imaging could be taken, with varying levels of intensity and focus, and with patience it could be determined that the obscured graph is **g**, and so the final word is a neuter noun *gæsil* — a noun that has not previously been recorded in Old English. In fact, once this reading has been made, it is possible to see tiny fragments of the **g** rune around the corrosion, but not enough to provide the reading to start with.

gæsil is readily explicable as a neuter noun formed from the root *sigillum* borrowed from Vulgar Latin as *sil* with the perfective prefix that is *ge-* in Standard Old English. This prefix is common on Old English nouns. While it can be semantically very light, its presence does imply that this object so named is not just an item of jewellery but one that somehow finishes something off: an apt term, then, for a strap terminal. A similar term may be the noun *gebæte, gebætel* for a bridle-bit. It is particularly interesting to see a Latin loanword, which in this case is likely to have passed into Germanic very early — certainly by the fourth century AD — and perhaps separately into different regions and branches of Germanic, picking up a Germanic prefix.

We have identified the text then as what would read in a normalised edited form as: *Hemele wrohte þis gesil*, 'Hemele made this strap-end'. One point of importance in relation to this short and in other respects banal text is that it adds a new term to the Old English lexicon. Contextually, the exceptional nature of the object and the fact that it carries only the inscription, where the closest counterparts have typical decoration on one face and are inscribed on the back, strongly implies that for Hemele this was some sort of badge or display of his craftsmanship. Perhaps ironically it appears to have been a display of his lack of runic competence at the same time. But that does not diminish the implications in respect of the relatively common use of runic literacy, probably around the late eighth century AD, and in southern England.

In terms of processes for determining and disseminating the data, the key point to emphasise is that none of the steps taken which make up this case study happened as a matter of regular course, other than the duty of the finder to report the Treasure find to a Finds Liaison Officer. It was not automatic that a specialist in runes would then be consulted to help assess the object, although of course most Finds Liaison Officers are diligent and resourceful in seeking such expert advice, not least in face of the massive diversity of material they are required to deal with. The processing of the find as a 'Treasure case' involved no stage that automatically responded to the special circumstances of this artefact being inscribed. A revision to the 1996 legislation is at the time of writing in May 2020 a matter of public consultation, and the point that its original provisions, which depended entirely on the precious-metal contents of a find, fail to take account of and to protect many other aspects of exceptional culture-historical importance and value is already fully recognised. It is very much hoped that reporting on the successful outcome of a readiness to address the needs of an inscribed object beyond standard procedures will help to improve and embed good practice in the operation of the scheme and in the law, as well as contributing to the critical reviewing and effective continued construction of widely available and informative digital archival resources.

DARK SEALS IN PORTUGUESE ARCHIVES

Maria do Rosário Barbosa Morujão

In medieval archives, in addition to parchments and papers, there are wax and lead seals, many of which are unread or unreadable, others missing. We could call them 'dark seals', after the title of this conference and in reference to the archivists' expression for an archive which is mostly or completely inaccessible.[1]

The word seal has a double meaning, designating both the matrix, usually engraved in metal, and the imprint which results from pressing the matrix on a material. That material was usually wax or, in modern times, sealing wax, but it could also be lead, gold or, in the case of applied seals, paper over wax or a mixture of flour and water that attached it to the documentary support[2].

It is difficult to determine how many seals were created during the Middle Ages, the period of European history when these artefacts were used the most. Some attempts have been made, namely by Michel Pastoureau, but they constitute nothing more than estimates. This historian, responsible for the development of modern sigillography, estimated that there were around 2 or 3 million extant medieval sigillographic imprints in western Europe, and that to have an idea of the total number of seals printed during that long period

---

[1] See, for instance, the definition presented by Pearce-Moses 2005, 102.
[2] For the definition of matrix and imprint, as well as of the various existing seals, see *Vocabulaire*, 1990. Several examples of the variety of seals and their materials can be found, for instance, in Bloche & Burette 2015.

of time, we should multiply that number by 100³. There is no shortage of proof that the number of seals created was far greater than those that subsist: first, because a large number of sealed documents have been lost over the centuries; secondly, because many documents have lost their seals, their existence witnessed solely by the suspensions to which they were attached, the holes through which these suspensions were placed, or the marks left by the seals on the parchment or paper (fig. 1). We also have summaries or copies of documents of which the originals no longer exist, mentioning the presence of seals and often describing them[4] – we will talk about these later. Finally, there is a large number of sigillographic matrices kept in museums, archives, libraries and private collections – many turn up all the time on archaeological sites or are discovered by using metal detectors – which often do not correspond to any known impressions[5].

Seals are fragile, either due to the materials they are made of (mostly wax) or the way they are attached to the charters. Pendent seals are especially fragile in the area where laces are inserted, in addition to being subject to knocks and falls. Applied seals, on the other hand, come loose easily due to the action of bibliophagic

---

[3] Pastoureau 1996, 276-77. These figures have been questioned as studies have progressed, pointing to a much higher number of seals, both produced and extant.

[4] On the importance of these terms for the knowledge of lost seals, see in particular Sanz Fuentes 1990; Pastoureau 1996, 291-93.

[5] On collections of existing matrices in several European countries see Carmona de los Santos 1994. For more recent dates see, above all, Laurent, Roelandt 1997 and Vilain 2014. A very important project is being carried out in England and Wales by the Portable Antiquities Scheme, which collects discoveries made by the public in a database (https://finds.org.uk/). Searching this database for 'seal matrix' on 01/22/2020 returned a total of 6835 files.

Figure 1

Last page of infant Ferdinand's will, showing the mark of his applied seal. Arquivo Nacional Torre do Tombo, Gavetas, Gaveta 16, maço 2, nº 13 (18 August 1437).

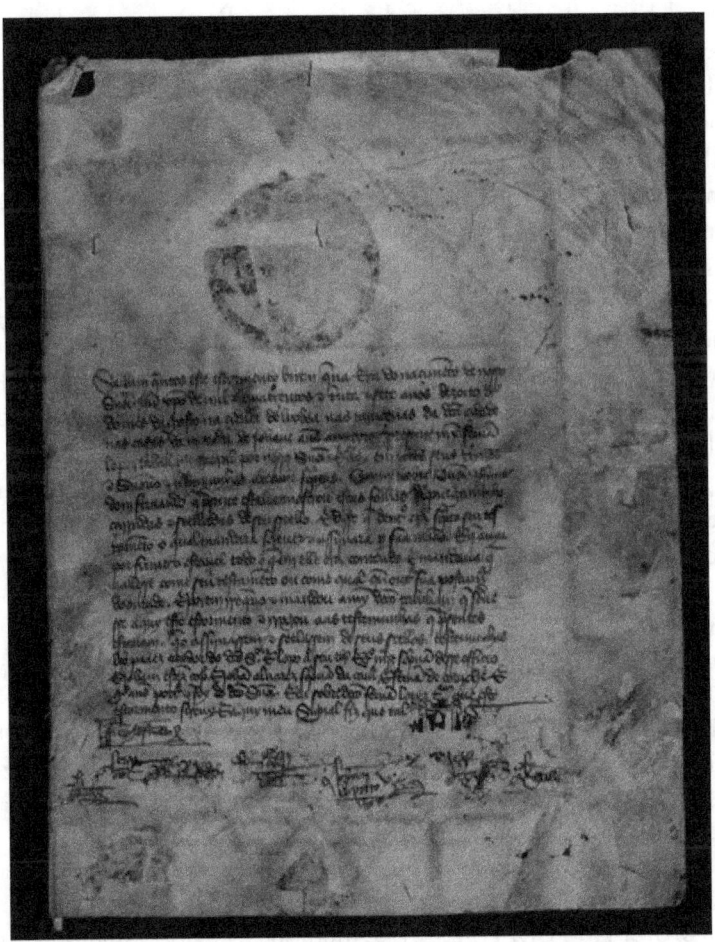

insects, or to the dryness of the wax layer that attaches them to the documents. Many of the impressions that didn't disappear were damaged over the centuries: broken, chipped, worn out, or reduced to mere fragments, both due to human neglect and to their own characteristics. With all due propriety, we can say that seals are a cultural heritage in danger of disappearing; Pastoureau had already stated, in 1996, that seals were in danger of perishing.[6]

The following pages are based on Portuguese seals, which began to be studied and catalogued mainly since the millennium.[7] In fact, sigillographic studies in Portugal have been late to develop. Contrary to many other countries, there is no complete catalogue of seals in any archive or library, and no campaign of casting has been carried out[8]. This lack of interest in sigillography has changed in recent decades, however, with the emergence of several studies[9] and a cataloguing project called *SIGILLVM PORTVGALIAE*, of which I am the coordinator[10]. In its first phase, between 2014 and 2016, this project focused on seals of secular clergy, but its scope is now being extended to all seals from the Portuguese *Ancien Régime*. Data emerging from this project show that more than half of the seals already catalogued have disappeared, and only 24% of the remaining ones are in good condition[11]. These results clearly demonstrate the urgency of

---

[6] Pastoureau 1996, 277, note 4.
[7] On developments on sigillography in Portugal see Gomes 2003, 2012 and 2018; Morujão 2012.
[8] The main work on Portuguese sigillography was, for decades, Távora 1983, often confused with a catalogue of Portuguese seals, despite only focusing on a small part of those, not royal, preserved in some Portuguese archives, and some matrices belonging to private owners.
[9] On the renewal of Portuguese sigillographic studies see Gomes 2003 and 2012; Morujão 2012.
[10] On *SIGILLVM PORTVGALIAE* see Morujão et al. 2014, Morujão 2016b, and the project's website: (http://portugal-sigillvm.net/).
[11] Morujão 2016b, 960-62.

protecting this heritage – a protection that necessarily implies its study.

But how can we study seals reduced to fragments, mutilated, worn or, even worse, no longer in existence? How can we guarantee that our sigillographic heritage will survive for future generations if we haven't been able to prevent its disappearance until now? How can we make the unreadable seals readable? How can we, in the present age of new technologies, bring these objects out of darkness and into light?

To answer these questions, I will define three different possible levels of action: 1) recording and cataloguing; 2) conservation and restoration; and 3) reproduction.

1. Recording and cataloguing

Before we can start preserving something, we must know what remains: no one can take care of something if they don't know it exists. This means recording and cataloguing work must be continued. Nowadays, the focus is essentially on digital catalogues, allowing for a more universal access and the possibility of adding pictures[12]. In cataloguing, we must include not only the impressions that remain attached to the charters but also those that were removed or fell. In fact, many archives have collections of detached seals. These seals exist either because time has worn out their cords or because somebody separated them from the parchments with the intention of preserving them or to allow the binding of sealed documents in

---

[12] Concerning digital sigillographic catalogues, see Hablot 2017 and 2019; Libert 2011 and 2017; McEwan 2015 and 2017; Morujão 2014 and 2016b, and the websites *Archives de l' État en Belgique* (http://www.arch.be/); *Sigilla: Base numérique des sceaux conservés en France* (http://www.sigilla.org/); *Digisig* (www.digisig.org); *Sigillvm: Corpus dos selos portugueses* (http://sigillvm.indexrerum.com/). For a reflection on the various types of seal research instruments that can be created today, see Delmas 1998.

factitious codices – without considering that they were amputating charters from one of their most fundamental elements. If many pendent seals are missing, the number of applied seals that no longer exist is even greater.[13] The tiny layer of wax or mixed flour and water that was used to paste the small piece of paper receiving the impression has very often partly or wholly detached itself. Identifying these detached seals can be very difficult, even impossible, especially if they are in poor condition[14]; digital catalogues can be very helpful by allowing a quick search of seals similar to these.

However, in addition to the existing seals, it is also important to recover the memory of those already lost. A catalogue should therefore also include all sealed documents whose seals have been lost, as well as mentions of those impressions. We did so in the *SIGILLVM POR-TVGALIAE* catalogue.

It's not always easy to know to whom these missing seals belonged, especially if a document has been sealed by more than one entity. The information on validation included in the corroborative clauses of charters is a precious source for this identification.[15] Unfortunately, these clauses were not mandatory. In some cases, the kind of seal used and its owner are mentioned: the king's lead seal, the bishop's great seal, the chapter's seal, etc. Sometimes the corroboration provides more details, explaining the presence of a seal that wasn't supposed to be there, and which could create doubts about the charter's authenticity. This happened, for instance, in a document from August 13th 1403 recording a decision made in Guimarães, a town in northern Portugal, by the archbishop of Braga; the charter should have been sealed by the archbishop and the town's municipality, but

---

[13] Some examples are given in Morujão & Saraiva 2002.

[14] As examples of good catalogues of detached seals, concerning departmental archives in France, see Baudin 2011; Rousseau 2013. In Portugal, the main collection of detached seals is kept at the Arquivo Nacional Torre do Tombo, waiting for the catalogue I am working on.

[15] On corroborative clauses see Carcél Ortí 1997, nº 246.

the prelate forgot his seal and instead used the one belonging to the collegiate of Guimarães.[16] Thanks to this explanation, taken into account when cataloguing this document's seals, we know about this practice of seal loaning[17] and we can count this impression, which has already disappeared, in our catalogue.

Furthermore, many documents that survived only through copies or summaries often mention their seals, identifying who they belonged to and sometimes describing their material, shape, iconography, legend and even the cords. As we have already stated, these mentions are of the utmost importance and should also be part of the catalogues, as they can give us proof of the existence of seals otherwise unknown to us, or seals which are believed only to have been used several years later. Even when other impressions exist, the information given by these descriptions can be precious, namely in the interpretation of iconography or in deciphering a legend.

For instance, we know from these sorts of references that Portuguese bishops started using seals more than 40 years before the earliest impressions we have: the mentions of episcopal seals date back to the 1140s, while the first remaining seals are only of the late 1180s[18]. Another example of the richness and importance of the information conveyed in these copies comes from an imperial notary in Bologna, in 1262, who when making an authentic copy of the will of a schoolmaster from the cathedral of Braga described the two seals that validated it.[19] The first, belonging to the schoolmaster, Pedro, of which no impression remains, had two sculpted figures, one of an angel and another of a woman: the iconography of the Annunc-

---

[16] Arquivo Distrital de Braga, Colecção Cronológica, caixa 26, nº 950.
[17] About loaning seals see Tock 2017.
[18] On this subject see Morujão & Saraiva 2014, 207-08.
[19] Arquivo Distrital de Braga, Livro I dos Testamentos, nº 2, fls. 1-1v (20 June 1262).

iation[20]. The second seal, of which we also have no impression, belonged to another Pedro, precentor of the collegiate of Guimarães. Its iconography is described as a bird with two other figures and birds[21]. The legends are transcribed in both cases; they follow the most usual model, which informs us that it is the seal of a given person, whose name and function are indicated.

The comparison of this information with the remaining impressions from the same matrix proves the accuracy of these notarial descriptions. A good example is the seal of Luca Rodrigues, abbess of the Cistercian monastery of Arouca at the end of the 13th century, of which there are some impressions and a very detailed description:[22] her seal was round, with the image of an abbess holding a crosier in her right hand and a book in the left one, over her chest, with a sun and a star above and below her on the side of the crosier, and a moon between two stars on the other side.[23] Fig. 2 shows us the

---

[20] 'In uno quorum erant due figure sculp[t]e, una angelica et alia cujusdam mulieris et hec littere SIGILLUM PETRI MAGISTRISCOLARUM BRACARENSIS'.

[21] 'In alio vero sigillo erat quedam avis sculpta cum duabus aliis figuris et avibus ibi sculptis et hec lictere que [...]abant SIGILLUM DOMINICI PETRI CANTORIS VIMARANENSIS'.

[22] Arquivo Nacional Torre do Tombo, Mosteiro de Arouca, Gaveta 6, maço 1, nº 16 (25 July 1291, Arouca). This is the best available impression of this seal.

[23] Arquivo Nacional Torre do Tombo, Mosteiro de Arouca, gaveta 2, maço 1, nº 6 (15 June 1294, Arouca); published by Rêpas 2003, doc. 123. This is the seal's description in Latin: '... sigillo dependenti dicte abbatisse monasterii supradicti (..) rotundum. Habet in circuitu has licteras: + S. ABBATISSE MONASTERII DE ARAUCA et in medio ipsius sigilli erat quedam imago abbatisse tenentis quemdam baculum in manu dextera et librum in sinistra ante pectus et ex parte baculi habebat ymaginem solis et unam ymaginem stelle superius et altera inferius ex parte vero sinistra habebat ymaginem lune et unam ymaginem stelle superius et aliam inferius'.

best-preserved copy of this seal, which allows us to see the degree of precision of its description.

Sometimes, these descriptions inform us of the seals' poor condition. The images are eventually difficult to understand, their legends already fading or destroyed. This happens, for example, in a

Figure 2
Seal of Luca Rodrigues, abbess of Arouca monastery. Arquivo Nacional Torre do Tombo, Mosteiro de Arouca, Gaveta 6, maço 1, nº 16 (25 July 1291).

14th century copy of a document granted by the Bishop of Coimbra on the 16th of May 1230, which tells us that part of the episcopal seal's legend was no longer readable, and that the seal of a monastic community was broken in half, the images in its field unrecognisable and part of the legend missing[24]. The legend of a 1258 seal belonging to the abbess of the monastery of Celas already had what the copyist called 'dead letters', impossible to decipher some 60 years later[25]. Another seal, belonging to King Fernando I (1367-1383), dating from 1376, took even less time to become deteriorated: it was already broken in 1404[26].

These descriptions lead us to the second part of this paper: the problems of seal conservation, of which, as we have just seen, there was already awareness in medieval centuries.

---

[24] Arquivo Nacional Torre do Tombo, Colegiada de S. João de Almedina, maço 1, nº 37, copy made in May 1372. The episcopal seal's legend is thus described: '... e da hua parte do dicto seelo pareçiam letras que deziam SIGILLUM PETRI e da outra parte do discto seelo pareciam a huum cabo contra cima do seelo outras letras que deziam SIS EPISCOPI porque as outras nom se pareçiam'. The conventual seal of the monastery of Arganil is thus described: 'seelo hera britado per a meiatade e porem nom lhi parecia o signal pero as letras que tiinha a redor dezian S. CONVENTUI DE ARGAN e nom mais'.

[25] Arquivo Nacional Torre do Tombo, Mosteiro de Celas, maço 12, nº 9 (19 April 1258, in a copy from 4 April 1318, published by Morujão 2001, nº 117: 'outro seelo era da honrrada e religiosa e honesta domna Elvira Lopiz abbadesa en outro tempo do moesteiro das Cellas de Guimarrães (...) en o cerco desse seelo eram as letras mortas e nom as podia entender'.

[26] Arquivo Histórico Municipal de Coimbra, Colecção de Pergaminhos Avulsos, nº 32 (2 January 1404, copying King Fernando's charter from 13 July 1376, 'seellada do seu verdadeyro seello pendente, ja bretado posto em çera branca colgado per hua fita de lynhas verdes'.

2. Conservation and restoration

There have been attempts to prevent the destruction of seals since the Middle Ages. The first solution to be applied, in Portugal and in other countries, was the use of thick rims of wax, creating borders that served as barriers around the impression. These rims could be damaged, but the impressions remained almost untouched, as can be seen in the 14th century episcopal seal reproduced in fig. 3.

Another rather common practice was the use of small bags made of cloth, leather or parchment, which Monnerie considered to be the worst of all protection methods[27]. Intended for protection, these bags unfortunately often had the opposite effect: the seals within them got too dry, broken or reduced to small fragments, even to dust on some extreme occasions.[28] A fragmented seal from 1321, belonging to Queen Isabel of Portugal (1288-1325), clearly demonstrates the inefficiency of parchment bags as protection (fig. 4)[29]. Sometimes, the relief of the seal becomes engraved on the leather or parchment, as can be seen on another royal seal from 1501 in fig. 5. Royal seals were by far the most protected by this method. We have no knowledge of Portuguese seal bags being painted or embroidered with the iconography or the heraldry of seals that exist in other countries[30]; on the other hand, there are sometimes surprisingly shaped wrappings, like the little shoe-shaped bag in the archival fonds of the monastery of Lorvão (fig. 6); the size of the sachet, much smaller than

---

[27] Monnerie 1994, 49.
[28] Monnerie 1994, 50: 'Personne, semble-t-il, n'a jamais extrait un sceau intact de ces sacs. Ce ne sont que fragments et poudre'.
[29] Arquivo Nacional Torre do Tombo, Mosteiro de Santa Clara de Coimbra, maço 22, nº 10. Concerning this queen's seals see Morujão 2014, 99-102.
[30] One of the best examples of these kinds of bags is the Great Royal Seal Bag of Edward I from 1280, kept at the Muniment Room in Westminster Abbey; see Browne, Davies, Michael 2016, n. 24 (p. 151).

Figure. 3 (right)

Seal of Jorge Eanes, bishop of Coimbra. Arquivo Nacional Torre do Tombo, Sé de Coimbra, 2ª incorporação, maço 57, nº 2130 (21 December 1353).

Figure 4 (below)

Seal of queen Isabel of Portugal. Arquivo Nacional Torre do Tombo, Mosteiro de Santa Clara de Coimbra, maço 22, nº 10 (24 April 1321).

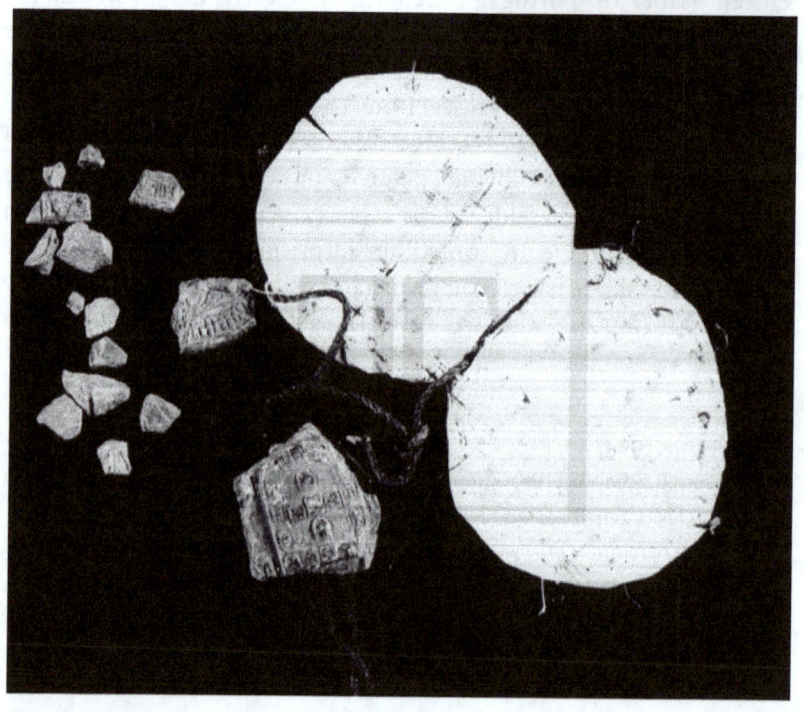

Figure 5 (right)

Seal of king Manuel I in a parchment bag. Arquivo Histórico Municipal do Porto, livro 7, nº 11 (1 February 1501).

Figure 6 (below)

Seal of king Fernando I in a shoe-shaped seal bag. Arquivo Nacional Torre do Tombo, Mosteiro de Lorvão, gaveta 1, maço 1, nº 17 (15 January 1377).

the seal of King Fernando kept inside, indicates that it was already fragmented when this protection was applied.[31]

From the 15th century onwards, the placing of seals in a box made of wood or metal became rather common; nevertheless, in the majority of cases, seals have disappeared just the same, detaching themselves from the box and the ties. In these cases, we can only know their shape and dimensions, and sometimes their colour if a small bit of wax was preserved, glued to the box.

Damaged, broken or fragmented seals – what can be done about them? Luckily, there are conservation and restoration techniques that can be applied to stop the degradation, restore as far as possible the seal's integrity and prevent further damage[32]. In Portugal, there are no conservation and restoration technicians specialised in this heritage; they only have a basic understanding of how to deal with these artefacts. The main exception is a project on lead seals that took place at the archives of the University of Coimbra[33]. This project focused on the royal and papal lead seals preserved in those archives, which began to present alarming conservation problems during the 1990s. The most likely hypothesis to explain their degradation is that they were affected by the strong humidity increase that the city suffered after the construction of both a dam upstream and a weir downstream, causing the waters of the Mondego river to rise. This shows how climate changes – an issue so important nowadays – can affect sigillographic artefacts. Although the corrosion of the seals cannot be reversed, it is possible to interrupt it and obtain good results in restoration interventions, as shown in fig. 7.

---

[31] On this bag see Morujão 2016a, 101-02.
[32] Concerning seal conservation and restoration, namely of wax pendent seals, see Monnerie 1994; Prévost 2008 and 2011; Bechetti 2006 and 2011.
[33] Santos 2008; Santos, Gonsalves 2011; Santos, Melo 2018. Other works on lead seals and the problems concerning their preservation include: Colson, Degrigny, Dubus 2001, and Moreno Cifuentes 2008.

Figure 7

Lead seal of king Sebastião (1572), before and after the restauration. *Apud* Santos, Melo, 2018, 546.

3. Reproduction

The third level of action proposed is the reproduction of seals, something that has been attempted very early on. There have been drawings of seals since the Middle Ages, especially in figured copies of documents and in cartularies[34]. Modern-era scholars have also made drawings, with more or less talent or accuracy[35]. Portugal moreover knew this practice, although it was carried out less systematically than in other countries.

---

[34] Chassel 1993.
[35] On the seal drawings of scholars from different countries see, for example, Wree 1641, Manni 1739, or the studies dealing with the drawings by Roger de Gaignières: Roman 1910, Ritz-Guilbert 2011.

The main author interested in Portuguese sigillography during the first half of the 18th century was António Caetano de Sousa, who in his volumes dedicated to the genealogy of the Portuguese royal house reproduces a remarkable set of 118 seals belonging to kings, queens and members of the Portuguese royal family from the Middle Ages to his own time[36]. One of these seals belonged to King Pedro I (1257-1267) (fig. 8) and it is the only complete representation of that king's wax seal[37]. Another example is the applied seal of King Afonso V (1438-1481) (fig. 9): the drawing shows it almost completely, but the legend is blank as it was no longer possible to read it[38].

Other authors also present seal drawings, but in a very limited number, although they may be of great importance because they reproduce missing seals. Such is the case for Queen Mécia de Haro's (c. 1240-1245) seal, known only through a sketch presented in Francisco Benevides's book about the queens of Portugal, published in 1878[39] (fig, 10).

Casting has been another method of reproducing seals. During the 19th and first decades of the 20th century, several casting campaigns took place, namely in France and Belgium[40]. Sigillographers like Louis Douët d'Arcq, Germain Demay or Auguste Coulon, just to mention some of the most important, did an admirable job in the

---

[36] Sousa 1738.
[37] Sousa 1738, fig. XXXIV; Morujão 2018, 30-31.
[38] Morujão 2018, fig. 21.
[39] Benevides 1878 127; this drawing was reproduced and studied by Morujão 2015, 93-95.
[40] On these campaigns see Nielen 2007; Libert 2011; Blanc-Riehl 2011 and 2012; Flammarion 2019. Castings were also made in other countries, like Russia: see Nosova 2011. On the seal-castings made by the United Kingdom National Archives see Jenkinson 1924 and *PRO23: Public Record Office: Surrogate Copies of Records: Moulds or Impressions of Seals deposited for examination* (https://discovery.nationalarchives.gov.uk/details/r/C11940).

Figure 8 (right)

Drawing of the seal of king Pedro I. *Apud* Sousa, 1738, nº XXXIV.

Figure 9 (below)

Drawing of the applied seal of king Afonso V. *Apud* Sousa, 1738, nº LXIV.

Figure 10

Drawing of the seal of queen Mécia de Haro. *Apud* Benevides, 1878, 127.

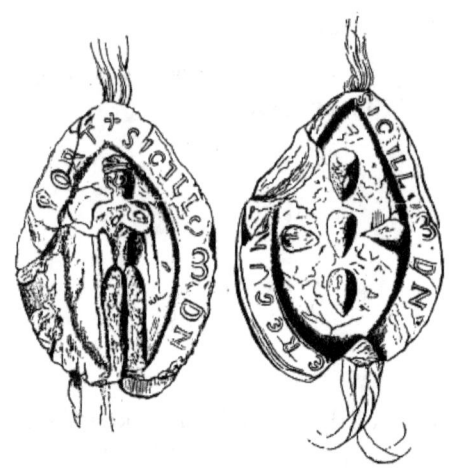

archives of those countries, casting and cataloguing seals[41]. A very substantial part of these casts is now available online through online databases such as SIGILLA, the digital database of seals existing in France[42], or the database of all the seal casts from Royal Belgium Archives[43].

Then came photography, an extraordinary revolution for sigillographic studies (as with other historical fields), allowing reproduction of seals in much more practical and inexpensive ways.[44] Thereafter, photography became the most used technique to obtain images of seals until the 21st century, with the development of digital

---

[41] Douët d'Arcq 1863-68; Demay 1873, 1877, 1881, 1885-86; Coulon 1912.

[42] SIGILLA (http://www.sigilla.org). On this database see Hablot 2017 and 2019.

[43] *Archives de l'État en Belgique* (http://www.arch.be/). On this database see Libert 2011 and 2017.

[44] There are so many examples of the use of photography in sigillographic catalogues and studies that I will only mention the important catalogue of Spanish seals, with an appendix of almost 400 photos, of Menéndez-Pidal 1918.

photography and reproductions and, mostly recently, increasingly accurate scanning permitting excellent images of seals.

At the same time, new technologies promise even more sophisticated reproductions, using techniques of digital imaging such as Reflectance Transformation Imaging (RTI).[45] This technique employs different lighting conditions to better reveal and decipher the legends, which are often in poor condition, but is also very useful for interpreting the seals' iconography. I can attest to RTI technology from my own experience, as I have already used it to study some matrices found in an archaeological excavation; without it, their identification would have been quite impossible.

In these days of huge technological advances, 3D scanning has also been coming to the fore, opening endless possibilities for sigillographic studies[46]. First, it gives a very different perception of the seal, allowing much more realistic and accurate reproductions. Secondly, this technology allows 3D printing in several materials, which are then usable for a range of practical purposes. Some archives already sell reproductions of seals: a good way to raise money that can be invested in the preservation and restoration of other impressions. Moreover, 3D imaging allows us to dream of virtually reconstructing a seal by combining different damaged impressions.

Other technologies have also been successfully applied to sigillography, such as material analysis[47], radiography and tomo-

---

[45] McEwan 2015 and 2018.
[46] Libert 2017. The SIGILLA database already has some seals digitized in 3D, following the Digiprint technique perfected by Jacquet 2011.
[47] These analyses have become ever less invasive, and increasingly performed both on impressions and matrices. On what has already been done in Portugal in this area, for lead seals see Santos 2008 and 2018; and for sigillary matrices, see the analysis of an exceptional gold matrix in Gomes, Portugal, Araújo 2018.

graphy[48]. These are techniques which do not exactly aim at the reproduction of what we see, but rather look inside the seals to study their material aspects, from the composition of their wax or metal to the way that the cords were placed within them.

There are also research projects combining sigillography and forensic sciences to study the fingerprints preserved on wax seals[49]. These projects open up very interesting insights, both as to the gestures involved in the preparation of seals – since it is possible to identify the fingers marked on the wax, allowing to know which of them were manipulating it – and as to the person or people who made them, as it is possible to verify if multiple seals attached to the same charter have identical fingerprints, or if the same person sealed several documents in close dates. In these cases, the knowledge that can be obtained goes beyond bringing dark seals into the light: it is a whole universe, bound up with the seal, that is made clearer and closer.

Even more can be known about this universe when researchers turn to suspensions, which have not yet been studied as they deserve. These are mostly made of textiles, in silk and hemp, obtained by weaving or twisting the threads, which we can date with great precision thanks to the dated documents they are attached to. Their study awaits.

By combining the three levels of action we described, we believe it to be possible to answer our question, at the start of this paper, as to how to bring dark seals into light. We must, however, act quickly, before the medieval sigillographic heritage further irretrievably deteriorates and disappears.

[48] These two technologies have been used mainly by Jacquet 2011, 2014, 2015. We know of no Portuguese example of their application to sigillography.

[49] Two projects have already carried out the research of fingerprints on seals. The first, led by Markus Späth, was based on the seal of the German city of Speyer; see *Verkörperung kommunaler Identität* (https://siegel.hypotheses.org). The second is an English project, *ImPRINT* (https://www.imprintseals.org); see Hoskin & New 2018.

THE CANON AND VARIANTS: BOUNDARIES AND INTERNAL VARIATION IN THE CORPUS OF MIDDLE ENGLISH *PATER NOSTER* VERSIFICATIONS[1]

Monika Opalińska

Introduction

This paper focuses on two issues related to data representation and cataloguing. First, it discusses some ways in which the *Pater noster* witnesses have been transformed in modern textual renditions. Second, it addresses the question of variance and cataloguing of the translations, and the problems this has created for the relative codification of individual pieces within the *Pater noster* corpus. The variety of extant translations makes every single witness a phenomenon in itself. Each composition therefore presents a philological challenge of its own but the problems exemplified by the five texts discussed in the following sections are representative for the entire group.

In medieval England the *Pater noster* was taught and disseminated among the laity in many different ways. The Benedictine Reform in

---

[1] I gratefully acknowledge the assistance of The De Brzezie Lanckoronski Foundation that allowed me to pursue manuscript research related to this paper in the British Library.

the late tenth century and the Fourth Lateran Council of 1215 each gave impetus to the making of vernacular translations, expositions and treatises based on this central Christian prayer. Unlike longer, more complex and theologically refined expositions, the short poetical versions of the Lord's Prayer in the vernacular have not attracted the scholarly attention that they merit. This lack of interest seems to be grounded in the conviction that they are endowed with very little hermeneutic or aesthetic value. On the one hand, they are based on a clearly identifiable Latin source and therefore do not stimulate any search for an original. On the other, many, although not all, are linguistically explicit and too stylistically austere to awaken philological curiosity. According to Rosemary Woolf (1968, 3), the rhymed versions of the prayer are not lyrics *per se*:

> As with so much medieval literature the religious lyrics have to be defined in terms of content not of form. When approached this way the lyrics can immediately be recognized as meditative poems, for their sources are invariably Latin works that are overtly and unmistakably meditations. The appropriateness of this description can also be seen in the fact that it excludes only a very small number of the poems normally called the lyrics, and all of those excluded are poetically inconsiderable. They are largely *versifications of the Pater noster* and Creed, confessions of sins, Levation prayers, and other ejaculatory and simple, extra-liturgical prayers. […]. (emphasis mine)

Putting aside their disputable aesthetic values, short versified versions of the *Pater noster* are important (albeit underestimated and largely unexplored) witnesses to popular devotion in medieval England. For this reason alone they deserve to be recovered from the dark archives where they have remained *in oblivione et pulvere* far too long.

Over thirty of such short-versified texts based on *Oratio dominica* are attested in different forms in diverse manuscripts. Some are written on flyleaves among random notes, others can be found in carefully designed manuals of catechetical instruction in which particular pieces are rendered in different graphic forms and occasionally in different languages. There are bilingual and macaronic variants, and texts with musical notation. On the fringe of the genre are mnemonic formulas in rhyme and alliterative prose, often featuring as marginal additions. Most of the texts are anonymous but there are also translations by James Ryman, John Audelay and John Lydgate.

An outstanding feature of medieval English *Pater noster* translations is that there are no identical versions either in prose or in verse (Cook 1891; Aarts 1969, 5). In some cases the actual differences are minor, in others – fairly considerable. This variation is equally characteristic for Old and Middle English sources, which is remarkable, especially since the latter form a substantial body of texts. By comparison, the twenty-three extant prose translations of the *Pater noster* in Old Polish recovered so far also differ with respect to morpho-phonological, syntactic and lexical forms (not to mention graphemic discrepancies between certain redactions), but the differences are far less prominent (Masłej 2016, 84-89).[2] In fact, they are on the whole so minor that all twenty-three Polish redactions can be regarded as variants of one and the same underlying text.[3] On the other hand, the extant English versifications are simply variations,

---

[2] Extant Old Polish texts of the *Pater noster* are dated to the 15th century but secondary evidence suggests that the first Polish translations of the prayer go back to the 13th century. No versified translations have been identified within the medieval period.

[3] The richness of this corpus of comparable variants is rather exceptional in Polish medieval tradition, given the history of archival losses in this country. Apart from the Lord's Prayer, multiple redactions are generally confined to canonical texts of prayers, the Decalogue, the canon of the mass and psalms.

based on the same ultimate source but with different lexical input, syntactic arrangement and rhythmical contour.

Neither the richness of the English corpus *en bloc*, nor the degree of variation among its component pieces have been reflected in editions or data registers. The literature on the subject is scanty and fragmentary. Printed editions and anthologies, most of which go back to the eighteenth, nineteenth and early twentieth centuries, are largely unrepresentative – based on obsolete methodology, they often ignore inherent elements of scribal input as well as specific codicological details. These are not merely cosmetic alterations: some witnesses are transformed beyond measure. Indexes of Middle English verse are often misleading, too, especially when essentially different texts are classified as variants on the basis of first-/last-line similarities.

A Middle English *Pater noster* lyric and the opacity of modern recensions

Our first example comes from Cambridge University Library, MS Add. 5943 – a fourteenth- or fifteenth-century miscellany consisting of sermons, religious and moral tracts, verses and songs (Ringrose 2009, 212-214).[4] The text of the *Pater noster* attested on fol. 167v was printed in Brown's anthology of fifteenth-century religious lyrics published in 1939. In his redaction, reproduced in fig. 1, the text is entitled *Our Father, Have Pity on Me* and divided into three stanzas: the first has a simple *abab* rhyming pattern, the second and third – presumably that of *ccd*, assuming that words *wylle* and *spylle* in lines 7 and 10, respectively, are monosyllabic. Practically nothing in

---

[4] Ringrose 2009, 84 dates the manuscript to the 14th c. Dobson & Harrison 1979, 15 argue on grounds of musical style and language that the manuscript itself must have been completed about 1400, though the songs contained in it may have been earlier.

Brown's edition, apart from a reference to Mayer 1906 in a brief editorial note on p. 310, hints at the immediate codicological context of the prayer or sheds light on its actual form attested in the codex.

Figure 1

Brown (1939, 84)

> 54.   *Our Father, Have Pity on Me*
> Cambridge Univ. MS. Add. 5943
>
> PAter noster, most of my3t,   [fol. 167ᵛᵒ]
> Þat al þys world hast wrot,
> help me, synful wrechyd wy3t,
> for synne þat I perysche nowt.   4
>
> Pater noster, haue pety on me,
> and helpe me synne for to flee
> and euer to worch þy wylle.   7
>
> Pater noster, yblessyd mote þu be,
> ffor þyn sone þat deyd on tre,
> help me, wreeche, þat y ne spylle.   10

In the manuscript this short variation on the theme of the *Pater noster* is followed by similar versifications of *Ave Maria* (fol. 168r) and *Credo* (fol. 168v) in Middle English. All three texts, most probably composed by the same author, are rendered with musical notation. In fact, they are part of a larger group of songs, copied into the penultimate gathering of the manuscript, which includes diverse lyrical compositions in Latin as well as French. Written down *ca.* 1400 they 'are of special value as one of only two collections of vernacular secular song still surviving from any period earlier than the end of the fifteenth century' (Ringrose 2009, 84-85; cf. also Dobson & Harrison 1979, Figure 2.

Figure 2.
Pater noster, Cambridge University Library, MS Add. 5943, fol. 167v. Reproduced by kind permission of the Syndics of Cambridge University Library

21).⁵ The collection belonged at some point to Thomas Turk, a Carthusian monk and fellow of Winchester College; the songs contained in it may have been performed by college members on festive occasions (Ringrose 2009, 85; Dobson and Harrison, 1979, 25-26, 62-63). Most pieces are polyphonic and composed for two voices – cantus and tenor. On folio 167v, which renders the *Pater noster* lyric, a copyist marked the part for the tenor by a majuscule *T* towards the end of the musical notation (see fig. 2, below). It is likely that the commentaries on the *Oratio dominica* (the Lord's Prayer), *Ave Maria* (the Hail Mary) and *Credo* (the Creed) in the form of lyrical songs were devised to teach young choristers the meaning of the prayers, on the one hand, and to give them practice in mensural notation, on the other (Dobson & Harrison 1979, 62).⁶

Although none of these details is explicitly set out in Brown 1939, 84, his redaction of the text tacitly hinges on an interpretation of the interface between the text and the musical notation discernible in the manuscript. On folio 167v the first four verses of the *Pater noster* are represented as a continuous single-line script directly under the staves. After a pen rest above the flat sign in the fourth staff the melodic contour changes and so does the rendition of the textual component: the remaining part of the text runs in two parallel rows beneath the consecutive staves. In other words, the duple rhythm coincides with triple textual division: after the pen-rest the melodic line may be implemented by two different textual variants, which correspond to stanza two and three in Brown's recension. The capitalised initial of the word *Pater* in line four, which goes along with the symbol of the pen-rest marked on the staff, highlights the major division of the

---

⁵ According to Dobson & Harrison 1979, 21, this group of lyrics 'is likely to belong to the last decade of the fourteenth century; for southern poems, as they are, their language is very advanced in its forms (especially the loss od -e).'

⁶ Cf. Bishop Grandisson's instructions concerning the choir boys' training in St. Mary Ottery in Devon (Dalton 1917, 100).

composition into two parts (it replicates a slightly more ornamental initial used at the very beginning of the text). The word *Pater* itself is written in mid-line and it is evidently devised as a common element to be repeated (along with *noster*) at the beginning of each of the two textual variants.

Brown's division of the text into three stanzas is thus justifiable in the light of palaeographical evidence, but the rationale for his editorial decision is not clear unless the manuscript is consulted. Moreover, his edition gives priority to the textual stratum and overshadows the musical layer which is fundamental to the understanding of the function of the composition and its relation to other pieces from the volume. An alternative interpretation, which gives precedence to the musical representation, has been proposed by Dobson and Harrison (1979, 218). In their study, which combines elements of philological and musicological analysis, *Pater noster, most of myght* is classified as a two-part Italian *canzona* (ibid., 65). Moreover, the authors argue that the scribe was more competent in transcribing the musical part than the text itself, which can be gathered from the discrepancies between the notes and words in several places. The omissions evidently escaped Brown's attention who discerned the general interrelationship but failed to recognize the actual alignment between the two tiers. Dobson and Harrison (ibid., 218), who fill in the supposed lexical gaps in their edition, propose a text that strays from Brown's recension in more than one way.

Finally, this piece has been registered as *Orison* (*Pater noster most of might*) in the *Index of Middle English Verse* (henceforth IMEV) by Brown and Robins (1943, no. 2738), *New Index of Middle English Verse* (henceforth NIMEV) by Boffey and Edwards (2004, no. 2738) and *Digital Index of Middle English Verse* (henceforth DIMEV) by Mooney et al. (1995-, no. 4348). DIMEV, partly following the two printed issues, classifies this text as a one ten-line stanza rhymed *ababccdccd* and tentatively suggests that 'the first four lines may be a burden'. This note, along with the subject tag 'song', reveals the musical character of the composition and so do, implicitly, references to two facsimiles (Mayer 1906, Rastall 1973) and the study on medieval English songs by Dobson and Harrison (1979).[7]

All things considered, it would seem that the *Pater noster* lyric from Cambridge, MS Add 5943 has been documented sufficiently. It has been registered in three consecutive issues of the *Index of Middle English Verse*. The text has appeared in two independent printed editions which might be regarded as complementary to an extent that each brings to light different aspects of the lyric – either its philological facet (Brown 1939) or its musical character (Dobson and Harrison 1979). Undue terseness in Brown's editorial note on the lyric is balanced by Dobson and Harrison's critical commentary which takes into account linguistic and musical details, on the one hand, and codicological and historical background, on the other. Despite its expanded critical apparatus, the latter study leaves many questions unsolved or at least open to further debate. These include, for example, the dating of the religious lyrics (musicological and linguistic cues seem to be at odds here and the literature is not unequivocal), the validity of corrections and emendations (reconstructed forms depend upon (1) the assumption that the exemplar from which the texts were copied was of poor quality and (2) a rather vague conception of the underlying metrical structure), the correlation between the music and the text (the editors assume that the latter has a secondary status but do not consider a possibility that it may have been an instance of *contrafactum*). Undoubtedly, in the light of these and other concerns, the composition from Cambridge University Library, MS Add. 5943 appears to be an excellent candidate for a serious interdisciplinary reanalysis and modernised (digital) editing.

One of the overarching issues regarding the composition attested in MS Add. 5943 is whether it should be included among Middle English *Pater noster* adaptations in the first place. Given its

---

[7] To these one might add Rastall 1990.

paraphrastic character, hardly following the Latin original, should it be considered a hymn to God the Father or a peripheral vernacular variant of the Lord's Prayer? Its contents might suggest the former, but its placement in the manuscript next to the paraphrases of *Ave Maria* and *Credo* – its two customary companion pieces – incline one to tentatively accept the latter categorisation. This, in turn, raises the question of variance and its limitations in the case of extant *Pater noster* pieces in general.[8] To what extant can texts from such a heterogeneous corpus, ultimately derived from one well-known Latin source but departing from it in different ways, be regarded as variants? Is it possible to establish objective criteria or is it a matter of intuitive, subjective assessment? Is variance in this case a gradient or a discrete category? Finally, can variance be measured only by the contents (or substance) or can it be a derivative of particular function(s) assigned to a given witness? All these questions become relevant in view of the classification of the *Pater noster* pieces adopted by Brown and Robbins 1943 and perpetuated in Boffey and Edwards 2004, and Mooney et al. 1995–. The two case studies discussed below show that classificatory criteria are not entirely transparent and the texts indexed as witnesses may be, in fact, quite incongruent.

Pater noster texts and their functions: *lectiones variae* or *lectiones singulares*?

The first case involves versified translations of the *Pater noster* attested in two early fourteenth-century manuscripts: Cambridge University Library, MS Gg. 4. 32, and British Library, MS Harley 3724. The former is a miscellany containing theological and ecclesiastical documents, and prayers in Middle English, Anglo-Norman and

---

[8] On the problem of variance and variants see Cerquiglini 1999 and Pearsall 2013.

Latin[9]. The first gathering in this volume presents several diagrammatic figures, such as the names of the instruments of the Passion in French written in a chess-like board, a coloured figure of a cherub, the tree of vices and virtues, and the *Pater noster* wheel.[10] After the diagrams comes a group of vernacular prayers: a Middle English translation of the *Pater noster* features at the top of fol. 21ra. The Harleian volume, attributed traditionally to Gerald of Wales and probably of Irish origin, contains *inter alia* parts of *Topographia Hiberniae*, the bull *Laudabiliter*, a treatise on the sacraments, some letters in prose, and religious verses in Latin and Middle English. Among the latter on fols 49r-49v there is 'a very ancient creed in English, with the Lord's Prayer in English rhyme'.[11]

In DIMEV (Mooney et al. 1995–, no. 4300) the *Pater noster* translations attested in these two manuscripts are registered as variants. From the general note at the top of the *Index* entry one learns a few basic details, namely, the attributed title ('*Pater Noster in anglico*'), the length and versification structure ('twelve lines in couplets rhymed aa'), the mode of exposition ('the clauses of the *Pater Noster* as remedies against the sins'), and the linguistic form ('macaronic': Latin). In fact, most of these details are relevant for the first witness only, i.e. the one attested in CUL MS Gg. 4. 32. Furthermore, the lists of editions given for each witness include

---

[9] For a codicological description see Hardwick & Luard 1856–67, vol. 3, no 1531, 177–82; Hanna 2005 includes the volume in his corpus of London texts of the period ca. 1330-75.

[10] These figures may have been originally made for another book (Scott 2007, 172, ft. 350; 173, ft. 361). A slightly later hand added an annotation *Turris Sapientiae* to the table of contents on fol. 1, possibly intending the words as a title to the volume (Hardwick & Luard 1856-67, 177).

[11] Cf. *A Catalogue of the Harleian Manuscripts in the British Museum* 1808, Vol. III, no. 3724.

Wright and Halliwell (1845, Vol. I),[12] a work which, despite its antiquity, has been continuously quoted in the literature on the *Pater noster* because it brings together several Middle English texts of the prayer.[13] One of them is, indeed, the version attested in CUL MS Gg. 4. 32 and this is the only printed edition of the text, as of yet. The Lord's Prayer from MS Harley 3724 has more ample editorial history since, apart from Wright and Halliwell (1845, 57), it also appears in Weever (1631, 152), Camden (1633, 24), Ellis (1867, 23) and Patterson (1911, 108).[14] For the sake of comparison, the corresponding fragments from editions of both texts are given in Figures 3a and 3b, below.

Judging only by the comparison of the first and the last two lines from both witnesses (in DIMEV only the lines from the Cambridge source are quoted), the texts seem close enough to be tentatively called (distant) variants. This ostensible similarity diminishes when they are examined in their entirety. First, in contradistinction to the simple translation from MS Harley 3724, the *Pater noster* from MS Gg. 4. 32 turns out to be an elaborate bilingual composition (see 4).[15] The vernacular text is divided into seven parts of different length, and

---

[12] There is an overlap of page range for both 'witnesses', i.e. DIMEV gives p. 159 for the text from CUL MS Gg. 4. 32 and 159-161 for BL Harley MS 3724, which is even more confusing because it implies that they are, indeed, the same texts. In fact, the text from BL Harley MS 3724 is quoted earlier in the volume, namely on p. 57.

[13] Other versified versions printed by Wright & Halliwell 1845 include: Cambridge University Library Hh. 6. 11, fol. 70v (p. 169), British Library, MS Arundel 292, fol. 3 (p. 235), British Library, MS Cotton Cleopatra B. vi, 201 (p. 22).

[14] Two of these editions have been issued more than once (i.e. Ellis 1867, 1869, 1871, 1874; Camden 1636, 1870); three have modern reprints, i.e. Ellis 1973, Camden 1970, and Weever 1979.

[15] Here and below, all scribal abbreviations have been silently expanded.

interspersed with Latin *lemmas* which epitomize the correlation between the seven deadly sins, the *Pater noster*, and the seven gifts of

Figures 3a–3b

Our Father in heaven riche, DIMEV no. 4300 (IMEV and NIMEV no. 2703): Wright and Halliwell 1845, 159, Vol. 1 (fragment)

> 39. (B β I a 1)   Harl. MS. 3724, fol. 44.
>
> Ure fader in hevene riche,
> Þi name be haliid ever i-liche;
> Þu bringe us to þi michil blisce,
> Þi wille to wirche þu us wisse,
> Als hit is in hevene i-do   5
> Ever in corþe ben it al so;

Patterson 1911, 108 (fragment)

> PATER NOSTER, CREED, &c.
>
> From MS. Gg. IV. 32, Bib. Publ. Cantab. temp. Hen. IV. This volume appears to have been the common-place book of a parish priest.
>
> *Oratio Dominica.*
>
> Oure fader in hevene riche,
> Thin name be i-blesced evere i-liche,
> Led us, Loverd, into thi blisce,
> Let us nevre thin riche misse.
> Let us, Loverd, underfon
> That thin wille be evere i-don,
> Also hit is in hevene
> In erthe be hit evene.

the Holy Spirit. The formula adopted by the scribe implements the conceptual framework pivotal to the medieval interpretation of the *Pater noster* in which each petition of the prayer militates against one specific sin and paves the way for one gift of the Holy Spirit.

However, there are other differences between the two texts and these do not merely involve minor scribal features (e.g. *oure* vs. *ure*; *þi* vs. *þin*) or lexical variation (*iblesced* vs. *haliid*) but also syntactic templates and stylistic devices. In effect, the rhythmical contour of each composition is implemented differently. Furthermore, the Harleian version in Fig. 4b transforms the petitions into simple rhyming clauses adhering in an unambiguous and uniform way to the original sevenfold structure of the prayer. The Cambridge version in 4a, on the other hand, is more elaborate: some of its petitions are expanded but the amplification is irregular and varies between two to six lines. The variability is enhanced by the intervening Latin lemmas, all of which are rubricated and thus visually prominent. The overall impression is therefore that of internal complexity and asymmetry.

Figure 4

Alleged variants of the *Pater noster*

a. *Pater noster*, Cambridge Univ. Library, MS Gg 4.32, fol. 21ra	b. *Pater noster*, British Library, MS Harley 3724, fol. 49v
Hic incipit Oratio Dominica in anglica lingua.	Ure fader in heuene riche.
Contra superbiam. Spiritus timoris domini.	Þi name be haliid euer iliche.
Oure fæder in heuene riche	Þu bringe us to þi michil blisce.
Þin name be iblesced eure iliche.	Þi wille to wirche þu us wisse.
Contra inuidiam. Spiritus pietatis.	Als hit is in heuene ido
Led us louerd in to þi blisse	Euer in eorþe ben hit al so.
Let us neure þin riche misse.	Þat holy bred þat lesteþ ay
Contra iram. Spiritus sciencie.	Þu send hit ous þis ilke day.
Let us louerd underfon	Fforgiue ous alle þat we hauiþ don
Þat þin wille be eure idon	Als we forgiuet uch oþir man.
Also hit is in heuene	Ne lete us falle in no fondinge
In erþe be hit euene.	Ak scilde us fro þe foule þinge
Contra tristiciam. Spiritus fortitudinis.	amen

Þe heuene bred þat lasteþ ay
Gif us louerd þis ilke day.
Contra auariciam. Spiritus consilii
Foguiue us louerd in oure bone
All þat we hauen here misdone
Also wisliche ase we forgiuen
Hwiles we in þis worlde liuen.
Al þat us is here misdo
And we biseken þe þerto.
Contra gulam. Spiritus intelligenciae.
Led us louerd to non fondinge.
Contra luxuriam. Spiritus sapienciae.
And sscild us fram alle euel þinge. Amen.

The bilingual character of the Lord's Prayer from CUL, MS Gg. 4. 32 is invisible in Wright and Halliwell's edition. This is due to a common convention which allowed editors at the time to truncate the elements of texts that were, in their view, extrinsic to a given composition. A well-known example of such textual mutilation is the anonymous poem *Stetit puella* from Munich, Bayerische Staatsbibliothek, MS Clm 4660. Raby (1959: 327), and a few other editors have printed the first two Latin stanzas of the poem but left out the third – macaronic – one.[16] Yet another editorial procedure can be seen in Sharon Turner's edition of a bilingual Old English paraphrase of the Lord's Prayer from Cambridge, Corpus Christi College MS 201 (Turner 1840, 203-205). In this case Latin lemmas, alternating in the manuscript with expanded vernacular passages, have been translated into modern English. Needless to say, both operations distort the original scribal redaction, meaning and function(s) of the source texts.

While Wright and Halliwell's recension of the Lord's Prayer misrepresents the manuscript evidence, the annotations in DIMEV

---

[16] For a discussion of this and other examples of textual mutilation, see Robinson 1994, 25-35.

are also misleading. The information provided at the top of the entry for item 4300 implies, among other things, that both texts are macaronic. This is not true of either witness. The text in CUL, MS Gg. 4. 32 is bilingual but not macaronic – the Latin verses are not welded with the vernacular ones to form grammatically logical structures as in, for example, the Old English *Phoenix*. Rather, they function as autonomous linguistic constituents. The other witness does not contain any Latin elements at all.

All these differences between the two *Pater noster* witnesses raise the question of whether it is legitimate to classify them as variants at all. Apparently, the similar rhyme-scheme might suggest a common source but a glance at other extant compositions from the corpus indicates that this was a recurrent versification pattern. This would suggest, in turn, that not only these two but also other pieces might be *lectiones variae*, if the metrical structure was the sole basis of classification. However, other aspects of the compositions should also be taken into consideration when a taxonomy is concerned. Leaving aside Latin, the architecture of the two English texts discussed here is divergent in many significant ways. But the point is that the Latin component is not merely a stylistic device. Latin lemmas in the first witness define its function as an instrument of theological exegesis and penitential guidance. *Oratio Dominica* from CUL, MS Gg. 4. 32 and a host of other prayers attested in its immediate manuscript context constitute a practical compendium that was most probably used by a priest tending to an Anglo-Norman congregation. The form of the prayer which so explicitly turns it into a spiritual weapon against the seven deadly sins and, at the same time, a medium to merit the seven gifts of the Holy Spirit may have been used in preaching or as an aid in a penitential service (cf. Hanna 2005, 5-6, 10, 13). By contrast, the compact monolingual version of the Lord's Prayer from the British Library, MS Harley 3724 does not bear any distinctive features that would allow for an equally obvious interpretation of how it may have been actually put to use. In the manuscript it forms a closely-knit unit with a prose translation of the Apostles' Creed followed by a brief explanatory note in Latin on three types of *Credo*.[17] Both vernacular pieces implemented the minimal catechetical programme for the laity from the Anglo-Saxon period (cf. Venerable Bede's Letter to Egbert in King 2006: 455; see also Rider 2010, 336) and they may have been added to the manuscript in connection with Hadrian IV's commendatory letter to Henry II concerning his mission to Ireland, an item which directly precedes the vernacular prayers in the manuscript.[18] In the light of these differences, the classification of the *Pater noster* texts from CUL MS Gg. 4.32 and Harley MS 3724 as witnesses seems less obvious than the entry in the *Index of Middle English Verse* might suggest.[19]

Translational praxis and relative variability

The second case involves versified translations of the Lord's Prayer attested in two thirteenth-century miscellaneous codices: Cambridge, Emmanuel College MS 27 (fol. 162ra) and Pavia, Bibliotheca Universitaria MS Aldini 69 (fol. 41v). As in the previous case, these two texts have also been classified as variants in the *Index of Middle*

---

[17] Incidentally, a similar redaction of the Apostles' Creed appears also among the prayers in MS Gg. 4. 32 but the names of the apostles are inserted in the text rather than added at the margin (as is the case in MS Harley 3724) and they are given in a different order. There are also differences between linguistic forms used in both versions.

[18] Similar examples of closely-knit units made of two or three basic prayers in the vernacular are attested in various manuscripts starting from the late Anglo-Saxon period, for instance, *Pater noster* and *Gloria Patri* in Cambridge, Corpus Christi College MS 201, pp. 167-169; *Gloria Patri*, *Pater noster*, *Credo* in Oxford, Bodleian Library MS 121 Junius, fols 43v-47r; *Pater noster*, *Ave Maria* in Cambridge University Library, MS Hh. 6. 11, fol. 70v.

[19] Nb, Brown & Robbins 1943 indicate that only witness 1 (CUL, MS Gg. 4. 32) is an expanded text of 18 lines. This information is not spelled out in Mooney et al. 1995-.

English Verse (Brown and Robbins 1943, no. 2704), its revised edition (Boffey and Edwards 2004, no. 2704) and the electronic edition (Mooney et al. 1995-, no. 4299). The general note provided for the item in DIMEV is confined to the basic data: the title (*Our Father in heaven I-hallowed be Thy name*), the subject matter (Lord's Prayer) and the versification structure (The *Pater Noster* in five couplets, two-line – aa). Like the attributed title, which is not attested in the form quoted above in either witness, the note on the versification pattern is misleading, too. The composition from the Emmanuel College manuscript is indeed made of ten lines that rhyme consecutively but the 'witness' from Pavia is shorter and contains only three rhyming couplets.

The longer text is part of a versified manual of religious instruction which contains other short prayers in Middle English, such as *Ave Maria, Credo, Confiteor, Decem praecepta, Septem peccata, In manus tuas, In nomine patris, Per crucis hoc signum fugit..., Vestio cibi poto, Septem opera misericordie, In elevation corporis domini,* all of which are rendered in two columns on fols. 162r-163v (James 1904, 25; Pfander 1936: 249). In addition, a short prognostic poem *In þe daye of seynte Svythone* follows the group on fol. 164. Other versified pieces are added to the margins elsewhere in the codex. These include a couplet on the seven deadly sins and five couplets on the Ten Commandments on fol. 111v, and two proverbial couplets on fol. 57v. Besides the prayers Emmanuel College MS 27 contains theological, devotional and pastoral material, including two popular treatises – summa *Qui bene presunt* by Richard Weatheringsett and *Templum dei* by Robert Grosseteste (James 1904, 22-27).[20]

The codicological background of Pavia, MS Aldini 69 is similar insofar as it contains miscellaneous theological and pastoral works,

---

[20] James 1904, 22-27 contains a full description of this composite volume; a number of important codicological details and references can be found in Goering & Mantello 1984.

including the two treatises by Richard Weatheringsett and Robert Grosseteste, mentioned above. The vernacular *Pater noster* appears as a marginal addition at the foot of fol. 41v. Although it is not part of a versified manual like its counterpart from the Emmanuel College, its inclusion in the volume cannot have been haphazard. First, it is written directly below the *Pater noster* section of *Qui bene presunt*, and secondly, on the preceding two folios there is another variant of the *Pater noster* in Latin added at the foot of folios 40v-41r. In both these sources the prayer is integrated into a pastoral model which demonstrates how the petitions counteract the seven deadly sins. In the Latin piece, the model has a form of a simple diagram in which the preposition *contra* links the *Pater noster*'s pleas with the cardinal sins to form short logical propositions. In Weatheringsett's exposition the model is more complex – it juxtaposes the petitions with the gifts of the Holy Spirit, the virtues, and the beatitudes, and concludes each line with the effect they exert on one of the seven deadly sins. Finally, in the short Middle English translation of *Oratio Dominica* reference to the seven deadly sins is also made explicit even though this is at odds with the original wording of the prayer. This expansion helps to bind the vernacular piece with confessional material in the volume and, at the same time, it acts as a metrical filler for the second couplet.

Thomson (1934), who printed the text of the Middle English Lord's Prayer from MS Aldini 69, noticed that it must have been a work of two scribes and, accordingly, rendered the interpolations in parentheses. The recension I propose in (5) follows that of Thomson with one exception: based on the distinctive handwriting, I would suggest that the whole of the final line and not just the last word 'Amen' is a secondary addition.[21] The emerging pattern indicates that

---

[21] Palaeographical and linguistic aspects of the versified *Pater noster* from Pavia, Bibliotheca Universitaria MS Aldini 69 are discussed in a more detailed way in another paper (Opalińska 2020). The problem of the seven deadly sins vis-

the original text was a fairly straightforward, albeit not entirely complete, prose translation of the Latin text from the Gospel of St. Matthew 6, 9-13. The second scribe filled in the gaps in the text by adding the missing word *deturres* in line 6 and the final clause. More importantly, he turned the crude prose rendition into a mnemonic verse by adding two other clauses – *scildes alle fro scame* and *forgif ous þe sennes seuene*, at the end of line three and five, respectively. The additions are functional not only at the rhythmical but also at the semantic level – the second scribe picked his words carefully, thus integrating the versified text into the conceptual framework of pastoral theology represented by the companion pieces in the volume. Notwithstanding his creative effort, the entire composition lacks cohesion. It is marked by repetition and tautology. The affixed parts stand out not only because they are rendered in different handwriting but also because they are autonomous syntactic units not merged with the rest of the structure. To put it another away, they can be easily identified via philological analysis even without the aid of visual palaeographical cues.

Figure 5.

Pater noster, Pavia, Bibliotheca Universitaria MS Aldini 69, fol. 41v

Oracio dominica in materna lingua
    fader þat hart in heuene blessed be þi name
    To þi kynedom mote (we) comen. (scildes alle fro scame)
    Þi wille be don in herþe as it is in heuene
    Gif ous to day houre echedaÿes bred (forgif ous þe sennes seuene)
    forgif ous oure dettes as we don our (dettures)
    (lad ous into no fonding bote into gode moures. Amen.)

à-vis the *Pater noster* petitions in this codex is examined in Opalińska (forthcoming).

Compared to the composition from MS Aldini 69, stitched by two different scribes, the *Pater noster* piece from Emmanuel College MS 27 seems to be a more homogeneous production, although not entirely consistent, either. Most of the text has been rendered in the same dark handwriting, but a noticeably paler ink and a more compressed script is discernible in the first two lines (marked in parenthesis in 6). This fragment looks as if someone had erased the original text and then tried to fill in the space with a longer sequence. Apparently, it seems that *punctus elevatus* (here represented by [:]), conventionally used by scribes to indicate a major medial pause, draws a division line between the translation proper and extraneous phrases/clauses added for the sake of metre. However, the symbol is placed in the middle of every single line (with the exception of line two which was added later) irrespective of its textual implementation.

Figure 6

Pater noster, Cambridge, Emmanuel College MS 27, fol. 167ra

> Ure fader in heuene : (yhalʒed) bo þy name
> þy (kynedom to us mote ^{come} for þar is blisse and game)
> Al þi wille boe ydo : boþe day and niʒt
> In heuene also on erthe : alse hit is riʒt
> Vre euer echedayes bred : þov ʒif vs to day
> fforgif us vre sunnes : so þov ful wel may
> Al so wis so we forgiveþ : here gultes alle
> þat aʒenvs helveþ agult : Wov sit bo bifalle
> Led us neuere Louerd : into no fondinge
> Ac lus · us · vt of vuele : and ʒif us þy blessinge ·
> Amen · / · So mote hit boe ·

In the light of palaeographical and philological evidence, it seems plausible to assume that, with the exception of line two, the composition from Emmanuel College, MS 27 is a work of one person. It is difficult to say whether it was copied from an exemplar or, given a rather conventional character of the lexical templates used in it, composed from memory *per analogiam* to similar pieces which must have been in circulation at the time. The methodology adopted by the Emmanuel College MS 27 scribe is similar but not the same as that of the Aldini versifier. The additions appear at line ends and, undoubtedly, function as metrical fillers. However, unlike in the Aldini *Pater noster*, the interpolated fragments are not simply self-contained clauses affixed to the preexisting structure. Rather, they are syntactic units consolidated with the rest of the text via linking words. This may be a simplistic method but it helps to construct a relatively more coherent, if not more inventive, vernacular composition than the one attested in the manuscript from Pavia. As Person (1953, 75) put it: 'the present poem is far superior to the *Pavia*, whose text differs so considerably from it that they have scarcely anything in common except their ultimate source'.

Conclusion

The corpus of short versified *Pater noster* compositions is a diverse collection. Some of the texts identified so far are unique and only distantly related to the Latin prayer. One such example is the song from Cambridge University Library, MS Add. 5943 – *Pater noster, most of myȝt*, discussed above. Owing to the paraphrastic character of this lyric its association with the corpus is not unambiguous. If it were attested on its own without the two accompanying paraphrases of *Ave Maria* and *Credo*, its reception might be quite different. In other words, the context in which it appears coerces it into a category even though it does not satisfy the 'ideal' criteria. A problem of a different nature arises when relatively similar pieces are classified as 'witnesses' representing the same underlying text. In such cases the classification hinges on the identity or, more often, mere similarity of the initial lines. Careful reading of such alleged variants in their respective manuscript renditions reveals fundamental differences in the elemental structures, beginning with the linguistic input, stylistic forms, rhythmical contours and mode(s) of composition. Since the descriptive criteria are not definitive, it is not always clear why certain pieces are singled out in the *Index of Middle English Verse* as exponents of the same exemplar. Given that comparable subsets of features are shared by other members of the corpus, one may conjecture alternative intersections within the generic category. For the present, the collection of extant versified *Pater noster* translations appears to be an unstructured variation group, a residue of what must have been once a rich repository of orally performed and memorially reconstructed texts subject to creative changes in the process of dissemination. In order to discover possible associations between its constituent parts and to appreciate the integrity of the entire corpus, one must look beyond editions and indexes, and place the emphasis upon the texts and their 'carriers' – manuscripts – in all their unpredictable richness and beauty. To accomplish the task, the dispersed sources must be retrieved from the archives and the evidence obtained from them must be fully displayed. Notably, clarity and precision in defining the selection criteria is a prerequisite for establishing the boundaries and the internal structure of the corpus.

L'EXPLORATION DES ARCHIVES MÉDIÉVALES EN FRANCE AVEC BIBLISSIMA PROJECT

Anastasia Shapovalova

Depuis plusieurs années, la Section de Codicologie, histoire des bibliothèques et héraldique de l'Institut de recherche et d'histoire des textes réalise le programme « Bibliothèques médiévales de France » (BMF). Ce programme a été commencé en 1987 avec la publication du Repertoire des Bibliothèques de manuscrits médiévaux en France, et au tout début valorisait l'immense corpus des informations sur les bibliothèques et possesseurs médiévaux accumulé par IRHT depuis son origine en 1937, en forme des fichiers de renseignements. Première étape est terminé, et la nécessité de l'exploration des sources est devenue primordiale. Actuellement le projet a pour objectif de recueillir dans les bibliothèques et archives les documents (d'une grande diversité) sur l'histoire des bibliothèques médiévales de France, les analyser et répertorier pour proposer aux chercheurs un corpus des sources médiévales et modernes permettant de reconstituer les bibliothèques françaises du Moyen Age et d'étudier l'histoire des collections de manuscrits médiévaux. Les documents découverts (inventaires et listes de manuscrits et de livres imprimés) font l'objet de notices analytiques et prosopographiques qui ont été publiées sur le site web Libraria.fr1 fermé actuellement. Les notices de Libraria seront transférées prochainement sous la forme de base xml dans la collection Thecae2 (préparée par les Presses Universitaires de Caen).

Depuis le printemps de 2020 les éditions de inventaires et de listes des livres en XML-TEI sont publiées dans la collection électronique et espace de l'expérimentation ThecaeLab.

Le programme « Bibliothèques médiévales de France » (BMF) est devenu un projet national avec l'arrivée en 2014 de l'Equipex Biblissima. L'observatoire du patrimoine écrit du Moyen Âge et de la Renaissance, Biblissima ou Bibliotheca bibliothecarum novissima, réunit les corpus de données scientifiques numériques sur l'histoire de la circulation des textes en Occident du Moyen Âge à la fin de l'Ancien Régime ainsi que les outils de travail sur les données, avec une grande ouverture aux humanités numériques. Avec le soutien de Biblissima le projet « Bibliothèques médiévales de France » a pu commencer la campagne d'exploration systématique des sources médiévales liées à l'histoire du livre et des bibliothèques en France et conservées dans les Archives départementales. Il s'agit d'une exploration intensive, intégrale autant que possible (vu l'état des documents), avec l'idée de se concentrer sur la possibilité de découvrir dans les fonds d'archives les documents mal ou pas connus, qui n'ont pas encore été l'objet d'une édition scientifique.

La présentation actuelle est fondée sur les résultats du travail d'exploration en Bourgogne, dans les Archives Départementales de l'Yonne à Auxerre. Nous avons choisi cette région, l'Yonne, parce que elle est connue par l'activité importante des scriptoriums monastiques au Moyen Age, et donc par la richesse des bibliothèques surtout ecclésiastiques mais privées aussi. Archives départementales de l'Yonne possèdent un fonds de documents très riche et bien conservé qui toujours a attiré l'attention des chercheurs. Ses explorateurs du 19e siècle, les archivistes – notamment Maximilien Quantin (1814 – 1891), Eugène Drot (1848 – 19..), Francis Molard (1845 – 1897), et un peu après Charles Porée (1872 – 1940), – nous ont laissé plusieurs publications y compris celles consacrées à l'histoire du livre au Moyen Age.

Comment trouver ces sources « inconnus » dans les archives qui attiraient l'intérêt de chercheurs depuis XIXe siècle ? La stratégie d'exploration des sources, effectuée aux Archives départementales de l'Yonne en Bourgogne est plonger dans *unread* et dans *unreadable*. Je me suis concentrée sur les fonds d'archives potentiellement intéressants pour l'histoire des bibliothèques médiévales, notamment des archives de clergé séculier, de clergé régulier, des établissements hospitaliers, des minutes de notaires, mais aussi les fonds qui pouvaient être potentiellement intéressants comme « Fonds divers » et « Pièces isolées et fragments ». Au total j'ai pu étudier presque 170 cotes (souvent une cote est une liasse des documents), cela fait des milliers des feuilles en liasses et reliées en registres du XIe siècle jusqu'au début du XXe siècle. Exploration de cette masse a donné 82 cotes utiles pour le projet « Bibliothèques médiévales de France », qui concernaient le livre manuscrit ou imprimé ou l'usage de livre médiéval. Nous pouvons repérer dans cet ensemble 3 types de sources:

1. Inventaires des biens, emploi des biens ;

2. Comptes et pièces de comptabilité, marchés diverses, reconnaissances des prêts.

3. Registres et procès-verbaux de visites pastorales.

Si les deux premières groupes des sources sont déjà bien connus par sa richesse en matière de l'histoire du livre, le troisième nous réserve encore beaucoup de surprises tout en gardant son haut potentiel pour la recherche dans le domaine d'histoire du livre et de culture.

Ce que est assez logique, des mentions de livres, y compris des listes des manuscrits, des nouvelles sources inconnues de chercheurs, ont été trouvés souvent dans les documents médiévaux mal écrits qui présentaient des difficultés de lecture et transcription et qui donc n'ont pas été lus avant. Comme ce document signalé par archiviste bourguignon Maximilien Quantin en 1873, et qui à cause de son très mauvais état, resté sans analyse et sans édition: il s'agit de la Reconnaissance par Jean de Montaigu, l'archevêque de Sens (1406-

1415), d'un prêt des livres par le chapitre pour son usage. Le document6 cite les livres liturgiques probablement conservés à la bibliothèque du chapitre et destinés à l'usage des archevêques de Sens et donc prêtés; étant défectueuse, cette charte permet de relever avec certitude la plupart des livres: un pontifical à l'usage de Sens, 3 missels, un ordinarium à l'usage de Sens, un bréviaire à l'usage de Sens, un graduel, les Évangiles, *Pro dedicatione ecclesiarum* et encore trois volumes qui ne peuvent pas être identifiés avec certitude. Cette liste donne des précisions sur le type de l'écriture et de sa couleur, sur le caractère incomplet des textes et sur la présence de la notation musicale. L'archevêque s'engage à les rendre à son successeur; on ne sait pas si les livres ont été tous rendus (Jean de Montaigu a été tué à Azincourt le 25 octobre 1415), mais on voit dans les inventaires de chapitre de Sens en cours du XVe siècle plusieurs livres qui pourraient convenir; et dans le catalogue de la bibliothèque de chapitre de 1760 on voit encore un Pontifical à l'usage de Sens du XIVe s.8 On ne sait pas si le prêt des livres par le chapitre de Sens à l'archevêque prenant ses fonctions, a été un pratique de longue date ou c'est un cas d'exception.

Chacun de ces groupes de sources fourni des témoignages sur les aspects divers de l'histoire du livre au Moyen Age et a son potentiel à exploiter; je vais me concentrer sur le moins étudié. En revenant au sujet de notre colloque, *unread and unreadable*, je voudrais dire que nous pouvons donner des explications très variées pour definir ce *unread*, non lu - l'écriture difficile, mauvais état de document, le fonds jamais répertorié et donc inconnu... Il est particulièrement intéressant d'observer que pour une partie de ces documents que nous avons trouvés en cours de notre projet il s'agit de sources qui ont reçu déjà une visibilité partielle et partiale, devenus « bien lu », en restant en même temps « invisibles », *unread*, pour l'histoire du livre et des bibliothèques. Grâce aux siècles de travail des érudits avec les fonds d'archives, plusieurs documents ont été étudiés, édités ou signalés sous un certain angle, avec une vision qui dépendait d'une recherche personnelle, mais ils réservent encore des surprises pour toutes sortes d'autres aspects. C'est exactement le cas de Registres et procès-verbaux de visites pastorales conservés aux Archives départementales de l'Yonne en Bourgogne.

Les visites est une source richissime en informations sur la vie matérielle et spirituelle du clergé et sur le fonctionnement des établissements religieux, avec le contenu diverse et compliqué à analyser. L'importance de cette source est liée au fait que le visiteur décrit la situation réelle, vue par ses yeux dans les églises et monastères visités pendant toute la durée de tournée de visite, ce que nous donne un vrai portrait de la vie religieuse de la région. Elle attirait souvent l'intérêt des historiens de l'église ou l'histoire économique; alors nous avons décidé de les analyser en recherche des informations sur les livres et les bibliothèques de Bourgogne médiévale, et finalement les visites ont devenus la source la plus riche en découvertes et intéressante, de toute la masse des documents de notre projet.

Les registres et les procès-verbaux de visites pastorales de l'époque médiévale ne sont pas très nombreux dans les Archives départementales de France car ce genre des documents n'a pas été vraiment destiné d'être conservé à l'époque. La lecture et l'analyse de ces documents ne sont pas toujours faciles: le procès-verbal était d'abord dressé sur place durant le déroulement de visite, dans une forme très abrégée, et ces notes étaient ensuite mises au net dans un registre spécial, qui reste toujours une copie au propre d'un texte antérieur et contient souvent des erreurs de lecture de copiste, erreurs dues à l'interversion de feuillets, les lignes sautées qui rendent le texte incompréhensible, mauvaise interprétation des noms ou des lieux.

Le diocèse de Sens de l'époque du Haut Moyen Age comprenait plus de sept cens paroisses. Son territoire correspondait aux départements de la Seine-et-Marne et de l'Yonne, et un peu l'Aube, l'Essonne, Loiret. Jusqu'à la Révolution il conservait sa structure ancienne comprenant cinq archidiaconés (Provins, Melun, Etampes, Gatinais, Sens), divisées en 13 doyennés. Les Archives départementales de l'Yonne conservent un ensemble important des registres et des procès-verbaux de visites pastorales de ce diocèse, les plus anciens datent du 1444 et les autres couvrent la seconde moitié du 15ᵉ s. et la première moitié du 16ᵉ s.9

On peut voir trois corpus des documents d'après le statut de visiteur:

- Les registres des visites pastorales effectuées soit par l'archevêque, soit par ses vicaires généraux, dans les abbayes, prieurés, églises collégiales, hôpitaux etc. Il s'agit des documents qui réunissent les descriptions des visites des archevêques Louis de Melun (1432-1474) et Tristan de Salazar (1474-1518) ou leurs vicaires généraux: G 36 (couvre les années 1444, 1483, 1484, 1488, 1493, 1494) et G 37 (1500 - 1520).

- Les procès-verbaux des visites faits par les archidiacres de Melun (G 81, 1483-1491), d'Étampes (G 74, 1491-1502), de Provins (G 84, 1483 - 1491) et par les doyens de Melun, d'Etampes, de Ferrières, du Gatinais en cours des visites des églises paroissiales (G 90).

- les procès-verbaux des visites des eglises paroissiales qui étaient sous la patronage du chapitre cathédral de Sens. G 714 – G 717 (1446 - 1781).

Le droit de visite est exercé par l'évêque, l'archidiacre ou doyen, elle est annuelle. La procédure de visite se définie par les instructions *Modus visitandi* (mais on ne connaît pas ce texte pour Sens), mais aussi par les statuts synodaux (Statuts synodaux de Sens de 1461 confirmés en 1485, les suivantes sont de 1524). Il faut noter que en réalité la structure de description de visite n'est pas la même dans les documents étudiés, mais on trouve quelques éléments toujours présents: *visitatio rerum* (examen des bâtiments, de leurs meubles et de leur décor, renseignements sur le revenu et sur l'administration), ensuite *visitatio hominum* (visite des clercs et auxiliaires, enquête sur leurs devoirs - étude de la célébration des messes, de l'administration des sacrements, moralité des prêtres, niveau intellectuel, de l'enseignement de la foi etc., les *inventa* (constatations), les *injuncta* (les ordonnances prononcées par le visiteur).

Quel est le place du livre et de son usage dans les visites ? On relève de nombreuses mentions des livres dans la partie de *visitatio rerum* aussi bien que dans la partie de *visitatio hominum*. Pour la *visitatio rerum*, les mentions de livres et parfois les listes de livres découvertes sur place se trouvent dans les *inventa*; pour les *visitationes hominum*, c'est l'examen du clergé qui présente un grand intérêt car il est souvent effectué à l'aide des livres liturgiques (ainsi, la *visitatio hominum* de l'église paroissiale d'Audeville, 1484, nous informe: ...*visitata fuit ecclesia parrochialis de Audevilla in presentia domini Guillelmi Martin presbiteri Lemovicensis vicarii seu firmarii dictae ecclesiae... Condempnatus fuit dictus capellanus in emendam pro eo quis est penitus illiteratus et ignorans et taliter fecit se promoveri per legatum ... et quia nescit legere canonem nec scit dicere verba sacramentalia canonis...*10). Particulièrement précieux sont les *injuncta* qui témoignent de contrôle de contenu et du soin de bon état des livres, contenant dans plusieurs cas non seulement l'ordre de faire un inventaire des livres et des ornements, mais aussi l'injonction de relier les livres, d'en entreprendre la correction ou l'achat.

Pour le plupart des cas l'information sur les livres est très basique (absence ou présence suffisante et en bon ou mauvais état), plus rares sont les listes des livres comme cette liste des livres trouvés à Étréchy (prieuré bénédictin Saint-Étienne, dépendant de l'abbaye Sainte-Trinité de Morigny), le 19 septembre 1484, qui inclut des livres liturgiques et d'autres livres de type non précisé (G 36, f. 55r).

Pour le plupart les livres rencontrés dans les registres des visites sont des missels, des graduels, des antiphonaires, des psautiers, mais aussi des manuels, legendiers, des « matrologes » (matrologium = martyrologium = obituaire dans l'ancien diocèse de Sens), des statuts synodaux (dans les injonctions apparaît systématiquement l'ordre les acheter), *Doctrinale simplicium*11, livres de droit. Un cas d'exception, un manuscrit de mystère à jouer, un exemplaire, est mentionné dans le registre de visite archiépiscopale à prieuré cure Saint-Pierre de Sormery en 1484: le registre signale qu'il a été demandé (par la paroisse?) la permission de jouer « une histoire de Job » (ludum seu Historiam Beati Job); les solliciteurs montrent un « papier » ou « exemplar » (papirum seu exemplar) qui contient le texte; le visiteur autorise un certain Johannes Pagot, ayant des compétences dans ce domaine, à améliorer l'« exemplar » (G 36, f. 60r).

Dans les *injuncta* et *emenda* on voit beaucoup de remarques des visiteurs qui se concentrent sur les problèmes suivants:

- absence des livres (se fait remarquer une inégalité importante, et l'absence des livres à cause de la pauvreté n'est pas si rare. Les livres manquent à cause des guerres, on repère aussi quelques cas de livres donnés en gage (monastère Saint-Jacques de Provins, 1488, G 36, fol. 96).

- les livres dont l'état de conservation est insuffisant (dans les injonctions on voit souvent les livres en mauvais état, sont mentionnés des taches, feuillets manquants ou placés dans le mauvaise ordre, l'absence ou vétusté de reliure, l'absence des initiales ou de la rubrication). On rencontre souvent les ordres de faire relier et réparer les livres; comme exception apparaît un ordre de *tympaniser* (i.e. gaufrer, estamper à froid la couverture de reliure12) le livre: pendant la visite à Saint-Martin-du-Tertre, prieuré bénédictin de Saint-Denis-en-France, situé à Montereau-Fault-Yonne, en 1494, il est ordonné de faire relier les livres, de les « tympaniser », et de faire faire les livres pour la messe (manuscrits ou imprimés ?). On sait que encore en 1444 le registre de visites pastorales a constaté que cette église était dans un grand état de désolation, tous les ornements, vêtements et les livres ayant été perdus à cause de la guerre (G 36, f. 3).

- corrections et additions (repérées en partie par Pierre Gasnault): 1) toute une chaîne des missels avec la même erreur dans le Canon a été repérée dans le doyenne d'Étampes: dans les paroles de consécration du vin « novi eterni testamenti » apparaît au lieu de

« novi et eterni », et « pro nobis » au lieu de « pro vobis ». Cette erreur est trouvée notamment dans les missels de l'église collégiale Notre-Dame d'Étampes en 1483: en cours de la visite il est constaté que le vicaire Cancianus Lesne, qui célébrait la messe en utilisant ce missel tel quel depuis le 25 juillet 1482 (jour de Saint-Jacques, où ce missel a été donné à l'église), a été taxé de 25 sols tournois pour lecture incorrecte (G 36, f. 27r/v); 2) additions dans les livres liturgiques de l'office de la Visitation de la Vierge et l'office de la Transfiguration liées à l'évolution de ces dévotions (Bouville, septembre 1486, G 74 fol. 95).

- problème de l'utilisation des livres liturgiques de l'usage autre que du diocèse de Sens (parfois sans précision, ou bien usage d'Auxerre, de Chartres, d'Évreux, même d'Utrecht).

Le plupart des livres cités dans les procès-verbaux sont des manuscrits, et on continue les réaliser assez longtemps (encore au XVIIe siècle on voit dans les documents conservés aux Archives de l'Yonne les commandes des manuscrits liturgiques, comme celle de « trois messes et les notes » donnée à « M. Nicolas, écrivain », en 1631 par l'église d'Avallon, G 2153); or, la fin du 15e s. est une période de la diffusion active de l'imprimerie et des imprimés en France.

Les procès-verbaux de visites conservés aux Archives départementales de l'Yonne est une source importante sur l'installation de l'imprimerie en France et en Bourgogne; on trouve notamment dans les registres de visites les traces de deux éditions incunables, le missel et le bréviaire à l'usage de Sens, dont aucun exemplaire nous n'est parvenu à ce jour.

Élucidée d'abord par Pierre Gasnault[13] et enrichie en cours de notre projet de l'exploration, l'histoire de ces deux éditions commence vers 1485. L'apparition et diffusion de missel et bréviaire à l'usage de Sens à la fin du XVe siècle est liée aux noms de l'archevêque de Sens Tristan de Salazar et de libraire parisien Vincent Commin. Les premières traces d'un missel et d'un bréviaire imprimé apparaissent dans les visites pastorales à partir de 9 septembre 1487 à Andonville

(Loiret), on les voit dans des injonctions ordonnant aux curés avoir ces livres (G 74 p. 106). L'initiative d'imprimer le missel et le bréviaire à l'usage de Sens appartenait au libraire parisien Vincent Commin et a du se réaliser vers 1485, d'après un arrêt du Parlement daté du 19 janvier 1485 (1486 n.st.). La lutte de l'archevêque qui a interdit l'achat et l'usage de ces bréviaires aux prêtres de son diocèse, a terminé en 1486 par la paix très probablement au profit réciproque: on voit dans les visites et dans les pièces de comptabilité de diocèse de Sens les traces de la vente et diffusion de ces éditions organisée par l'archevêque dans son diocèse.

Cet effort de l'archevêque a contribué beaucoup pour fixer l'usage liturgique du diocèse avec l'introduction imposée de missel et bréviaire imprimés, renforcée par l'interdiction aux prêtres d'acheter ou utiliser les autres livres liturgiques sous la peine d'amende. Les archidiacres et les vicaires utilisaient les visites annuelles pour vendre les missels et les bréviaires imprimés, ordonnant dans les injonctions l'acquisition du missel imprimé à l'usage de Sens auprès le doyen ou même chez le marchand qui venait spécialement pour cette occasion (probablement de Paris?). Les pièces de comptabilité conservées aux Archives départementales de l'Yonne attestent de la vente des imprimés donnés aux doyens par l'archevêque en 1486-1490 (ainsi Jean de Bray, chapelain de l'archevêque, reçoit de Guillaume Des Marquais, doyen, 35 livres, à cause des bréviaires qu'il a distribuez en son doyenné de la Rivière de Vanne (1486, G 421).

Un exemple de la campagne de diffusion de missel imprimé est présenté dans le procès-verbal de visite faite par Gabriel Nicolas, archidiacre d'Étampes, dans les églises de son archidiaconé en 1490 (G 74). On voit que les curés reçoivent systématiquement l'injonction d'acheter un missel à l'usage de Sens, parfois avec la précision sur le type – imprimé, et la convocation de le faire à Étampes: à l'église paroissiale d'Intville-la-Guétard, injonction est prononcée de venir à Étampes samedi prochain et acheter un missel imprimé à l'usage de Sens; à l'église paroissiale d'Aulnay-la-Rivière, c'est aussi une injonction d'aller à Etampes samedi et acheter un missel à l'usage de Sens chez le doyen d'Etampes. Ces missels se vendent par le doyen d'Étampes ou par le marchant qui vient à l'Étampes spécialement pour cette affaire (27 août 1490, à l'église paroissiale de Césarville, apparaît une injonction d'aller à Étampes samedi après la fête de Saint Loup et Saint Gilles, et acheter un missel à l'usage de Sens chez un marchand qui viendra à Étampes exprès pour cette affaire).

Vers 1493 les missels et les bréviaires imprimés semblent de pouvoir prendre sa place dans la vie du diocèse et devenir une obligation: ainsi en décrivant la visite à Saint-Loup de Preudhon, prieuré bénédictin de St-Pierre-le-Vif, en 1493, un registre de visites pastorales nous informe que, il a été trouvé un missel partiellement sans valeur ou en mauvais état (« nil valet nisi partim »); le visiteur ordonne au prêtre fermier (« firmarius ») Johannes d'avoir un missel imprimé (« missale in impressione factum ») dans un délai d'un mois sous la peine d'amende (G 36, f. 120v). Cette « obligation » n'a pas toujours a été appréciée par les curés qui voulaient garder ses anciens bréviaires manuscrits (G 90, p. 123).

Aucun exemplaire de ces éditions n'est parvenu à nos jours. La même chose pour ces centaines des livres manuscrits ou imprimés lus et utilisés dans les paroisses et monastères du diocèse de Sens au Moyen Age, dont les seuls traces de l'existence et de l'usage apparaissent conservés dans les procès-verbaux des visites pastorales, la source mise au lumière grâce à l'exploration des archives.

En conclusion, il nous semble que même si l'exploration de grand fonds d'archives médiévales ne peut pas devenir une action définitive, l'exploration du document médiéval peut être bien complète. Il nous faut envisager de l'étudier dans son intégralité, sous tous les points de vue, prenant en compte toute la variété de données à analyser – pour le sortir définitivement de l'ombre de l'oubli.

II. Endless Deserts, Oceans and Mountains: The Metadata Crisis

Training Generic Models for Handwritten Text Recognition Using *Transkribus*: Opportunities & Pitfalls

Achim Rabus[1]

Introduction

This paper is concerned with computer-assisted transcriptions of medieval (and modern) handwriting. Since its main target groups are rather philologists than computer scientists, I shall restrict myself to a minimum of technical details.[2] The application used in the analyses reported on is *Transkribus* (www.transkribus.eu), a piece of software that can be used for working with manuscripts. While there is a free basic version, charges depending on the amount of data transcribed.[3] The Java-based expert client is available for all major platforms and features a graphical user interface exhibiting, among others, a frame

---

[1] I would like to thank Stefanie Anemüller, Martin Meindl, Elena Renje, the creators of the models used in this paper, and the Transkribus staff. The usual disclaimers apply. Funding for this paper includes the Humboldt Foundation (Research Group Linkage Program DigiPalSlav, www.digipalslav.uni-freiburg.de.

[2] This may sometimes lead to a somewhat inaccurate technical description. The technical reader is referred to Sánchez et al. 2019.

[3] For details, see https://read.transkribus.eu/about/coop/.

for the digitised version of the manuscript and another frame for the transcription as depicted in Figure 1.

Figure 1

GUI of *Transkribus* (letter by Athanasius Kircher, http://diglib.hab.de/edoc/ed000005/startx.htm)

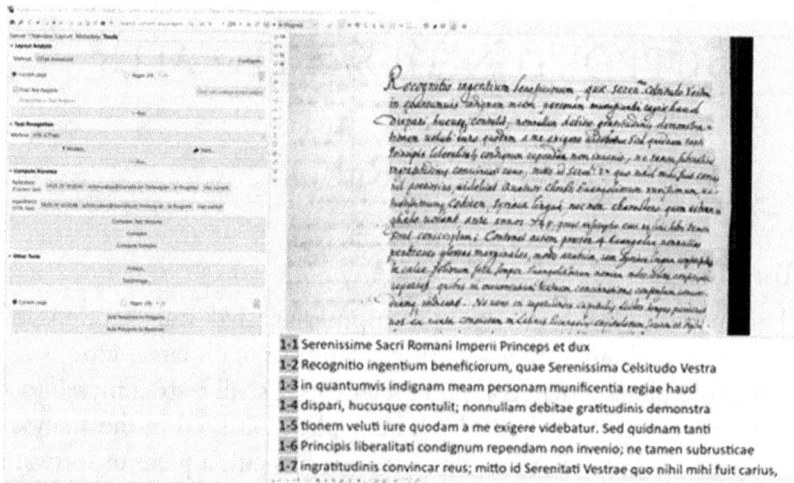

While there are many other software applications capable of providing an interface for manually transcribing medieval (and other) manuscripts, the most interesting feature of *Transkribus* making it important for successful mass digitisation[4] is its model training capabilities. Given a sufficient amount of training data, i.e. several thousands of line-by-line transcribed words of a manuscript along with the corresponding digital images, models can be trained that allow for automatically transcribing manuscripts in a similar script. This process is called Handwritten Text Recognition (HTR). As opposed to traditional instances of Optical Character Recognition

---

[4] Muehlberger et al. 2019.

(OCR) of printed text, HTR does not read single characters, but rather whole lines. *Transkribus* applies machine-learning techniques, specifically Neural Networks, to compare the digital image with the corresponding symbol used for transcription. During numerous epochs[5] of training and testing (the default number of epochs when using the current HTR+ engine in *Transkribus* is 50), the models learns the correspondences of the visual signal and the corresponding transcription more and more precisely. While, at the beginning of training, the Character Error Rate (CER) of the model is very high and quite quickly drops drastically, the more epochs the model runs through during training, the smaller the drop in CER becomes. As is characteristic for such instances of Machine Learning, a typical learning curve of a model trained with *Transkribus* looks as follows:[6]

Figure 2

Learning curve of a model trained in *Transkribus*

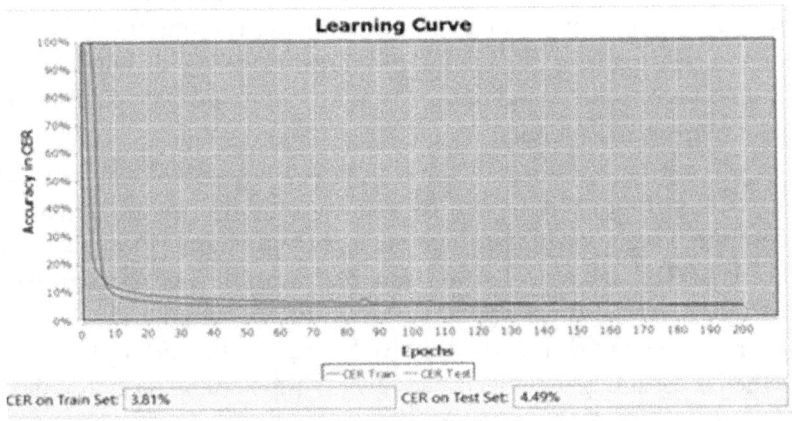

---

[5] According to *Praat: Doing Phonetics by Computer*, an epoch is 'is one complete presentation of the data set to be learned to a learning machine' (http://www.fon.hum.uva.nl/praat/manual/epoch.html).
[6] For further details on model training see Rabus 2019.

When provided quantitatively and qualitatively sufficient training data (the *Transkribus* FAQ recommends at least 15,000 word tokens, but, as we will see, specific models can reach a decent CER with less than that), good models reach a CER ranging from 3% to 5%, and sometimes, depending on the script complexity and the quality of the images, even less. This means that, in theory, only three to five out of 100 characters in a manuscript from a similar hand are read incorrectly. In order to assess the real-world performance of *Transkribus* models, I will provide examples from different manuscripts and languages.

A model tailored for a specific manuscript has been trained by me using parts of the St. Gallen Parzival manuscript taken from the Parzival edition project, www.parzival.unibe.ch. It took around three hours of manual work to copy the parts of the Parzival edition used for the model, clean the data and paste them into the *Transkribus* application. The training of models in *Transkribus* is triggered locally, but takes place on servers located in Innsbruck, which means that one does not need to have their computer up and running until the end of the training process. Training of large models with hundreds of thousands of tokens, and hundreds, if not thousands, of epochs, may take more than 24 hours.

The current specific model was trained using 25,000 tokens of the Parzival edition and it yielded a CER of 0.8%, which equals a computed accuracy of less than one incorrectly transcribed character every 100 characters. As one can see, most letters are rendered correctly, even superscripts such as in *tro̊m* (line 1-5). The abbreviation *vn(d)* has been resolved correctly by adding brackets, which is because the model has seen *vn(d)* quite often during training. As one can see, there does not need to be a visual similarity between the digital image and the transcription sign; during training, the

Figure 3

Example of transcription of Parzival manuscript using a specialised model (Parzival_Test1)

Words	Lines	Epochs	Train CER	CER	Language
25,334	4,746	200	0.79%	0.83%	MHG

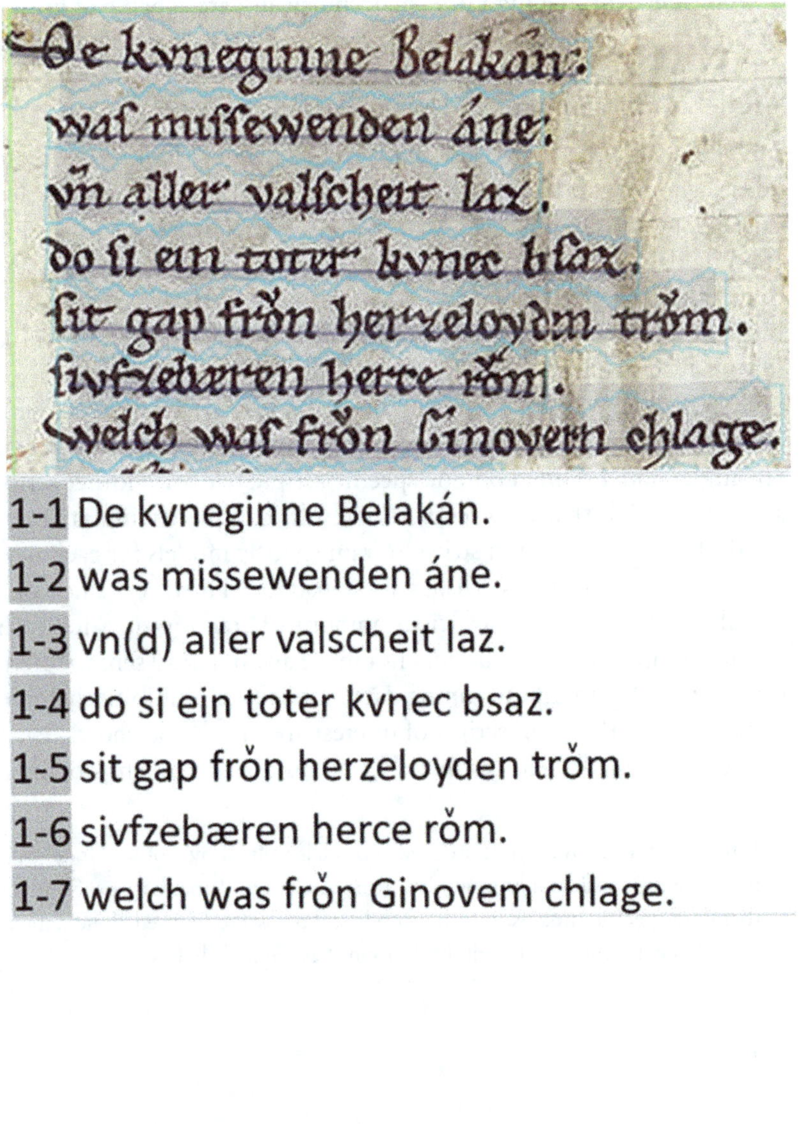

1-1 De kvneginne Belakán.

1-2 was missewenden áne.

1-3 vn(d) aller valscheit laz.

1-4 do si ein toter kvnec bsaz.

1-5 sit gap frŏn herzeloyden trŏm.

1-6 sivfzebæren herce rŏm.

1-7 welch was frŏn Ginovem chlage.

models learn correspondences of visual cues in the digital image and signs used for transcription independently of optical similarity.[7]

Judging from this example, it should have become clear that, under ideal circumstances (i.e. if there is a manuscript of excellent quality, the script style is very clear and regular, and the transcription used for training does not contain errors), the models trained using *Transkribus* exhibit a high level of accuracy and are capable of greatly facilitating transcription tasks, thus even leading to mass digitisation.

Model training: issues and possible solutions

However, as impressive as such results might look, the main advantage of good *Transkribus* models – their being specifically tailored to the manuscripts that need to be transcribed, by using training data written by the same hand – may become a serious flaw. Since, by design, the models adapt to specific script styles, it is difficult to reuse specific models with other manuscripts and retain a low CER. Usually, the hand present in the training data is recognised with a very low CER, whereas other hands are recognised with considerably more errors. Often, the error rates obtained when reusing a model trained on one specific script style for another script style are so high that they render the results completely unusable. In an ideal world, one would strive to train specific models for each new hand or manuscript one wishes to transcribe. However, since one usually does not have a sufficient amount of training data for each possible script available, this does not make any practical sense. Often, the time needed to input training data manually is prohibitively high. In other cases, the manuscripts of interest are simply too short – even if one transcribed them completely, the number of tokens obtained

---

[7] It has to be noted that there are several models trained by Tobias Hodel that make use of considerably more data from the Parzival manuscript. Some of them are specific models, in other models, Tobias Hodel used these data as part of generic models. I shall dwell upon these models below.

would not amount to sufficient training data for decent models. These factors severely inhibit the use of specific *Transkribus* models for mass digitisation.

Because of that, in order to achieve the goal of computer-assisted mass digitisation, *generic models*, i.e., models suitable for transcribing a variety of script styles, are of crucial importance. If users could simply use an already pre-trained model and apply it to their own data without the need to train their own models, the number of digitised manuscripts could rise significantly and fast. In this context, the issue of user-friendliness is crucial: while it is not extremely complicated to train a model in *Transkribus* (one does not need to fiddle around with command-line commands; everything can be done using a GUI), it might nevertheless be prohibitively complicated for certain users who are not very computer-savvy. Since it is clearly easier to apply already available pre-trained models than to train one's own models, the availability of functional generic models might make the difference for a considerable amount of users as to whether to use computer-assisted transcription and digitisation methods or not.

Generic models can be trained by simply combining training data from similar but different script styles, e.g., different varieties of Gothic or cursive script or – for Cyrillic – a combination of Uncial and Semi-Uncial script. When training generic models (or specific ones, for that matter), it might be helpful to 'recycle' transcriptions of manuscripts made for completely different purposes, be it the creation of a printed or an online edition. In doing so, one can obtain the critical mass of training data rather easily and fast without being forced to produce the bulk of the training data manually. Usually, generic models consist of several hundreds of thousands word tokens of training data and are trained for more than 300 epochs – there exist generic models that have been trained for more than 1,000 epochs. During training, the models learn that different visual cues (i.e., the different script styles of the heterogeneous training data resulting in different glyph forms) are transcribed with one and the same character or string of characters, respectively. Because of that, generic models are expected to cope with variation – and, thus, completely new and unseen script styles – better than specific models. In order to test this hypothesis, I shall provide examples from both Slavonic and Western manuscripts.

The following test has been conducted using parts of the Church Slavonic manuscript Pogodin 27. It is written in the older variant of Cyrillic semi-uncial script, the so-called *staršij poluustav*.[8] Simply put, this is an intermediary script form of traditional (Old) Church Slavonic *ustav* (Uncial) and newer *poluustav*, the latter being influenced by South Slavonic traditions. The generic model I trained for Old Cyrillic contains newer *poluustav* and *ustav* training data. Additionally, I added training data from an early printed Bible, namely the Elizabeth Bible from 1751, exhibiting glyph types similar to the newer *poluustav* manuscripts. There are no instances of *staršij poluustav* in our training data. In order to assess the performance of the generic model, I use a smaller, specialised model for comparison.

Figure 4

Pog. 27 transcribed with the generic model Combined_ChSl_VKS_E_1

Name	Words	Lines	Epochs	Train CER	Test CER	Language
Combined_ChSl_VKS_E_1	503466	93674	600	4.31%	4.00%	Church Slavonic
VMČ_Test_5+	252179	53576	400	3.62%	3.91%	Russian Church Slavonic

---

[8] Barkova 2013.

The performance of the model Combined_ChSl_VKS_E_1 is as follows:

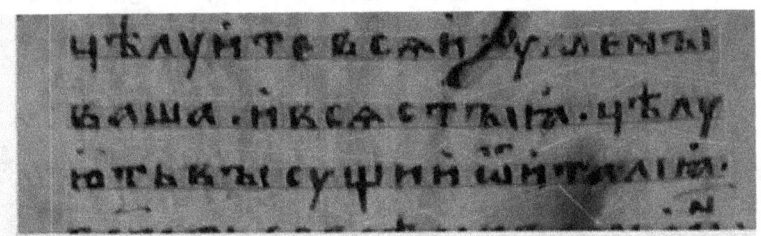

1-5 цѣлуйте всѧ иу· ленъ
1-6 саша· й всѧ стыӷа̑· цѣлу-
1-7 ють въ сущию҄ ѿитачлї.

The following is the performance, of the smaller, non-generic model VMČ_Test_5+:

цѣлүите вса иоу. мьно

заша. и всастъїіа. цѣлу-

ють въ соуѱи ю ѡ итилї.ка.

This example shows that, while the overall quality of the transcriptions is not comparable to the ones discussed elsewhere[9], it is obvious that the generic model performs better than a smaller, specialised model. For instance, цѣлуите is recognised correctly.

In another experiment that shows the advantages of a large generic model, I analyse the East Slavonic Manassija Chronicle manuscript from the middle of the 14th century, also written in *staršij poluustav*:

---

[9] Rabus 2019.

Figure 5

Transcription of Manassija Chronicle, GIM Sin. 38, State Historical Museum Moscow

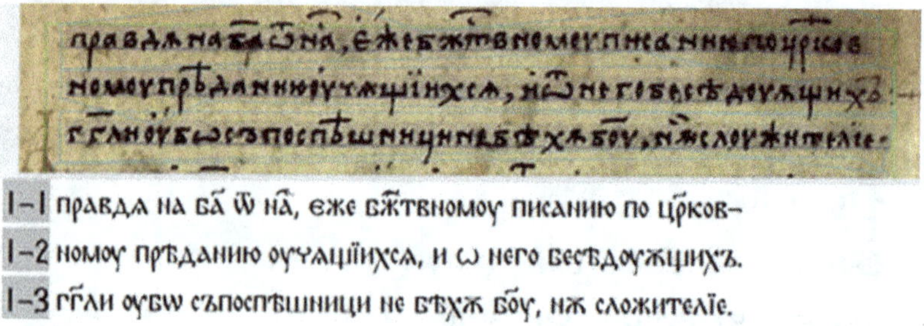

l-1 правда на ба̃ ѿ на̃, еже бж̃твномоу писанию по цр̃ков-
l-2 номоу прѣданию оучащїихсѧ, и ѡ него бесѣдоужщихъ.
l-3 гл̃ли оубw съпоспѣшници не бѣхж бо̃у, нж сложителїе.

Here, the large generic model Combined_VKS_E_2 together with large parts of the printed Elizabeth Bible was used, which resulted in better accuracy than the use of a generic model without the printed Elizabeth Bible.

Name	Words	Lines	Epochs	Train CER	Test CER	Language
Combined_VKS_E_2	600336	109212	1000	3.80%	6.03%	Church Slavonic
Combined_Full_VKS_2 [10]	393079	75422	400	4.90%	3.92%	Church Slavonic
Elizabeth_Bible_1	107899	17876	400	2.62%	2.47%	Russian Ch. Slavonic
VMC_Test_+	173287	38374	200	3.77%	3.82%	Russian Ch. Slavonic

[10] In Rabus 2019, the models have other names. They correspond the following way: Combined_Full_VKS_2 corresponds to Comb1; VMC_Test_4+ corresponds to VMC1.

The smaller generic model Combined_Full_VKS_2, without data from the printed Elizabeth Bible, performs as follows:

правда на бд о нд҇, еже б҄жтьномоу письнию по ц҄рков-
номоу пр҄еданию оу҄чащїихса, и ѿ него бес҄едоу҄ащи хо
г҄ли оу҄бѡ съпосп҄ешници не б҄ехѫ б҄оу, нѫ слоу҄жителїе.

Each letter marked in red corresponds to an error the latter, smaller generic model committed that the former, larger generic one did not. Conversely, each letter marked in green corresponds to (non-)errors the other way round. Errors committed by both models have not been marked.

A specific model trained exclusively with data from the printed Elizabeth Bible (Elizabeth_Bible_1) is completely useless, while the specific model trained on the *Velikie Minei Čet'i* (newer *poluustav*, VMC_Test_4+) performs as follows:

правда на бд о нд҇, еже б҄жономоу пис҄нин но ѱрков
номоу пр҄еданию оу҄чащїижса, и ѿ него бес҄доу҄ащи 30.
г҄ланоу҄ бѡ съпосн҄ ѡници не б҄е а б҄оу, нъ слоу҄ жителю.

It is obvious that this model adds a couple more errors to the already existing errors produced by the 'smaller' generic model.

For these Slavonic test cases, large generic models perform better than smaller ones, and smaller generic models perform better than specific ones. This holds true even though some of the specific models have a considerably lower CER than the generic models. The versatility of the generic models nevertheless leads to better performance.

With respect to languages and manuscripts written in Latin script, similar results can be obtained. The following is an example of

Humboldt's handwriting[11] when writing Kurrent. The correct transcription is as follows:

Figure 6

Correct transcription of Humboldt's handwriting.

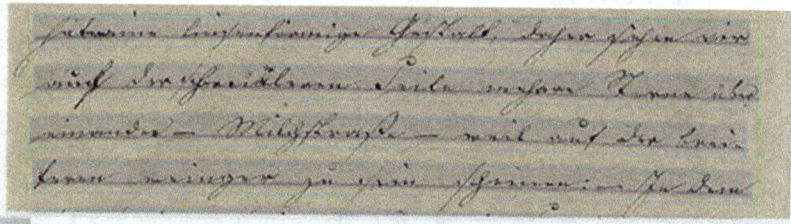

1-1 hatben eine linſenförmige Geſtalt, daher ſehen wir
1-2 auchf der ſchmaleren Seite mehrere Sterne über
1-3 einander – Milchſtraße – weil auf der brei-
1-4 teren weniger zu ſein ſcheinen. – In dem

Note that in the original online edition, the <b> in the first word in 1-1 as well as the <ch> in the first word in 1-2 have been crossed out. I use one small, specific and one large generic Kurrent model to transcribe this hand:

Name	Words	Lines	Epochs	Train CER	Test CER	Language
Kurr_1800_Ms._Freiburg_UB_497,3	13089	1621	200	2.95%	4.69%	German
TEST_German_Kurrent_XIX-larg_0.1	2928711	480824	200	7.44%	9.98%	German

[11] Haaf & Thomas 2016. The online edition can be found at http://www.deutschestextarchiv.de/book/view/nn_n0171w1_1828?p=10 .

When using the small, specialised model for Kurrent Kurr_1800_Ms._Freiburg_UB_497,3 trained on another hand, the transcription results are as follows[12]:

> hatniien fuernefernign fnshalt dahe gihenwer
>
> ung der sgenmleren xien miühren duri über
>
> nundner Dlilchsernsuch auf der haue
>
> burin runmger zu idein ssihuen stu dien

While some of the letters and even some words such as prepositions and articles are recognised correctly, the overall amount of errors is rather high and the results are not very usable in practice. A very large generic model trained with different styles of Kurrent, by Tobias Hodel (TEST_German_Kurrent_XIX-larg_0.1) performs as follows:

> habame Lisenförmige Gestalt, daher sichen ver
>
> auch der schreibleren Feile mehrre Ferne über
>
> einander- Milchstraße — weil auf der Brei-
>
> feren weniger zu ssem scheinen. In dem

Even though there are quite a few errors, it becomes obvious that the generic model performs considerably better that the specialised model. The fact that the large generic model uses more than 200 times the training data clearly overcompensates for its considerably worse CER when it comes to real-life performance with unseen data.[13]

---

[12] This model was trained during a tutorial at Freiburg University led by Pia Eckhart and Ina Serif. Charly Beck, Alina Bruderer, Alexander Gerhardt, Olivia Kirsten, Sophie Lutz, and Yuping Zhou participated in the tutorial.

[13] The CER of the generic model would most likely become better if the model were re-trained with more epochs. As mentioned before, large generic models specifically benefit from a high number of epochs. In the meantime, the

While these are encouraging results that speak in favour of the use of generic models, there are several issues that have to be taken into account when training and using them. First, as a rule, generic models are constituted using training data from different sources, different projects and different linguistic and academic ecosystems – the editorial principles (e.g., how to resolve abbreviations, deal with diacritic signs, encode/represent special characters, etc.) usually vary to a considerable extent. This heterogeneity inevitably introduces noise which, for its part, may confuse the model and thus lead to a higher CER. Let us take the Cyrillic example from above (Figure 5): As we have seen, the overall performance of the large generic model is better than the performance of the other models tested here. However, some characters are represented correctly in the other models as opposed to the large generic model. This holds for the green ѿ in line 2. This is a ligature of Cyrillic small omega ѡ and superscript ᵀ . This ligature is quite common in Church Slavonic texts and has often been seen during training in all Church Slavonic models discussed here. However, the large generic model uses the broad version of ω, which complies with the visual image of the character more exactly. Curiously, the character ω does not occur in the transcription of the Elizabeth Bible: the only addendum in the large generic model as compared to the smaller one.[14] In the specialised models trained on the *Velikie Minei Čet'i* that are also part of the training data of the large generic model, this character does however appear. There is no rational explanation for the large model to use this character instead of the correct one except that the large inventory of different characters used – sometimes for similar or identical manuscript glyphs – confused the model.

model has been retrained with both more training data and more epochs; see Hodel et al. 2021.

[14] The similar character ѽ is sometimes present, though.

Other arguably more systematic errors that can be observed when training and using generic models are *language-specific* and *hyper-correct errors*. Language-specific errors are due to the fact that, during training, the models learn the letter combinations specific for the individual languages.[15] In English, for instance, the letter combination *sh* is much more common than in German, while in German, *sch* is much more common than in English. When training monolingual generic models and applying them to manuscripts in a different language, some language-specific letter combinations are likely to be recognised incorrectly. A good example in support of this claim is the analysis of a Dutch text using a generic model for Dutch:[16]

---

[15] After writing the first draft of this paper, Transkribus has implemented the possibility of using transcription models with or without so-called language models. Generally speaking, a transcription model with language models enabled will be more focused on linguistic features such as language-specific letter (or word) combinations and less focused on script-specific characteristics. Enabling the language models will typically lead to better recognition with unknown hands in the same language the model was trained on, but to even worse results with text in a similar script but different language.

[16] The text is included in Philipp Balde's *Naauwkeurige beschryvinge van Malabar en Choromandel* (Balde 1672). Its image can be found at https://www.oldfonts.com/antiquepenman/handwriting-as-art/; reproduced with the kind permission of Brian Willson.

Figure 7

Transcription of Dutch 17th century handwriting (model NAN/NHA_GT_M3+)

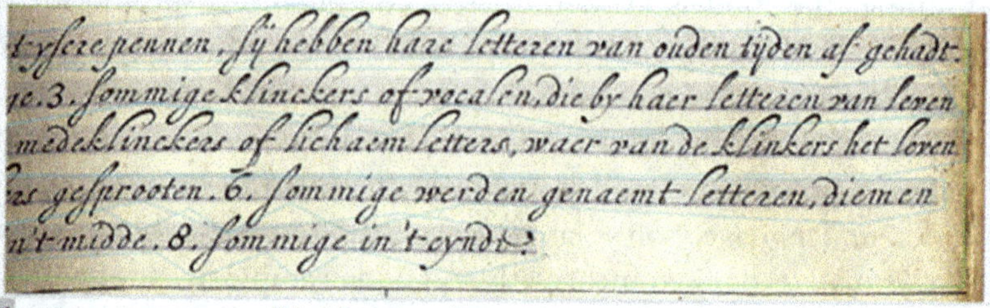

[handwritten manuscript image]

1-1 met gesere pennen, sij hebben hare letteren van ouden tijden af gehadt
1-2 dnge De sommige klinckers of rocas en, die by haer letteren van leven
1-3 de medeklinckers of Schaem letters, waer van de klinkers het beven
1-4 kers gesprooten. 6. sommige werden genaemt letteren, diemen
1-5 int midde. 8. sommige in 't ernde:

Words	Lines	Epochs	Train CER	Test CER	Language
475769	79154	1100	7.83%	6.15%	Dutch

The generic Dutch model – at the time of writing available to all users of *Transkribus*, thanks to Vincent Noppe – transcribes this very clear and easy-to-read manuscript quite well. Specific Dutch letter combinations such as <ij> in *sij* and *tijden* (1-1) are recognised correctly.

However, when using large generic models trained by Tobias Hodel on German handwriting, the following results are obtained:

Name	Words	Lines	Epochs	Train CER	Test CER	Language
Comb_Deutsch_Latein_XX_M2	769739	118967	400	8.35%	5.86%	German

Generic Models for Handwritten Text Recognition 199

TEST_ German_ Kurrent_XIX-larg_0.1	2928711	480824	200	7.44%	9.98%	German

The following is the result of the model Comb_Deutsch_Latein_XX_M2:

> metgfere pennen, Sy hebben hare letteren van onden biden uf gehadt
>
> ge 3. hommige Kinchers of rocalen die Er kaer lesseren san leren
>
> amDahlinaher of Schaemleuers, war vande klinkersher leren
>
> bers gesprooten. 6. Jommige werden genaemt letteren, diemen
>
> it midde. 8. Jommige in Fepndr.

For a generic model based on that large amount of data and given that the handwriting is highly legible, the results are somewhat underwhelming. As can be seen, the typical Dutch letter combination <ij> is incorrectly rendered in all instances. Other errors can be observed as well.

The same holds for another generic model trained on German Kurrent manuscripts from the 19th century (TEST_German_Kurrent_XIX-larg_0.1) that had performed so well with Humboldt's handwriting:

> Aere pennen, sy kebben hare letteren van onden tÿden af gehaden
>
> Ageesommigeklencters of vocasen die by kaer letteren san leven
>
> Achlineters of Schaimletters, waer vande Llenters her loren
>
> Bergesprooten. 6. sommige werden genaemt fetteren, diemen
>
> Amdde. 8. Jommige in t gndo.

Here, the mediocre results are understandable, since the Dutch writing does not have many similarities with typical Kurrent writing styles.

The fact that the models are somewhat dependent on language is confirmed when looking at German manuscripts. Here, a letter written by Ingeborg Bachmann is analysed using the model Comb_Deutsch_Latein_XX_M2.

Figure 8

Letter by Ingeborg Bachmann, by courtesy of Dorotheum Wien, Auktionskatalog 4.12.2012

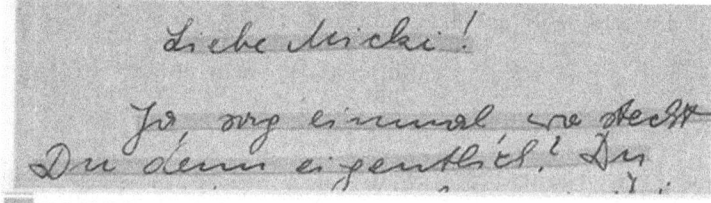

1-2 Liebe Micke:
1-3 Ja sog einmal wo stecht
1-4 Die denn eigentlich? Iu

The results are not perfect, but definitely usable. The Dutch model NAN/NHA_GT_M3+, however, misreads German words such as *eigentlich* (1-4) and renders them differently, in a 'less German' and overall worse fashion:

> Liebe Micat.
>
> se wij emmel e veift
>
> Du dens e Ceutles. Dij

The same holds for typical Modern German handwriting. The German model Comb_Deutsch_Latein_XX_M2 performs better, while the Dutch model NAN/NHA_GT_M3+ commits language-specific errors:

Figure 9
Modern German handwriting,
https://commons.wikimedia.org/wiki/File:Handschrift_(1).jpg

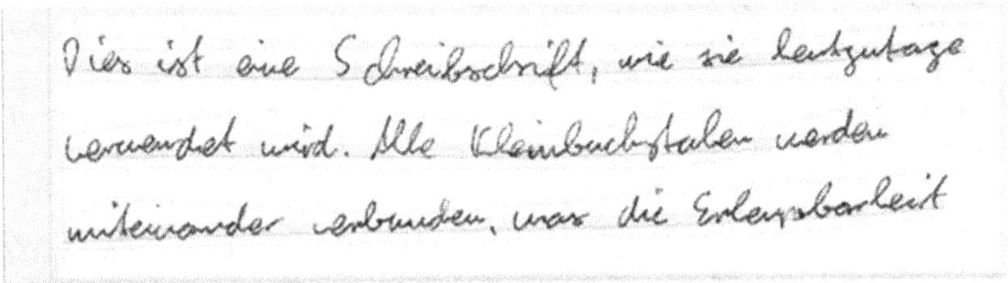

[handwritten sample]

1-1 Dils ist eine S cverbschrift, wie sie leutzutage
1-2 beinendhet und. Alle Kleinbeebstaben werden
1-3 miteinander Lenbunden uas die Erlenbarleit

ier is oul 3 erlbrerifr, wie tie lentjulage

Cermendet wjd. slle Cembackstalen werden

itsmarder verbanden ar die Erlagebarlent

It is obvious that less German-specific letter combinations are recognised using the Dutch model.

Language-specific errors can also be observed when analysing Latin sources. The following models were used for the next experiment:

Name	Words	Lines	Epochs	Train CER	Test CER	Lang.
Athanasius Kircher Letters	6050	587	200	1.68%	5.54%	Latin
TEST_German_Kurrent_XIX-larg_0.1	2928711	480824	200	7.44%	9.98%	German
Comb_StAZH-StASO_kurr_XVI	1177899	185744	200	14.69%	8.61%	German with small parts of Latin
Comb_Deutsch_Latein_XX_M2	769739	118967	400	8.35%	5.86%	German
NAN/NHA_GT_M3+	475769	79154	1100	7.83%	6.15%	Dutch

The specific, small model that I trained on letters by Athanasius Kircher exhibits the following results when transcribing another letter by Kircher from 1639[17] not seen during training:

Figure 9: Kircher's Hand

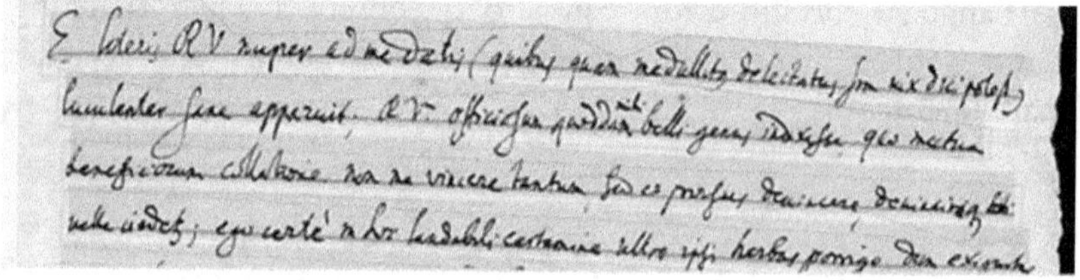

---

[17] *Voynich MS: 17th Century letters related to the MS* http://www.voynich.nu/letters.html

> Aliteri erei ditae auperi ad me dalis (quibus, quam medullitu delectatus sun vix dici potest.
>
> luculenter sane adparuit. erenitat Vestrae officiosum quoddam belli genus indixisse, quo metua
>
> beneficorum collastione; non me vincere tantum, sed et proisus devincure devinciraque hbi
>
> velle videt. ego certe in hoc laudabili certamine ultro ipsi horbus porrigo dum exiquitus

While numerous errors can be observed, several words and even phrases have been transcribed with decent quality[18], which shows that even very small specialised models with less than 10,000 tokens of training data may be helpful.

Transcription quality gets worse when using generic models not tailored towards the Latin language. The German Kurrent model (TEST_German_Kurrent_XIX-larg_0.1) performs as follows.

> 7 sderi RV zuper ad me dalii (geibich guan medulltz delectatus him nic dreiplest,
>
> tumlenter sane appermit. D V. officiosem georden betli genus mahfen ges mecten
>
> benesiiomm Shitione non mn vincere tentun sad es persais dininene deineirig ih
>
> uete undet; ege wrte mhrr tandebilicertamme uller ishi herbar pörrige diem eLigucter

To be fair, Kircher's handwriting is not in written in Kurrent, which explains the results.

---

[18] Cf. the almost correct resolution of the abbreviation in line 2 Vestrae.

The German sixteenth-century Kurrent model Comb_StAZH-StASO_kurr_XVI, also trained by Tobias Hodel, performs remarkably well in recognising the Latin text:

> soleris e. v nuper ad me datis (quibus quam medullitus delectatus sim nir dicipolß

> luculenter sane apparuit. E V. officiosum quoddam belli genus indrise quo metua

> beresicorum collitione non na vincere tantum sad et prrsurs druincere devinciriq e

> vebe ciodet, exo certe in dur saudebili cestamine ullro issi herbas porigo dum edigurtes

This might be due to the fact that there are a couple of Latin documents in the training data which seemed to enable the Kurrent model to recognise the Latin morphology quite well, even though the visual style of the letters differs.

The German Latin script model Comb_Deutsch_Latein_XX_M2 yields the following results:

> 5 Weri RV zuper ud me dahy (geibug quan medallitz deleitatung Som nie diei pbef,

> lumlerler Sene appernit. AV. officiofun zwoddm belli genug dertiße ger mehen

> berefionm Whone. don zu vireere Fantum zu es frfen denisene denistirag

> velle wndet; ex certe in dor Sandehli certaaie allro ishi herbos porrige dem Exgurte

The Dutch generic model NAN/NHA_GT_M3+ performs as follows:

> 7. loterij R V ruper adve datij (gribns gaan medllitg de lectate, som rir dr: plos
>
> Cuinlenter sare apparnit. A V: oppciosen goeddan belli genag adrissn ges weeker
>
> berehioue Aehore ten na vireere tanten sed e pisses duireere dchirlirig be
>
> vele uedet; en eerte inter sandeblj certaaiie ulloo ijs herbos ponigo den clguste

As we can see, the overall results are mediocre at best. However, some typical Dutch letter combinations can be observed such as in *goeddan* (2) or *eerte* (4), which speaks in favour of the hypothesis that the language-specificity of the models may lead to worse recognition performance when applied to manuscripts written in other languages.

Within one specific language, other interesting errors might occur when using generic models, namely hypercorrection errors. For the purpose of this paper, I understand hypercorrection errors as wrong transcriptions brought about by wrong assumptions the model made about the correct transcription. That is to say, the model has learned a linguistic/orthographic rule and over-generalises it during the transcription process, which results in a wrong transcription.

An example of such hypercorrected forms can be found when transcribing the Russian Church Slavonic Gennadian Bible from 1499 using the generic model that includes data from the printed Elizabeth Bible from 1751. Written in clear *poluustav*, it should not pose any significant problems to large generic models. As can be seen, the overall transcription quality is quite good, with hardly any errors and correct word separation.

Figure 10

Transcription of parts of the Gennadian Bible with hypercorrect errors

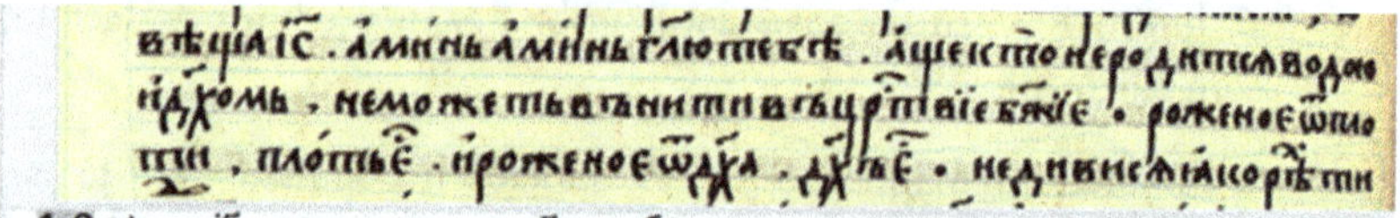

1-8 вѣща і҃с. аминь аминь гл҃ю тебѣ. аще кто не родитсѧ водою

1-9 и д҇хомь, не можеть вънити въ цр҇ствіе бж҃іе. рожѐное ѿ пло-

1-10 ти, плоть е҃. и рожѐное ѿ дх҃а, дх҃ъ е҃. не дивисѧ ꙗко рѣ́х ти

However, the generic model Combined_ChSl_VKS_E_1 consistently renders рожєноє, the participle form 'born', as рожєноє with a superscript ᲆ. From the perspective of Synodal Church Slavonic in the 18th century, the time of the compilation of the printed Elizabeth Bible, the writing with ж̑ is the correct rendering of the South Slavonic continuant of Common Slavonic *dj. During the standardisation of Russian Church Slavonic in the 18th century, the originally East Slavonic rendition with ж, often applied in older varieties of Russian Church Slavonic and present in the Gennadian Bible, was replaced with the South Slavonic form with superscript ᲆ. Since the generic model used here apparently learned that the form with ᲆ is correct, it chose to add those letters even though there is no visual cue that would suggest the existence of that letter in the digital image. Obviously, these errors are less severe than other, language-specific errors discussed above. However, when training large models with a certain degree of homogeneity and a low amount of noise in the data, striving for a very low CER, one might want to take the factor of hypercorrect errors into account. Smaller generic models such as Combined_Full_VKS_2 do not show this hypercorrect error in this case.

Conclusion

In this contribution, I discussed certain implications of training and using generic models for transcribing a variety of manuscript types written in different languages using *Transkribus*. While there are several caveats with generic models, and their CER is usually higher than that of specialised models, I hope to have demonstrated that generic models are helpful, especially in situations where there is not much training data available to create a specialised model best suited to the data that needs to be transcribed. Thus, the CER of a model is not always a good predictor of real-life performance, especially when we are faced with a model trained on diverse handwriting styles.

Often in transcription practice, an interesting compromise solution may be to use a generic model to pre-transcribe parts of the data needed, then manually – or with the help of interactive-predictive technologies – correct the data and use this new, corrected data to train a new specialised model with a low CER.

The analyses reported in this paper suggest that the models learn certain language-specific traits such as letter combinations, letter frequencies and words, which leads to the model usually performing considerably worse when confronted with manuscripts written in a script similar to the hands included in the training data, but in another language. This leads to the recommendation to prefer models trained with data written in the same language as the data one would like to transcribe. A first step in this direction would be to create generic language-specific models; in a second step, one could try to combine the data used for these models in order to create large multilingual – or even multiscriptal – models.[19] However, due to heterogeneous editorial principles and training data, noise will inevitably be present in the data. Together with hypercorrect forms

---

[19] Experiments with Fedor Polikarpov's trilingual and triscriptal *Leksikon Trejazyčnyj* (Polikarpov 1704) by Irina Podtergera and her team yielded promising results.

that can also be brought about by generic models, this may sometimes lead to less than perfect results.

Nevertheless, generic models in HTR applications such as *Transkribus* are a crucial step when it comes to efficient mass digitisation. Since *Transkribus* is very user-friendly, it can be used by non computer-savvy philologists, which may lead to the application actually crossing the non IT-specialist chasm and going mainstream.[20] Drawbacks such as the lack of scope for fine-tuning the models (i.e., in order to mitigate the language bias) might be minor in view of its user-friendliness.[21] From a pragmatic viewpoint, generic models trained with *Transkribus* are important tools for anyone who wishes to greatly speed up their digitisation processes. Since the models can easily be shared via the *Transkribus* platform, all scholars interested can benefit from already existing models. If the academic community concerned with different flavours of written cultural heritage joins forces to create and distribute generic *Transkribus* models, this may mark an important cornerstone for the digitisation of Medieval Studies.

---

[20] Jenset & McGillivray 2017.

[21] At the moment of writing, another promising HTR application named *Kraken* developed by Benjamin Kiessling exists (see http://kraken.re/) as well as Romanov et al. 2017. *Kraken* is a command line tool that allows for precisely controlling specific aspects of model training. It has been implemented in a user-friendly GUI platform called *eScriptorium* (see https://escripta.hypotheses.org/). It will be a worthwhile endeavour to compare the capabilities of *Transkribus* and *eScriptorium*.

THE SPACE BETWEEN: JEWS, CHRISTIANS, AND MUSLIMS IN MEDIEVAL SPAIN. MOOCs, CITIZEN SCIENCE, AND DIGITAL MANUSCRIPT COLLECTIONS

Roger L. Martínez-Dávila

Introduction

The medieval cathedral archives of Spain, especially those in the royal Castilian city of Burgos and La Mancha's ancient intellectual center located in Toledo, remain Dark Archives to all but a few academicians who know the hidden doors that guard access to almost a millennium of interreligious history. There are fundamental cultural, institutional, specialist, and technological impediments that hinder our understanding of these Dark Archives collections. Within them are evidence of remarkable – typical – moments of inevitably interfaith cooperation. For example, in just three minor transactions recorded between 1397 and 1427, amounting to no more than one or two manuscript folios, we find evidence of the intimate economic and personal relations that bound Catholic archdeacons, Jewish noblemen and ladies, and Muslim craftsmen together. We learn that when Toledan church chapels required repairs as well as finer embellishments, the churchmen turned to well-known experts like Hamete Abelhat, a Muslim carpenter, to implement the work, and to trusted confidants such as Jewish Don Mayr de Levi and Lady

Jamila to finance the efforts. In Burgos, the same pattern of collaborative relations transpired when church administrators sought out their neighbor, Abraan Aben Seca, a Jewish nobleman, to lease church vineyards to generate revenues. Or, when the cathedral required the meticulous expertise of a master carpenter, canons explicitly named the Muslim Hamete de Cordova as the best tradesman for numerous projects. Year after year, these customary and well-worn norms stitched Jews, Christians, and Muslims together and they now lie dormant in dozens of cathedral archives that house thousands of bound volumes detailing a millennium of rich social history.

Deciphering this secret history – of the collaborative nature of interreligious of life in medieval Spain – is a significant, but resolvable, Dark Archives problem. This article explores how several constraints to working with cathedral manuscripts might be overcome via cost-efficient micro research initiatives that focus on global digital interconnectivity, free web-based education, and a whole-hearted commitment to democratising palaeographical expertise and research collaborations using a citizen-science approach. First, I discuss how scholars can engage the public by revealing the complicated nature of the history of the Middle Ages, subsequently I discuss how Massive Open Online Courses are used to facilitate learners' acquisition of palaeographic expertise and those learners' collaborative work transcribing manuscripts, and lastly, I outline the digital organisation, documentation, and publishing of manuscripts and transcriptions using the Dublin Core schema in the University of Colorado-Colorado Springs Digital Collections.[1] Via this endeavor, known as the *Deciphering Secrets* project, I present a citizen science

---

[1] A special thanks to Ms. Mary Rupp, archives librarian at the University of Colorado-Colorado Springs, for her fundamental efforts in co-developing the metadata description guidelines and the *Deciphering Secrets* collection.

model that offers a fruitful future for research efforts in academia and our globally interconnected world.

Massive Open Online Courses (MOOCs) and compelling medieval history

Capturing the attention of the public

One of the principal questions that often arises when seeking to advance citizen science is: How can scholars capture the attention of the public and convince them to participate in research initiatives? In my experience, the answer is in seeding the deep intellectual and cultural curiosity of the university-educated public. Humans are naturally cooperative, collaborative, and curious. We care about the humanities – history, the arts, philosophy, and language – because they embody the noblest goals of our globalised culture and our yearning to serve the higher purpose of making positive democratic, egalitarian, and socially beneficial contributions to our world. Yet, as technological change and internet-connectivity have advanced, we recognize that the essence of our humanity is being swallowed whole as our lives become less focused on people and more on technological devices like the Apple iPhone. A short trip on the Metro Madrid, lunching in a cafeteria, or even sitting in our own flats, reveals the pervasiveness of this phenomenon where humans stare intently into little video screens and do not acknowledge or talk to each other. Who is serving whom in this world – do we serve technology, or does it serve us?

The key to drawing the digitally connected public to citizen science projects is a fundamental recognition that humanity is in desperate search for individual meaning and purpose, as well as opportunities to share their personal realisations through social connection. Meaning, purpose, and sociality cannot be satisfied through the canned whimsies of devices. Today's global world, at least prior to the COVID-19 pandemic, is a panorama of human cultures in dialogue with one another. Naturally, cultural differences and distinctiveness evoke powerful emotional responses that range from love, amity, indifference, confusion, and hostility. Through the lens of medieval Iberian history, the public can explore and engage with each other and scholars via the safety of the temporal distance of the Middle Ages. This far-away place provides a safe intellectual and emotional arena for the public to evaluate and reflect on contemporary intercultural issues through the medium of medieval Spanish Jewish, Christian, and Muslim relations. In effect, our 2020-selves inhabit the history of medieval Spain so that we can contemplate the best and worst of human relations.

The *Deciphering Secrets* (DS) project, which I created in 2014 and this article discusses, examines issues of medieval interreligious history and promotes civic engagement in the research process. The central focus of DS, and by extension its MOOCs, is 'scholars and the public collaborating to better understand Jewish, Christian, and Muslim coexistence during the Spanish Middle Ages (500-1500 CE)'. Since summer 2014, DS have delivered MOOCs to share the interreligious history of Spain (also known as Islamic al-Andalus and Jewish Sefarad). DS works alongside of museums like the Museo Sefardí (Toledo). the Museo de Santa Cruz (Toledo), the Museo de Burgos, and the New Mexico History Museum to present compelling cultural knowledge. Further, this research effort energizes current and former MOOC learners to assist with transcribing and investigating medieval manuscripts pertaining to medieval Jewish, Christian, and Muslim interrelations. We teach introductory, intermediate, and advanced Spanish palaeography (or, reading old handwriting) to our learners so that they can 'decipher secrets' from medieval manuscripts. Through our collaborations with Spanish cathedral, municipal, and national archives, DS is making new collections available for investigation. Presently, our research is focused on interreligious affairs in the cities of Plasencia, Burgos, Toledo, and Granada, and their broader connections to the Iberian Peninsula.

What DS has learned is that the public wants to contribute to scholarship. When queried about their perspective on the value of 'crowdsourced research', learners in our DS Massive Open Online Courses (MOOCs) and transcription project resoundingly supported it.[2] DS believes this is largely due to the fact that our learners' intellectual and emotional attachment to the issues of intercultural cooperation and conflict. Specifically, 82.5% of our learners believe it is *very important* for academic researchers to incorporate the public into scholarly investigations. A full 100% believe these scholarly-public collaborations are *very or somewhat important*. When asked if they wanted to participate in other types of research:

- 85% indicated they wanted to contribute to additional palaeography transcription projects,
- 65% stated they wanted to assist with editing and creating final versions of transcribed manuscripts, and
- 75% wanted to help index the contents of manuscripts that have not been abstracted.

After completing one course, 77.5% of our learners stated they were *very likely* to return and take additional DS MOOCs that follow the trajectory of intercultural life in medieval Spain. The public desires to participate, therefore, the question is: how do we engage our audiences so as to motivate them to dedicate their limited time to scholarly pursuits? We must offer them compelling histories that relate to the challenges of our contemporary world.

---

[2] This student survey data collected during the summer 2016 edition of the *Deciphering Secrets: Unlocking the Manuscripts of Medieval Burgos* MOOC on edX.org at https://www.edx.org/course/deciphering-secrets-unlocking-the-manuscripts-of-3. The current version of the MOOC on coursera.org is accessible at https://www.coursera.org/learn/burgos-deciphering-secrets-medieval-spain.

How Jews, Christians, and Muslims came to live alongside each other in medieval Spain

Perhaps the best manner to explain how scholars can excite the imagination and efforts of the public is via the central storyline of the DS project and its MOOCs – specifically, how Jews, Christians, and Muslims came to live amongst each other in medieval Spain. By retelling this history of 800 years of interreligious life, we can note the hallmarks of storytelling that connect the public to its quest for personal meaning, purpose, and social connection.

Like our diverse societies of 2020, medieval Spain was the child of many cultures, civilisations and peoples.[3] First populated by Celtic and Iberian peoples before the ninth century BCE, the Iberian Peninsula assumed a greater Mediterranean character with the arrival of the Phoenicians around 800 BCE (Phillips and Phillips 2016: 14-15). The Carthaginians from North Africa, standard bearers of the Phoenician empire, later conquered and claimed Iberia in 236 BCE, which set off a civilisational conflict with the Romans until the end of the third century BCE. The Latinisation of the peninsula transpired over six centuries and right up until the end of the fourth century of the common era. The Jewish population, which had accompanied Phoenician traders prior to the common era, grew substantially in Iberia after the year 70, the year the Romans destroyed the Second Temple in Jerusalem and Jews were forced to resettle across the Mediterranean world (Gerber 1994: 2). Therefore, immediately through this window into one millennium of history, our MOOC learners perceive the brevity of a human lifetime, the

---

[3] In terms of historical periodisation, late medieval Spain might be best captured as the time period between the seminal Spanish Christian military victory over the Islamic Almohads at *Las Navas de Tolosa* (1212 c.e.) and the Catholic Monarchs' (Isabel and Ferdinand) political consolidation of Spain after the capture of Granada, the expulsion of the Jews, and the encounter with the Americas (1492 c.e.).

frailty of what we perceive as 'civilisation', and the dangers of religious intolerance and the pain felt by diasporic communities.

Continuing, we encounter the early medieval character of Iberia as when it came into focus from the fifth through eighth centuries, when the Roman empire was overrun by the Vandals and later, the Visigoths. The latter established their capitol in the ancient city of Toledo (415-711). According to mythic tradition, the city is where Hercules slept before his eleventh labor. The Visigoths refused to acculturate with the Romanised Iberian-Celtic peoples and not until 585, with King Roderick's conversion from Christian Arianism to Catholicism, did both the political elite and the native populations share the same faith (Phillips and Phillips 2016, 34, 37, 74). In 711, Islamic Umayyad and North African Berber calvary forces led by Tariq Abu Zara invaded the Iberian Peninsula at the Straits of Gibraltar and began their rapid elimination of the Visigothic monarchy that was plagued by internal dissension and dynastic claims (Collins 1994: 17–18, 28, 45). In a conquest that lasted no more than ten years, Iberia would become Islamic *al-Andalus,* a mixed religious community with almost unimaginable cultural splendor, in the central and southern portions of the land mass, and ragtag Christian kingdoms, militantly preserving their varied cultural and linguistic traditions in the northwestern coastal regions and Pyrenees Mountains. For our learners, mythic history is invoked through these references to Hercules, the Celts, and Romans, and the span of the known human story is brought to the attention of learners as they begin to appreciate the privileged place of the Iberian Peninsula. Moreover, political intrigue, a sense of abrupt religious and political transformation, and the tradition of the contest of civilisations are invoked. Therefore, learners are brought into dialogue with consequential issues.

Similarly, appealing to distinct learning communities is also critical to engaging the public's participation. Among the most motivated members of the public are distinct cultural and religious communities, and in the case of Iberia and my own research expertise, I concentrate on retelling the mixed heritage of Hispanic communities and the noble story of Sephardic Jews. Thus, these MOOC learners appreciate the structure of medieval Spanish history and that it was predicated on the dynamic interaction, both positive and negative elements of co-existence (*convivencia*), of Jews, Christians, and Muslims (Hillgarth 1985, 33). And as one of the remaining refuges for the European Jewry (England expelled Jews in 1290 and France in 1306), Spain prior to the late fourteenth century offered one of the few regions in western Europe where Jewish communities could live and prosper (Phillips and Phillips 2016, 83, 97).

Lastly, this early medieval history retold to learners is complemented with noteworthy leaders that awaken notions of grand periods that shaped our memory of the past. Great war captains, knights, kings, caliphs, and religious leaders pepper Spain's history, including Tariq Abu Zara (early eighth century), the famous Berber warrior at the vanguard of the Umayyad conquest of Iberia; Pelayo (r. 718-737), the semi-mythical founding champion of the Spanish Christian *Reconquista*; Frankish Charles Martel (r. 718-741), the Mayor of the Palace, and the victor of the Battle of Poitiers (732); Islamic Caliph Abd al-Rahman III (r. 912-929) and his magnificent Caliphate of Cordoba (929-1031); Moses Maimonides (b. 1135 – d. 1204), the Jewish polymath and author of the *Guide for the Perplexed*; and Castilian King Alfonso X 'The Wise' (r. 1252-1284) who promoted himself as the monarch of three religions. Born from this environment of constant political and cultural tension was a European world unlike any other on the continent.

The fourteenth & fifteenth centuries: from crisis to consolidation

What drives the thrust of DS MOOCs and its manuscript studies is a period in Spanish history that remains consequential and relevant to learners in the twenty-first century. The research derived from our Deciphering Secrets manuscript collection, which will be addressed subsequently, presents a fourteenth- and fifteenth-century Spain in deep conflict with itself as it wrestled with a global pandemic, political disintegration, and most notably, tremendous religious violence inflicted on the Sephardic Jewish community. The seeds of change began with the sudden and unexpected death of King Alfonso XI in 1350 from the Black Plague. Between 1347 and 1350, the plague claimed the lives of approximately 25 million in Europe, or 25 percent of the population (Olea and Christakos 2005, 291). In fact, the pandemic returned twice more to Castile, in 1374 and 1384. The COVID-19 pandemic of 2019 and 2020 makes this medieval history very present in our time: we understand how precariously human life teeters from the joy of good health to unexpected death. Over the course of the fourteenth century, the Iberian population withered from an estimated 5.5 million to 4.5 million (Pamuk 2007, 294). Across Europe, Jewish communities were scapegoated as the cause of the illness. Samuel M. Cohn Jr. writes that 'Jews were accused of poisoning food, wells and streams, tortured into confessions, rounded up in city squares or their synagogues, and exterminated en masse' (Cohn 2007: 4, 8). In Germany, southern France, and Spain, in particular, the 'burning of Jews' was carried out. It is through this miserable past that learners in our MOOCs acknowledge the frailty of human judgment and the power of fear and racial and religious hate.

In the midst of this turmoil, political control and rule of Iberia's most important kingdom of Castile and Leon came into question. The splintering of society feels profoundly contemporary – especially at the end of this second decade of the 2000s as right-wing, extremist, anti-immigrant, and nativist political parties and leaders feed the hunger of disaffected Europeans and Americans. Learners in DS MOOCs perceive the past as returning to influence the future.

For example, the *Crónica de los reyes de Castilla* relates that on March 26, 1350, the Castilian monarch was cut down by the plague:

> [While] laying siege to Gibraltar and] after the battles and conquests by the noble prince Lord King Alfonso of Castile and León . . . it was at the village and the noble, notable, very strong castle of Gibraltar, the plague entered among the Muslims and Christians. . . . By the will of God this pestilence of the greatest mortality returned and fell upon our most noble Lord King Alfonso (Cronicas de los Reyes de Castilla: 390).

Upon Alfonso XI's death civil war broke out, with the king's legitimate son Pedro I 'The Cruel' battling his half-brother Prince Enrique II of Trastámara for the kingdom and crown.[4] Neither of the competing claimants could secure the kingdom. Pedro I was only fifteen years old, and many leaders considered him too young to rule, whereas his older half-brother was the son of the deceased king's mistress, Leonor de Guzmán (Hillgarth 1985, 374-76). Hostilities between the half-brothers commenced as early as 1353, when Enrique fielded 600 knights and 1,500 Asturian men-at-arms in the village of Cigales to meet Pedro I's military companies coming from the nearby city of Valladolid (Cronicas de los Reyes de Castilla, 431). By 1360, after he had three of his half-brothers executed and signed a peace accord with the Kingdom of Aragon, Pedro I seemed to be in a strong position to gain the upper hand (Ruiz 2011, 80). The remaining impediment to his consolidation of control of Castile was his brother, Enrique II. Among the many complaints raised by Enrique II was that his half-brother was far too sympathetic to religious minorities and

---

[4] In his valuable work, Clavero 1974 argued that prior to the civil war there were old noble clans and after its conclusion came a new generation of noble houses known as the new nobility.

was overly dependent on Jewish advisers and Muslim men-at-arms (Hillgarth 1985, 372, 385). On several occasions during the civil war, Enrique II besieged Jewish communities in Toledo and Burgos (Singer and Adler 1901). It was ironic that Enrique II, in his eventual victory over Pedro I, would turn to elite Jewish converts to Christianity as he rebuilt his devastated prize, the Kingdom of Castile and León. Thus, this uncomfortable story begins to introduce a fresh and unexpected narrative to *Deciphering Secrets'* learners: How did Jews and their descendants come to survive these calamities, and in some cases, rise in an anti-Jewish Castile?

The royal contest was also a pan-European conflict as several Spanish Christian kingdoms, England, and France politically and militarily wrestled with each other on the continent during the opening of the Hundred Years' War (Hillgarth 1978, 375, 380). England and France both courted Castile as a strategic ally in their continental war, which in 1362 pulled Pedro I into an alliance with King Edward III's England and in 1363 prompted France to recognize Enrique II as the legitimate heir to the crown of Castile. Not until 1369 was the internationalised conflict for the crown resolved, when Enrique II and Pedro I fought the fateful Battle of Montiel (Cronicas de los Reyes de Castilla: 589–592).

The war reached its apex in a breathtaking moment of fratricide. At Montiel, Pedro I was defeated and took refuge in his castle. When Enrique II sent his emissary, Mosén Beltrán, to his half-brother to negotiate, Pedro sought Beltrán's assistance to betray Enrique II, making him a generous offer. As the chronicler Pedro López de Ayala detailed, 'Pedro...said if he [Mosén] will liberate him from here, safely and securely...he would give to him, and those who succeeded him, the villages of Soria, Almazán, Atienza, Montagudo, Deza, and Serón...as well as two hundred thousand Castilian *doblas*.' Beltrán agreed to the treachery but informed Enrique II of the plan and led him to Pedro's refuge. There the two met face to face. According to Pedro López, the bitter war had inflicted damage on both men's memory, and Enrique II did not recognize his half-brother. In the presence of Pedro I, one of Beltrán's knights said to Enrique II, 'This man is your enemy', and to this statement Pedro I replied, 'I am. I am.' With a dagger, Enrique II struck his half sibling in the face; 'the two fell to the ground . . . and there died King Pedro on the twenty-third day of March of the said year.' For *Deciphering Secrets*' learners, the tale is matched with Jean Froissart's artistic depiction in *Chroniques* penned just four years after the event. (See Figure 1.) With Pedro's death in 1369, Enrique II became the fountainhead of the Trastámaran dynasty, culminating in the unification of Spain under Isabel of Castile and Fernando II of Aragon in 1469 (Phillips and Phillips 2016, 83).

Figure 1

Pedro slays Enrique II as depicted in Chroniques de Froissart
(KB 72 A 25).

DS' learners are subsequently confronted with an arresting image of cultural and religious revolution, that raises the questions: how did the twin stresses of political dissolution and disease facilitate a redirection of Spanish history predicated on Jewish and Christian blending? The Castilian nobility was exhausted by almost two decades of civil war and its ranks were rebuilt with a 'New Nobility' composed of elite Jewish families who converted to Christianity, or Jews who converted to Christianity (Martínez-Dávila 2018, 35). Unfortunately, there was a serious constraint – Enrique II had the power to grant noble titles but lacked financial resources. Enrique II and his three heirs thus devised an ingenious method to regenerate the noble class. Their approach and calculation were simple: in return for political loyalty and financial assistance to entice these families, Enrique II promoted lower-class noble Christian families and elite New Christian (or converso) clans to become his new nobility. The social experiment was wildly successful, even if it came at the expense of the traditional Old Nobility and ran counter to anti-Jewish polemics during the civil war and thus angered Christian commoners. At the heart of rebuilding the nobility was the rapid integration of elite conversos into royal and church institutions. Among the greatest contributors to these institutions were the Santa María and Carvajal families of Burgos and Plasencia, Spain, who hailed from the ha-Levi rabbinic family and the Old Christian Carvajal family of lower noble knights.[5] Thus, late fourteenth- and fifteenth-century manuscripts in

[5] In *Creating Conversos: the Carvajal-Santa María Family in Early Modern Spain* (Martínez-Dávila 2018), I unravel the complex story of Jews who converted to Catholicism in Spain between the fourteenth and sixteenth centuries, migrated to colonial Mexico and Bolivia during the conquest of the Americas, and assumed prominent church and government positions. Rather than acting as alienated and marginalized subjects, the conversos were able to craft new identities and strategies not just for survival but for prospering in the most adverse circumstances. The text offers an extensive,

cathedral archives in Burgos, Plasencia, Toledo, and Granada are particularly ripe for investigating late medieval religious identity-shifting and interreligious relations.

The counterpoint to the new opportunities for elite conversos in Spain were the disastrous anti-Jewish pogroms of the 1390s and Disputation of Tortosa (1413–1414). During the pogroms of the 1390s it is estimated that as many as 100,000 Jews were killed, 100,000 converted to Christianity, and another 100,000 fled to Muslim territories or went into hiding (Gerber 1994: 113; Roth 2002: 33). For example, Benzion Netanyahu summarizes the era as follows:

The losses of Spain's Jews in 1391 far surpassed those the Jews had borne elsewhere [in Europe]...Within two or three years from 1391, Spain's Jewish community, the largest in the world, was reduced by nearly one third—in both geographic and numerical terms, the greatest catastrophe that had hitherto befallen European Jewry (Netanyahu 2002: 127).

Unfortunately, these claims minimize the complexity of interreligious relations during this era in Spanish history. Addition-

> elaborately detailed case study of the Carvajal–Santa María clan from its beginnings in late fourteenth-century Castile. By tracing the family ties and intermarriages of the Jewish rabbinic ha-Levi lineage of Burgos, Spain (which became the converso Santa María clan) with the Old Christian Carvajal line of Plasencia, Spain, the monograph demonstrates the family's changing identity, and how the monolithic notions of ethnic and religious disposition were broken down by the group and negotiated anew as they transformed themselves from marginal into mainstream characters at the center of the economies of power in the world they inhabited. They succeeded in rising to the pinnacles of power within the church hierarchy in Spain, even to the point of contesting the succession to the papacy and overseeing the Inquisitorial investigation and execution of extended family members, including Luis de Carvajal 'The Younger' and most of his immediate family during the 1590s in Mexico City.

ally, the impact of the Disputation of Tortosa cannot be underestimated in terms of the chilling effect it had on European Jews. Although previous efforts, like one in Paris (1240) and another in Barcelona (1263), had established a precedent for forcing Jewish religious leaders to debate the validity of their religion, the coerced debate in the Aragonese city of Tortosa was exceptionally effective (Maccoby 1998, 23). The effectiveness of this campaign was tangible: over the course of the year many elite Jewish leaders and thinkers converted to Christianity, including the poet Solomon de Peira, Vidal Joseph (of the Benveniste and Cavallería families), and Fernando de la Cavallería (Roth 2002, 55-58).

A closer inspection of interreligious affairs during this era, made possible via DS MOOCs' selection and targeting of municipal and cathedral manuscripts, presents a more complete perspective on the complicated societal arena in fifteenth-century Spain. Were conversos traitors to their former coreligionists? Some historians have charged the elite converso Pablo de Santa María, a rabbi turned Catholic bishop, and his lineage as treacherous defectors. The historian José Amador de los Ríos castigates Pablo by connecting him to the Dominican Vincent Ferrer, the intense proselytizer of Jewish communities. Jose Amador argues that Ferrer's mission to convert Jews closely corresponded with Castile's implementation of the anti-Jewish Ordinances of Valladolid, which Queen Mother Catalina and Prince Fernando de Antequera proposed in 1412 to regulate Jews (Amador De Los Rios 1876, 12, 42, 493-502, 618-26). Amador de los Ríos states that Pablo de Santa María developed these policies as a means to attack his former coreligionists; the ordinances focused primarily on limiting Jews' social and economic interaction with Christians and conversos, as well as moving Jews to separate neighborhoods. He proposes that both Pablo and his son, the Placentino bishop Gonzalo García de Santa María, were intent on 'squeezing and reducing to sterility' the Jewish community throughout Castile.

However, the historical record in fifteenth-century Castile demonstrates more complex facts on the ground. Yitzhak Baer, author of *History of the Jews,* states that Castilians implemented just two of the Ordinances' comprehensive provisions, 'namely, the removal of Jews to separate quarters, and their exclusion from tax farming and from the service of the State and the court' (Baer 1966: 169). Though draconian, at minimum, these provisions do not seem to have been uniformly enforced.

Inside of Castile, the Santa María clan appears far less ruthless than Amador de los Ríos articulates; this fact is revealed via a royal order collected at the Archivo Histórico Municipal de Burgos. The Santa María were also creators of new protections for Jewish communities. The majority of the violence against Jews concluded at the end of the fourteenth century after Enrique III of Castile repeatedly demanded that his subjects cease their harassment of both Jews and new converts to Christianity (Cronicas de los Reyes de Castilla, 177). In a July 30, 1392, royal decree sent from the city of Segovia to Burgos, the king mandated the following to all persons living in the kingdom: 'No person shall obligate Jews to become Christians by force, nor make them listen to a sermon against their will, nor mistreat them, because it is counter to Christian charity' (AHMB Legajo HI-2960, unfoliated).

As the king was still three years from the age of majority, his royal advisers and teachers seemingly had a weighty impact on the decision to call an end to the violence (Lea 1896, 216; Cantera Burgos 1952: 24-25). Among those advisers was Chief Justice Diego López de Estúñiga, one of the New Nobility and founder of the Counts of Béjar and Plasencia, and Bishop Pablo de Santa María. In other specific cases, Enrique sent communiqués that enhanced these basic religious protections. Not only would the youthful king refuse to tolerate further forced conversions, but he directed Alvar García de Santa María (the historian-bureaucrat) to enforce his decision to allow forced converts to return to Judaism. On this issue, the king's pronouncement stated, 'Many [Jews] had converted and now wanted to return [to their faith]. . . . Not one person should harass them, and if some amount of them were to return [to Judaism], no one should seize them (AHMB Legajo HI-2960, unfoliated).

Although the monarch was concerned about the safety of the Jewish community, the call to protect Jews also explicitly acknowledged their vital role in the economy. For instance, the crown used a religious poll tax levied on Jews to pay for its wars against Islamic Granada, as well as to fund other royal initiatives (AHCB, vol. 48, fol. 250; AHCB, vol. 46, fol. 424; AHCB, vol. 5, fol. 51–51v.). In this way, the *juderías* in each community contributed to the royal coffers. For example, in the early 1400s, the Jewish community of Plasencia paid the king 10,250 *maravedís* annually in *cabeza de pecho* (poll tax) (AHNOB, Osuna, Caja 300, docs. 8 (6), 9 (5), no folio; AHNOB, Osuna, Caja 299, docs. 1 (4), 1 (6), 2 (1), no folio; AHNOB, Osuna, Caja 303, doc. 51, no folio; AHNOB, Osuna, Caja 303, doc. 42, no folio). Jewish subjects were valuable assets that necessitated royal protection on economic grounds.

Through this window of religious violence, conversion, and reforming of the Castile's noble families and institutions, *Deciphering Secrets* MOOCs explain why medieval cathedral and municipal manuscripts are the quintessential source for understanding interreligious relations. The manuscripts expose the messiness of Jewish, Christian, and Muslim life during the later Middle Ages in Spain.

Integrating the public in novel manuscript research via MOOCs (2014-2020)

Overview of MOOCs

By assembling a compelling intercultural history with a corpus of our curated collection of cathedral and municipal manuscripts from archives in Burgos, Toledo, Plasencia, and Granada, we employ Massive Open Online Courses (MOOCs) to encourage and support citizen scientists' efforts to create rough and diplomatic transcriptions. Our first MOOC integrating online education with crowdsourced transcription of manuscripts for research purposes took place in the summer of 2014. Since then DS has delivered several MOOCs via the coursera.org-University of Colorado System and the edX.org-Universidad Carlos III de Madrid collaborations. Table 1 displays the eight MOOC course editions we authored as well as learner enrollments, course completion rates, and the specific manuscript collections we investigated. It is worth noting that starting in spring 2018 each coursera.org MOOC enrolls a new cohort of learners every six weeks, or about eight-course sessions each calendar year. Between summer 2014 and early fall 2020, approximately 32,350 learners from over 140 nations have participated in the MOOCs. Even as the range of MOOC course offerings have proliferated over the past five years, for example as of April 2020 on coursera.org there are approximately 4,000 MOOCs, our enrollments have remained strong (Lohr 2020). From fall 2017 to fall 2020, we engaged 11,350 learners via our three MOOCs on coursera.org.

Similar to other MOOCs, student completion rates have diminished over time from a high of 19% for the very first MOOC in 2014, to present completion rates ranging from 1.1% to 2.9% in 2020. The lower completion rates in 2020 are reflective of a change in the MOOC business model; initially learners could complete a course for no fee (no cost) but since 2015 learners must purchase a course in order to complete the course. As our courses do not certify any formal credentials there is little incentive for learners to pay for course content. Therefore, DS has fewer course completers. Moreover, our newest courses, *Burgos: Deciphering Secrets of Medieval Spain and Toledo: Deciphering Secrets of Medieval Spain*, focus intensively on palaeographic studies and more difficult hands (scripts) from the early fifteenth century. The palaeographic difficulty of these courses is considerable and may lead to learner attrition.

Over six years, these citizen scholars transcribed most of the 600+ page *Libro I* of the *Actas Capitulares* of the cathedral chapter of Plasencia as well as dozens of manuscripts from the cathedral and municipal archives of Burgos and Toledo.[6]

Table 1

Deciphering Secrets MOOCs: editions, enrollments, completion rates, and manuscript collections

MOOC	Edition	Enrolled learners	Course Completion Rate	Manuscript Collections
Unlocking the Manuscripts of Medieval Spain (Coursera)	Summer 2014	10,600	19%	19th-century copy of the 600+ page *Book One (1399-1453) of the Capitulary Acts* of the Archivo de la Catedral de Plasencia (Spain)
Unlocking the Manuscripts of Medieval Spain (Coursera)	Spring 2016	6,000	8%	Same as prior MOOC.

[6] Many of Deciphering Secrets' crowdsourced manuscript collections are routinely updated on the research section of our website. See https://grants.uccs.edu/deciphering-secrets/deciphering-secrets-medieval-spanish-manuscript-and-transcription-collection/.

Course	Term	Enrollment	Completion	Description
Unlocking the Manuscripts of Medieval Burgos (edX)	Summer 2016	1,700	14%	13th-, 14th- and 15th-century manuscripts from the Archivo de la Catedral de Burgos (Spain) and the Archivo Municipal de Burgos (Spain).
Unlocking the Manuscripts of Medieval Burgos (edX)	Spring 2017	1,400	3%	Similar materials to the prior MOOC on Burgos.
Unlocking the Manuscripts of Medieval Toledo (edX)	Fall 2017	1,300	3%	13th, 14th and 18th/19th-century MSS from the Archivo y Biblioteca de la Catedral de Toledo (Spain), Archivo Municipal de Toledo (Spain), and the Archivo Historico de la Nobleza (Toledo, Spain)
Coexistence in Medieval Spain: Jews, Christians, and Muslims (Coursera)	Continuous enrollment since Fall 2017	7,800	2.9%	Introduces the history of medieval Spain and palaeography.
Burgos: Deciphering Secrets of Medieval Spain (Coursera)	Continuous enrollment since Spring 2018	1,500	1.1%	Similar materials to the prior MOOC on Burgos.

Toledo: Deciphering Secrets of Medieval Spain (Coursera)	Continuous enrollment since Summer 2018	2,050	1.9%	Similar materials to the prior MOOC on Toledo.
Total	Years 2014-2020	32,350	No avail.	N/A

In terms of curriculum and pedagogy, the MOOCs provide online history education and palaeographic instruction. In five- to eight-week courses, learners learn about the complex nature of Jewish, Christian, and Muslim relations through brief Spanish and English documentary-style videos with English and Spanish subtitling,[7] readings (including original sources), and participatory discussions via online forums and social media (e.g., Facebook's *Revealing Cooperation and Conflict Project* group-page). These activities challenge learners to examine the significance of medieval material culture and manuscripts: for example, how was a private eleventh-century mosque in the city of Toledo transformed into the thirteenth-century Capilla de Belén in the Convento de Santa Fe used by King Alfonso X 'The Wise'? (See Figure 2). Or, how should we understand an eleventh-century royal privilege that dedicated income generated from a mill and taxes collected from the Jewish community of Burgos

---

[7] For example, the following *Deciphering Secrets* videos that feature local museum directors (i.e., Museo de Burgos), archivists (i.e., Archivo Municipal de Burgos), cultural delegates (i.e., Centro Sefarad Israel, and Casa Arabe), and scholars (i.e., Consejo Superior de Investigaciones Científicas) hosted on Youtube.com. See: *Deciphering Secrets: Burgos - A tour of the medieval city of Burgos (Spain)* (https://youtu.be/SQDVIhhc8GY); *DS Burgos - Treasures of the Archive of the Cathedral of Burgos (Spain)* (https://youtu.be/ZZQHu2WyvvI); *DS Burgos Muslim Artifacts Become Christian Museo de Burgos UC3M Standard* (https://youtu.be/3z5s7PuiZEY).

for the burial of Christian pilgrims traveling on the Camino de Santiago?[8] (Figure 3). By using engaging materials and raising intriguing questions, these MOOCs entice and encourage learners to take on the challenge of learning medieval Spanish palaeography and transcribing original manuscripts.[9]

Figure 2

Composite Image of the 13th-Century Capilla de Belen in the Convento de Santa Fe (*Museo de Santa Cruz, Toledo, Spain*).[10]

[8] The privilege described is cataloged as Archivo Historico Municipal de Burgos SJ 1/1. In this 1091 royal donation, King Alfonso VI concedes valuable resources (a grazing reserve, a mill, a communal oven, and Jewish tax collections) to the Monastery of San Roberto de Casa Dei, located in the vicinity of the city of Burgos. See the *Deciphering Secrets* Youtube.com video *DS 6 - Burgos - AMP - Manuscript SJ-1-1* (https://youtu.be/watch?v=jV5A WmjBddg).

[9] The present Courersa.org-University of Colorado MOOC titled *Burgos: Deciphering Secrets of Medieval Spain* is accessible at Coursera (www.cour sera.org/learn/burgos-deciphering-secrets-medieval-spain).

[10] Photograph by the author, Roger L. Martinez-Davila. Video discussion of the chapel posted at *DS 1 Museo de Santa Cruz Islamic Art Architecture Part 3* (https://youtu.be/U5xrchhjaQM).

Figure 3
Archivo Municipal de Burgos, Mss. SJ 1/1 (1091 C.E.)

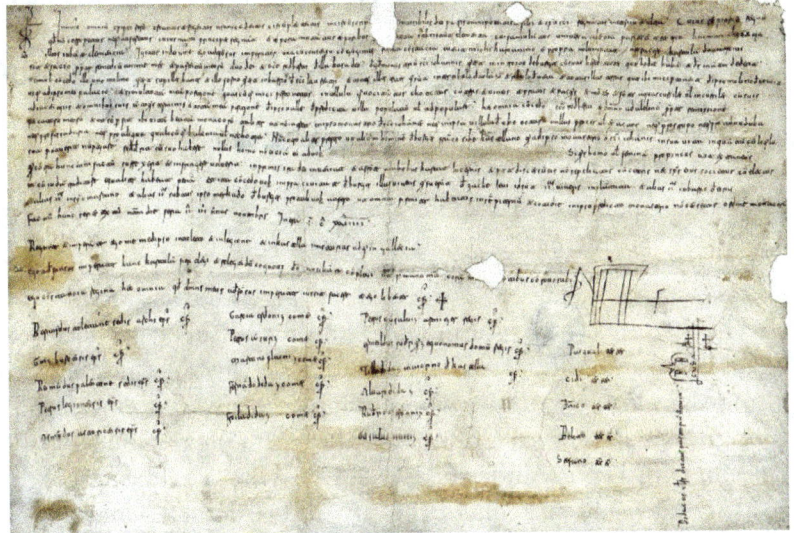

Toledo: Deciphering Secrets of Medieval Spain MOOC

Our eight-week MOOC, *Toledo: Deciphering Secrets of Medieval Spain*, utilizes our latest curriculum that delivers historical and cultural lectures and readings, intensive palaeography training and exercises, and collaborative transcription projects. What might be quite surprising to university educators is the intensity and rigor of our MOOC courses: learners pursue on average 45 hours of instruction over eight weeks. The primary learning objectives, which are linked to distinct video lectures, readings, and assessments, ensure our course content follows a well-defined pedagogy. Of the 18 learning objectives, six in particular are directly linked to palaeographical and transcription efforts:

- Recognize that palaeography is both the study and interpretation of older forms of handwriting.
- Interpret thirteenth-century letter-forms, numbers, and abbreviations.
- Interpret fifteenth-century letter-forms, numbers, and abbreviations.
- Interpret 18th-19th century letter-forms, numbers, and abbreviations.
- Apply the SILReST Palaeography Method to deciphering manuscripts.
- Evaluate a 15th-century manuscript using SILReST.

The first three weeks (or modules) of the course focus exclusively on historical and cultural studies that articulate why this interreligious history is valuable to those who are intellectually and emotionally concerned about Jewish, Christian, and Muslim interrelations. Week 1 begins with a course introduction and an abbreviated history of the ancient and medieval roots of the city of Toledo. This includes an introduction to medieval Europe, the Byzantine Empire, and the Islamic world. We also explore the Visigothic Kingdom that called the city of Toledo its capital. During Week 2, we study Jews, Christians, and Muslims in medieval Toledo until 1212. We witness the Islamic conquest of Visigothic Spain, the formation of Islamic al-Andalus, the birth of the Christian Reconquest, and Toledo under the Umayyads and successor kingdoms. We also virtually explore Islamic architecture at the Museo de Santa Cruz as well as other local sites. Week 3 evaluates medieval Toledo in relation to broader affairs on the Iberian Peninsula. We evaluate the rule of Castilian King X 'The Wise' and his legal codes, and the *Cantigas de Santa Maria*. We also virtually visit the Museo Sefardí and consider how 'cleanliness of blood' statutes impacted recent converts to Christianity (conversos).

Weeks 4, 5, and 6 transition learners to investigations of the cathedral and municipal archival collections, learning and practicing palaeography, and studying our SILReST Palaeography Method. Over the course of sixteen hours of instruction during these three modules, we have determined our learners can master thirteenth-, eighteenth-, and eighteenth-/nineteenth-century palaeographic interpretation; we define 'mastery' as an average error rate of approximately 12%. Our prior published work on the SILReST Palaeography Method determined that our student transcriptions of fifteenth-century manuscripts revealed a 12.1% average error rate; learners correctly identified 87.9% of all the letter-forms, numbers, and abbreviations from fifteenth-century manuscripts (Martinez-Davila et. al. 2018, 27).

The key to the course is the SILReST Palaeographic Method. This method teaches palaeography to non-specialists in two to three weeks of instruction. SILReST is an initialism, each letter represents one of six strategies. Figure 4 presents method. SILReST is now integrated into each MOOC's toolkit of practice exercises, examinations, and transcription projects. These MOOCs often attract former learners to re-enroll and thus their palaeography proficiency undoubtedly improves with each course.[11]

The final modules of the course, weeks 7 and 8, are dedicated to individual and collaborative research projects using novel manuscripts that are matched to learners' respective skill levels: eighteenth-/nineteenth-century (introductory level), thirteenth-century (intermediate level), or fourteenth-/fifteenth-century (advanced level). Using our thematically curated digital library of manuscripts from the

---

[11] A video overview of the SILReST method, which is presented to the learners, is viewable at *Deciphering Secrets: Burgos - SILReST: Six Essential Strategies for Advanced Paleography* (https://youtu.be/N4PgmILwaKw). A video tutorial demonstration of how to use SILReST with a fifteenth century Spanish manuscript is available at *DS Burgos - Learning a Castilian Spanish Script from the 15th Century - Part 1* (https://youtu.be/aI9nS98H1Is) and *DS Burgos - Learning a Script from the 15th Century - Part 2* (https://youtu.be/iy4wDa9oXX0).

Archivo y Biblioteca de la Catedral de Toledo (ABCT) and the Archivo Municipal de Toledo (AMT), learners are provided with initial abstracts of documents as well as specific guidance about what types of information can be garnered from the documents. For example, in the present edition of the course learners are presented with fourteen folios from the 'Obras y Fabricas' collection of the ABCT that detail cathedral transactions relating to the repair, rental, and use of church real property in the year 1379. Similarly, palaeographic 'cheat sheets' are offered to learners so as to give them a primer as they attempt to transcribe all of the folios presented. Figure 5 presents a sample abstract of a selection of manuscripts, Figure 6 a palaeographical primer, and Figure 7 a sample image of our method of blocking text for the purposes of recording transcriptions.

Figure 4

SILReST Palaeographic Method

- S. Strategy #1 - Scan the entire document before attempting to transcribe it. It is important for you to become familiar with how the scribe writes. Repeatedly scanning a document will accustom your eyes to the 'hand' of the scribe.
- I. Strategy #2 - Identify those letter-forms, abbreviations, and numbers that you can immediately recognize. This is very straightforward, but it is the beginning of finding your way into the document. Finding easy-to-recognize letter-forms will help you to appreciate how much you can already see and spur you along to uncover other letter-forms and words.
- L. Strategy #3 - Locate common words to (a) understand how the scribe connects their letter-forms together and (b) recognize other alphabetical letter-forms and numbers.

This strategy helps you identify letter-forms that are hard to recognize. If you are flexible in terms of how a common word might be spelled, then, you will be able to see many curious spellings of words you know. More importantly, you can find new letter-forms using this strategy.
- R. Strategy #4 - Recognize the abbreviations used in the document and if they vary within the document. Finding and marking abbreviations makes your task easier because it reminds you that some words on the page are not complete words at all. Rather, they are almost nonsensical connections of letter-forms. Find the abbreviations so that your eyes and mind do not attempt to create words that do not exist on the page.
- S. Strategy #5 - Search for English-Spanish cognates (those words that share similar meanings and spellings in English and Spanish) to identify more letter-forms and connections. Cognates are helpful because you can work 'backward' into reading letter-forms on the page. For example, if you know the word might be 'jurisdiction' in English and therefore is 'jurisdicción' in Spanish, then you can begin to identify hard to read letter-forms within the word on the page.
- T. Strategy #6 - Type or write your transcription and leave plenty of room to add edits. Creating a transcript will help you fill in the blanks as you work through those last, hard to read letter-forms and words.

Figure 5

Abstracting of Archivo y Biblioteca de la Catedral de Toledo Obras y Fabricas 929 ('Posesiones del Refitor').

Manuscript Overview - Archivo y Biblioteca de la Catedral de Toledo OF 929

- Manuscript Reference Numbers: Archivo de la Catedral de Toledo Obras y Fabricas 929 ('Posesiones del Refitor').
- Volume OF 929 is for the year 1379.
- The 'Obras y Fabricas' collection pertains to the Cathedral of Toledo and all aspects of its many properties. The specific sub-collection we are reviewing is under the heading of 'Posesiones del Refitor', or the cathedral organisation and churchmen responsible for the real property of the church. This section describes economic transactions (property rentals, sales, exchanges, etc), houses, businesses, communal ovens, mills, vineyards.
- There are 14 folios available and they are quite legible. Each image is a unique folio, or page, from one of the newly released manuscripts from the Archivo y Biblioteca de la Catedral de Toledo. Please choose at least one folio (page) for this assignment.
- We have selected this limited set of images because they are a hand-written index that details the location of houses, lands, and other real property owned by the Cathedral of Toledo in the year 1379. By collecting a solid transcription of this section we (1) learn more details about daily life in Toledo and (2) begin to creating a Geographic Information System (GIS) map showing where these historical events transpired in the city.

Guide to the Folios (What is on each page?):
- Individual Transactions. Each block of text is an individual transaction or event.

- Geographic Headings. On most pages, you will see headings with references to place names like Folio 13v, which describes 'del Santa...' and 'del la Juderia'.

Preliminary Findings:
- Folio 13 Verso - There appear to be three transactions relating to Jews in the juderia. Two Jewish nobles in the records: 'Dona Jamila' and 'Don Mayr de Levi'
- Folio 14 Recto - There is a reference to the aljama, or perhaps the Muslim quarter. There are two names here as well. One is Don Mose Abybadal.
- Folio 17 Recto - On 'Calle Fra...' there is a reference to 'Mose tundidor' or Mose the cloth shearer. There is also another person, perhaps, Mose Abadias.
- Folio 17 Verso - The prior record continues on about Mose Abadias.
- Folio 37 Verso - There is a reference to the collection of 'decimos' taxes and 'Judios'. Decimos were a form of tax on all produced goods, crops, and animals in the diocese.
- Folio 38 Verso - There is a reference to a 'molino', or a grain mill, and somehow it is connected to Mose and Jamylla (previously mentioned). Perhaps they are leasing it as 'tax farmers'?
- Folio 39 Recto - There are more molinos here.
- Folio 40 Recto - There is a reference to the place 'Alcala' and the person, 'Hamete Abelhat Moro'. This is a Muslim man.

Figure 6

Palaeographic Primer for Archivo y Biblioteca de la Catedral de Toledo Obras y Fabricas 929, Folios 37v-38r.

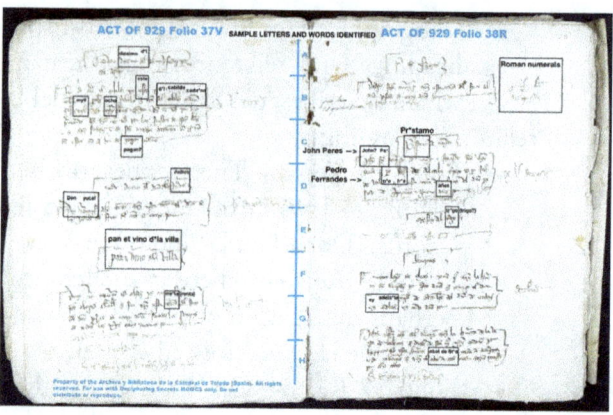

Figure 7

Blocking for Mss. Archivo de la Catedral de Toledo Obras y Fabricas 929, Folios 39v-40r.

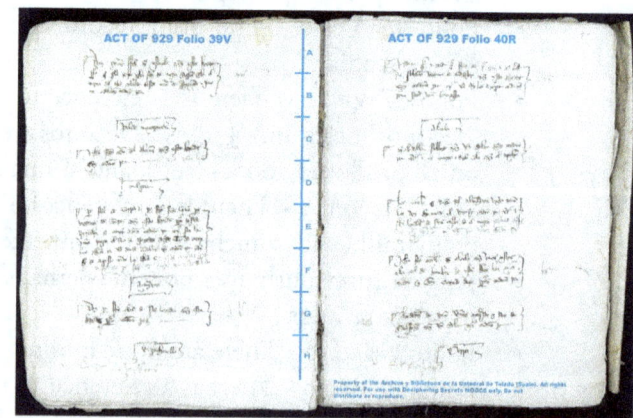

To ensure that learners create manuscript transcriptions that are standardised, but not overly complicated to record, we employ a basic transcription approach.[12] Learners prepare individual transcriptions of selections of manuscripts, denoted as text blocks, and then share these in online discussion forums for peer-review. Therefore, learners can comment and assist one another in exploring the complicated nature of more illegible pen markings. The instructions we provide to learners are reported in Figure 8. In their transcription formatting, learners begin to encode the text, which is necessary for developing finished transcriptions.[13]

Figure 8

MOOC Transcription Guidelines
- Choose 4 Text Blocks. For your manuscript image, try to transcribe the text in four (4) of the blocked areas as best as you can. For example, areas A, B, C, and D. Or, for example, E, F, G, and H.
- Formatting your transcription:
  o First Line. The first line should indicate what text blocks you transcribed. For example: 'Blocks A, B, C, and D'
  o Use Line-Breaks. Type in your transcription as a line-by-line recording. In other words, use line-breaks.
  o Marginalia. You do not need to type in marginalia (the writing on either side of the main section of text). If you choose to record marginalia, include

---

[12] For a discussion of various norms within Spanish transcription see López Villalba 1998, 285-306.
[13] For more on the importance of clear, simple guidelines for crowdsourcing projects see Duxfield 2018, 78.

the word and a colon, 'Marginalia:', in front of the text.
- Abbreviations. If you know the abbreviation, please type the abbreviation and then spell the entire word out. The spelled-out word should appear inside of (parentheses). For example: 'dho (dicho)' or 't* (testigo)'.
- Missing Letter-forms and Words. If you cannot read a section of the manuscript text, then you should type one period ' . ' for a missing individual letter. If you cannot read more than one letter, or an entire word, then you should record three periods ' ... '.

• Post Your Transcription in the Forum.

Provide Feedback to Other Learners. Comment on the transcriptions of your fellow learners in that same forum. Please be kind and offer constructive criticism.

Scholarly-curated digital collections

The culmination of the *Deciphering Secrets* (DS) project's citizen-science efforts is manifested in the creation of a scholarly-curated digital collection within the UCCS Digital Collections. The DS Collection is composed of a repository, software platform, and metadata schema. The UCCS is a R2-designated public higher education institution with a modest research profile that offers a limited number of doctoral and masters programs, an enrollment of 12,000 students, and a faculty of approximately 800 persons. Unlike R1-designated public universities, such as the University of Colorado-Boulder, UCCS lacks the substantial funding and staffing that typically support large research programs. Rather, this humble institution is representative of many middle-ranked universities in the United States that equally balance teaching and research. The UCCS Digital Collections is a member of the Mountain Scholar regional open access repository that offers a solid platform for our preservation, cataloguing, and distribution of medieval manuscripts and transcriptions:[14] this eight-member academic consortium provides access to digitised collections and other scholarly and creative works within the states of Colorado and Wyoming. Mountain Scholar utilizes the DSpace software platform.[15] Lastly, we use a customised Dublin Core metadata schema, which has a vocabulary of fifteen properties for use in resource description.[16]

Among the principal research contributions of the DS manuscript and transcription collection, available at doi.org/handle/10976/167140, is that it offers digital access to manuscripts that are otherwise inaccessible unless a researcher travels to view these physical ecclesiastical and municipal manuscripts on site in Spain. The DS collection also responds to the larger issue of the limitations of existing archival indices that were primarily created for administrative and not scholarly purposes such as the study of interreligious history. In this respect the DS collection is unusual as it assembles and describes church, municipal, and royal administrative records from the fourteenth through sixteenth centuries for the cities of Burgos, Toledo, Plasencia, and Granada. These particular dioceses and city centers were important communities where significant historical events were either directed or occurred. Burgos was the royal administrative center of the Kingdom of Castille and Leon, and a diocese led by elite conversos like the Santa María clan. Toledo held a long-standing position as an intellectual capital built upon Jewish, Islamic, and Christian shoulders and was the first locality that implemented 'blood purity statutes' in the 1450s that blocked the participation of conversos in municipal government. Plasencia generated the administrative and ecclesiastical leadership that

---

[14] For more on Mountain Scholar, see https://mountainscholar.org.
[15] For more on DSpace, see https://duraspace.org/dspace/.
[16] For more on the Dublin Core schema, see https://dublincore.org/.

propelled medieval Spain into an imperial power during the early sixteenth century. This direction was specifically embodied in the converso personages of Cardinal Bernardino López de Carvajal (1456-1523) – who secured for Queen Isabel and King Fernando II the title of 'Catholic Monarchs' and the *Inter caetera* papal bull (May 4, 1493) granting them control over most of the Americas – and Lorenzo Galíndez de Carvajal (1472-1528), the historian of Queen Isabel and King Fernando II who cleansed royal and noble genealogies of Jewish ancestries and was first de facto royal governor of the Spanish dependencies in the Americas per his position of *Correo Mayor de Indias*. Granada, the last of the Islamic kingdoms ruled by the Nasrids (1230-1492) at the Alhambra, is where Isabel and Fernando rode triumphantly into the city on 2 January 1492, and completed the eight-hundred-year Spanish Christian reconquest of Iberia from Islamic civilisation. Moreover, on 31 March 1492, at the Alhambra the Catholic Monarchs issued the Edict of Expulsion that decreed all Jews leave Spain within four months, and by 1502, a similar order was issued pertaining to the remaining Muslims (a majority of the city's population) who did not convert to Christianity. Thus, by assembling disparate secular and ecclesiastical archive collections from these four cities into a new one, centering on those manuscripts pertaining to interfaith life in late medieval Spain, a new digital archive can be realised and shared globally. Although it is presently a small collection, it will grow substantially over the next five years.

The raw DS collection of manuscripts consists of approximately 5,750 digital, high-resolution photographs of folios from the four cities' cathedral and municipal archives, as well as the national archive holding the familial archives of the nobility. The photographs, often captured under normal research conditions and without specialised lighting, were recorded on a Sony a7 rII digital camera (designed for low light conditions) at a 42.4-megapixel resolution. See Table 2.

Table 2

Deciphering Secrets collection: raw count of folios by source.

Locality	Archive (manuscript collection)	Raw count (fols)
Burgos	Archivo de la Catedral de Burgos (Libros, Registros)	750
	Archivo Historico Muncipal de Burgos (Sección Histórica)	500
Toledo	Archivo y Biblioteca de la Catedral de Toledo (Obras y Fabricas)	250
	Archivo Municipal de Toledo (Archivo Secreto)	500
	Archivo Historico de la Nobleza-Toledo (Baena, Bornos, Covera, Frias, Griegos, Luque, Osuna, Polop, Priego, Torrelaguna)	350
Plasencia	Archivo de la Catedral de Plasencia (Actas Capitulares)	2,300
	Archivo Municipal de Plasencia (Libros de Actas Capitulares)	600
Granada	Archivo Municipal de Granada (Actas del Cabildo)	500
Total	---	5,750

During 2019, the first preliminary efforts began to create metadata standards to organize and describe the DS collection, as well as to publish manuscript images prepared as PDF-As (an archival form of the popular file format that is used for long-term preservation) and transcriptions. During spring and summer 2020, the twenty-eight folios and crowdsourced transcriptions were abstracted using our custom metadata descriptors and published in Mountain Scholar. For example, these metadata extensions center around medieval European themes, ecclesiastical organisational and content factors, and highly specific issues of interreligious relations. Table 3 presents the collections' metadata descriptors as well as sample metadata elements for one of the collection's folios.

Table 3

Deciphering Secrets Collection Dublin Core Metadata Descriptors and Sample Data for the manuscript, Archivo de la Catedral Burgos, Registro 10, folio 156 verso.

Dublin Core metadata element[17]	Metadata definition (collection specific notes)	Sample data
dc.contributor.author	Individual(s) responsible for making significant contributions to the item. (Spanish archives proper name.)	Cabildo de la Catedral de Burgos (Espana)
dc.coverage.temporal	Temporal topic may be a named period, date, or date range. (Time periods – century, descriptive terms. Gregorian calendar.)	1400s, fourteenth century, Medieval, Middle Ages
dc.date	A single date or inclusive dates indicating when the item was created. (Gregorian calendar.)	1447-29-12

---

[17] Within Mountain Scholar, several elements are repeatable so that extended data can be collected. For the *Deciphering Secrets* Collection the following elements are repeated to capture nuanced data: dc.description, dc.rights, and dc.subject.

dc. description	A brief free-text note or descriptive statement that characterizes more fully than the title does the scope or content of the item. (Abstract provided by the local archive in modern Spanish.)	Manda dar al maestre Brahem, moro carpintero, dos cargas de trigo para que vaya junto con el reparador del cabildo a comprar la madera necesaria para reparar sus posesiones. Y una carga de trigo para el yesero. Ordena al arcediano de Burgos Juan Ruiz, que haga relación de las edificaciones necesarias en la casa de Quintanaortuño. (Note: Original Spanish-language abstract provided by Archivo Historico de la Catedral de Burgos, translation by UCCS staff.)
dc. description	New English abstract prepared by the University of Colorado that focuses on interreligious issues.	Document describes a business transaction between the Catholic Church and a Muslim Carpenter. It also provides insight into Church leadership in Quintanaortuno.
dc. description. abstract	A summary of the item. (English translation of abstract prepared by provided by the local archive.)	Order issued to master Brahem, Muslim carpenter, two loads of wheat to go to the council

		repair man to purchase the wood and a load of wheat for the plasterer to repair buildings. The order was issued by Archdeacon of Burgos, Juan Ruiz, who is responsible for the necessary buildings in the house of Quintanaortuno.
dc. description	Length in pages notes, blocks transcribed.	One page, folio 156 Verso.
dc. identifier. citation	Bibliographic citation for the item. Recommended practice is to include sufficient bibliographic detail to identify the resource as unambiguously as possible. (Citation used by the archive that includes include folio or page number.)	Registro 10, Folio 156 Verso
dc. identifier. uri	DSpace generated, unique bookmarkable handle; generated at point of submission/approval. The unique identifier of the item. (Permanent stable url for the item.)	https://hdl.handle.net/10976/167151
dc. language	Language of the item. (Use 'Romance Language' for early Spanish language family.)	Romance Languages
dc. publisher	Name of hosting entity. (Publisher of digital format.)	University of Colorado Colorado Springs, Kraemer Family Library

dc.publisher.original	The entity responsible for making the item available. (Entity presently in possession of the item.)	Diocese de Burgos (Espana)
dc.relation.ispartof	A related resource in which the described resource is physically or logically included. (Citation used by archives for collection or volume including the transaction.)	Registro 10
dc.rights	Information about rights held in and over the item. Typically, rights information includes a statement about various property rights associated with the item, including intellectual property rights; it can also include a license. (Education and research declaration use only.)	UCCS-CS The University of Colorado Colorado Springs is providing access to image files of the *manuscripts* for educational and research purposes only. Some of the material contained in these images may be protected by U.S. and International Copyright Law.
dc.rights	(Declaration of rights of the entity presently in possession of the item.)	Original document held by Archivo Historico de la Catedral de Burgos. UCCS-CS The University of Colorado Colorado Springs is providing access to image files of the _manuscripts_ for educational and research purposes only. Some of the material contained in

		these images may be protected by U.S. and International Copyright Law.
dc.rights	(Declaration regarding reproduction and crediting of source.)	Use of this image is restricted to non-commercial, public access and does not include the right to reproduce. Any materials used, for academic research or otherwise, should be fully credited with the source.
dc.source	A related item from which the described item is derived. The described item may be derived from the related item in whole or in part. Recommended best practice is to identify the related item by means of a string conforming to a formal identification system. (Identity of holder of item and collection or volume including transaction.)	Archivo Historico de la Catedral de Burgos, Registro 10
dc.subject	The topic of the item represented using keywords and/or key phrases. (Keywords and descriptive terms in English.)	Muslim, carpenter, barter, exchange, construction, Quintanaortuno
dc.subject	(Keywords and descriptive terms in Spanish.)	Moro, carpintero, trigo, cambio, permuta, construccion

dc.subject	(Proper names used in documents.)	Juan Ruiz, Brahem
dc.title	A name given to the item. (English title assigned to the item.)	[Repair/Construction agreement with Muslim Carpenter]
dc.title.altern ative	An alternative name for the item. (First line of the item in English.)	Order issued to the master Brahem, carpenter, two loads of wheat to go to the council repair man
dc.type	The nature or genre of the item. (Physical description of item.)	Manuscript

Among the innovations of this new digital archive are the fundamental framing of collection descriptors (metadata) through the lens of Spanish Jewish, Christian, and Muslim economic, social, religious, and political relationships during the Middle Ages. The collection's contents uniquely focus on manuscripts that record interfaith economic transactions detailing property leases, sales, individual and communal agreements, and other routine dealings documenting payment for services or religious poll taxes. At this time, there is no other collection like DS that specifically examines this interreligious dynamic. We employ several metadata elements to categorize manuscripts and transcriptions along these lines, namely, dc.description, dc.subject, and dc.title. These elements, which are presented in English and Spanish, describe the items according to religious identities and proper names of the reported individuals. An important characteristic of medieval Spanish manuscripts is that when an individual who is not a Christian is reported in a document, the recording notary will almost universally notate their religious status (Jew/judio, Muslim/moro, Muslim convert/morisco, Jewish convert/converso) and their Hebrew and Arabic given and surnames using a Latin-alphabet phonetic spelling. While these religious details exist in the original manuscripts, they are routinely omitted from abstracts and indices prepared by the institutions because these data were not important or relevant for the institutions' purposes.

While Mountain Scholar will display the full range of our metadata, only a limited set is harvested by portals such as Europeana (www.europeana. eu/en) and the Digital Public Library of America (https://dp.la/). In addition, the collection's content is now searchable on Google Scholar as that search engine continuously 'crawls' our institutional collections. For example, a search for 'moro Burgos' on Google Scholar will locate and link to the sample manuscript described in Table 3. Therefore, our efforts have realised a crucial foundational goal of making our scholarly-curated collection searchable using universally accessible search tools (Google Scholar) and accessible via an open-source digital repository (Mountain Scholar).

As transcriptions are harvested from the citizen-science efforts in our MOOCS as well as from student efforts in our traditional university courses, they are converted into semi-diplomatic 'rough' and diplomatic 'final' transcribed folios. Presently there is a backlog for organising and finalising transcriptions for a substantial number of folios from Plasencia in particular (approximately 500 folios), and to a lesser extent, from Burgos and Toledo (several dozen). As this effort moves forward, each calendar year it is anticipated that two hundred manuscript image folios and transcriptions with comprehensive metadata will be integrated into DS collection.

Concluding thoughts

There no longer need be Dark Archives accessible to just a few privileged academicians with substantive palaeographic training and knowledge of unique collections. Nor do the impediments of limited financial resources and time need to obstruct the investigation of exclusive archival collections. By building collaborative partnerships with cathedral and municipal archives, employing free MOOCs to attract and engage interested learners, and maximising the connectivity of minor research university digital repositories, we can advance the accessibility and study of medieval manuscripts. Moreover, it is a replicable research model for modest research initiatives. Certainly there are limitations to this approach, namely, the creation of 'silos' (separate fragmentary collections), incompatible description methods, difficulty in finding small collections, and the challenges of integrating citizen science into the research production process. However, if our goals are to generate new findings from medieval manuscripts, employ new digital methods of collaboration, and implement new forms of publication and dissemination, then there is no rationale to delay any longer. Let us light the way into these Dark Archives.

DIGITAL ARCHIVES AND DAMAGED TEXTS: CAPTURING, PROCESSING, AND SHARING MULTISPECTRAL IMAGE DATA

Alexander J. Zawacki and Helen Davies

Over the past twenty years multispectral imaging (MSI) has come to prominence as the most productive way of recovering lost text and images from manuscripts that have been palimpsested or erased, stained or burnt, whether by monks of the twelfth century or bombing raids of the twentieth. Prior to imaging, such texts may constitute different kinds of 'dark archives': scholars might know full well what work has been effaced from the page but be unable to read it, or the text may be too illegible to identify at all.[1] As with any new technology, the business of cultural heritage recovery brings problems, practical and conceptual, along with its solutions: the

---

[1] Such was the case with the famed Archimedes Palimpsest, which had been known since 1906 to contain otherwise-lost works by the mathematician. Some of this could be discerned by the naked eye (and by photographic techniques), but it took a digital MSI project — the first of its kind — to recover the majority of the undertext. In the process, the team discovered a truly dark text that scholars had not supposed lay hidden in the manuscript: a lost work by the Athenian orator Hypereides. Netz, Noel & Tehernetska 2011. See also Noel & Netz 2007; Easton & Noel 2010; as well as Easton, Christens-Barry & Knox 2011. For the Hypereides text, see Care et al. 2008. Images produced by the project have been made freely available at www.archimedespalimpsest.org.

problem of data storage and availability, for example, and the ethical issues entailed by the production of digital facsimiles that bear little visible resemblance to the original objects as seen with the unassisted eye. Because of the newness of the technology, its expense, and the small number teams who deploy it, few scholars have yet begun to undertake the important thought-work and problem solving necessitated by these issues. This paper presents a basic overview of the technology in the hope of both making it more familiar to the broader academic community.[2] Using our experiences as members of a cultural heritage recovery team as a baseline, we discuss questions of methodology and address some of the problems — particularly the issue of big data — raised by MSI and its use, as a kind of propaedeutic to further conceptual labor.

The present authors are members of the Lazarus Project, a team located at the University of Rochester and lead by Dr. Gregory Heyworth.[3] The project employs a multispectral unit built by Mega Vision, Inc., which is particularly notable for its being portable and thus enabling the imaging of cultural heritage objects *in situ* around the world. The system is set up around a copy stand, on which is placed the object to be imaged (Figure 1).[4] For illumination, the

---

[2] For a comprehensive overview of past MSI projects by various teams around the world, Davies & Zawacki 2020.

[3] It is also, with scholars and scientists at the Rochester Institute of Technology (RIT), a founding member of Rochester Cultural Heritage Imaging, Visualization, and Education (R-CHIVE). More information on the project, as well as a full listing of its active members, can be found at www.lazarusprojectimaging.com.

[4] The kind of support into which the object is placed varies depending upon what form that object takes. Codices are held in a cradle, which support the spine of the codex as the pages are turned for imaging. These cradles can be more or less technologically advanced; the most sophisticated ones, like that used by the Sinai Palimpsests Project, employs computer-controlled motors

system employs light-emitting diodes (LEDS) which are set into four panels, two on each side. If the object is translucent, a transmissive light source may be employed below it. The camera (a 50-megapixel monochrome sensor) is centered directly above the image plane of the object, and between the lens and object sits a filter wheel. A Macbeth color checker chart is placed within the frame of the image to ensure chromatic fidelity. Additionally, the Lazarus Project has championed the use in cultural heritage imaging of Spectralon, a substance which is maximally reflective (i.e., white) across all bands. This is used for calibration during the processing stage in order to set a universal white point for all captured images of each manuscript folio.

Proper material handling protocols are crucial to prevent damage to the manuscript and ensure high-quality images. The spine of the book is supported by a specially designed book cradle which holds the codex in place and level while each folio is imaged. The folios must of course be held flat, or as flat as possible. Towards that end, the Lazarus Project uses fine wooden knitting needles or thin plastic 'fingers', weighted down with sandbags and placed with their tips just barely touching the edge of the pages in order to obscure as little of the object as possible.[5] We also employ a laser-assisted system to check that the focus is constant between folios. The cockled state of many manuscripts means that the focus can never be perfect, of course, but it is possible to much ameliorate much unevenness through the strategic placement of weights.

to rotate the spine support; see Sinai Palimpsests Project 2015–20 (www.sinaipalimpsests.org).

[5] We are also in the process of producing bespoke devices, specifically designed to delicately hold down parchment or paper for the purposes of imaging.

Figure 1

The multispectral imaging system belonging to the Lazarus Project at the University of Rochester.
1: The main light panels, used for the reflectance stage of imaging.
2: auxilliary light panels, used to induce fluorescence.
3: The transmissive light source, with the top of the cradle used to hold the manuscripts in place visible behind.
4: The camera, lens, and filter wheel.

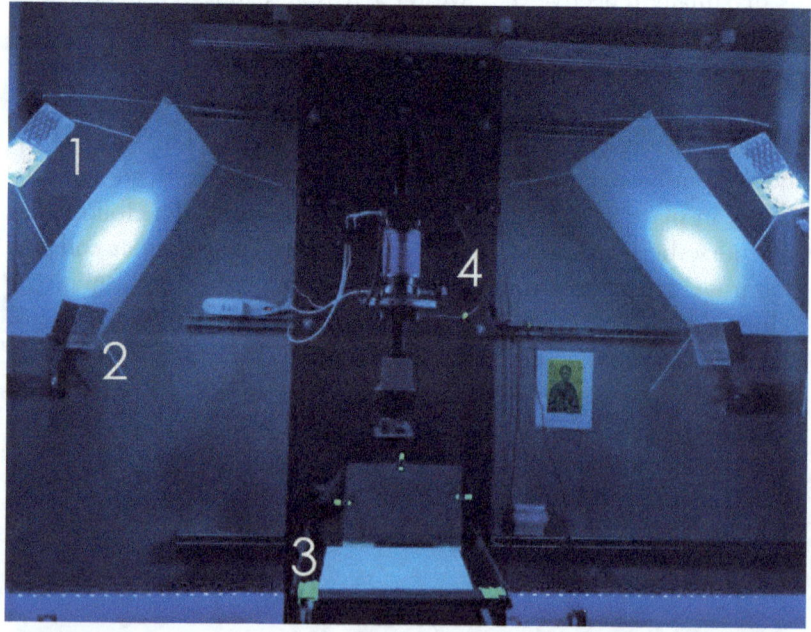

The manuscript is imaged one folio at a time and in three stages, each of which employs a different kind of illumination. In the first stage, that of reflectance, the upper two LED panels are used. These emit light in sixteen discrete wavelengths, moving from the ultraviolet (365

nm) through the visible spectrum into the infrared (940 nm).[6] An image of the folio is captured under the illumination of each wavelength.

The second is fluorescence, and is more complex. Substrates such as parchment, paper, and canvas possess the property of fluorescence: they absorb light at shorter wavelengths (e.g., ultraviolet) and re-emit it at longer ones (e.g., blue or green), making it appear to glow. This is the principle behind basic ultraviolet photography, long used as a method of recovering faded text from manuscripts. Advanced multispectral systems take this method farther, however, by interposing a series of filters between the object and the lens. Each of these filters block out certain wavelengths of light while allowing others to pass through, essentially squeezing more information out of the object than is allowed for by basic ultraviolet photography.[7]

For translucent materials like parchment a third stage involving transmissive light may be employed. In this stage, a thin acrylic screen attached to an LED light bar is slid beneath a given folio, directing light upwards through it.[8] Unfortunately for conservators but fortunately for those in the business of recovering lost texts, iron gall ink is corrosive, and over a long enough period of time will eat into

---

[6] The full list of wavelengths used during the reflectance stage is as follows (all in nanometers): 365, 420, 450, 470, 505, 530, 560, 590, 615, 630, 655, 700, 735, 780, 850, and 940.

[7] The Lazarus Project uses six filters in sequence: UV block (Schott GG400, which blocks ultraviolet light], UV pass (Hoya U360, which allows only ultraviolet light through), red (R25), green (G58), blue (B47), and orange (O22).

[8] In four wavelengths: 940, 735, 580, 450. Shorter wavelengths (like ultraviolet) are not used because their capability for penetration is poor compared to the longer and they cannot pass through the thickness of parchment or paper.

its substrate.⁹ In extreme cases, this can result in letters being wholly eaten away and the parchment reduced to lace, as has happened to some extent with the 'Ambrosian Palimpsest' which is the most important witness to Plautus' extant plays.¹⁰ More often, however, the damage is less severe, and generally invisible (or nearly so) to the unaided eye. If the ink had sufficient time and the proper conditions to corrode the parchment prior to the manuscript's being palimpsested, the parchment where the ink once lay will be slightly thinner than its surroundings. If, then, light is shone through the folio, the erased letterforms will appear as 'ghosts', brighter than the parchment around them — even if no trace of the original ink remains.¹¹ The camera and lights are controlled by a laptop or computer running Photoshoot, a bespoke MSI program designed by Mega Vision, Inc. Images are saved to the computer or an external drive as they are captured.

But capturing the images is only the first step. The next — processing — is crucial, and produces yet more reams of data. For it is almost never the case that any one image will restore the damaged or erased text to illegibility (though they may certainly improve on what is visible to the naked eye); if that were the case, standard ultraviolet or infrared photography would for the most part suffice. The real act of resurrection for which Lazarus is named comes in the form of statistical processing, which entails the application of various

---

⁹ On which see, e.g, Kolar et al. 2006. A rundown of the chemical processes involved can be found at Banik 1998 and Reissland, Ligterink, Phan & Luu 2010.

¹⁰ For an early attempt at digitally recovering this manuscript, see Fontaine & Scafuro, eds 2014.

¹¹ Transmissive illumination is also, as one would imagine, very effective at revealing watermarks.

algorithms to the collected image data.[12] These include principal component analysis (which reduces a complex dataset to a few maximally uncorrelated variables preserving most of the variance of the whole set, but with less redundancy),[13] independent component analysis (a method of 'revealing hidden factors that underlie sets of random variables'),[14] minimum noise fraction transformation (a modified form of PCA that filters noisy bands from the output),[15] and blur and divide (a process that divides the dataset by a reduced-resolution version of itself in order to reduce background features of the text such as staining and emphasize foreground features such as text).[16] The processing stage may be lengthy and laborious depending on the condition of the manuscript and the extent to which the target

---

[12] First, all images of a given folio (across all wavelengths) are digitally 'stacked' into what is called a cube. Next, calibration is performed using the Spectralon visible in the image. This calibrated cube forms the basis of all subsequent processing. For more in-depth discussions, see Easton & Kelbe 2014; Giacometti et al. 2017; and Craig-McFeely 2012.

[13] See Jolliffe 2002. See also Hyvärinen, Karhunen & Oja 2001, 124–44. The method was first put forth in Pearson 1901, and developed by Harold Hotelling in two publications: Hotelling 1933 & 1936.

[14] Hyvärinen Karhunen & Oja 2001, xvii. See further 1–12 and 147–64.

[15] Green, Berman, Switzer & Craig 1988; and Lee, Woodyatt & Berman 1990.

[16] For statistical processing, the Lazarus Project primarily employs ENVI (ENvironment for Visualizing Images), produced by Harris Geospatial Solutions, but other programs are available. One such is ImageJ, an open-source program developed by the National Institute of Health (www.imagej.nih.gov/ij/index.html). Keith Knox is developing a free Java-based program called *Hoku* that can be used to batch-process multispectral imaging (see www.cis.rit.edu/~ktkpci/Hoku_Software.pdf). Drs. Tania Kleynhans and David Messinger have developed an open-access NEH-funded image processing software called *R-CHIVE Spectral Analysis ToolKit* which it remarkable for its ease of use. It is available at R-CHIVE.com.

text has been effaced or etiolated.[17] Different processed and raw images may be combined to produce pseudo-color images in order to maximize contrast. Finally, a graphics editor such as Adobe Photoshop or the open-source GIMP (GNU Image Manipulation Program) may be used for anything from simple, globally-applied visual tweaks (contrast and brightness adjustment, hue rotation) to more drastic intervention (tracing faded letters, using the color selection tool to remove the overtext from a palimpsest).[18]

The result of all of this labor will be an image or a series of images that look drastically different from the object they putatively represent. This fact poses some ethical concerns, which Lazarus and some other teams working in the field have tried to navigate by adhering closely to standards of reproducibility and transparency. Just as well-designed scientific experiments should be repeatable in different laboratories by different people, so scholars and end-users of processed multispectral images should — at least in principle — be able to reproduce the results of an MSI team's efforts rather than having to trust wholly in the wizardry of the individual processors. For statistical processing, the first goal is generally quite attainable. In ENVI, algorithms like PCA and ICA take as their starting point a

---

[17] Further, the same folio may need to be processed multiple times, either because initial attempts failed to produce the desired results or because, as is often the case, they restored some aspects of the text but not others. One processing method might recover the rubrication on a page, for example, but leave the black text obscured. This produces multiple images which the scholar studying the object will need to consult.

[18] MSI teams generally eschew alterations as major and subjective as the latter, though they may be performed under certain conditions and with clear documentation (see below). Julia Craig-McFeely of the Digital Image Archive of Medieval Music (DIAMM; www.diamm.ac.uk) has produced with Alan Lock a freely available guide to using Photoshop for the purpose of recovering cultural heritage objects; see Craig-McFeely & Lock 2006.

region of interest (ROI), a two-dimensional polygon drawn over the object under study which effectively tells the program on what areas

Figure 2. A folio from a palimpsested manuscript at the SLUB. Clockwise from top left: the folio under natural light, a monochrome processed image (produced using angle mapping), a pseudocolor processed image (spectral angle mapping and minimum noise fraction transform), and the same pseudocolor image after postprocessing in Adobe Photoshop (contrast, brightness, HDR toning, hue, shadows, and sharpness all adjusted).

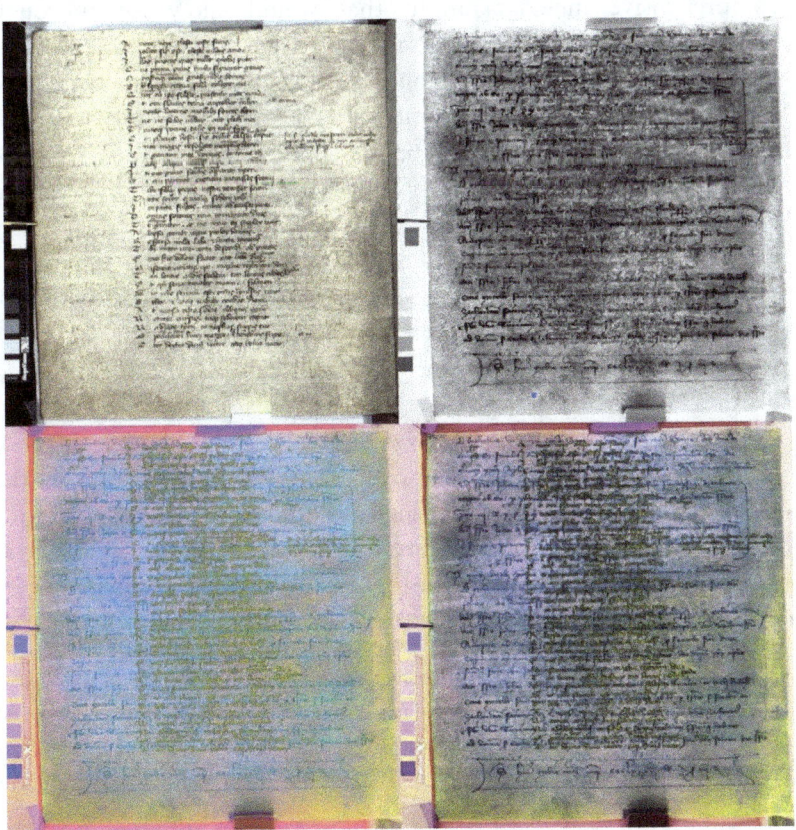

it ought to focus.[19] These ROIs can be saved independently of the images and constitute very small files (on the order of less than a kilobyte). Any number of scholars can take the original image files and the ROI and, by applying the same statistical processing methods, arrive at identical results.

Of course, one scholar needs to know exactly what processes another applied to a given dataset in order to achieve the same result. Thus transparency, in addition to being a desirable aim in its own right, is essential to reproducibility. Unfortunately, neither ENVI nor any similar software known to the authors allows for the kind of comprehensive metadata input that would allow for thorough documentation of every processing step. In lieu of such a tool, Lazarus has devised standardised file naming conventions which at a glance supply comprehensive information about the images, and statistical processing methods utilised. The filename begins with the name of the object or manuscript (e.g., Hengwrt) and is followed by the folio number, the initials of the scholar who performed the primary processing, and (sometimes a series of) abbreviations or initials denoting different applied processes.[20] Anyone familiar with the naming convention can therefore know what folio of what manuscript a given file contains images of, as well as who performed the processing and what exactly they did. It is a system that makes up in effectiveness for what it perhaps lacks in elegance.

However, the filename solution is complicated somewhat by the use of postprocessing programs such as Photoshop or the open-source equivalent GIMP. This software can greatly improve legibility as compared to files processed using ENVI alone, but listing every

[19] With palimpsests, for example, drawing an ROI or a series of ROIs that include the undertext but not the overtext often produces best results.

[20] For example, an ENVI cube folio 22r of the Hengwrt manuscript processed by Helen Davies using (in order) PCA and ICA would bear the name Hengwrt_22r_HD_cal_PCA_ICA. *Cal* refers to the calibration using the Spectralon, mentioned above.

adjustment made (contrast, brightness, hue rotation, shadows, highlights, levels, sharpness, tint, de-noising, color selection, etc.) would quickly made the filename unwieldy. This is doubly true if one wanted to note by how much each effect changed the image (e.g., contrast up ten, brightness down twelve).[21] Lacking a better solution, the Lazarus Project simply saves the Photoshopped file separately from the ENVI file, retaining the latter should there arise a need to compare the two. A note is made in the filename that the image was altered in Photoshopped, but we avoid trying to fit exhaustive descriptions of what precisely was done. Still, as Photoshop is a veritable byword for manipulation, falsification, and even fraud, teams using this invaluable tool should be able to provide, when asked, a full accounting of what was done to each image.

If a team acts transparently and retains all relevant data, reproducibility should be achievable. Some potentially thorny issues arise when considering *local* (as opposed to global) image changes, that is, changes applied to one particular portion of the image rather than the image as a whole. An example will serve by way of explanation: in 2017, Gregory Heyworth's Digital Media Studies (DMS) class (composed of a mix of under- and post-graduates, mostly the former) processed a musical score imaged by the Lazarus Project at the Sächsische Landesbibliothek – Staats- und Universitätsbibliothek (SLUB) Dresden. This manuscript, of a concerto by the Baroque composer Georg Philipp Telemann, had been heavily water damaged during the Second World War. Much of the ink had been washed off, and much that was left was obscured by mold. The DMS students were able to recover the score in its entirety, though most of the staff had vanished irretrievably. Other students, from the University of Rochester's Eastman School of Music, performed the piece at a

---

[21] Some of these, like hue rotation or tint, are not easily quantifiable — how helpful would the note 'hue shifted towards yellow a bit, then tint made a little greener' be?

fundraising event in New York City and later at a festival in Rochester. Before presenting the score to the musicians, however, we at the Lazarus Project used Photoshop to add the staff back in.[22] This we deemed acceptable for the purpose of performance, though not for scholarship. Even so, the performers were clearly informed of the fact and the precise nature of the image alteration. Every team or individual working on digital restoration will likely face similar quandaries. Our belief remains that total transparency, achieved through documentation and data retention, offers a route between the Scylla of necessity and the Charybdis of misdeed. Just as in the traditional sciences, MSI teams should be prepared to explain and justify all of their methodological decisions.

It goes without saying that imaging, processing, and post-processing all produce reams of data, the long-term retention and distribution of which is fraught, both ethically and technically, with similarly difficult choices. The raw images of a single folio alone constitute up to four GB of data. Saving each processed image cube can compound this number many times over. Even a single manuscript, then, can easily run into a terabyte, and a team committed to the imaging and processing of cultural heritage objects will need to commit itself to acquiring and maintaining in perpetuity ever more terabytes of storage.[23] The result is a problem alien to many (though certainly not all) who work in the humanities: that of big data. In the digital humanities, the concept of big data has traditionally been associated with the work of Franco Morretti, who

---

[22] Particular credit goes to Kyle Huskin and Alison Harper, PhD candidates at the University of Rochester, for this effort.

[23] It is worth noting here that the International Image Interoperability Framework (IIIF) has largely solved the display problems for these large files. IIIF provides a mechanism to easily render and view these files around the world via the Mirador (and related) viewers. However, this does not solve the actual large file size findability and storage issues. For more information on IIIF see https://iiif.io/.

famously introduced the term to computer-assisted literary studies.[24] Moretti and his lab specialised in corpus analysis; their datasets are textual in nature.[25] Big *image* data, however, presents a very different kind of problem from that in which Moretti was interested. Serious institutional commitment is required not only to make such large datasets available in the first place but to keep them available in the long term.

The primary limiting factor is, of course, money. Some initiatives — like the Archimedes Palimpsest and the Sinai Palimpsest Projects — received funding from the National Endowment for the Humanities specifically to make data freely available online. The precise method by which the images are made accessible may vary: the Archimedes project simply listed a collection of jpegs which can be downloaded, while the later Sinai Palimpsests Project developed an interactive online viewer that gives users the ability to dynamically compare visible light, multispectral, and processed images.[26] Hosting such large amounts of data is expensive; devising creative ways of interacting with that data adds further costs, and requires more technical know-how. Discussions around multispectral imaging tend to focus, perhaps naturally, on the *imaging* portion, but that is only the beginning. The long-term aspects of the project — namely, whether or how much of the data will be made available online at all, and if so how and with what funding — should be considered in the early planning stages and factored into budget calculations.

Ideally, teams may commit to storing their data and making it accessible, though this commitment will not always be practicable or

---

[24] Franco Moretti, Graphs, Maps, Trees: Abstract Models for a Literary History (New York: Verso, 2007).

[25] The Stanford Literary Lab is now under the direction of Mark Algee-Hewitt. More information can be found at https://litlab.stanford.edu/.

[26] The Archimedes Palimpsest Project images can be found at http://archimedespalimpsest.net/. The Sinai Palimpsest Project viewer and images can be found at http://sinaipalimpsests.org/.

durable. And not only because of cost: numerous issues may influence decisions about data availability. MSI teams at times work with private collections, the owners of which may allow the publication of scholarly work based on the images but not those images themselves. MSI teams are asked, not infrequently, to work under non-disclosure agreements, providing imaging services for a private individual, museum, or institution who then makes the ultimate decision about the disposition of the data.

In addition, making datasets available too soon runs the risk that the scholar(s) working on them might get scooped, beaten to the punch by unaffiliated researchers. To this end, the Lazarus Project proposes (and follows) an 'embargo' protocol applied in certain areas of technical imaging, especially astronomy, for example the Hubble and James Webb Telescopes.[27] Data from these taxpayer-funded initiatives are made freely available to the public after a year-long abeyance. This proprietary period of withholding gives investigators attached to the teams the opportunity to work and publish on the data prior to its becoming widely available, while still fulfilling the project's open access mandates. This two-pronged approach ensures that, after a short delay, the MSI data will enter the larger cultural archive as both images and academic discourse. These embargoes, like all decisions regarding data management, should of course be discussed with the institution hosting the cultural heritage object under consideration, and clear agreements should be reached prior to the commencement of imaging.

As noted above, the Lazarus Project prefers to work only on projects in conjunction with a dedicated scholar or scholars who will shepherd the results through to publication. Except under particular

---

[27] 'On the subject of data, the Webb Telescope will follow the policy in place for the Hubble, which is to embargo data for a one-year "proprietary period" for the benefit of investigators working on funded projects. After that, the data is to be released to the public' (Phillips 2016).

circumstances — say, when a manuscript or cultural heritage object is in imminent danger of further damage — we broadly avoid working without a planned endgame. Thus even though budgetary constraints or other issues may prevent our making available online all of our data from a given project, we try to ensure that the fruits of that labor at least reach an academic audience.

This may seem an obvious and easy decision. Yet it is far from unheard of for manuscripts to be imaged by teams who, for one reason or another, never manage either to release or publish on their data. And while some manuscripts may be difficult to access — stored in far-flung libraries, or kedged up in the weeds of institutional bureaucracy — they remain accessible in theory, if not always available in practice. A collection of images stored on a forgotten hard drive owned by a team now bereft of funding and overworked may as well be on the moon. The result is a new kind of dark archive, or what we would call a 'digital palimpsest'. We cannot expect institutions always to allow repeated and liberal access to their cultural heritage objects, and once a manuscript has been imaged by one team it may be a very long time before another is granted similar permissions. This is especially true of particularly valuable or fragile objects. If the data is rendered inaccessible, of the images obtained are of poor quality, scholarship on the object may be hampered for years.

Much of this is uncharted territory. Libraries and universities have only recently begun to acquire MSI systems at all, much less incorporate them into their broader institutional workflow. The British Library, for example, has a simple online form for ordering (and paying for) digital images of the manuscripts in their collections, but while they possess an excellent MSI system helmed by the imaging scientist Christina Duffy there is no formal channel for requesting multispectral images. The logistical problems are obvious, since as noted above imaging a manuscript produces a dataset many times larger than does standard digitisation, and those images must be further processed in order to be optimally utile. The costs involved, to say nothing of the necessary time commitment on the part of staff, are considerably higher than with traditional digitisation or the scanning of microfiche. Institutions like the BL might commit to hosting, or delivering upon request, the raw MSI data; scholars could then carry out the processing themselves, or pay an additional fee for imaging scientists at the institution to do it for them.[28]

The obvious benefits of MSI to the study of cultural heritage objects and the ever-decreasing cost of the necessary equipment ensure that the technology will continue to proliferate.[29] An increasingly diverse collection of institutions large and small will find themselves grappling with all of the issues discussed above. Questions like those surrounding data availability and the ethics of postprocessing should be conducted openly amongst interested scientists and scholars, and teams should be transparent about all aspects of their methodology, in order for best practices to be reached and agreed upon. Above all, we must work to avoid the creation of digital palimpsests either through flawed imaging protocols or unavailable data. Only by practicing a rigorous imaging and processing methodology and an open exchange of data can we bring the lost texts in our archives into the light and ensure that nothing is left in the dark.

---

[28] Transference of the data requires channels more technically complex than just email, such as the use of an FTP server.

[29] In January 2020, the Rochester Institute of Technology received a significant grant from the National Endowment for the Humanities to develop systems which would cost as little as $5,000. The project is led by David Messinger, a member of the Rochester Cultural Heritage Imaging, Visualization, and Education (R-CHIVE), with which the Lazarus Project is affiliated.

SELVA OSCURA: IN AND OUT OF A DARK ARCHIVE

Debra Taylor Cashion

Figure 1

METAscripta, with user annotation tools enabled by IIIF/*Mirador*, applied to Vat. lat. 3199.

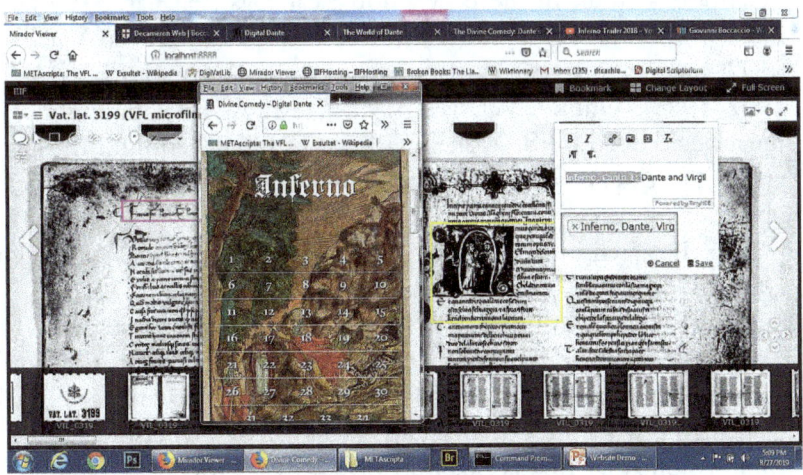

Although the manuscripts of the Biblioteca Apostolica Vaticana (BAV = Vatican Library) have enjoyed a long history of dedicated scholarship, many remain unstudied by scholars who have no way of knowing the manuscripts even exist. *METAscripta*, meaning 'metadata about manuscripts,' intends to help bring BAV manuscripts out of the shadows of *l'archivio oscuro* and into the light of digital access. A large-scale digital humanities project of the Knights of Columbus Vatican Film Library (VFL) at Saint Louis University, *METAscripta*'s immediate goal is to digitize and create online discovery access to 37,000 pre-modern manuscripts on microfilm, originally photographed at the BAV in the 1950s by the founders of the VFL.[1]

For present-day scholars, even well-researched BAV manuscripts, such as Vat. lat. 3199, a fourteenth-century manuscript of Dante's *Divina Commedia*, are often difficult or impossible to find in the online or printed catalogs of the Vatican, because about three-quarters of the BAV's collection of approximately 80,000 pre-modern manuscripts have either inadequate catalog descriptions or no catalog descriptions at all. In the BAV printed catalogs, Vat. lat. 3199 falls into an information gap of 7,542 records lacking between Vat. lat. 2192 and Vat. lat. 9734 (Biblioteca Apostolica Vaticana [BAV], 1902–1988). Online, Vat. lat. 3199, like most BAV manuscripts, must be accessed by BAV shelfmark, and cannot be found through an author, title, or keyword search (BAV, *OVL: Opacvatlib*). These obstacles to access cast a shadow of archival darkness on Vatican manuscripts, reminiscent of the *selva oscura* (dark wood) in which Dante is lost at the opening of the First Canto of the *Inferno*.[2]

The BAV 'dark archive' is especially unfortunate, because the Vatican collections are full of manuscripts of great historical and cultural significance. Vat. lat. 3199, for example, is an exceptional manuscript with an extraordinary pedigree of ownership. It was commissioned by Boccaccio, who gave it to his friend Petrarch as a

---

[1] For more information online see Cashion & Pass n.d.
[2] This paper is based on a presentation given at Oxford University: 'Dark Archives: A Conference on the Medieval Unread and Unreadable', (2019, 10-12 September). I want to thank Stephen Pink, Juliana Dresvina and Anthony J. Lappin for inviting me to participate in this exciting conference.

gift and included a persuasive dedication to Petrarch explaining that Dante was actually a great writer, even if he wrote in Italian instead of Latin (Eisner, 2013, 13-15). Later, in the early 16th century, the manuscript was copied by the Dante scholar Cardinal Pietro Bembo to serve as a press-copy for his friend Aldus Manutius, the renowned publisher of Renaissance Venice (Clough, 1984, 305-31). Aldus used Bembo's autograph copy, today Vat. lat. 3197 (also in the BAV catalog information gap), to print in 1502 the first Aldine edition of the *Divine Comedy*. Entitled *Le Terze Rime*, Aldus printed it with a typeface, newly invented by his type cutter Francesco Griffo, which became known as 'italic' because its slanted letters were quickly associated with works of Italian vernacular literature (Kidwell 2004, 219).[3]

The VFL microfilm collection, designed to serve as a practical entry to the study of Vatican manuscripts, is also obscured by a lack of descriptive metadata, and at present the VFL database can only be searched by Vatican shelfmark or VFL microfilm roll number. The *METAscripta* project, however, will ultimately produce a website where registered users can find BAV manuscripts in their area of interest, study manuscripts in context with other digital works and resources, and contribute new descriptive information to catalog records of BAV manuscripts. *METAscripta*'s metadata tools will help users find their way through thousands of uncatalogued and undiscovered Vatican manuscripts and continue along a path of enlightened preservation, access, shared cultural heritage, and scholarly exchange. The result is a new digital working environment for interactive scholarship about Vatican manuscripts, based on relationships between the Vatican and American scholars that began over 60 years ago.

---

[3] A beautifully illuminated copy of the 1502 edition of *Le Terze Rime* is in the collections of the Newberry Library, Chicago (VAULT WING ZP 535.A354). Some images are available at Cachey & Jordan (1996).

Eight years after WWII ended, the Vatican Film Library of Saint Louis University was founded in 1953 under the supervision of Lowrie J. Daly, S.J. (1914–2000), professor of medieval history, and Charles J. Ermatinger (1921–2002), professor of philosophy and first Librarian of the VFL.[4] Ermatinger's background contributed to the motivation for the original project, which was to microfilm as much as possible of the Vatican Library's collection of pre-modern manuscripts. During World War II, Ermatinger served as a member of the 'Monuments, Fine Arts, and Archives Section' of the associated allied forces assigned to protect and safeguard European civilisation's most important artistic and cultural treasures from the ravages of war and the greed of the Nazis ('Charles Joseph Ermatinger (1921–2002)'). If you would like to know more about the *Monuments Men*, there is not only a real foundation and website dedicated to their history, but also a Hollywood movie with George Clooney, Matt Damon, and Cate Blanchet (Clooney 2014).[5]

Having close experience of the destruction of major European libraries, such as the monastery of Montecassino located about 90 miles south of Rome, Ermatinger saw the need for the replication of culturally valuable texts in order to help preserve them for the future. We know from records in St. Louis that Pope Pius XII himself had concerns that the 'conditions in Europe are much too unsettled and chaotic for sustained study, scholarship, and research....If the Holy See could in any way encourage, foster and help scholarship and research in the United States, he would be happy to cooperate' with the people in St. Louis (Moynihan, 1956, March 16). Thus plans were made to set up a fully equipped microfilming shop at the Vatican, as well as to build a new library in St. Louis, which according

---

[4] For more information on the founding of the VFL see Nance (1991).
[5] See the movie trailer, 'Monuments Men: Lost Treasure Featurette' (2014, 8 January) on *YouTube* (https://www.youtube.com/watch?v=c9ZpyVJrMaQ) based on the book by Edsel (2009).

to the letter signed by Pope Pius, would become 'a spacious temple of learning, a storehouse of the good, the true, the beautiful.' (Nance 1991, 188). This temple became Pius XII Memorial Library, and the master negatives to the microfilms, made with the Kodak silver-gelatin process and stored undisturbed in a vault since the 1950s, are the source materials for the *METAscripta* project.

Presently in development, the *METAscripta* website will enable users to view digital images of any manuscript in the VFL microfilm collection. The technical workflow, developed over the past 4 years, is briefly described as follows. In order to create robust and sustainable archival masters, VFL microfilms are digitised with a Mekel Mach 12 scanner and edited with proprietary software to produce raw TIFFs ('Mekel Mach 12'). The Quantum software, bundled with the Mekel scanner, includes automated boundary detection that allows us to crop each microfilm frame and remove unwanted duplicates or cancelled frames before the films are converted to raw TIFFs. Using Adobe Bridge and Photoshop, the raw TIFFs are processed, batch numbered and embedded with technical metadata that has been mapped to display in the Windows 'Properties' template, so that every image is fully identified as a digital object, no matter where it might be opened.[6] Then each folder of images, usually comprising one digitised manuscript, is manually edited for lighting corrections and clarity in Adobe Camera Raw, in order to produce images of maximum legibility for researchers. The fully processed Raw TIFFs are then saved as Master TIFFs, and these are used to produce various derivative image files, including JPEGs and PDFs. These are made

---

[6] For user awareness, the 'Date Digitized' from this technical metadata is also copied to the descriptive metadata displayed for the user on the METAscripta website. For an insightful discussion of managing digital data about manuscripts see Noel (2019). I am grateful to Will Noel, Lynn Ransom, Douglas Emery, and the whole team at the Schoenberg Institute for Manuscript Studies for their continued collegiality and support over many years of common interest in digital manuscript studies.

web-accessible using various software, including IIIF open-source image protocols (International Image Interoperability Framework), *Omeka S* web publishing tools, and *Mirador*, a IIIF-enabled image viewer with interactive display tools.[7] IIIF allows us to build a digital image platform that is interoperable with other IIIF repositories, including *Digivatlib*, the Vatican Library's own digitisation project, which *METAscripta* has been developed to support (BAV, *Digivatlib*).[8] Omeka S enables us to develop *METAscripta* using an out-of-the-box digital platform designed for cultural heritage projects and adaptable to IIIF.[9] The versatile *Mirador* viewer not only enables viewers to compare VFL microfilms with manuscripts digitised at other IIIF repositories, but also allows users to dynamically add annotations to any manuscript(s) they can open in *Mirador*. With *Mirador* annotation tools, users can search the internet for other resources, such as transcriptions, translations, still images, videos, or audio files, and link these to specified selections of any manuscript (Fig. 1).[10]

[7] I am especially grateful to Ben Bakelaar, METAscripta software architect and developer, for his work on the implementation of these digital resources and general collaboration with the technical aspects of the project. I also owe huge thanks to David Gohara, former SLU Director of Computational Research, for his dedication to this project.

[8] I am very grateful to the staff at the Vatican Library for their enthusiastic support of this project, including Vice Prefect Ambrogio Piazzoni, Metadata Librarian Paola Manoni, and Director of Photography Irma Schuler. I would also like to thank Francesca Manzari and her family for their warm hospitality while I was visiting Rome.

[9] Omeka S is integrated with IIIF through a series of plugins developed by Daniel Berthereau ('Modules', n.d.).

[10] Figures 1-3 are screen shots from my laptop running the Simple Annotation Server developed by Glen Robson, IIIF Technical Coordinator (Robson, n.d.). Many thanks to Glen for his help with this application, which I was

An important goal for *METAscripta* is to acknowledge researchers as information producers as well as consumers. The *METAscripta* Scholar's Workbench is thus designed not only for data access and retrieval but equipped with tools for data manipulation, transformation, and collaboration. These tools will serve to make *METAscripta* a personalised workspace for scholars doing online manuscript research.[11] A user interested in studying Vat. lat. 3199, the Dante manuscript once owned by Boccaccio, can compare the digitised VFL microfilm, adding annotations to the text, with the *Digivatlib* version of the same manuscript, adding annotations to the decoration, illustration, and physical characteristics – or the user can compare the microfilm of Vat. lat. 3199 with *Digivatlib* version of Vat. lat. 3197, the manuscript prepared by Pietro Bembo for printing the 1502 Aldine edition. To this comparison could be added a third manuscript, Ricc. 1035, preserved not at the BAV but at the Biblioteca Riccardiana in Florence, of interest as one of three autograph copies of the *Divine Comedy* written and illustrated by Boccaccio in his own hand (Fig. 2).[12] The Scholar's Workbench also allows registered users to save their work to personal accounts, choosing to keep their annotations private or make them available to other users.

introduced to at the Beinecke Library workshop, 'Mirador for Medievalists' (Albritton & Davis 2018).

[11] The workspace displayed in Figure 1 shows Vat. lat. 3199 opened in Mirador with annotations applied to the dedication by Boccaccio to Petrarch on Flyleaf c, verso and to Fol. 1, recto, with the opening of the First Canto of the Inferno. The pop-up window displays an open hyperlink to *Digital Dante* (Barolini 2019).

[12] Ricc. 1035 is digitized in IIIF at the World Digital Library ('The Divine Comedy', n.d.).

Figure 2

METAscripta, with user annotation tools enabled by IIIF/*Mirador*, applied to Vat. lat. 3199, Vat. lat. 3197, and Ricc. 1035.

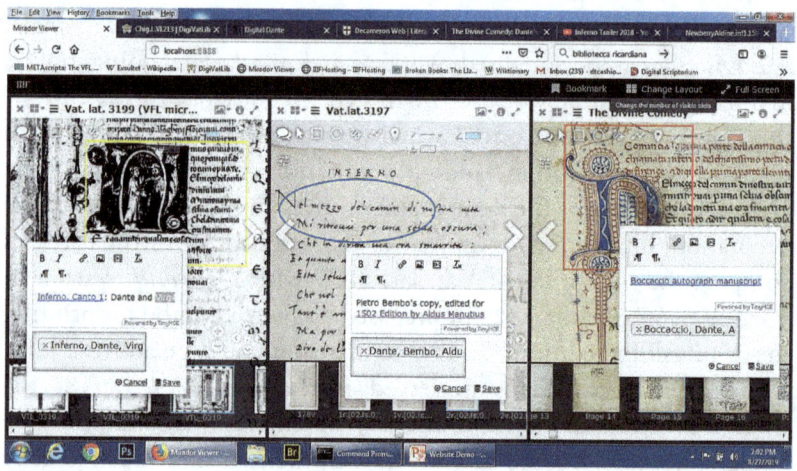

For a different research project, a user could use *METAscripta* to study Exultet Rolls, again using three manuscripts: Vat. lat. 9820, digitised only on VFL microfilm, Barb. lat. 592, and Vat. lat. 3784, the latter two digitised at *Digivatlib*. The three manuscripts were originally made in the tenth to the eleventh centuries, designed as pulpit scrolls to display to the congregation while the deacon sang the liturgy for lighting the Paschal candle on Easter Eve (Kelly 1996, 3-11; 245-253). Because they were working aids to worship, the three scrolls are all incomplete, revised, reconstructed, and rewritten for use in later periods. In order to study any one of them it is necessary to refer to other manuscripts to establish a context for the missing pieces, overpainted images, and fragmented texts. As we saw with the Dante manuscripts, *METAscripta* provides a digital environment in which that can happen, so that the three rolls can not only be compared but also annotated and linked to resources on the internet to help clarify the illustrations and reconstruct the text (Fig. 3).[13]

Figure 3

METAscripta, with user annotation tools enabled by IIIF/*Mirador*, applied to Vat. lat. 9820, Barb. lat. 592, and Vat. lat. 3784.

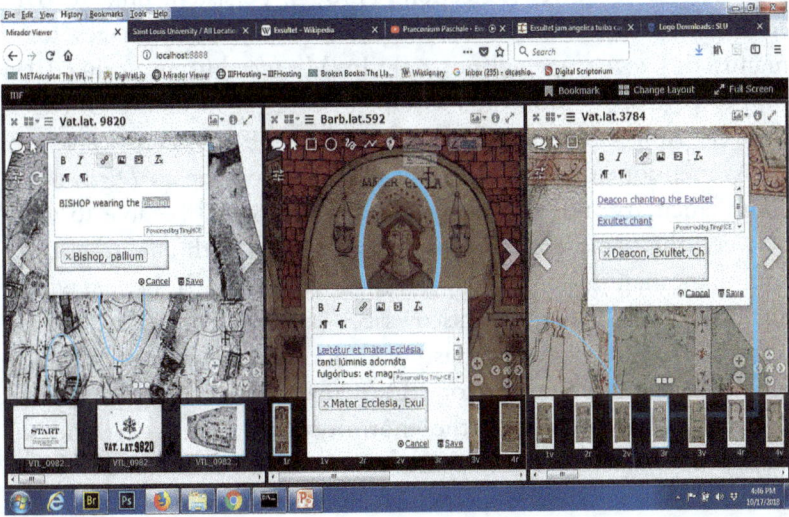

Besides the *Mirador* annotation tools, other open-source resources developed by the IIIF community include the Bodleian Library's IIIF Manifest editor, which we used to make the first JSON manifests needed in order for the *Mirador* viewer to display the digitised VFL

---

[13] The annotations illustrated in Fig. 3 include embedded links to: 1) a SLU library record (Schoenig 2016); 2) a *Wikipedia* article with the text and translation of the Exsultet text ('Exsultet', n.d.); 3) a *YouTube* video of a Deacon singing the liturgy on Easter Eve at St. Peter's in the Vatican ('Praeconium Paschale: Exsultet', 2013, 1 April); 4) the complete text and melody for the same chant in the *Cantus* database ('Exsultet jam angelica turba caelorum', n.d.).

manuscripts on microfilm (Bodleian Library Digital Manuscripts Toolkit).[14] The Bodleian editor generates a manifest from uploaded IIIF images and allows for adding customised embedded metadata, important to *METAscripta* in order to search the manuscripts using discovery tools as explained below. Once a complete IIIF manifest is created, it can be used as a template to generate manifests for all the manuscripts in a given collection. Through persistent links to IIIF-compliant image files, a IIIF manifest enables the images for a manuscript to be opened not only in *Mirador* but any other IIIF-supported display tool, such as Open Sea Dragon or the Universal Viewer ('Apps and Demos').

As mentioned above, *METAscripta*'s relationship to *Digivatlib* is complementary, not redundant, because users will be able to work between the two digital repositories, as well as with any other IIIF-compliant manuscript sites, to suit their needs.[15] *METAscripta* will be especially useful for users to discover BAV manuscripts related to their research because *Digivatlib* has not included the systematic creation of new catalog records for BAV manuscripts. This is quite understandable because of the enormity of the collection and the highly specialised labor required to catalog ancient texts. The traditional library access points of author/title, which for printed books are declared by title pages, are not easily determined for pre-modern manuscripts, which often do not self-identify their contents, place of origin, or date of production. Thus the cataloging of one of

[14] For more information about IIIF manifests see, 'IIIF Presentation API 2.0' (n.d.). I am grateful for the guidance of Andrew Hankinson of the Bodleian Library regarding the IIIF Presentation API.

[15] Besides *Digitvatlib*, a selection of IIIF manuscript repositories now include: 1) The Houghton Library ('Medieval and Renaissance Manuscripts'); 2) The Parker Library (*Parker on the Web: Manuscripts in the Parker Library at Corpus Christi College, Cambridge*); 3) The J. Paul Getty Museum, ('Getty Manuscripts')); 4) The Bodleian Library ('Western Medieval Manuscripts'.); e-Codices (*e-Codices*).

these challenging works demands the skills of an expert who must not only read pre-modern languages but also decipher elaborate book-hands and idiosyncratic scripts in order to identify the text.[16] The *METAscripta* project takes a different approach, one that still relies on skilled palaeography, or the assessment of scripts, but uses this and other evidence, such as illuminated decoration, to efficiently index manuscripts by language, century, and country of origin.[17] This cursory metadata allows catalogers to classify manuscripts as historical artifacts and helps users to discover materials in their areas of interest, while deferring description of the contents of the text to the scholar/expert. Using this expeditious method, SLU graduate students working on the project have so far cataloged about 6,500 manuscripts in the past 3 ½ years.[18]

The detailed description of the contents and all other attributes, however, is still the ultimate goal, and this will be made possible through user contributions. *METAscripta* will include a separate crowd-sourcing tool that will enable scholars to submit descriptive cataloging information about any BAV manuscript, without previous

---

[16] For an introduction to manuscript description, see Clemens and Graham (2007), 129–133.

[17] Selected resources in Latin palaeography include: Bischoff 1990, Brown 1990, De la Mare 1973, Derolez 2003, and Thomson 1969.

[18] I am grateful for the work of Blake Hartung, Amy Nelson, Beth Petitjean, Margaret Mary Summers, George Summers, John Thorpe, and Nathalie Whitaker, who as SLU graduate students have all contributed to researching and writing catalog records for the METAscripta project. I would also like to recognize the work of other SLU graduate and undergraduate students who have worked on various components of this complex project: Kirsten Buckner, Conor Dorn, Bing Han, Genna Hilbing, Jerris Kirkwood, Jacob Kopfensteiner, Bailey McCulloch, Emma McGilvray, Francesco Moro, Evie Nguyen, Kate Perko, Annie Pham, Sugandh Raj, Xander Sisco, Olivia Smithhisler, Katherine Tang, Sai Tanikonda.

training in library cataloging (Fig. 4). The discovery metadata

Figure 4

METAscripta, detail of model for the crowd-sourcing metadata template, which applies links to authority files and controlled vocabularies to the user-contributed metadata.

A CONTEXT Expandable field: + click to add multiple inputs	B CONTRIBUTE DATA User types free text in here	C LINK TO RECORD IN Dropdown menu for authorities	D COPY-PASTE PURL Add link to authority file
City:	Vatican City	VIAF	http://viaf.org/viaf/136038551
Institution:	Catholic Church	VIAF	http://viaf.org/viaf/130782063
Repository:	Biblioteca apostolica vaticana	VIAF	http://viaf.org/viaf/146085455
Shelfmark: +	Vat. lat. 3199	BAVdig	http://digi.vatlib.it/view/MSS_Vat.lat.3199
Nickname: +	Petrarch's Dante	BAVopac	http://www.mss.vatlib.it/gui/console?service=shortDetail&id=36507
Patron (first owner): +	User types free text in here	Dropdown menu for authorities	Add link to authority file
Dedicatee: +	User types free text in here	Dropdown menu for authorities	Add link to authority file
Provenance: +	Boccaccio	VIAF	http://viaf.org/viaf/64002165
Provenance: +	Petrarch	VIAF	http://viaf.org/viaf/39382430
Provenance: +	Pietro Bembo	VIAF	http://viaf.org/viaf/54144140
Insignia (coat of arms, etc.):+	User types free text in here	Dropdown menu for authorities	Add link to authority file
Date acquired: +	User types free text in here	Dropdown menu for authorities	Add link to authority file
Ex libris name: +	User types free text in here	Dropdown menu for authorities	Add link to authority file
Library Stamp: +	User types free text in here	Dropdown menu for authorities	Add link to authority file
Binding: +	User types free text in here	Dropdown menu for authorities	Add link to authority file

discussed previously is automatically fed into a crowd-sourcing metadata template to which users can add more information. The template is faceted according to context, carrier, and content, so that users are guided to focus on these various aspects of description separately.[19] User contributions are standardised and controlled through linking to online vocabularies and authority files such as *VIAF* (*VIAF: Virtual International Authority File*) and the *Getty Art*

---

[19] For an extended discussion of this method for cataloging medieval manuscripts see Cashion 2016.

and Architecture Thesaurus ('Getty Vocabularies', n.d.).[20] Built with the technology of Linked Open Data (LOD), these digital ontologies serve to unambiguously identify an author or describe a script, no matter what terms, spellings, languages, or even alphabets users employ to write them.[21] In order that one user cannot overwrite the contributions of another, the *METAscripta* crowd-sourcing catalog allows different users to catalog the same manuscript. Thus differing attributions or unresolved opinions about any other information will display for users to formulate their own judgments. We aspire to build this part of the project according to the Resource Description Framework (RDF) standards compliant with LOD, but this component may need to wait until the second stage of project development ('Resource Description Framework', 2014, 25 February).

Although *METAscripta* was to be presented at the cancelled IIIF conference to be hosted by Harvard and MIT in Cambridge, MA, 22-24 June 2020, it was launched in the Fall of 2020, and the digital development is almost complete. I am extremely grateful for the continued series of IIIF international conferences, working meetings, and community calls, and to the IIIF community for their generous collegiality, encouragement and support.[22] With a newly awarded

---

[20] I am especially grateful to Patricia Harpring of the Getty Research Institute for her knowledgeable guidance and support of this component of the METAscripta project, and to Elizabeth Morrison and David Newbury of the J. Paul Getty Museum for their generous guidance and encouragement concerning the implementation of IIIF.

[21] For explanations about Linked Open Data see Heath (n.d.) and 'The Getty Vocabularies as Linked Open Data (2019, 2 October)'. For the original Ted Talk about Linked Open Data see Lee (2009, 12 March).

[22] Individuals not mentioned previously but who have generously shared their experience with IIIF include Daniel Gullo, John Meyerhofer, Rashmi Singhal, and Jeffrey Witt. The collegiality of the international IIIF

grant from the SLU Research Growth Fund, *METAscripta* aspires to help lead Vatican manuscripts out of *archivio oscuro* and into the light of full access and retrieval through innovative metadata tools, based on cooperation and collaboration with users, scholars, and the community of people dedicated to the study of pre-modern manuscripts.[23]

community has really been an unexpected and inspirational experience—this project would not be possible without it.

[23] For support of this project at Saint Louis University I am grateful to David Cassens, Dean of University Libraries, Gregory Pass, Assistant Dean for Special Collections, David Gohara, Director of Computational Research, Kenneth Oliff, Vice President for Research, Jasmin Patel, Assistant Vice President for Research Strategy, and John McEwan, Associate Director of the Center for Digital Humanities. I am also very thankful for funding from the SLU Research Growth Fund supported by Rex Sinquefield, Board of Trustees and generous benefactor. I am also extremely indebted to Erica Lauriello, Donna Neely, and Ann Scales for indispensable administrative support.

III. The Future Worlds of Medieval Scholarship

CORPUS PHILOLOGY, BIG DATING AND BOTTOM-UP PERIODISATION

Mark Faulkner

All philological inquiry, whether classical or otherwise, is now a special case of corpus linguistics (Crane, Bamman and Jones 2013, 53)

The label 'philology' has been attached to a very wide range of approaches over the last two hundred years, ranging from a soaringly ambitious interdisciplinarity that saw all forms of cultural production as interconnected to (at least in the eyes of its detractors) an obsolescent if not obsolete obsession with textual minutiae.[1] But in its modern and narrowly linguistic sense, philology's principal goal is the description and contextualisation of the linguistic forms that can be found attested in historical texts. Thus, confronted with the spellings *long*, 'long' and *hronas*, 'whales' among a handful of annotations to a copy of Bede's *Historia ecclesiastica* in a mid-twelfth-century hand, a philologist might note that the spelling <o> for /a/ before a nasal consonant is generally accepted as an early West Saxon or Anglian feature (e. g. by Hogg 1992, §5.5) and, having considered other similar evidence, reason that the annotations are less likely to be spontaneous interjections than to have been copied from an earlier exemplar, recall that the language of early manuscripts of the Old

---

[1] From among an extensive bibliography on this topic, see particularly Ziolkowski 1990, Frank 1997, Pollock 2009, Drout & Kleinman 2009 and 2010, McGann 2014, and especially Turner 2014.

English Bede is Anglian in character, check the correspondence between the annotations and that text, and discover it was their source (Faulkner 2017a). In most work on medieval English conducted over the last century, as in that article, this contextualisation of linguistic forms has usually been effected through reference to published grammars, dictionaries and handbooks, yet five decades of work dedicated to the creation of machine readable texts, and to the development of corpus linguistic techniques and computer technology have now made it feasible to partially automate some of this contextualisation, and thereby to assess the distribution of features not treated in the grammars and to verify what is claimed about those that are. This paper provides an introduction to these techniques, which it subsumes under the label of 'corpus philology', in the context of 'big dating', an approach that seeks to explore the potential of studying the distribution of high frequency linguistic features to better place the composition of texts in time and space.

The dating scene

A clear understanding of when and ideally where and by whom the relevant texts were composed is a necessity for any literary history. This understanding is at present only partly available for medieval texts in general, and particularly those in Old and Early Middle English, which are the specific focus of this paper.[2] Thus, the date of composition of the 'Old English' Life of St Neot (Warner 1917, 129-34), extant only in a single manuscript of mid-twelfth-century date, remains controversial, with Godden (2011) arguing for its

---

[2] While there is an extensive literature on the dating of particular Old English poems, particularly *Beowulf* (e.g. Neidorf 2016), and some equivalent work exists for early Middle English (e.g. Parkes 1983; Cartlidge 1996) studies of the dating of prose texts are much less common (notable exceptions include Pelle 2015). The tacit consensus – for both prose and verse – often seems to be that medieval texts are not closely datable.

composition between 1015 and 1030 and Younge (2012) for an early-twelfth-century date. The cases for these putative dates are essentially circumstantial, with Godden and Younge arguing that particular features of the text, like its borrowings from Ælfric and Wulfstan, and attitude towards particular historical figures, like King Alfred, are more likely to have arisen at one date rather than another. While the Life's language has been featured in these discussions (Godden 2011, 201-2; Younge 2012, 353-4), it has not done so prominently, even though it potentially offers very important evidence. Features that might warrant consideration include words like *gelustfullung*, 'desire' (Warner 1917, 129/18), not found in Middle English; words like *gebīgan*, 'bow, bend' (Warner 1917, 133/13), used here in the sense 'to convert', found in Old English mainly in the works of Ælfric and perhaps attested in Middle English in this sense only in late copies of Old English works;[3] features of phrasal syntax like *bebēodan* + accusative (Warner 1917, 131/27) where dative is usual in Old English;[4] morphosyntactic features like the use of subjunctive *sēo*, 'he may be' (Warner 1917, 129/6), when s-subjunctives are very rare in Early Middle English (Förrstrom 1948, 221); and spellings like *-big*, 'by' (Warner 1917, 132/28), which is not the Vespasian scribe's usual spelling, and thus putatively an authorial feature, at present of unknown distribution in surviving Old English.[5] Since the dictionaries and handbooks presently available do not comment on

[3] DOE (Cameron et al. 2018) **ge·bīgan**, D; MED (Kurath et al. 2001) **beien**, 3, though only the third quotation, from a pre-Conquest homily (Pope 1967-8, no. 8) exemplifies the relevant sense.
[4] The accusative 'hine' in 'se king ælfred dyde þa swa se halge hine bebead' (Warner 1917, 131/27) is not explained by any of the uses of the accusative mentioned in DOE **be-bēodan**. Note however the two other occurences of *bebeodan* in the Life take the dative (Warner 1917, 131/5, 16).
[5] The usual spelling for the scribe who copied the Life is *beo*; for further discussion of his orthography and the significance of deviations from it, see Faulkner 2017b.

the distribution of these features in surviving Old and Middle English, there is for the moment no way of knowing if these and the hundreds of other forms that comprise the Life's 2,000 words provide significant evidence regarding its date.

We ought to be able to date medieval texts more precisely than we currently can. By way of parallel, let us briefly consider, by taking two sample pages more-or-less at random, the differences between the language of an early-twentieth-century novel, *My Man Jeeves* (Woodhouse 2006 [1919], 35) and an early-twenty-first-century one, *Milkman* (Burns 2018, 111). The former's use of 'dashed' as an adjective, the abbreviation 'O. P.' for the 'opposite prompt' in a theatre without further explanation, reference to a 'drawing-room' and 'Sunday Clothes' all suggest it is not a contemporary work; the latter's references to entities like 'motorcar parts', things being 'world-famous', a 'boyfriend' and (perhaps) topicalisation of the verb in 'shifted too, my fears did' suggest a date at least somewhere into the twentieth century. Data can often be found to support these intuitions; thus a Google Ngram for the word 'boyfriend' shows it was essentially unused before the 1940s and only begins to increase in frequency in the late 1960s.[6] Combine this with a consideration of forms found on the other 348 pages of *Milkman*, and it is not difficult to imagine one could come to a fairly secure sense that it post-dated the millennium or even that it was a work of the late 2010s.[7]

One might object that we do not have enough Old and Middle English to date the surviving texts more accurately, but a comparison of the surviving corpus of medieval English with that of modern

---

[6] It should be noted that doubts have been expressed about the reliability of drawing conclusions like this from these n-grams (e. g. by Gooding 2012, Pechenick et al. 2015 and Pettit 2016).

[7] We should also expect to be able to distinguish the date of *My Man Jeeves* and a more recent parody, like Faulks 2013, in much the same way as art historians can tell the difference between genuine paintings and subsequent imitations.

English suggests this scepticism is not wholly valid. Google's Ngram viewer draws on everything presently available through Google Books, which in 2012 comprised at least 8m volumes and almost 0.5tn words of English (Lin et al. 2012, 170), and has only got bigger since. As we will see, existing corpora for Old English enable us to harness at most 5m words, those for Middle English perhaps 15m words. Yet, this is not quite such a counsel of despair as it may seem, since for the eleventh century we can digitally search approximately 1.8m words out of perhaps 5m words that survive in manuscript, which represent what remains of perhaps 67m words copied in that period and thus about 2.7% of all textual production from that period (Faulkner 2020). As of 2012, Google had digitised 6% of all the books ever published (Lin et al. 2012, 170), more of course than the 2.7% of all the Old English that perhaps once existed which we might claim to control, but not as large a difference of magnitude as one might expect.

The available data

At present, the principal sources for contextualising the chronological and geographical spread of particular Old or Middle English features are handbooks and dictionaries. The major handbooks (e. g. Campbell 1959; Mustanoja 1960; Luick 1964; Brunner 1965; Mitchell 1985; Hogg 1992; Hogg & Fulk 2011; Ringe & Taylor 2014) are largely works of synthesis, which for their evidence rest primarily on nineteenth-century dissertations and monographs which exhaustively detailed the way particular medieval texts spelled the reflexes of the various Germanic vowels and consonants. While still essential, these handbooks do not cover all the features that might be of interest, are frequently unwilling to commit about the distribution of particular variants, and rest on datasets that are both limited and, given changes in the methods of editing texts since the nineteenth century, of questionable accuracy. For lexical features, we can turn to the Dictionary of Old English (Cameron et al. 2018) and Middle

English Dictionary (Kurath et al. 2001), though both – for different reasons – still need to be supplemented with corpus-based approaches if one is to comment authoritatively on the attestation of a particular word.[8]

The main data sources available to supplement the picture provided by the handbooks and dictionaries are the Dictionary of Old English Corpus (DOEC: diPaolo Healey et al. 2009), Manchester Eleventh-Century Spellings Database (C11DB: Scragg et al. 2004) and Linguistic Atlas of Early Middle English (LAEME: Laing 2013-).[9] The DOEC, which contains upwards of 3m words and 3,000 texts, claims to offer at least one copy of every 'Old' English text, though there are certainly omissions, such as the document *An is ece cyning*, discussed in more detail below. C11DB transcribes 978 texts from 272 manuscripts from the long eleventh century (a period it defines as spanning 980-1099), collectively 1.8m words, many of which are variant texts of works found in the DOEC, but here taken from different manuscripts than those which underlie the editions used there. LAEME includes 0.75m words from 169 texts from manuscripts dating between 1150 and 1350. While these resources do not offer data big by the norms of computer science, by the

---

[8] As an example, consider that for all but the rarest words, no dictionary, not even the peerless DOE, gives any more than illustrative citations, meaning that to comment authoritatively on a particular word's distribution, a corpus-based approach is a necessity.

[9] Also worth mentioning here is the Corpus of Middle English Prose and Verse (McSparran et al. 2006), which comprises at least 14m words of Middle English, largely digitised from Early English Text Society editions published in the nineteenth century. I relegate it to a footnote since it is a serious challenge to deploy in a robust way, thanks to the spelling variation endemic in Middle English. Pending funding to make C11DB available again officially, it has, with Professor Scragg's permission, been made available via the author's personal website (https://mark-faulkner.com/c11db).

standards of the data underpins philological handbooks, they are massive.

It is not however entirely straightforward to use these data sources to generate large datasets that can speak to the chronological and regional distribution of particular linguistic variants, in part because the user interfaces with which they are supplied were not built with this use in mind. Thus, the DOEC itself permits a very limited range of searches and offers very little scope for processing the results, but the compilers very generously make the most recently superseded release, from 2000, available for download via the Oxford Text Archive, and this can be loaded into a corpus linguistic programme like *Antconc* (Anthony 2019) to be searched in a far wider array of ways. Much the same is true of LAEME, which makes its component files available for download and use outside of the web interface through which it is mounted online. Since neither these resources nor the methods employed here to search them will be familiar to some medievalists, in what follows I first outline how one can use them to collect big data to study two particular linguistic features, then look at what the methods bring to the problem of dating of one particular text.

Mapping linguistic features 1: /hl-/

One of the features that distinguishes Old and Middle English is the presence in the former of a series of initial consonant clusters /hl-, hn-, hr-/ which simplify in the latter to /l-, n-, r-/ (I omit Old English /hw-/, which has a more complicated history in later English). Jordan (1974, §195) suggests:[10]

---

[10] See also Luick 1964, §704 which dates the change to the eleventh and twelfth centuries in all dialects except Kentish, where he says it occurred in the fourteenth; Anm. 1 gives a very full list of relevant forms. Hogg 1992: §7.48 non-committally notes in words with /h-/ as well as /hC-/ 'occasional example

> In hl, hn, hr, the h was silent generally already about 1000 (*laford* [Anglo-Saxon] Chron[icle] 1014, in the 12th cent., inversely *hnacod*, *hregen* [...])

His statement rests, however, on the slender foundations of three forms from two manuscripts, one perhaps a ghost,[11] the other two from a mid-twelfth-century south-eastern manuscript,[12] so one might wonder about the date he gives and whether it holds for the whole of England.[13] Fortunately, C11DB and LAEME, and the methods advocated in this paper, offer scope for testing it.

The compilers of C11DB manually inventoried all the spellings the texts it contains include into what it calls 'Lemma Groups'.[14] Thus Lemma Group 701 is devoted to *hlaford*, 'lord' and the compounds of which it is a part, the whole Lemma Group comprising 36 different

---

of the failure of initial [h] to be represented in spelling', noting a few texts where it is found with particular frequency. See also Brunner 1965, §217 Anm. 2.

[11] *Laford* does not occur in annal 1014 of manuscripts A, B, C, D, E or F of the Chronicle. The only instance of this spelling in the texts of the Chronicle in DOEC (which lacks a text only of manuscript B, which ends with annal 977) is in annal 1124 of the Peterborough Chronicle (Irvine 2004, 126/2).

[12] Both are from London, British Library, Cotton Vespasian D. xiv: Warner 1917, 2/16 (*hregn*); 4/8, 49/4, 125/4, 130/31, 137/10 (all *hnacod*; etymologically-correct *nacod* occurs once, at 125/4).

[13] Jordan's reliance on the evidence of 'occasional' spellings warrants note, as a methodological difference between traditional philology, where one-or-two such spellings are sufficient to establish the completion of a sound change, and corpus linguistics, which places much more emphasis on the ratio of 'new' spellings to 'old'. To my knowledge, the rights and wrongs of both approaches have not received sustained consideration by the practitioners of either discipline.

[14] For another example of how big data for the spelling of particular phonological segments (in this case /æɑ, æːɑ/) can be collected from C11DB and LAEME, see Faulkner (forthcoming).

spellings, including (expected) *hlaford*, but also forms like *hlafurd*, *laforas* and so on. To study how words that historically began /hl-/ are spelled in C11DB, we first identify all Lemma Groups containing at least one <(-)hl(-)> spelling, then check the relevance of each (excluding, for instance, the Lemma Group containing *fuhlas*, 'birds', where <-hl-> appears for /-xl-/). This leads to a list of 41 pertinent Lemma Groups, comprising 402 separate spellings, which, when searched for in the C11DB text files, leads to a list of 3,127 occurrences across 527 texts in 118 manuscripts, of which 3,018 (96.5%) are spelled <hl->. These spellings can then be examined by text, revealing for example that the copyist of the Will of Ælfric, Bishop of Elmham in Norfolk, composed 1023x1038 (and extant in a contemporary single-sheet), used <hl-> just once, beside two <l-> spellings.[15] One can also look at the frequency of <hl-> spellings by date, which reveals a significant decline in consistency only in manuscripts copied in the late eleventh century, when only 92 (85.2%) of 108 relevant forms are spelled <hl->, or by manuscript provenance.[16]

LAEME is lexically-tagged, so recovering comparable data for Early Middle English is relatively straightforward, the only obstacle being that words that historically began *hl-* are tagged in two distinct ways, with their Old English form if they do not survive in present-day English and with their present-day English descendent if they do. Having identified the 81 relevant tags ('lexels', in LAEME's parlance), we search the LAEME files for their occurrence, finding 3,158 forms across 118 texts, which we can examine by text, by manuscript date and by the place with which LAEME associated the language of each.

---

[15] Sawyer 1968, no. 1489 ed. Whitelock 1930, no. 26: *laforde* (70/19), *lafordas* (70/21), bedside *hlefdigen* (72/5).

[16] One question that at present remains to be answered is how representative the manuscripts transcribed for C11DB are of texts copied in the eleventh century more generally.

The picture that emerges is that <hl-> spellings are rare in early Middle English and very seldom, in a given dating window, occur in more than 10% of relevant examples, suggesting very significant change between the eleventh and twelfth centuries, as represented in C11DB and LAEME respectively. Such striking differences between late Old English and early Middle English have been a relatively common finding in the early stages of this work, and what exactly they indicate remains an open question.[17] But the data does suggest that, all other things being equal, Jordan's blanket date of c. 1000 for the simplification of initial *hC-* clusters seems doubtful. From the point of view of dating, moreover, any text that consistently uses <l-> for *hl-* is more likely to have been composed in the twelfth century than the eleventh (or, alternatively, that its language was very thoroughly modernised in that period). Similar generalisations may also be possible about <n-> for *hn-* and <r-> for *hr-*; the data is available from C11DB and LAEME.

Mapping linguistic features 2: *heom*, 'them'

While in earlier Old English the dative plural of the third-person pronoun is usually *him*, in eleventh- and twelfth-century manuscripts it is frequently *heom*. According to the grammars, the latter form is late West Saxon and appears from 1000 onwards.[18] Its consistent

---

[17] Possible answers might include the difference being not real but a consequence of the selection of texts in LAEME (and to a lesser extent, C11DB), the disparity in dialectal origins of the majority of Old English texts and those that survive for Early Middle English, a significant change in the praxis for writing English after the Norman Conquest (indicative of discontinuity between Old and Middle English scribal traditions) or, less likely, substantial (perhaps contact-induced) change in the language itself.

[18] Campbell 1959, §704 ('late West Saxon especially after 1000'); Brunner 1965, §334 ('im 10 Jh. vereinzelt, vom 11 Jh. an häufig'); Hogg & Fulk 2011, §5.17(4) ('starts to appear in some Ælfrician texts and is frequent thereafter').

presence or absence in an Old English text may therefore be a dating criterion. Prior to using it in this way, it is important however to test the validity of the generalisation the handbooks make about its distribution. This can be done using corpus philological methods.

Heom occurs 1,798 times in the DOEC (this figure does not include instances the compilers placed in angled brackets to indicate they derive from editorial emendation). One could read through each of these matches to verify that each is dative plural, but such a procedure would be extremely laborious and perhaps eliminate only one or two datapoints from consideration. Ideally, we would examine the frequency of *heom* relative to all other forms of the dative plural used in a particular text, but here the homography of another very common form of the dative plural, *him*, with the usual dative singular of the personal pronoun, would make this a work of days rather than hours. Instead we can calculate the frequency with which *heom* occurs per million words, assuming that texts will tend to use the dative plural of the third-person pronoun with approximately equal frequency and that a higher frequency for *heom* per million words corresponds to a scribal preference for this form over other potential alternatives.

To explore the distribution of *heom* over time and space, we need metadata. The DOEC attaches only minimal metadata directly to the texts it contains, but each is equipped with a number (e. g. B3.4.37) which cross-references it to the 'List of Old English Texts' (Cameron 1973). This in turn provides a cross-reference to an appropriate handlist or catalogue that in turn supplies an indication of the date and (where available) origin or provenance of the witnesses that preserve the text. Thus for non-documentary texts, it provides a list of manuscripts in which that text is preserved, and the numbers of those manuscripts in Ker 1957's *Catalogue of Manuscripts Containing Anglo-Saxon*, while for documentary texts, it makes reference to Sawyer 1968's annotated list of Anglo-Saxon charters. The list also indicates which edition the compilers of the DOEC took their text from and, by consulting that edition, it is usually possible to identify which witness it used as its base manuscript and, with the help of the handlists or catalogues mentioned above, to assign the language of the received text to a particular date and place.[19] It is at present possible to download from the 2009 web version of the DOEC a spreadsheet containing word counts for each of the texts, and by augmenting this with metadata derived in the manner described in the preceding sentences regarding the dates, origins and/or provenances of the witnesses which underlie each edition, it becomes a tool that allows the distribution of forms like *heom* to be plotted over space and time. Thus B3.4.37, an anonymous homily printed by Napier (1883, no. 46) as 'Larspell' contains one instance of *heom* in its 2,601 words of Old English, a rate of one *heom* every 384 words. Napier's base manuscript was his 'B', then Cambridge, Corpus Christi Cambridge, MS S. 14 and now MS 419, a manuscript of the first half of the eleventh century whose language is otherwise attested in seven other texts in the DOEC and which is one of ninety-nine manuscripts containing writing of this date represented in the corpus.

The easiest way to get an overview of *heom*'s distribution is to plot its occurrence per million words by the date of the witnesses in which it appears, reducing some of the surface discord by normalising these dates into twenty-five year windows (Fig. 1).[20]

On first glance, it may seem a little odd that the dates on the x-axis range from 400 to 1800, but one must remember that the earliest text in the DOEC is the inscription on a piece of deer bone found in

---

[19] It should be noted that the 2000 version may sometimes use a more recent edition of a particular text than that mentioned in Cameron 1973. Bibliographical details of these are available in the headers to the component html files.

[20] The chart excludes 42 datapoints where the editions used by the DOEC are based on multiple witnesses or where it is unclear what witnesses the editions used.

Figure 1

Frequency of *heom* per million words, by date of witness underlying DOEC text

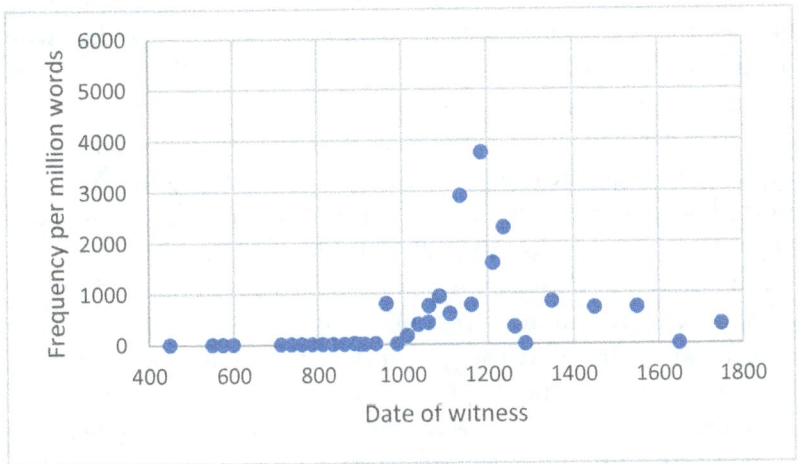

a cremation urn at Caistor-by-Norwich (E8), dated by Page (1999: 179) to the fifth century, and that not insignificant numbers of Old English texts only survive in post-medieval transcripts, most famously perhaps *The Battle of Maldon.* Having discounted the outlying datapoint for the mid-tenth century which derives entirely from the frequent use of *heom* in Farman's portion of the Rushworth Gospels (Oxford, Bodleian Library, D. 2. 19), dated 's. x' by Ker (1957, no. 292), it is clear that the handbooks are essentially correct that *heom* is used with any frequency only after 1000.[21] The data also helps us

---

[21] The only other instance from a witness predating the millennium, excepting the example mentioned in the next footnote, is a single instance in Sawyer 1968, no. 878 (ed. Sawyer 1979, 46/24), a charter of King Æthelræd for his minister, Wulfric, granting land at Abbots Bromley in Staffordshire, dated 996 and extant in a contemporary witness. In Early Middle English, as a

identify the earliest use of *heom*, which is to be found in the will of Ælfred, ealdorman of Surrey, written 871x889 and extant in a contemporary single-sheet and is, interestingly, like the Rushworth Gospels, a Mercian text.[22] On its own, the distribution of *heom* does not perhaps prove much, but, as I show below, taken in tandem with other linguistic variants, it may have the power to illuminate when particular texts were written.

Before moving to an example of how these corpus philological approaches might help date a text, two methodological points are worth highlighting. First, at the moment the data collected for each linguistic feature speaks primarily to its distribution in the surviving manuscripts, that is its place in scribes' passive repertoires rather than authors' active repertoires.[23] In trying to use it to date the composition of texts, we are therefore using what is for the moment quite a crude implement, though one that has, as we shall see, the potential to be quite effective. Second, while we are striving to design methods for assessing the distribution of particular features as precisely as possible, we are not necessarily aiming for the rigorously-vetted data that a historical-linguistic study would require, where each datapoint is verified to ensure it represents the feature in question, and coded according to multiple variables, such as (for example) information structure or prosodic weight, to check that factors other than mere date and place of composition do not explain a particular form's appearance in a particular context in a particular text. Coding and

LAEME search for $/P23Oi shows, *him* was the exception rather than the rule, occuring in just 15 (2.0%) of 759 forms with the form *hVC*.

[22] 'twa þusendu swina ic heom [*scil*. Werburge 7 Alhdryðe uncum gemenum bearne] sello' (Brooks & Kelly 2013, 2.809/9 = Sawyer 1968, no. 1508).

[23] Its potential value for localising texts (or at least to better understand the geographical currency of particular linguistic variants at particular times) suffers from similar limitations, since for most texts we do not know the location in which the author wrote and often only have a later provenance for the manuscript in which it is preserved (and sometimes not even that).

checking several thousand or more forms for five or more variables is simply not feasible for hundreds of different linguistic features; we rely instead on the hope that large datasets, or at least some large datasets, will reflect (however crudely) broad changes in the distribution of particular variants across time.

Corpus philology in action: a case study of dating

Sawyer 1968, no. 136 is ostensibly a diploma of King Offa in favour of St Albans, dated 793, granting estates in Hertfordshire and Middlesex, ordaining they should be held in perpetual freedom, exempt from all taxes and that, insofar as was possible, the monastery should be and remain Benedictine.[24] Until the early 1990s, the diploma was known only as a Latin text, preserved in three surviving St Albans cartularies and a series of *inspeximus* copies made from the fourteenth century onward. However, a Bollandist transcript of a now-lost St Albans cartulary discovered in 1993 revealed two separate English texts of the diploma, one (which I shall call, after its first words, *Gode rihsiendum on ecnesse*) a relatively faithful translation of the Latin, but incorporating additional estates granted by Offa in a separate diploma (Sawyer 1968, no. 138), the other (which I shall name, on similar grounds, *An is ece cyning*) rather less close textually, but nonetheless confining itself to the estates mentioned in Sawyer no. 136.[25] The Bollandist responsible for the transcript (unsurprisingly) did not know Old English, and several letters are consistently difficult to distinguish in his handwriting, so that while Crick, in her edition of the St Albans charters in 2007, was able to resolve a considerable number of textual problems, she nonetheless described parts of *An is ece cyning* as 'garbled in transmission and

---

[24] It is edited by Crick 2007, 109-11.
[25] Brussels, Bibliothèque Royale, 7965-73 (3723), fols 151-216, brought to scholarly attention by Keynes 1993. *Gode rihsiendum on ecnesse* and *An is ece cyning* are edited by Crick 2007, 119-23, 112-24.

extremely difficult to construe' (Crick 2007, 113, as well as 114, 115). However, in a forthcoming article, I offer new editions of both it and *Gode rihsiendum on ecnesse*, which while not settling all the challenges they pose, significantly improve on Crick's texts.[26]

The Latin of S136 has long been thought to be spurious, at least in its received form.[27] It is betrayed by the inconsistency between its incarnational date (793), indiction (3) and regnal year (Offa's thirty-third),[28] by the appearance of among the witnesses of eight kings of Mercia between Coenwulf (796-821) and King Alfred (overlord 880-899), but not in entirely the correct sequence,[29] by the structure of its

---

[26] Pending this article's publication, I cite the texts of both *An is ece cyning* and *Gode rihsiendum on ecnesse* from Crick, but note any places where the readings I propose differ.

[27] Kemble (1839-48, 1.197-9) marked it with the asterisk he used to denote documents that were 'ascertained forgeries, or ... liable to suspicion' (1.cxv). Earle (1888, 395) classed it with fourteen other 'transparent fabrications' from St Albans. Haddan and Stubbs (1869-1878, 3.480) looked on it slightly more favourably, judging the evidence 'strongly against' its authenticity, but not 'conclusively condemnatory'. Stevenson (1914, 702n61) placed it in a list of 'late and clumsy fabrications'. Gelling (1979, no. 162) denoted it as 'fundamentally a fabrication', while acknowledging that the opening formulation and dispositive section might be genuine. Scharer (1982, 272-73) dismissed it as a fabrication, like the rough forgery (*grobe Fälschung*) Sawyer 1968, no. 138, another St Albans document to which he argues it is closely related. Opinion remains divided about the extent to which this might be true, Cubitt (1995, 274) denounces the document as 'a blatant forgery', while Taylor (1995, 142) has argued that forgery at St Albans was 'on a modest scale and basically interpolative'. Barrow (1999, 108) treads a middle path, labelling the document a forgery, but suggesting it has some basis in fact.

[28] As Keynes (1993, 271) 271 notes, 793 was instead indiction 1 and Offa's thirty-third year, calculated from his accession to the throne in 757, would have been 789-90.

[29] As Crick (2007, 116) notes, the source was probably a regnal list.

dispositive section,[30] by its pronouncement that the land is given with 'perpetual freedom' and should be free 'from all tribute and obligation to a king or a bishop or an earl or to judges or to noblemen, or even to officials and for works which are accustomed to be assigned, including indeed campaigns and all public ordinance',[31] and by various other features, including its style (Scharer 1982, 273).

If, as the consensus is, Sawyer no. 136 is likely to be largely spurious, one question that naturally arises is at what date or dates it was confected. The outer limits for its production are its ostensible date of 793 and that of its earliest witnesses, both of which belong to the mid-thirteenth century.[32] These however likely replicate a compilation of the twelfth century (Keynes 1993, 262; Crick 2007, 42-3). Crick has narrowed the dating window still further, arguing that its forgery must postdate the production of S916, an authentic diploma of King Æthelred for St Albans dated 1007, which describes the restoration of lands in Hertfordshire, earlier granted by Offa to St Albans, but makes no mention of any charters of the Mercian king, but predate the Norman Conquest, after which St Albans is unlikely to have sanctioned either episcopal or royal influence on its choice of abbot.[33]

Beyond a brief and somewhat lapidary comment by Keynes, the language of the English versions of S136 has not featured in these

---

[30] See Scharer 1982, 272-73, esp. 273n24.
[31] 'Ab omni tributo et necessitate seu regis, seu episcopi, ducis, iudicium, comitum, exactorum etiam et operum que indici solent, necnon et expeditionis, et omni edicto publico' (Crick 2007, 110/10-12); 'perpetuo … libertate' (Crick 2007, 110/12).
[32] Dublin, Trinity College, MS 177, fols 63r-64r; London, British Library, MS Cotton Nero D. i, fol. 149r.
[33] Crick (2007, 61) and her no. 11. Barrow (1999, 108 and 115n18), acknowledging advice from Crick, suggests a late-tenth-century date for S136.

discussions regarding its date.[34] Once errors introduced by the Bollandist copyist and perhaps the twelfth-century cartulary scribe have been eliminated, that language is essentially the late West Saxon that served as a type of standard language in England from approximately the mid tenth century to the early twelfth. Deviations in *An is ece cyning* are usually regular: the accusative singular masculine of the demonstrative pronoun is consistently *þæne* not *þone* (112/18, 27, 29; 113/1), there is some interchange of <e, æ, a> in low-stressed forms (e. g. *efter*, 'after' (112/18), *et*, 'at' (112/33), *þer*, 'there' (112/15),[35] *þet* (112/31) beside *þæt* (112/15) etc), /v/ is usually <u> rather than <f> as it had been in Old English,[36] subjunctive plural

---

[34] 'The language of the vernacular versions of Offa's grants suggests that the forgeries existed in some form or other by the end of the eleventh century (or not far into the twelfth)' (Keynes 1993, 273).

[35] There is another instance earlier in the document of *þer* (Crick 2007, 112/7), but Faulkner (forthcoming) suggests this should perhaps be read *þet*.

[36] The relevant spellings are *heofena* (112/2), *luuige* (112/2), *hauað* (112/5), *sylues* (112/11), *syluum* (112/13, 27), *loue* (112/13), *sirreua* (112/16, on which see below), *lufige* (112/19), *liue* (112/25), *lyfe* (112/25, where it is Crick's emendation of *lysue* and *lyue* is an equally feasible alternative) and *heofonan* (113/3). According to the testimony of C11DB, spellings with <-u-> are rare in eleventh-century manuscripts, with it found intervocallically on only 71 (0.4%) occasions, to 15,918 instances of <-f->, and with only five texts using <-u-> in 50% or more of the occasions where the relevant environment occurs. This may perhaps understate its frequency, a least between a vowel and a voiced consonant, since a search of the DOEC shows that <-u-> spellings are found in *sylf*, 'self' at least 23 times before the Conquest. Pending more detailed data, the balance of probability nonetheless remains that the predominance of <-u-> spellings in the extant text of *An is ece cyning* is a consequence of a reviser working at some point between the mid-eleventh and mid-twelfth-century.

present ends *-an* rather than *-en*,[37] and God is *Drihten* (112/1, 3, 9) rather than etymologically-correct *Dryhten*. Also notable is unsyncopated, unumlauted *hauað*, '[he] has' (112/5). This general regularity suggests the scribe who copied the twelfth-century cartulary that ultimately underlies the Brussels transcript in large part faithfully reproduced what was in front of him.

In general terms, the consistent use of standard Old English spelling in *An is ece cyning* suggests it was composed when that variety was in current use, that is some time between the mid-tenth and early-twelfth century. The homogeneity of its language suggests it cannot have been subject to significant interpolation after this date. The exception that proves the rule here is *An is ece cyning*'s exemption clause, which frees the granted lands from any interference from various parties, including the *sirreua*, 'sheriff' (Crick 2007, 112/16). *Sirreua* is by some margin the most advanced spelling in the entire text, in its use of <s> for /ʃ/, its omission of the *-ge-* typically found in pre-Conquest occurrences of the noun, and its reduction of the oblique weak noun inflection *-an* to *-a*, which is not otherwise found in *An is ece cyning*.[38] The chronological distribution of <s>-spellings has only been partly mapped in earlier work.[39] Corpus philological

---

[37] The relevant forms are *gebyrian* (112/9); *ceosan* (112/27); and *wyllan* (112/28).

[38] Oblique forms of weak nouns otherwise exclusively end *-an*: *naman* (112/3, 6, 11, 31), *gewunan* (112/5), *eorþan* (113/1). See also nominative plural *geferan* (112/27).

[39] Scragg (1974, 46) does not mention <s> in his consideration of spellings for /ʃ/. It is noted, however, by Jordan (1974, §181), Bourcier (1978, 102) and Upward & Davidson (2011, 157), who observe 'marked regional differences' in the use of the different spellings available, but do not comment further on their distribution, either geographically or chronologically. Dietz (2006, 158-9) lists a number of <s>-spellings in eleventh- and twelfth-century manuscripts, though noting they are rare until around 1150. Fisiak (1968,

methods let us improve on this picture, noting that among 16,308 spellings for words with initial /ʃ/ in eleventh-century manuscripts, C11DB contains just three (0.02%) that begin <s->.[40] The earliest manuscript in LAEME to contain <s-> spellings is that of the Trinity Homilies, from the final quarter of the twelfth century.[41] Pending a better method for determining its emergence, <s-> can thus, with some certainty, be described as a twelfth-century innovation. The earliest secure spelling of 'sheriff' without *-ge-* that can be found in the DOEC is in a manumission from Exeter in which Alice, the sister of Richard, sheriff of Devon (occ. 1107 x 1128), frees one Hrothwulf, palaeographically datable to the first half of the twelfth century.[42] While no ready way is yet available for obtaining a 'big' data picture of the denasalisation of weak noun endings, it is clear from the evidence of the initial <s-> and the omitted *-ge-* that *sirreua* is unlikely to have entered the document before 1100. This fits neatly with the

§2.57) says <s> is found in the South-East and North and restricted to unaccented syllables and words.

[40] These are *sæcdom* (i. e. *sceacdom*, 'flight') in Gen 31.21 in the Old English Heptateuch in Oxford, Bodleian Library, MS Laud misc. 509 (ed. Marsden 2008, 59, based on this manuscript); *seortran*, 'shorter' in the copy of Ælfric's *De temporibus anni* in London, British Library, Cotton Caligula A. xv (ed. Blake 2009, 84/209, printing *scyrtan* from his base manuscript, Cambridge, University Library, MS Gg. 3. 28); and *seolde*, 'must', in the copy of Ælfric's First Series Homily for St Stephen's Day in Oxford, Bodleian Library, MS Bodley 340 (ed. Clemoes 1997, 201/97). The form *seatan* in Lemma Group 1181 appears to be a ghost, since it does not occur in any of the texts included in C11DB, nor can it be found in DOEC.

[41] For /ʃ-/, Hand A has <s-> x 25 (27.8%), <sc-> x 5 and <sh-> x 60. On the scribes of this manuscript, Cambridge, Trinity College, MS B. 14. 52, see more generally Laing & McIntosh (1995).

[42] Pelteret (1990, no. 96), a manumission preserved in Exeter, Cathedral Library, MS. 3501, fol. 4r and edited by Earle (1888, 258). For Richard's dates, see Green (1990, 35).

historical context that saw the importance of sheriffs increase considerably after the Conquest so that by the twelfth century they were the 'chief financial officers in the localities' and thus a potential thorn in the side of monastic houses (Green 1990, 10), as well as fitting with Crick's suggestion (2007, 62, 65) that the immunity clauses of the Latin of S136 and *An is ece cyning*, which bear a close resemblance to *Ad hoc nos* (the bull Calixtus II issued in favour of St Albans in 1122), were subject to further tampering into the first quarter of the twelfth century. Its distinctively modern spelling suggests other late interpolations into *An is ece cyning* would be readily detectable.

An is ece cyning conversely contains one form which suggests its forger may have been drawing on earlier written materials. It occurs in the opening invocation of 'ure drihten Crist, þe ecelice rihsað a buton ende' (112/1). The Brussels manuscript in fact reads 'riihsað', but Crick emended it to 'rihsað' on the grounds that the copyist had misread insular r as <ri>.[43] Geminate spellings are sometimes found for long vowels in Old English manuscripts, but less frequently in the eleventh century, though the unusualness of the form's use of <-hs-> for /-ks-/ means it is possible 'riihsað' is the correct reading.[44] Spellings with <-hs-> for /-ks-/ have generally been described as 'early

---

[43] Faulkner (forthcoming) reinstates the manuscript reading.
[44] Both Campbell (1959, §26) and Hogg (1992, §2.4) say such spellings are confined to early manuscripts. Later instances are found in the mid-eleventh-century manuscripts London, BL, Cotton Tiberius B. i, where the spelling *tiid* is frequent in the *Menologium* (e. g. Karasawa 2015, lls. 5a, 45a, 57a etc), and London, British Library, Cotton Tiberius A. iii, where there are several such spellings (e. g. *æbyliigða, þiinum, biicgan*: Chardonnens 2007, 311/224, 322/602, 412/228) among the glossed dreambook and lunary prognostics on fols. 27v-35v, as well as in the directions for the use of a charm added to Cambridge, Corpus Christ College, 391, pp. 617-18 around 1100, with its imperative *geciig*, 'call' (ed. Zupitza 1892, 364/3). This list is by no means exhaustive.

West Saxon', but the DOEC shows that it also occurs in tenth-century compositions, like Æthelwold's account of the revival of monasticism, and was very likely part of the active repertoire of at least one early-eleventh-century scribe and in the eleventh and even twelfth centuries continued to be reproduced in copies of earlier texts.[45] But it remains rare in eleventh-century manuscripts, occurring just four times in C11DB (of 613 instances of the verb), all in the copy of the Old English translation of Gregory's Pastoral Care produced at Exeter for Bishop Leofric in the third quarter of the eleventh century, so there is some possibility it was not the natural usage of the author of *An is ece cyning* but borrowed by him from a model.[46] This is a supposition strengthened by the use of written

---

[45] Campbell (1959, §416); Brunner (1965, §209); Hogg (1992, §2.51, §7.6). The form 'rihsigende', 'reigning' occurs in the opening peroration of Æthelwold's account of King Edgar's establishment of monasteries (ed. Whitelock et al. 1981, 143/10). A search of DOEC shows the s. xi[1] scribe of the copy of Ælfric's *Sermo de die Iudicii* in Cambridge, Corpus Christi College, MS 178 (ed. Pope 1967-8, 599/213) has *rihsað* here but *ricsað* two lines later; the other witness, Oxford, Bodleian Library, MS Hatton 115 has in both cases *rixað*, which appears to have been Ælfric's preferred spelling, to judge by the manuscript of *CH* 1 produced under his own supervision (Godden 2000, 756). A mid-twelfth-century instance of the reproduction of a <-hs-> spelling is in the Eadwine Psalter's gloss to Ps 64.4 (Harsley 1889, 106).

[46] In C11DB, the dominant spelling for the medial cluster is <x> (86.8%), with most of the remaining instances spelled <cs> (11.1%). The manuscript of the Old English translation of Gregory's Pastoral Care is Cambridge, University Library, MS. Ii. 2. 4 (the spellings there, *ryhsodon, rihsiað* (x2) and *rihsode* correspond to Sweet 1871-2, 27/14, 27/15, 33/13; in each case Oxford, Bodleian Library, MS Hatton 20, the copy King Alfred sent to Worcester, has <-cs->). In C11DB, the spelling <-hs-> is considerably more common in forms of *axian*, and it also occurs in *weaxan*.

sources by the forger of the Latin text of Sawyer no. 156.[47]

But even if the forger used earlier materials, and his forgery was augmented in the first quarter of the twelfth century, its linguistic centre of gravity is clearly in the eleventh century. The document uses a number of words not found in early Middle English texts, including *gedafenlic* (112/2),[48] as well as *estfullum* (112/13) in its Old English sense of 'devout, pious' rather than its Middle English one of 'pleasure-seeking, fastidious, delicate',[49] not to mention the hapax legomena *ealdorcyre*, 'choice of leader' (112/29),[50] *minsterlagan*, 'monastic jurisdiction' (112/7),[51] and (if it should not be emended)

---

[47] Crick (2007, 116) shows that the forger of the Latin text of S136 used a late-eighth-century synodal document and a Mercian regnal list, so it would not be altogether surprising if *An is ece cyning* also had written models. To this it might be added that the spelling *ond*, 'and', which conjoins the grant at *Heanhamstede* to that at Cassio in the three major manuscripts deriving from the lost cartulary of the Latin of the document (Crick 2007, 109/7), seems likely to go back to a source of the tenth century or earlier, a possibility latent in Gelling's suggestion (1979, no. 162) that the dispositive section might rely on some genuine material.

[48] MED **idafenlīch** cites only two late copies of Old English texts, both works of Ælfric (Morris 1867-8, 221/34 = Clemoes 1997, 181/86; Belfour 1909, 72/27 = Irvine 1993, 73/354).

[49] Crick (2007, 112/13) prints 'þe ic geo frige est fullum mode Gode syluum to loue', which Faulkner and Boorman respace to 'þe ic geofrige estfullum mode Gode syluum to loue'. On the semantics, see DOE **ēst-full**, 2; MED **ēst-ful**.

[50] The DOE has no entry for *ealdorcyre* but lists no less than 24 other compounds of which *ealdor-* is the first element. It does not however include any in which *-cyre* is the second element.

[51] *Minsterlagan* is printed by Crick (2007, 112/7) as two words, but Faulkner (forthcoming), guided by the absence of an inflection on *minster*, restores it as a compound. Compounds with *mynster-* as their first element are common in Old English; particularly close parallel formations include *mynsterland*, 'land owned by a monastery' and *mynsterþeaw*, 'monastic custom'.

Angolleodan, 'English people' (113/1).⁵² Precisely what proportion of the vocabulary of Old English texts late-eleventh- and twelfth-century writers inherited remains unclear, but a text that uses a range of words not otherwise attested in compositions of this period is more likely to have been written earlier. *An is ece cyning*'s inclusion of these words thus suggests a terminus ante quem somewhere around 1100. Its use of *minsterlagan*, moreover, suggests a date during or after the reign of Æthelred (978–1016), when according to Pons-Sanz (2013, 158), *lagu* became 'fully naturalised as a legal term'.⁵³ If *eorl* is not like *sirreua* an interpolation into the exemption clause, and if it is equivalent to the *dux* to whom the Latin waives any obligation, its use may point to points to a date of composition after the accession of Cnut in 1016, though this is somewhat complicated by its appearance in collocation with 'ceorl', a formula of very considerably longer

---

⁵² *Angollēodan* is printed by Crick (2007, 113/1) as two words, but Faulkner (forthcoming), again guided by the absence of an inflection on the first element, treats it as a compound. It is possible this unattested *Angollēod* should be emended to the commoner *Angelþēod*. In any case, neither the compound *Angelþēod* nor the element *Angel-* appears to survive into Middle English.

⁵³ While *lagu* is usually strong feminine in Old English, unambiguously weak forms are also attested from at least the millenium, for instance the gloss '*Decretum .i. institutum . **statutum** . diffinitum . iudicium . positum . consilium . placitum .* geþoht *. laga . gesetnes . sollicitum*' from the Harley Glossary, copied c. 1000 in the West of England (Oliphant 1966, 118-9 (gloss D2)), the gloss 'legum: lagena oþþe æa' in the glosses to Prudentius copied early in the eleventh century, probably at Canterbury (Meritt 1959, no. 12) and twice (as the second element of a compound) in an anonymous homily, 'To eallum folke', from the mid-eleventh-century London, British Library, Cotton Tiberius A. iii (Napier 1883, 274/7, 11). On weak forms in early Middle English texts from the West Midlands, see Dance (2003, 85).

standing.⁵⁴ Two spellings, consistently used in *An is ece cyning* and therefore perhaps more likely to be authorial rather than scribal, also suggest an eleventh-century date. *Heom*, which is the spelling of the dative plural of the personal pronoun on its two occurrences in *An is ece cyning*, is, as we saw above, found with any frequency only in manuscripts from the first quarter of the eleventh century onward.⁵⁵ For the grammars, accusative singular masculine *þæne*, the sole form used in *An is ece cyning*, is late and mostly West Saxon.⁵⁶ The 'big' data methods here help us narrow down its currency chronologically and show <æ> spellings were rare in the tenth century manuscripts but peak in books copied between about 1025 and 1100.⁵⁷

The linguistic evidence presented above thus suggests that *An is ece cyning* was composed in the eleventh century, confirming the plausibility of Crick's more contextual dating of 1007x1066. This linguistic evidence is still rather slighter than one might like, largely because the document's general adherence to 'standard' Old English means it contains only a few forms sufficiently distinctive to warrant further investigation. However, even if it is slight, this evidence in favour of an eleventh-century date seems, if not conclusive, at least

---

⁵⁴ For discussion of *eorl*'s use and meaning in *The Battle of Maldon* and the implications for the poem's date, see e. g. McKinnell 1975, Clark 1983, Fulk 1992, 415-18. For its collocation with *ceorl*, see DOE **eorl** 1a.

⁵⁵ Crick (2007, 112/27, 29). The first is printed by her as *þeom*, but emended to *heom* by Faulkner (forthcoming).

⁵⁶ For earlier comment on the form and its distribution, see Campbell 1959: §380 ('late West Saxon'); Luick 1964, §112A1 (*þæne* found 'in der späteren Sprache sowohl in Westsächsischen wie im Anglischen'); Brunner 1965, §337A2 (*þane* and *þæne* 'beide in späten Texten häufigen'); Hogg & Fulk 2011, §5.8n1 (*þæne* a 'further development' from *þane* in late West Saxon).

⁵⁷ LAEME has only a single spelling with <æ>, from Lawman's *Brut* when Godlac 'forheow þænne mæst; a-two riht amidden' (Brook & Leslie 1963-78, 120/2293), so it is most unlikely to be a twelfth-century innovation in *An is ece cyning*.

compelling. An earlier date would require us to posit a later revision in which the orthography was updated with near perfect accuracy and words like *mynsterlagan* were substituted in. A later date seems ruled out by the presence of vocabulary not attested in Middle English and the different orthographical practices apparently operating when *sirreua* was interpolated. As the corpus philological methods being advocated here become more refined, features that at present do not seem significant will become so, and we may be able to refine on the broad eleventh century dating proposed here.[58]

Looking forward: big dating and bottom-up periodisation

The approaches described above and subsequently applied to *An is ece cyning*, while novel in the size of the datasets they use, remain to some extent traditionally philological in their analysis and interpretation of those datasets.[59] This section closes the paper by looking at two future approaches that are somewhat more abstract: cluster analysis and bottom-up periodisation.

Cluster analysis (e. g. Everitt 2011) is a widely used statistical technique that looks for patterns in datasets too large to eyeball. An economist, for instance, might have a dataset of 25 different economic indicators for the 28 EU countries. While any one of these

---

[58] In particular, the analysis above has taken no cognizance of negative evidence, that is forms that (say) commonly occur in texts composed in the mid-eleventh century, but are absent from *An is ece cyning*.

[59] One example is the rejection of a possible instance of *heom* from Cameron (1973, B9.2.2) found when searching the DOEC for *heom*. The edition underlying this text (Bately 1980) is largely based on the mid-tenth-century Tollemache Orosius (London, British Library, MS Additional 47967), and my metadata codes it with this information, but checking the edition reveals that for a short section, including this instance of *heom* (25/12), she follows a manuscript of a century later, London, British Library, MS Cotton Tiberius B. i, where in any case, as her apparatus criticus notes, *heom* has been altered from original *hiom* (fol. 21r/1).

variables could be plotted against any other (for instance, GDP per capita against inflation rate), no human could envision and interpret the three hundred paired variables necessary to a full understanding of this data. Cluster analysis makes this possible, essentially by envisioning each country's data as a vector in twenty-five dimensions and measuring the similarity between the shapes of those vectors. It then pairs the two closest-shaped vectors, and this process is repeated until the analyst decides when it should stop, usually at a point where the distance between the clusters involved in the putative merger reaches a particular threshold.

In the case of the dating problem being described in this paper, one would have a series of texts (for instance, the more than three thousand texts in the DOEC) and a series of linguistic variables measured for each of those texts, including perhaps the relative frequency of <hl-> spellings for *hl-* and the frequency per million words of *heom*. This is some way off, but we can apply a very primitive clustering technique to *An is ece cyning*, by tabulating for every text in the DOEC the frequency of *heom* per million words, the relative frequencies of *pæne* and unsyncopated, unumlauted *hafað* for the third-person singular present of the verb 'to have', three distinctive features of its language.[60] Rather than cluster them statistically, since the number of variables is small we can simply observe that only 21 texts in the DOEC have all three features, the average date of the manuscripts which preserve them being 1064. Of course, some of these texts, like the Eadwine Psalter gloss (Harsley 1889), contain only a small proportion of relevant forms, in its case four instances of *heom*, and one each of *pæne* and *hafað*. In fact, only one text uses *heom* more than a thousand times per million words and has as its preferred forms both *pæne* and *hafað*. That is the anonymous Life of St

---

[60] It would be worthwhile also to include the relative frequency of <hl-> spellings for *hl-* here, but this would require aligning the metadata of C11DB and DOEC, which I have yet to attempt.

Pantaleon (Matthews 1965-6), uniquely preserved in the mid-eleventh-century, London, British Library, Cotton Vitellius D. xvii, a manuscript of unknown origin and provenance.[61] This kind of analysis does not tell us anything particularly absolute in itself, but it certainly suggests further valuable lines of inquiry, not least investigating how many other features *An is ece cyning* shares with the Life of St Pantaleon and whether these shared features are a consequence of a common place of origin, a common stage in their transmission, or more general connections in scribal practice between different houses.

The second technique mentioned as a future possibility above, bottom-up periodisation, is an application of a special kind of cluster analysis known as Variability-Based Neighbor Clustering or VNC (Gries & Hilpert 2008; Gries & Hilpert 2012; Hilpert 2013, 32-109). VNC takes data regarding one or more variables in texts of different dates and clusters it to help identify the different stages by which a linguistic change progressed. Thus in one particular study, Gries and Hilpert took data on the frequency of *get*-passives (e. g. *get drunk*) from the TIME corpus, which is divided into decade-long segments, and showed on the basis of VNC that there were four salient phases in the adoption of the construction, with significant changes around 1940, 1990 and 2000 (Hilpert 2013, 32-8). One issue of major interest to both literary and linguistic scholars is the periodisation of Old and Middle English (Malone 1930; Kitson 1997), and it is possible to imagine that if the big dating approaches advocated in this paper succeed in identifying credible composition dates for a significant number of texts, then VNC could be used to provide an indication of when the boundary (or boundaries) between

---

[61] Another text very similar linguistically is the anonymous homily *In Parasceve* (Scragg 1992, 7-43 [odd pages]), the versions of which in both Oxford, Bodleian Library, MS Bodley 340+342 and Cambridge, Corpus Christi College, 162 share the use of *heom*, frequent *þæne*, and *hafað*.

Old and Middle English should be placed and thus a bottom-up rather than top-down indication of where the division between the set of textual practices we know as 'Old English' and the set we know as 'Middle English' should be located.

This is however very much a possibility for the future. Cluster-analysis-assisted big dating is a more immediate prospect, given the availability of the corpus philological techniques showcased in this paper for collecting the large datasets it will need. Even if it does not succeed in dating any texts, it will undoubtedly help us identify linguistic similarities between texts that more traditional methods have not noticed. To return to the epigram with which I began this paper, philology has always been about placing particular linguistic forms in context. What has changed, and what perhaps makes it *now* 'a special case of corpus linguistics' is that our ability to place those forms in context has advanced remarkably over the past twenty years. For that, we are grateful to generations of philologists, editors, corpus builders and computer scientists.

HIDDEN IN PLAIN SIGHT: THE OBFUSCATION OF MANUSCRIPT EVIDENCE IN THE MODERN CRITICAL EDITION

Michael G. Sargent

If we think of the dark archive as somehow analogous to dark matter (that some 85% of the matter of the universe, as measured by gravitational attraction, is invisible to any other kind of observation) then we may note and begin to describe the bulk of textual matter in our archives that is invisible to the world of named, known, and edited texts as the dark archive. I would like here, however, to draw attention to the way that texts that we think of as known are in fact also composed of dark text. And a major *actant* of the obfuscation of this dark text is the modern critical edition.[1]

From a theoretical point of view, we may note that the critical edition—in fact, the act of editing itself—is an instance of the compulsion to recall and re-inscription that Jacques Derrida characterised as the *mal d'archive* (*Archive Fever*, as it is translated in the English version of his essay of that name):[2] 'It is to have a

---

[1] As described by Bruno Latour, an *actant* is any one of the human or non-human causes or agents of change that surround and interact with human subjects: its meaning differs from that of *agent* in that it does not imply intention. See Latour 2005, 54–55.
[2] Derrida 1995, 91.

compulsive, repetitive, and nostalgic desire for the archive, an irrepressible desire to return to the origin, a homesickness, a nostalgia for the return to the most archaic place of absolute commencement.' Textual scholarship in general, and editing in particular, are driven by the compulsion to recover from the archive and produce for present use the original form of the past text. But the original form of the text can never be recovered: it can only be discovered—and what the textual critic can discover (even as a wholly practical matter) is never the singularity of the original text. Like memory, it is overwritten by every attempt at recovery. As present-day neuroscience has observed, what we recall is never the original memory; what we recall is what we remember from the last time we recalled the no-longer-original memory.

In practical terms, and particularly for medieval literature, we may note that what we hold in the archive is seldom the 'originary' form of a text in the first place: few surviving manuscripts are in the hand of the original author, or are linked with the author in terms of provenance or patronage. And even these do not necessarily provide unitary, original evidence of the text. Take for example two of the surviving manuscripts of one text that I have edited, Nicholas Love's early fifteenth-century *Mirror of the Blessed Life of Jesus Christ*, the expanded, anti–Wycliffite English version of the pseudo-Bonaventuran *Meditationes vitae Christi*. One of these manuscripts (Cambridge University Library Add. MS 6578) belonged to Mount Grace charterhouse in Yorkshire, where Love was prior, and was written during his priorate; the other (Yale University, Beinecke Library Takamiya Deposit MS 4) belonged to Joan Holland, countess of Kent, the widow of the founder of Mount Grace, and was probably presented to her when her husband was interred before the altar there around 1410 (again, while Nicholas Love was prior). These two, the most closely-associated manuscripts to the point of origin of Love's *Mirror*, represent two completely different recensions of the text—

recensions that are both probably authorial, but which differ substantially.³

In practical terms, we must also note that what we hold in the archive seldom represents a conscious effort at collection and preservation. In the case of medieval English texts, what we have are manuscripts of works that appealed to the interests of seventeenth-century collectors of dispersed medieval libraries (Robert Cotton, Robert and Edward Harley, Hans Sloane, Matthew Parker, William Laud), minus in some cases those manuscripts that appealed to the interests of other collectors (such as the works of contemplative writers like Richard Rolle and Walter Hilton that Augustine Baker requested of Robert Cotton for the reading of the English recusant nuns of Cambrai),⁴ plus manuscripts that have remained in private hands, even when (like the important Barking Abbey copy of Nicholas Love's *Mirror* when it was in the hands of the Foyle family) they break the surface of public knowledge for a short time like a sea-turtle drawing breath, then disappear again into the depths.⁵ This can

---

³ See Love 2005, 116 and 153; Sargent 2004 (updated and corrected in Sargent 2014). On the other hand, Bodleian MS e Museo 35, made, apparently, for Thomas Beaufort, who succeeded Thomas Holland as Duke of Exeter, and whose beneficence made him the 'second founder' of Mount Grace contains a text virtually identical to that CUL Add. 6686. See Love 2005, 105–06.

⁴ See the letter from Baker cited in Sargent 1974, 291–92: 'I am in their behallfe become an humble suitor vnto you, to bestowe on them such bookes as you please, either manuscript or printed being in English, conteining contemplation, saints' lives, or other devotions. [Richard Rolle of] Hampole's workes are proper for them. I wishe I had [Walter] Hilton's *Scala perfectionis* in latein; it woulde helpe the vnderstanding of the English; and some of them vnderstande Latein [capitalisation, punction, and spelling of names modernized].'

⁵ The Barking Abbey manuscript belonged to Sibyl de Felton, abbess from 1393 until her death in 1419; it was eventually purchased by Foyle's

have peculiar results. As I have argued before in the case of Walter Hilton's late-fourteenth century *Scale of Perfection*, what survives to us probably represents particular recensions of the text better than others—that, for example, because of the reputation of the English Carthusians for sanctity, their copies of Hilton's *Scale* in particular are probably better preserved than other copies made for other readers—including copies textually closer to the origin. The same is also probably true of the manuscripts surviving from a particular textual cluster associated with the city of London.[6]

Even more problematic than the fact that what is to be found in the archive is almost invariably not the originary text (provided, again, that there ever was a single originary text) is the modernist compulsion to produce a simulacrum of the originary text out of what is to be found in the archive—the critical edition. Such an edition is based on a liberal humanist grand narrative of authorial creation, scribal corruption, and editorial restoration.[7] The term 'critical edition' is also problematic in that it has been appropriated to a particular kind of edition. Although it ought by rights to be applicable to any edition based on an analytic, critical assessment of the archival evidence, the term 'critical edition' has become applicable only to those editions that are based on the use of coincidence in shared error

  booksellers, and remained (largely unknown) in the personal library of the Foyles at Beeligh Abbey, Essex, until the death of Christina Foyle in 1999. See Love, 2005, 126–28; Christie's sale, July 11, 2000, lot 72; present ownership and location unknown. See Gillespie 2006.

[6] Hilton 2017, cxix–cxxix; Sargent 2019.

[7] For a parallel formulation of the problematics of the modern critical edition, see the statement of 'Editorial Aims and Principles' in the introduction to Millet, (ed.) 2005, xlv–lxi. See also Millett 1994, and the studies in McGann (ed.) 1985a and 1985b. In speaking of the discourse of the transmission of the text here as a 'grand narrative', and below, of 'local narrative' alternatives, I am consciously appropriating categories of description most cogently delineated in Lyotard 1984.

among the surviving witnesses to construct a 'stemma codicum'—a 'family tree of books'—in order to argue back through reverse genealogy to the original from which all surviving copies descend.

The ideal of textual authority is of course not uniquely modern: the discrimination of greater and lesser degrees of authenticity of texts and readings was already practiced in the classical world, and manifested itself in various practices of control over scribal activity up to and including the medieval monasteries and the early universities, and of course the renaissance re-discovery and edition of classical texts.[8] But the ability of the printing press to produce uniform copy in large volume by mechanical means, requiring a substantial capital investment in the means of production, and with profits accruing to the investors and owners of the means of production, but only on completion of a print run—the paradigm of industrial capitalism—gave a new form to both authorship and textual authority. Current-day discussions of the 'print revolution' often focus on the capacity of the printing press to produce large numbers of books for a low price, but we should pay equal attention to the capability of the press to produce uniform, authenticated, authorised text (and remember that the word *auctor* applied originally in Latin primarily to the authorisation, and not the original writing of a text—a conceptualisation that neatly parallels the definition of *archive*, derived (as Derrida notes) from the name of the residence of the authorities, the ἀρχαί).[9]

In fact, printed editions have always stood in the way, blocking our view of the variation that is the natural state of text, occluding the

---

[8] See Reynolds & Wilson 1991. For the late medieval period in particular, see Bataillon & Rouse 1988, Rouse & Rouse 1991), Oswaldus de Corda 2001, and Beadle & Piper 1995.

[9] See Eisenstein 1979, 80–88. As Eisenstein notes, critics differ in their views of the importance of the ideal of textual authority and uniformity. See also Chapter 5, 'Perfect and Imperfect' in McKitterick, 2003, 139–65; Carlson 2006, 35–68; Kuskin 2008.

manuscript text by its self-presentation as the unvarying representation of the 'real' (that is, the ideal) text. We should note, too, that when print was first used to produce uniform, authorised text (and we should remember that the first printer's bill issued in England, Caxton's advertisement of the Sarum *Ordinale* of 1477 offered text that 'ben wel and truly correct') it promised to meet a need already recognised for Bibles, liturgical books, laws, religious regulations and university texts in manuscript. The words 'author' and 'authorize' have diverged in emphasis over time, but they are etymological twins. In the course of the development of humanist modernism, particularly during the period of Romanticism and after, the singular writer came to have the greatest importance, and authorised, published text came to be measured by its conformity to what could be reconstructed of authorial intention.

In the case of modern books that came from the hand of a known, singular author, the primary question came to be whether to honour his first, or his last known intention: the first, or the second edition of the *Lyrical Ballads*, for example; or which version of Whitman's *Leaves of Grass*. In the case of most classical and medieval texts, for which the originals usually do not exist, the question has been how to reconstruct the authorial text from the detritus left by scribal incompetence. The critical edition is not something that actually exists in the archive. It represents the archive, but in doing so, it occludes the archive.

In the centuries since the invention of moveable-type printed books, scholars have developed various methods for authenticating (and thereby authorising) texts that have survived from former ages, primarily for classical and scriptural texts. The culmination of the exploration of methodologies in the eighteenth and nineteenth centuries, characteristic of the modern period in its dependence on the metaphor of arboriform growth, was recension.[10] It is the recensionist edition that depends upon the identification of persistent patterns of coincident error to identify groups of manuscripts conjectured to descend from hypearchetypes in which these errors first occurred, and upon a similar conjecture of relationship among the hypearchetypes to create a stemma at the top of which stands the archetype from which all surviving copies descend. Recension implies a narrative of paternity, of descent, inheritance and legitimation;[11] but in a deconstruction of its own authority, recension can only establish legitimacy by focusing its attention on the identification of patterns of transmission of error—the descent of the illegitimate. It is common error, according to recension, that provides the evidence of the pattern of transmission.[12]

Nearly a century ago, Joseph Bédier,[13] in a sarcastic aside, compared the stemmata of manuscript relations produced by recensionist analysis to 'un arbre qu'on a pris coutume, je ne sais pourquoi, de dessiner à l'envers, racine en haut, branches en bas.' It is, as Michel Foucault points out,[14] the working of the modern *épistémè* that it organizes knowledge according to arboriform lineages of evolution—but stemmata are not ascending, but descending lineages. What is it that determines the orientation of the line of development?

---

[10] See Timpanaro 2005, Alter 1999; Hanna 1996, 63-93; Ingham 2006; Sargent 2013. Lindner 2016, 52–53 has pointed out that the first actual usage of the phrase 'stemma codicum' (codicum familiæ stemma) is in Eduard Wunder's edition of *M. Tulli Ciceronis Oratio pro Cn. Plancio* (Leipzig, 1830), xviii.

[11] Greetham 1996 notes the patrilineal tendency of recension and suggests the exploration of matrilineal descent.

[12] See Reeve 2011.

[13] Bédier 1928, 165.

[14] Foucault 1971, 1966.

As is too often the case with Bédier, his observation that textual stemmata are customarily drawn with their point of origin at the top and their historical actualisations (the surviving manuscripts) below is remarkably astute, but he does not analyse it: he does not ask 'pourquoi'. The answer is, of course, that while the teleological narrative of evolution is one of progression from 'lower' life-forms to 'higher', the narrative of textual descent – like that of the pedigree, the tree-diagram with which the textual stemma shares its downward orientation – is one of legitimation by the elimination of bastard lineage.

The flaw in the recensionist approach, according to Bédier, is that it mechanically led to the growth of stemmata where every branching was bifid: critical theory had created a veritable forest of binary trees– –'silva portentosa!' For the bifid, inverse teleological narrative of the recensionist stemma, Bédier (and he has been followed in this by a large number of modern editors) substituted the heroic narrative of the 'best text', in which the base text of an edition is chosen, not because of the unreconstructable vagaries of lineage, but because of historical, biographical or philological criteria largely peripheral to the history of the making of copies of a text from preceding copies. The authenticating narratives supporting best-text editions tend to frame themselves in terms of authorial biography or of regional, dialectal, national, or institutional history.

A different approach to manuscript textuality, influential particularly among scholars working in the Romance-language tradition of textual criticism, but increasingly among editors working on medieval English texts, is that identified with the names of Paul Zumthor and Bernard Cerquiglini.[15] Zumthor and Cerquiglini both emphasize the tendency of the manuscript transmission of medieval literature to *mouvance*, to *variance*. Both, unfortunately, founded their arguments in the perception of the oral (or at least partially oral)

---

[15] Zumthor 1992, 41-49, Cerquiglini 1999.

conditions of production of medieval literature that make it particularly susceptible to variation, rather than — more appropriately, I believe—observing (and this is important) that variation is the normal state of text, which is only artificially (and partially, at best) inhibited by print.

The greatest influence on the practice of editing medieval English texts in the past half-century, however, derives from the narrative of massive, inevitable, wilful (when not simply obtuse) scribal corruption—a degree of textual corruption that only the most perceptive of textual critics can attempt fully to repair—that underpins the Athlone edition of *Piers Plowman*.[16] Where recension depends upon the delineation of paternity and best-text editing upon a historical or biographical narrative, the editorial stance taken by George Kane and those associated with him in the *Piers Plowman* project is best characterised by one of its proponents as 'the way of genius',[17] for it is a narrative of the recovery by critical conjecture of the mind of the poet, which had been lost in the scribal corruption of the text.[18] Edition is no longer a process based on physical evidence: it is a meeting on a higher plane of the superior minds of the poet and the critic.[19] Where earlier strictures for the identification of textual error had been founded on observations about the physical process of copying a text, conjectural criticism is based in a New–Critical aesthetic sensibility that functions entirely within the mind of the critic and can lead to editions that contradict all of the manuscript

---

[16] Kane (ed.) 1960; Kane & Talbot Donaldson (ed.) 1975. Revised editions of these two volumes were published together with the C Version in Russell & Kane 1988.

[17] Patterson 1985. See also Kane 1976; Hanna 1992; Hanna 2010.

[18] The Introduction to Kane (ed.) 1960, 115–46, provides a list, with numerous examples, of the kinds of errors, aesthetic rather than palaeographic, to which medieval scribes were prone.

[19] Pearsall 1985 responds to this tendency; to which Kane (1989) replies.

evidence.[20] This is where modern textual criticism shows itself most similar to grand historical narrative: in support of the *telos* towards which it aims and its consistency as a narrative, it requires the critic to substitute his account of what must have been for the actual data that survive.

The problem of the tendency of critical edition to occlude the manuscript evidence on which it is based is, of course, not peculiar to the conjectural method of the Athlone *Piers Plowman*. In producing the recensionist full critical edition of Nicholas Love's *Mirror of the Blessed Life of Jesus Christ*,[21] based on the α-text manuscript Cambridge University Library Add. 6578 (since the α text is Love's final version), I corrected away some three hundred variants characteristic of all α manuscripts, but which the agreement of β and γ manuscripts (which together agreed with the underlying Latin text of the *Meditationes vitae Christi* where applicable) showed to be erroneous. In doing so, I created a text of the *Mirror* of which Nicholas Love may well have approved, but which may well not have existed in his day.[22] This is the nature of the modern critical edition: it is a chimera of a uniform, authorised text, a construct of the collusion of the editor and the printer. The more perfect it is, the

---

[20] Patterson 1985 demonstrates the relationship between the assumptions on which the Athlone edition of *Piers Plowman* is based and New Critical poetics. It should be noted that the presumption that each version of *Piers Plowman* must be a poetic improvement upon what preceded it led to the emendation of some 300 readings where the editors determined that the reading of the B-text is inferior to a different reading in which A and C agree. At no point was the reading of B considered superior to a reading in which A and C agree, even when all of the B witnesses agree in a single reading.

[21] Love 2005.

[22] Noting Langland's tendency to revision of his text, Pearsall 1985, 100, remarks that, 'One can be sure that if Langland saw the Kane–Donaldson B text, the first thing that he would want to do would be to revise it.'

more fully it counterfeits the manuscript evidence upon which it is based.

By whatever method, the purpose of the modern critical editor has thus always been to distinguish true readings from false, the authentic from the erroneous, to enshrine the true in the critical text, and to banish the erroneous to the critical apparatus, or not to print them at all.[23] Yet neither authenticity nor error exists prior to the editor's work of discrimination: they are both projections of the editor's judgement on the material before him or her. Certainly there are readings that are erroneous, in the sense that no-one would expect an intelligent, non-satyric author to misspell the words he uses (granted the vagaries of late Middle English orthography), to commit grammatical errors, or otherwise to write nonsense. One should think that sentences without verbs, or explications of the Ten Commandments lacking a crucial 'not' following the phrase 'Thou shalt' were probably not what their authors intended.[24] The vast majority of textual variations in late medieval vernacular prose, however, are not as clear to decide as that. The editor may also wish to exclude from consideration as authorial those forms that vary from an author's known dialect (although the author's dialect is usually known from the text under study). But

---

[23] Modern textual criticism distinguishes here between variations that are the result of authorial revision and those that result from scribal corruption of the text. The representation of the latter is only required for the establishment of the critical text; or it may be represented in the apparatus because it is intrinsically interesting. See, for example, Pearsall 2013, 202. The assumption is that authorship is real, but manuscript readings are ephemeral. I would reverse this ontology to argue rather that the readings of the manuscripts are real, and that the authorial text is hypothetical.

[24] In Chapter 35 of Nicholas Love's *Mirror*, for example, where he castigates the Jewish elders with a quotation from Prov. 21:30, 'haþ not of ȝou þe wiseman wryten þat þere is no wisdam nor consele aȝeyn God?', all manuscripts read 'haue ȝe not wryten of þe wiseman'. The reversal of who is writing about whom cannot be correct.

despite the sometimes pontifical affirmations of some editors of their own inerrancy, and the multiplication of rules for distinguishing both conscious and unconscious forms of scribal corruption of the text, the discrimination of 'true' from 'false' readings is usually a matter of the editor's sense of the author's 'voice'—a fallible instrument at best. For the majority of textual variants, the most that can be said is that to the editor who has the experience of reading many surviving copies of a medieval text, some variants are more cogent than others. Questions of error tend to be independent of manuscript attestation; the usual consequence of error is that the text fails to make sense. Questions of cogency often do involve attestation, and usually involve decisions about the preferability of one out of several readings all of which do make sense.[25]

But in the end, the modern, printed critical edition, whether produced by recension or by modernist/aestheticist conjecture, is not something that actually exists in the archive. It represents the archive (in the Deleuzean sense of representation),[26] but in doing so, it occludes the difference (again in the Deleuzean sense) that constitutes the archive.

A different tradition of textual presentation, much derided by the critical editors of the German philological tradition at the end of the nineteenth century, but employed in a number of prominent publications of the founders of the Early English Text Society, was the printing of multiple variant versions of verse texts in parallel columns.[27] Capitalising on his own egalitarian values while making a

---

[25] Kane & Donaldson 1975, 63 fn. 100, revise the traditional *dictum* that 'readings should be weighed, not counted' to 'readings should be weighed, not manuscripts counted'. I would respond that the responsible editor ought to do both.

[26] Deleuze 1994.

[27] See Spencer 2015a, 792, where she notes, 'English editors, then, had tended to produce parallel texts or diplomatic transcriptions, with variants from

virtue of the fact that England in the late nineteenth century did not have the cadre of university-trained philologists to produce critical editions according to the criteria of the German school, F.J. Furnivall led an effort, through EETS and the Chaucer Society, to produce diplomatic editions of all of the earliest and best manuscripts of Chaucer's *Canterbury Tales* and *Piers Plowman*, or at least sample sections of their texts, in ledger-book format where possible.[28] Furnivall's *Six-Text Canterbury Tales* eventually expanded to include two more manuscripts,[29] and Furnivall also published the separate narrative units of the *Tales* in no fewer than forty-three volumes.[30] The culmination of this effort, as well as parallel work on Chaucer's other works, was Walter Skeat's *Complete Works*.[31] Skeat himself published two sets of extracts from *Piers Plowman* for comparison, one of twenty-nine manuscripts, and another of forty-five, and three separate editions of the A, B, and C versions of the text, before producing his three-text edition.[32]

Not all texts published in multiple versions were intended for eventual critical edition, however. In notable cases of philological or historical interest the presentation of the totality (or a significant part, at least) of the surviving manuscript evidence was an end in itself. Richard Morris's four-manuscript edition of the *Cursor Mundi*, for example, made available to scholars the most extensive poetic text available in Northern English dialect.[33] Derek Pearsall has also noted

other copies, which were not usually allowed to invade the text.' Other examples are given in Pearsall 2013, 199-201.

[28] Furnivall (ed.) 1869–77. See Spencer 2015b; Singleton 2005.
[29] Including Furnivall ed. 1885, and 1901–02.
[30] Chaucer Society, 1st series 2-13, 16-20, 26-28, 30, 32-36, 38, 40-43, 50-55, 66-71 (London: Trübner, 1868-77).
[31] Skeat (ed.) 1894–1900.
[32] Extracts: Skeat (ed.) 1866; revised 2nd edition, Skeat (ed.) 1885; Versions A–C: Skeat (ed.) 1867, 1869, 1886.
[33] Morris (ed.) 1874–93.

the tendency to publish popular Middle English romances in parallel-text format.[34] Several versions of *Mandeville's Travels*, a text that shows nearly unparalleled variation in form,[35] have been published in separate volumes.[36] The series of separate volumes comprising the various manuscripts of *Ancrene Wisse* provides both an illustration of the early Middle English reflex of literary West Saxon and a major vernacular text of the *cura mulierum*.[37]

The publication of the various versions of the *Canterbury Tales*, *Piers Plowman*, *Cursor Mundi*, and *Ancrene Wisse* in the late nineteenth and twentieth centuries all function as multiple best-text editions, with minimal representation of the variant readings of other manuscripts. They provide an example of an alternative to the grand narrative of the critical edition: a set of local narratives of the textuality of a given work. They realize Furnivall's egalitarian ideal that every reader should be his own amateur textual critic. At the same time, a number of the early editions based on partial surveys of the surviving manuscripts have eventually been replaced by more critical

---

[34] Pearsall 2013, 199–200.
[35] See Higgins 1997.
[36] Hamelius ed. 1919–23; Seymour (ed.) 1963; 1973; 2002; and 2010.
[37] Day (ed.) 1952 (Cotton Nero A.xiv); Wilson (ed.) 1954 (Gonville & Caius ms. 234/120); Baugh (ed.) 1956 (Royal 8.c.I); Tolkien & Ker (ed.) 1962 (CCC 402); Mack & Zettersten (ed.) 1963 (Cotton Titus D.xviiii); Dobson (ed.) 1972 (Cotton Cleopatra C.vi); Zettersten (ed.) 1976 (Pepys 2498); Zettersten & Diensberg (ed.) 2000 (Vernon); as well as d'Evelyn (ed.) 1944; Herbert (ed.) 1944; Trethewy (ed.) 1958 (Latin, French and Welsh respectively). The Tolkien edition of Corpus Christi College 249 was to have comprised a discussion of the language of the text, but the editor was diverted by other matters; the lack was supplied by d'Ardenne (ed.) 1961. Hope Allen's interest in the publication of the literature of women's spirituality in the medieval period in all its specificity, and a concomitant infusion of American funds, provided a second impetus for publication of all manuscript witnesses.

modern editions. *The Prick of Conscience*, for example, was edited by Richard Morris in 1863 from ten manuscripts in the British Museum, plus one other in private hands (out of 115 surviving witnesses).[38] A century and a half's worth of examination of the manuscripts has led to Ralph Hanna and Sarah Wood's recent 'reading text'.[39] Likewise, Susan Powell's recent edition of John Mirk's *Festial* stands as the culmination of a century of scholarship beginning with Theodor Erbe's edition and continuing through a burgeoning series of studies of the text and its manuscripts (primarily by Powell and her collaborators Martyn F. Wakelin and Alan J. Fletcher) over the past half century.[40] It was not until some time in the 1960s, apparently,[41] that E.J. Dobson conceived of the project of producing the critical edition of the *Ancrene Wisse* that was eventually produced by Bella Millet in 2005.[42]

In the most prominent edition of a Middle English work to acknowledge the tendency of medieval texts to *mouvance*, Millett's edition points particularly to the great deal of variation (including probable authorial intervention) shown among the manuscripts in the "'dynamic' textual tradition' of a work of practical instruction in the religious life, in manuscripts copied over a period of more than two centuries, and translated as well from the English original into French and Latin. Millett's solution was to produce not a recensionist critical text, but a 'corrected edition', based on Cambridge, Corpus Christi College, MS 402, that presents a historical text.

Equally, on the other side, there has been an editorial tendency on the part even of editors who espouse recension to pare back on the

[38] Morris (ed.) 1863; Lewis & McIntosh 1982.
[39] Hanna & Wood (ed.) 2013; see Hanna 2013.
[40] Erbe 1905; Powell 2009–11.
[41] Dobson (1962) reported that he had undertaken the (at that point) incomplete collation of manuscripts of the *Ancrene Wisse* specifically as a contribution to the J.R.R. Tolkien Festschrift.
[42] See particularly Millett 2005 (above, fn. 17) and 1994.

presentation, or even the collation, of the evidence of manuscripts that do not contribute to the construction and support of the critical text. In producing her edition of *The Cloud of Unknowing* and related works, Phyllis Hodgson collated all manuscripts partially, for the sake of establishing the critical text; but '[a] full collation of all the variant readings of the fifteen English texts of *The Cloud*,' she reported, 'would certainly not justify the great amount of space it would occupy.'[43] Margaret Connolly's recensionist critical edition of *Contemplations of the Dread and Love of God*, a variable text comprising twenty-four chapters, several of which occur independently in varying numbers of manuscripts, was based on a collation of the fifteen complete surviving manuscripts and one incunable print. The *Contemplations*, however, is equally represented by twenty-five manuscripts comprising extracts ranging from one to several chapters; these were collated, but not represented in the edition. Connolly has described their various forms in a recent article.[44]

It should also be noted that the tendency of a number of recent series of editions of Middle English texts (e.g. the short-lived Garland series in which the first edition of Nicholas Love was published, the Heidelberg series, all but one of the Exeter series, and the TEAMS series) are all best–text editions, in which one manuscript is chosen from the archive to speak for all.

In the recent Early English Text Society edition of the second book of Walter Hilton's *Scale of Perfection*, I have presented a text based on British Library MS Harley 6573, a manuscript that my predecessor, Stan Hussey, had dismissed for recensionist reasons as an inaccurate copy of the less-authoritative of the two textual families

---

[43] Hodgson (ed.) 1944, xxiv. The 'cloud of variants' (as Hodgson termed it) in which a full collation would have resulted would have required scarcely fewer lines of apparatus than of text per page (just under, as opposed to just over 20 lines).

[44] Connolly (ed.) 1993, and 2018.

into which he saw the manuscripts as falling (precisely as Bédier noted was the tendency of recension).[45] A complete new collation of the manuscripts demonstrated rather that Harley 6573 differed less often from the consensus of all manuscripts, and was apparently closer than any other to the original from which the Carmelite friar Thomas Fishlake, who probably knew Hilton at Cambridge, made his Latin translation. I still corrected the text. It was suggested to me that after forty-odd years of (sporadically) reading Hilton and ten years of collating the manuscripts of *Scale* II, I probably had a pretty good sense of Hilton's voice; but I did not correct the text when I found the readings of the other manuscripts (even *all* the other manuscripts) more cogent: only when I felt that the reading of Harley 6573 was false to Hilton's meaning. I still corrected the text some 200 times; but every reading of every manuscript is registered in the critical apparatus.[46] In making these decisions, I was consciously addressing the issue of what a postmodern edition would look like, in a paper, rather than an electronic format.

But the fundamental opposition remains: the printed modern critical edition can only—in Deleuzean terms—represent the medieval text. It is not the text, but a simulacrum erected between the text and the reader. It may be an entirely credible simulacrum, but it is not the text. Only the specific manuscript instantiations of the text, each one a repetition of another (or others) before it, in all their diversity, are the text. And diversity is precisely what the modern critical edition aims to suppress. Even a best-text edition is not the text as such, because it presents a single instantiation, shorn of its location in the textual matrix, privileged by the editor as a representative of the others. But this is a problem inherent in the print medium: it inevitably privileges a particular form of the text. Even though all

---

[45] See Hussey 1992.
[46] At a rate of approximately twenty lines of small type per twenty-five lines of text per page.

variants of all manuscripts of *Scale* II are presented in my edition, for example, fewer than 100 lemmata are reported on an average page of 300 words, totalling approximately 250 notices of variation (most variants occur in more than one manuscript) out of a total archive of some 6600 archived words of text.[47] Only an electronic edition based on a complete transcription and collation of all manuscripts would be able report all of this evidence—but without some sort of editorial method, it would be equal in size to the archive that it records. On the other hand, a truly postmodern edition might only be possible in some rhizomorphic electronic form that would base itself upon all surviving manuscript material,[48] and would make all of that material available to the reader simultaneously, under the guidance of the editor.[49] But even such an electronic edition would still privilege the 'default' form of the text: the form that appears on screen when the edition is booted up. Either by the unmitigated presentation of an electronic text that is simply a copy of the entirety of the archive of the text, or by editorial selection of one text that represents the archive of the text, the edition deconstructs itself.

Of current electronic editorial projects in Middle English literature, the *Piers Plowman Electronic Archive* headed by the late Hoyt Duggan has produced seven single-manuscript transcriptions (out of a total of nearly fifty manuscripts) over the course of several decades, and a recensionist critical edition of the B-text.[50] Tokyo

---

[47] I have used Walter Hilton, *Scale: Book II*, 117 (Hilton 2017) as the specimen from which these totals are derived. At this point in the text, there are twenty-two manuscript witnesses.

[48] Sargent 2013. See also McGann 1997 and 2014.

[49] Despite the fears of some modernist textual critics that the editor, as Derek Pearsall says of the editor of a parallel-text edition, will become 'a mere stage-hand' (2013, 201), the editor will never lose his or her place as the most experienced reader of the text, the only one who has worked with all the manuscripts.

[50] *Piers Plowman Electronic Archive* (piers.chass.ncsu.edu).

Medieval Manuscript Reading Group's electronic parallel text version of *Ancrene Wisse* (available in a series of paperback fascicles) has recreated the multiple printed text in a new medium.[51] The 'Canterbury Tales Project' headed by Peter Robinson, on the other hand, is intended to produce an electronic version of recension, with the characteristic binary methodology of recension embedded in the coding of its cladistic programme.[52] Bella Millett has recently described the problems in the major current electronic editorial projects dealing with medieval texts, beginning with their foundation in the editorial *mentalité* of the printed page and continuing into present-day concerns with technological limitations (and particularly obsolescence), perceptions of impact, and sustainability of editorial projects;[53] her analysis ends on a note of melancholic, Arnoldean ambivalence. I suspect that the solution to the problems of the electronic critical edition will eventually be worked out by a younger generation of scholars, who have grown up on electronic media and think in the *mentalité* of those media, rather than by those who have been trained on pencil-and-paper collation and the printed critical edition. For us (for me, at least) the task is to produce critical editions that attempt to bridge the gap between the modernist and the postmodern, to preserve and demonstrate in our work the editorial tools and techniques of print-based textual criticism from which the electronic editor can assemble his or her own tool-kit.

Going forward, in my view, scholars producing postmodern, electronic editions should take as their ultimate goal the presentation of the complete archive of the text: images and transcript, with links for material composition, scribal hand, dialect, provenance, co-occurrence with other texts in the same manuscripts, and ownership history. The edition should open up to a default text and its

---

[51] *Ancrene Wisse* 2000 and 2001; Kobouchi & Ikegami (ed.) 2005.
[52] Robinson N.d. The most recent post on this website dates from 2006.
[53] Millett 2013.

apparatus—the choice and presentation of this text is still the work of the editor, as the single most experienced reader—but other readers should also be able to 'flip' the text to see it in any of its manuscript instantiations, each with its own apparatus. This would require both software that would allow any entry in the critical apparatus to became the base-text for an alternative reading, and the complete transcription of every manuscript of the text—linked, of course, to images of the actual manuscripts. Ideally, I would envisage the nodes of an electronic text that included all of this information as a display of arcologies in a three-dimensional cyberspace (to borrow a term from William Gibson's *Neuromancer* novels),[54] on which the reader could dock, and among which he or she could navigate as their curiosity took them. Such an edition would thus be one face of the exploration of the dark archive. In such an edition, the default text should not be thought of as "the" text, occluding its silent brethren (or glancing back, like Orpheus, to see Euridice disappearing into the darkness): it should be the form of the text that the editor suggests, as the one person who has searched furthest in the archive, that the reader see first.[55]

Finally, keep in mind that I am not arguing that resources should be diverted from the exploration of those parts of the archive that, at this point, are still truly dark; but that we should remain aware that darkness also resides in the clean, well-lighted places with which we think ourselves already familiar.

---

[54] Gibson 1984, 1987, 1989; see Biddick 1998, 165–84; and Benedikt (ed.) 1991.

[55] For a provisional version of a rhyzomorphic presentation of the affiliations of the manuscripts of *The Scale of Perfection*, see Figure 1 overleaf. Note that the figure is presented in two dimensions: in a three-dimensional display, it would be mapped onto an ovoid shape like half of a rugby ball.

Figure 1

Hypothesis of affiliational patterns of the surviving originally complete manuscripts of Books I and II of Walter Hilton's *Scale of Perfection* (*Scale* I based on Dorward and Bliss, unconfirmed). Legend: Legend: *Scale* I only – *Scale* II only – *Scale* I and II

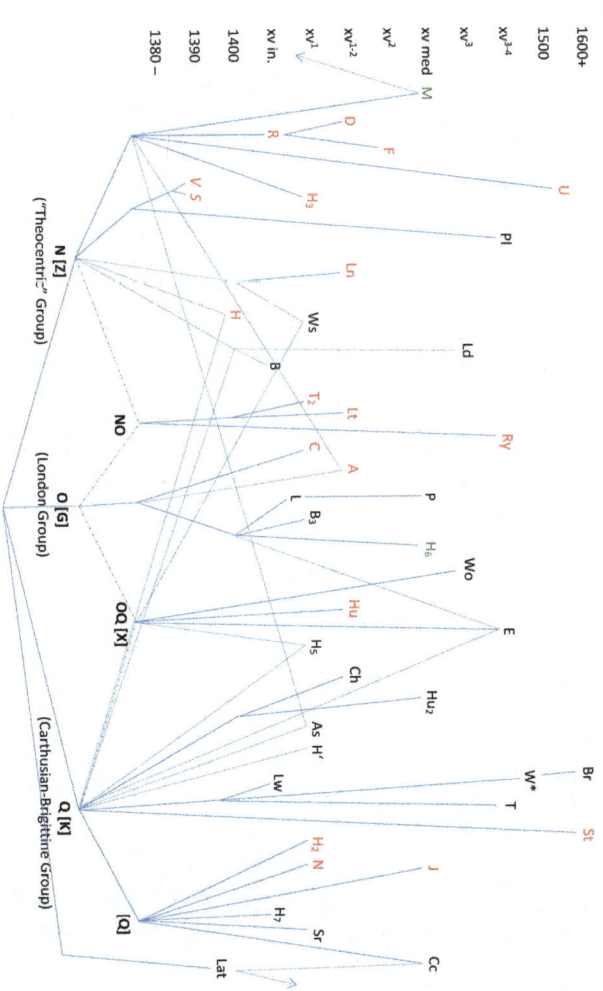

The Beautiful Glitch: Human and Machine in Luciano Floridi's Philosophy of Information

Lapo Lappin

Luciano Floridi's philosophical work, stretching over the past twenty years, is almost synonymous with the philosophy of information. Even though the roots of this branch of philosophy go back considerably further (Gottfried Wilhelm Leibniz springs to mind as a possible candidate, although Alan Turing is Floridi's favourite), Floridi is the first to give the philosophy of information an unmistakable character. He defines the objective of a philosophy of information as two-fold (Floridi 2002, 137):

> [T]he philosophical field concerned with (a) the critical investigation of the conceptual nature and basic principles of information, including its dynamics, utilization, and sciences, and (b) the elaboration and application of information-theoretic and computational methodologies to philosophical problems.

The project is, therefore, not only to bring philosophy to the informational approaches, but also to bring the informational approaches to philosophy. While the first criterion may have its predecessors, the second criterion is original to Floridi. Floridi is the first to elevate the philosophy of information to a kind of 'first philosophy', as a gold standard for the solution of ancient as well as novel philosophical problems (Floridi 2010, 153). Twenty years later, Floridi is now far from alone: his research programme has gained considerable traction, charting the course for the entire field.

This paper will focus on two aspects of Floridi's polyvalent thought. These are the two aspects that arguably relate the most to the project of digital humanities. The first aspect is Floridi's analysis of the difference between human and digital, in terms of Floridi's concept of *semantic capital*. The second aspect is the philosophical implications of the digital revolution, in particular Floridi argument that the digital revolution comports a *re-ontologisation*, a philosophical development from an ontology of things to an ontology of relations. These two sections will be followed by an attempt to relate these two aspects to each other. I argue that the two aspects cannot be accommodated without a certain amount of friction. In closing, I offer two ways out of this dilemma suggested in Floridi's work.

1. Man and Machine

We live in a world where the presence of technology is ever more ubiquitous. We are constantly connected to the digital, always leaving footprints of data behind us. According to Floridi, we have thus in a defining stage in history – into *hyperhistory* – where our well-being is completely *dependent* on informational technology. In previous junctures in history, our well-being may have been *related* to informational technology (books, letters, and so on); today, they are necessities in a previously unknown manner (Floridi 2014, 1-3; Floridi 2015, 51-53).

Perhaps Floridi's philosophy of history can be enriched with a reappraisal of the role of the archive, arguably one of the most vital forms of informational technology. Even before the advent of hyperhistory, human well-being was not only related too, but entirely dependent on the archive (in all its multifaceted purposes: administrative necessity for the working of the state, for taxation and documentation...) and its proper functioning. Instead of a strict association of hyperhistory with the digital revolution, it is perhaps more helpful to highlight the vitality of pre-digital technologies, and stretch the conception of hyperhistory further into the past.

Another way of configuring the shift from history to hyperhistory, one that would align well with the digital revolution, would be a shift in the shape of the archive itself. Smartphones are, after all, not primarily a communicational device; there are rather pocket-archives, carrying around, storing, filing the user's information. Philosophers Andy Clark and David Chalmers refer to smartphones and other informational equipment as 'extended minds'. Perhaps a more fitting phrase would be 'restricted archive'. In any case, the digital revolution implies a reconfiguration of the archive. While previously centralised locations, archives are now decentralised, from physical they have become 'dephysicalised' (*vide infra*). The motor of the digital revolution is a revolution in the nature of the archive.

Dovetailing neatly with this observation, Floridi predicts that we are currently living alongside the last generation that recognizes a difference between being online and being offline. For the newer generations, this division has been all but erased. We are now permanently online, or, rather, not only online, but – in Floridi's neologism – *onlife* (Floridi 2015, 5).

The symbiosis of humans and machine has never been closer than it is today. All of which raises the question of where the human is placed in this brave new world. Where is the distinction between human and machine, now that biological life is to an ever-greater extent *onlife*? To pose this question is by no means to invoke science-fiction scenarios of humanity mulcting into cyborg hybrids, as Floridi is all too keen to remind the reader. (While disavowing the legacy of science fiction is an understandable dialectical move, it does seem to be something of a misunderstanding of the role of science-fiction; after all, the cyberpunk smog-scapes of *Bladerunner* are hardly about some hypothetical far-future scenario.) The question is a pressing and down-to-earth one, prompted by our immanent transactions between the digital world right now. It is also not a question without practical political repercussions: the rapid explosion in the AI sector, and the real risk of a radical re-juggling of the labour market, help bring the question to centre stage. Lastly, it is without doubt a question of interest to the humanities' explorations of the virtual realm.

So, where are the borders between human and machine? Floridi's answer is resolute: humans, in contrast to machines, are endowed with the capacity to create and process meaning. Machines, by contrast, cannot process meaning at all; they can solve problems, but not understand problems. 'Our present technology is actually incapable of processing any kind of meaningful information, being impervious to semantics, that is, the meaning and interpretation of the data manipulated', Floridi writes (Floridi 2014, 136). In other words, humans are good at semantics, machines are good at syntax: 'whenever the behaviour in question is reducible to a matter of transducing, encoding, decoding, or modifying patterns of uninterpreted data according to some set of rules [...] computers are likely to succeed' (Floridi 2014, 137).

Floridi's answer is needs to be put in relation with his analysis of AI. The 'intelligence' in 'artificial intelligence' is somewhat misleading. Artificial intelligence is, in fact, rather stupid. What AI can do is not solve challenges *intelligently*, according to Floridi. What it does is solves challenges that, *for a human*, would require a degree of intelligence. This does not imply that AI simulates intelligence. It is rather a de-coupling of intelligence from problem solving, two capacities which are always coupled in humans.

In doing so, Floridi sides with a particular faction of the AI community, the proponents of so-called 'weak' AI. This faction argues that the goal of AI is not to emulate human intelligence itself, but rather to reproduce the *outcomes* of human intelligence. This is in opposition to the 'strong' AI community, whose vision is to simulative cognitive human functions in an artificial system. As

Floridi points out, there are absolutely no empirical reasons to subscribe to strong AI, and only a kind of fideism can justify the proponent's confidence in technological progress. In reality, all the impressive results of AI to date have been uniformly due to 'weak' approaches. All 'strong' approaches have uniformly failed.

It is worth spelling out the difference between human and machine in a little more detail. Humans, as mentioned above, have an innate proficiency in handling and generating meaning. Floridi's name for this ability is *semantic capital*, by analogy to economic capital. Semantic capital is defined as 'any content that can enhance someone's power to give meaning to and make sense of (semanticise) something' (Floridi 2018, 483). The term 'content', in this definition, is equivalent to 'well-informed and meaningful data'. This kind of data could be anything from points of ink on a page to lights in the darkness. When meaningful, these points of data cluster together together as semantic capital. Floridi provides a wealth of examples (Floridi 2018, 484):

[T]he game you played when you were a child; the sound of a bell in the village in which you spend your holidays; a song, so intimately mixed with a significant experience, which you keep hearing again in so many difference circumstances of your life; the inevitable taste of any Proustian moment ('The taste was that of the little piece of madeleine which [...] my aunt Léonie used to give me', *In Search of Lost Time*); the movies you have watched, the gossip you shared; the smell of a new car; the first feeling of a new wedding ring around your finger.

It is on the basis of semantic capital that we can successfully discriminate between humans and robots. Floridi is unequivocal on this point: 'persons have semantic capital animals and robots do not, but most importantly cannot' (*ibid.*) Semantic capital gives us the theoretical framework to make sense of the shortcomings of strong AI touched upon above. '[R]obots only handle syntax, syntactical flames can leave no scar, in the same, sense in which the simulation of a fire cannot burn', Floridi writes, with a nod to the semantic capital of Dante's *antica fiamma* (Floridi 2018, 485).

The notion of semantic capital lends itself as a powerful theoretical tool to the digital humanities. The possibilities of syntactic processing on textual material verge on the infinite. The role of the scholar must increasingly become one of discernment – a semantic discernment – among the possibilities of syntactical processing. The core of the digital humanities lies precisely in the juncture between the syntactical capacities of machines and our abilities semanticise. Ulrike Wuttke argues that the humanities will to a greater extent to follow the pattern of the sciences and begin treating 'data' as a first-class research product. This data, as Floridi points out, needs to be meaningful. While digital tools can cull data that we could not, its meaning is invested by humans.

2. Re-ontologisation

Let us return to the ubiquity of the informational technology in our societies, and what this means for philosophy. In its magnitude and effects, Floridi compares the digital revolution to previous historical revolutions in our way of seeing the world (Floridi 2019, 210-11). This process was set in motion by Copernicus *De revolutionibus orbium celestis* in 1543, which inflicted the first serious blow to the geocentric model inherited from Ptolemy and Aristotle, where the earth was considered to be the central (and lowest) point in the cosmos. The second revolution was inaugurated by Darwin's *On the Origin of Species* in 1859, which changed the way we view life on earth; the third was the revolution is due to Sigmund Freud, who uncovered the role of subconscious psycho-sexual drives in the realm of human behaviour. (The psychoanalytical revolution is interchangeable with the neuro-scientific one in Floridi's genealogy, depending on one's personal preference in respect to Freud.)

Floridi christens the digital revolution, by analogy to these historical precedents, 'the fourth revolution'. Like its three predecessors, this revolution brings with it radical philosophical changes. The most profound of these is a transition with regards to our 'Ur-philosophy', Floridi's name for our most basic philosophical attitudes. Floridi argues that we are dealing with a *re-ontologisation* – a shift in our ontology, a shift in our perspectives on what entities and relations make up the world in its fundamental constitution (Floridi 2007). Up to the dawn of the digital revolution, our Ur-philosophy was an Aristotelian-Newtonian one: it was a philosophy that dealt primarily with individual substances, with 'things'.

The digital revolution, Floridi explains, is in reality an *informational* revolution. Information and communication technologies (ICTs), through their ubiquitous presence, 'are leading our culture to conceptualize the whole reality and our lives within it in ICT-friendly terms, that is, informationally' (Floridi 2014, 40). The result of this (re)conceptualisation is the concept of the *infosphere*, understood as the sum total of informational interactions. 'Maximally, the infosphere is a concept that can also be used as synonymous with reality, once we interpret the latter informationally.' Floridi turns Hegel on his head: 'The real is informational and the informational is real' (Floridi 2014, 41) This informational proliferation brings with it a shift in ontology: the ontology of 'things' is supplanted by an ontology of relations. It is now the *relations* between nodes in a relational web that catch our interest, rather than the individual substances connected by these relations. In what follows, I will outline three consequences of the re-ontologisation due to the informational revolution: *dephysicalisation, typification*, and a development in our standard of existence.

The first effect is an increasing process of *dephysicalisation*, 'in the sense that [objects and processes] tend to be seen as support-independent'. A music file, for instance, is no longer as dependent on its physical substrate as it was, say, when CDs were in circulation. The increasing dephysicalisation of things also has deep philosophical implications: the ontological problem of personal identity, for example, has always been closely connected to the co-presence of the body and the person. In the age of the denizens of Zoom – the age of 'Zoombies', as one philosopher calls it – presence is no longer linked to bodily presence in any meaningful sense. Technologies of telecommunication open up the possibility of presence at a distance, of personal presence without bodily presence. In the process, the Newtonian Ur-philosophy of locality is slowly eroded (Floridi 2014, 50).

Dephysicalisation, in a way, cuts to the very heart of the dilemma that confronts the digital humanities, especially in the project of digitalising manuscripts and artefacts. It has often been pointed out that the manuscript is necessarily a three-dimensional physical object. To digitize it is to denude it of its physicality. By losing its physicality the manuscript therefore ceases to be a manuscript proper. In this sense, to capture the artefact seems, paradoxically, to be precisely to lose it *qua* artefact. But, if Floridi is right that physical presence can no longer serve as a meaningful criterion of presence, at least on terms of personal identity, one may wonder why one should cling to the physicality of the manuscript as a necessary condition for its presence. Could the manuscript, like the CD, become independent of its substrate?

The second consequence of philosophical import is the *typification* comported by the digital. This concept brings our attention to the fact that the distinction between an original and copy no longer holds in the digital realm. When one creates a copy a physical artefact, such as a sketch of a painting, the original remains in its place; we are now simply in possession of a newer copy. In the digital world, copying does not take place in quite the same way. When one duplicates a file – which one is the original? Does the question even make sense? The two files remain indistinguishable (apart from certain possible encryptions we do not necessarily have access to). In philosophical terms, the distinction between *types* and *tokens* is no longer applicable. The informational revolution inverts of the platonic scheme of archetype and cascading degrees of simulacra; there is no longer such thing as originality, there are only copies (Floridi 2014, 50).

Again, the bearing on the question of manuscript digitisation is obvious. Floridi's examples are limited to the enclosed sphere of digital space. The interesting question, however, is the interplay of the physical and the digital. Is the relation of sketch to artwork really transferrable to the relation of artefact and digitalised artefact? One may wonder whether the digital revolution itself comports a reworking of the whole notion of archetype and simulacrum. Paradoxically, the digitised manuscript sometimes brings us closer to the archetype in its original form. Multi-spectral imaging, for instance, allows us to glean features no longer accessible in its physical copy. The ontological relation between the physical 'original' and its digitised 'copy' seem at any rate to be more complicated than a simple schema of original and copy.

One possible way out of this dilemma that has been suggested is to treat the digital version of a manuscript as an 'incomplete' version. A digitised manuscript, the argument goes, is only a part of the manuscript. The manuscript in its entirety remains the physical artefact. Only a book can be a 'whole'. Alas, there is a hitch. Without needlessly entering into mereological intricacies, a reasonable case can be made that the whole is the sum of its parts. Perhaps it is more than the sum of its parts; in any case, it certainly cannot be *less* than its parts. But if we are willing to say that the digital version is 'but' a part, we also need to say that it is a part of the whole (the book). A necessary (and perhaps unwanted) consequence of this line of argument is that the physical manuscript now forms a whole *with the digitised manuscript*, which, as a part, has become a requirement for the totality of the object.

Neither the configuration of digitised manuscripts as 'copies', nor configuration of them as 'parts' seem especially sound. Perhaps we should further explore the possibility of digital artefacts being objects in their own right. They are *digital objects*. The simple fact that the digital manuscript unlocks a wealth of potentialities that the physical manuscript cannot access, should maybe edge us into thinking that we are dealing with two different things. After all, it would at any rate appear that the same object cannot both have and not have certain properties. The details of an ontology of the digital remain to be flashed out. The difficulty lies in the fact that, as Floridi points out, digital entities do not conform to our Newtonian prejudices. What instead seems basic is reference and relationality. Here, technologies like block-chain, and other efforts to contain the history of the digital object within the object itself, pose provocative philosophical challenges, which theoretical approaches in the digital humanities must seriously engage with.

Returning to Floridi's analysis of the digital revolution's consequence of philosophical import, we see a shift in the standard of existence, the criterion we use to grant the existence of something. The story goes something like this: for ancient and medieval philosophers, to exist fully was to be immutable; for modern philosophy, the hallmark of the real became perception (as Floridi admits, this is a very rough sketch). The informational revolution, by contrast, makes us think of existence in term of *interactibility* (although this view has strong roots in antiquity, fulfilling a line of argument initiated in Plato's *Sophist*). 'Our philosophy seems to suggest that 'to be is to be interactable', even if that with which we interact is only transient and virtual.' (Floridi 2014, 53). As proof of this Floridi adduces the monetary transactions in online multiplayer games: considerable sums of ('real') money are spent for what in reality are just bundles of code, but in our interactions become characters, artefacts, and so on.

Lastly, it is worth mentioning a final philosophical facet of the informational revolution, one that Floridi has, to my knowledge, not explicitly set out in print. Nonetheless, all the dots are in place. We need only connect them. The previous revolutions were characterised by reductionist intents: they very interested in reducing the number of postulates and entities to a bare minimum (Darwin's *Origin*, for instance, was interested precisely in finding a single general law behind the vicissitudes of the animal world). The informational revolution, on the other hand, seems to be animated with the exact opposite concerns. It no longer wants to boil down principles to a bare few. It is excessive: it moves humans into new spaces, colonising them, dwelling in them. Information is not a reductive power but fundamentally creative one.

Some reductionist elements may admittedly present – the claim that 'everything is information', perhaps. Nonetheless, there seems a deeply rooted aspect of ontological excess. The aesthetics of the Internet prize extravagance, they are baroque rather than minimalist. We are no longer interested in keeping things simple, organised along a logic of linearity. We want elliptical circles. It is less of a Copernican revolution and more of a Ptolemaic one: an efflorescence of invisible ellipses, symbolic connections, the incessant movement of the web should constantly be pointing back to itself (think of Wikipedia's sprawling relational charts of self-reference).

It is important to understand the connection between Floridi's re-ontologisation and the *re-aesthetisation* described here. Every ontology is animated by a certain aesthetic, and vice-versa. This specific aesthetic can be traced throughout the digital realm, from Silicon Valley to meme culture. We do not want to reduce; we want to bud out into unknown areas of reality, unlocking new realms of experience: the internet of things, certainly, but also Elon Musk's Neuralink project (which will enable objects to be moved by the mind, through networks of neural implants), or Ray Kurzweil's messianic advent of the 'singularity' (which will, somehow, enable the uploading consciousness into the cloud) (Kurzweil 2005, 147-49). Again, it is not the feasibility of this fabling that is at stake, but the exponential aesthetic that suffuses it.

As for the memes: the aesthetic paradigm that dominates this Internet subculture is one of free borrowing and modification: an ongoing reciprocal borrowing for the purpose of opening potentialities. Memes are 'pictures' designed precisely to be shared, even stolen – modified, improved, transcended. It is this guiding logic of *surfeit*, of a constant excess of information and association, which is, perhaps, a glimpse of a new Ur-philosophy. This explains the Internet's ebullient reaction to the European Union's legislation on digital copyright. The law tried to hammer digital goods into the Newtonian logic of a physical private property, into a zero-sum game of finite goods. That is to say – the very opposite of the ontology of the Internet.

3. Frictions

It is now time to relate the two aspects outlined above to each other. Our main question is whether the strong distinction between human and machine outlined in the first section really can coexist alongside the re-ontologisation advocated in the second section.

As touched on above, the revolutions in question have come hand in hand with reductionisms. In all too broad brushstrokes: Freudianism was keen to reduce all behaviour to subconscious drives, not to mention the entire genres of reductionism laying claim to the Dawinian legacy; the neurological revolution spawned extreme reductionist positions in the philosophy of mind, like *identity theory* (mind and brain are absolutely indistinct) or even *eliminativism* (consciousness is a *bona fide* illusion). We must ask the question of whether the fourth revolution brings with it a reduction and devaluation of the human place analogous to the ones allegedly brought to pass by previous shifts in paradigm.

Revolutions, Floridi writes, have 'introvert' and 'extrovert' effects on our world-view. The extrovert aspect – that dealing with our view of the world – has been dealt with above, in the re-ontologisation of the world to an informational system. The introvert aspect, on the other hand, has to deal with our own self-perception and view of our proper place in the order of things. The revolutions in world-view have also brought revolutions in self-perception: first humans were demoted in their place at the crown of creation, then as the highest of beasts, then as the 'masters of their own house'. Floridi envisions an analogous devaluation of the place of the human, by analogy with the three original revolutions: 'The fourth revolution has brought to light the intrinsically informational nature of human identity. It is humbling, because we share such a nature with some of the smartest of our own artefacts' (Floridi 2014, 96).

This conclusion comes in and of itself as no surprise. If we are to focus solely on relations, especially informational ones, there is really nothing that sets us apart from other *inforgs* – chatterbots, smartwatches or any of the other technological fauna endemic to hyperhistory. After all, ever since its inception, Floridi's philosophy of information was designed to be as 'free as possible from a self-indulgent, anthropocentric obsession with us and our super-duper role in the whole universe' (Floridi 2010, 153). The problem that immediately arises is whether the distinction drawn up in the first section, which seems to be a fundamental distinction between humans and other creatures can be maintained at the same time.

Perhaps the point can be elucidated through a comparison with ontological projects resembling Floridi's. The Pandora's box of a radically relational ontology was first rattled by Deleuze and Guattari, then blasted open by several currents in continental political thought.[1] These ontological projects are, always or for the most part, coupled with resolutely anti-humanist philosophies. In Bruno Latour's actor-network theory, for instance, humans as independent agents are dissolved into an anfractuous web of relations. In Donna Haraway's anti-metaphysics, the concept 'human' is a remnant of a patriarchal ontology, an obsolescent category that should be traded in without further ado (Haraway 1991, 152-53). What I am looking for here is not a matter of guilt by association; I simply want to bring out

---

[1] A radically anti-humanist version of this project can be found in Land 2001, 322.

the tension between the two aspects of Floridi's thought: on the one hand, a relational ontology intent on dethroning the human, and, on the other, a deeply humanist philosophy that places human value (Floridi 2010, 165-168), grounded in the unique ability to bestow and weave meaning, in the centre.

Now, there is no doubt of Floridi's aversion to any trans-, post-, or anti-humanism. Going on a few throwaway comments, Floridi does not seem particularly impressed with any of these projects, writing them off as fanciful speculation. Which may well be the case; the question remains, however, of where the cut-off point exactly is: can Floridi crack open the lid just enough to let out an informational ontology, but slam it shut quickly enough to keep the proliferation of the anti-humanist trajectory?

The question is especially relevant for further explorations in the digital humanities. If the purpose of the humanities is to explore the human and its permutations, it is relevant to know if such a thing even exists! If a radically relational ontology turns out to be the only game in town, this would imply a fundamental reconfiguration of the subject. This is a provocative idea, but by no means a novel one. Donna Haraway, for instance, suggests christening the discipline *humusities*, in accordance with the principles of anti-anthropocentrism, ecologism, relationality, and the whole ball of wax (Haraway 2016, 13). But perhaps it is not time to jump ship just yet. There are two strategies suggested in Floridi's work that could chart a potential middle way between the two horns of the dilemma. I will turn to each of these in turn.

The first of these strategies can be gleaned from Floridi's ethical work. One of the hallmarks of Floridi's ethics of information is the fundamental role accorded to the value of human dignity. The question that confronts him as a consequence of this is very similar to the one we are posing here, although formulated in an ethical ambit. Floridi asks: given an ontology of relations, how do we ground the value of human dignity? After all, this is a value that has gone hand in hand with anthropocentric cosmologies, the very world-views eroded by the four revolutions. Floridi, therefore, requires a non-anthropocentric ethics, that can ground a special (ethical) place for humans without according them any special (ontological) place (Floridi 2020, 147-155).

Floridi's suggestion is that instead of an anthropocentrism, we should veer towards an anthropo-*eccentrism*. The special status of humans is not due to any perfection or centrality; it is rather due to the fact that humans are precisely marginal and aberrant. The value of humans is not due to some special property. It is rather due to a fundamental *lack*: we are an incomplete species – an open software, so to speak – always looking to accrue new semantic capital (Floridi 2020, 152; Floridi 2019, 97-100). Our species is just special enough to justify speaking of human dignity; this exceptionalism, however, is grounded in an ontological fluke, rather than any crowning moment in a Great Chain of Being. Humans are a singularity, a *hapax legomenon* in Galileo's ciphered book of nature: we are 'a fantastic anomaly, *the beautiful glitch*' (*ibid.*).

This is an interesting and provocative suggestion. It remains to be seen, however, whether the fancy footwork involved amounts to anything more than a contrived bulwark to escape the ineluctable logic of an informational ontology. Then again, an anthropo-eccentric ethics may well be a fruitful project, of use far beyond the confines of an ethics of information. The meta-ethical underpinnings of an ethics of *eccentricity*, however, remain yet to be developed. This may prove to be a particularly prickly feat: any such argument needs to consider the status of humans among other species in an amoral sense (configuring it in a moral sense must, if anything, be anthropocentrism), and, on the basis of this, affirm the special nature of the human with respect to other species in a properly moral sense.

A second way out of the dilemma described above can be found in the work of Alan Turing, a figure Floridi elevates to the fountainhead of the informational revolution. One of Turing's chief contributions to a philosophy of information is the notion of a 'level of abstraction'. This is understood as a specification of the parameters in which a given question is posed (Floridi 2019, 41-45). The most memorable example of this is of course the (in)famous Turing test. Instead of asking the question 'Can a machine think?' in some sort of absolute sense, Turing designed a level of abstraction, the Imitation Game, where that question could be posed more precisely (Floridi 2019, 22). The notion of levels of abstraction is not least an important one in the digital humanities: at what level are we analysing a given artefact? It could be at the level of chemical composition, provenance, DNA traces, at any given semantic or stylistic level, and so on.

Perhaps this strategy could be used to navigate the Scylla of anthropocentrism and the Charybdis of anti-humanism. Depending on the levels of abstraction that interest us, we can accommodate a degree of specialness on some levels and a degree of devaluation on others. When we ask the question at the level of: 'are humans are better at processing meaning than machines or?' – the answer is yes, and a kind of anthropocentrism may be allowed. If we ask: 'what things in the world are made of information?' – the answer is no, and this is humbling. In other words, there is no such thing as the friction I have tried to outline above. There is only a possible blurring of different levels of abstraction, as often happens with philosophical questions.

As for this second strategy, its success hangs on whether interfaces are conceived of in a purely pragmatist way, or whether they can be understood in a platonic sense. That is to say: are there any privileged points of view when it comes to understanding the human, levels of abstraction that cleave closer to reality than others ? If not – and Floridi seems to waive the notion of any LoA being more 'privileged' than any other – then we remain vulnerable to a serious challenge: given the plurality of possible interfaces, one cannot argue for the primacy of one over the other. Under the interface of the *humusities*, for instance, there is simply no such thing as a 'human being', only a mesh of relations. That is fine, relative to their level of abstraction. Under the interface of the humanities (traditionally conceived) this may not be the case. Nonetheless, there seems to be no real way of arguing against the proponents of a different interface.

This does not necessarily amount to relativism, as Floridi is right to point out. But it certainly is a kind of radical pragmatism, and one that does not hold up to scrutiny. This is because the philosophy of information seems to be claiming a kind of platonic high-ground (telling us how the world really is, in its ontological constitution), although, according to its own logic, is in fact just one interface among others, which we can opt in or out on relative to our interests. This is obviously problematic: if one's interest happens to be precisely doing philosophical anthropology the platonic way (that is to say, discover what the human is *in an absolute sense*, according to the platonic 'interface'), there is little or nothing a pragmatist's level of abstractions can complain about.

Furthermore – even if these foundational obstacles can be surmounted – it would appear that something stronger than a simple co-existence of different LoA is required if the fourth revolution is to have the introspective devaluation it is supposed to have. We cannot just say that, given interface A, we are indistinguishable from other informational beings; given interface B, we are not. This cannot be sufficient for any evaluative conclusion about the place of the humans among other beings. After all, we share several physical properties in common with a clod of earth. This is hardly an especially humbling insight. There are several levels of abstraction where we share absolutely nothing with a clod of earth – our capacity for levels of abstraction being one of these properties. There thus seems to be a need for a kind of absolute ontological commitment, one where the informational perspective (anti-anthropocentric) is not just one interface among other (anthropocentric) ones. What is required is the kind of reductive absolutism implicit in the offshoots of previous revolutions: the physicalist reductionism that declares objects are *only* their physical properties and interactions, for example, is much more effective in entailing the anti-anthropocentrism *desideratum*.

Conclusion

This paper has outlined Luciano Floridi's thought in relation to the question of the human and the digital. The first section treated Floridi's notion of sematic capital as the basis for a distinction between humans and machines. I argued that the notion is invaluable to the digital humanities, as it puts the interplay of syntactical and semantic capital into perspective. The second section outlined the effects of the digital revolution, arguing that the philosophical implications sketched out by Floridi have bearing on the question of the relation between physical and digitised manuscripts. The final section outlined certain frictions between the preceding section, asking whether Floridi can consistently uphold both the sharp divider between machines and humans and, at the same time, an anti-anthopocentric ontology of relations.

This tension leads to an undeniable ethical or anthropological worry. But also relevant to the digital humanities is a considerable methodological worry. Relational ontologies (Haraway, Latour, etc.) bring with them the problem of an infinite proliferation of relevant information, with no real means of recognising the wheat from the chaff. One needs to spell out answers to why some levels of abstraction more privileged that others: why are we interested in certain questions in the humanities (provenance and production of manuscripts) and not others (how many occurrences of the letter *a* are on a given page)?

The discrepancy in Floridi's argument results from a philosophical engagement with the relation between the human and the digital. While Floridi does not manage to sow together the two lines of argument, his reflections may provide inspiration for the underpinnings of the digital humanities. After all, the symbiosis of human and computational that is in focus in both projects. If this relation is to be taken seriously, the flow of information cannot be unilateral. Floridi's notion of the twofold purpose of a philosophy of information – to bring computational tools to philosophy and vice-versa – could be a useful model for the digital humanities. Adelaide Coe has argued that the digital humanities should be the study of humanities through digital tools, rather than the study of the human *interactions* with the digital. As we have seen, computational tools do not lend their services neutrally. They require a complex interaction of semantic and syntactical capital. According to Floridi, cross-pollination between the two realms is not only necessary, but also desirable.

BIBLIOGRAPHY

Note. Unless otherwise stated, all websites listed below were current as of 1 December 2022. Publication dates of web content are given where known.

Aarts, F.G.A.M. 1969. 'The *Pater noster* in Medieval English Literature'. *Papers on language & Literature* 5, 3-16.

Albritton, Ben & Lisa Fagin Davis. 2018. 'Mirador for Medievalists: IIIF, shared canvas, & digital images'. *The Medieval Academy of America*. https://www.medievalacademy.org/page/miradormedievalists [Accessed 12 December 2019]

Albritton, Benjamin L. 2020. 'Found Within: discovery and complex objects'. DA20 Presentation. https://www.youtube.com/watch?v=mNYQ cej7GxE

Alter, Stephen G. 1999. *Darwinism and the Linguistic Image: Language, Race, and Natural Theology in the Nineteenth Century*. Baltimore.

Amador De Los Rios, José. 1876. *Historia social, política y religiosa de los judíos de España y Portugal 2*. Madrid.

Anderson, Marjorie O. 1980. *Kings and Kingship in Early Scotland*. Rev. edn. Edinburgh.

Anthony, Laurence. 2019. *AntConc*. Version 3.5.8. https://www.laurenceanthony.net/software [Accessed 7 January 2020]

'Apps & Demos'. *International Image Interoperability Framework*. https://iiif.io/apps-demos/#awesome-iiif [Accessed 12 December 2019]

The Archimedes Palimpsest Project. http://www.archimedespalimpsest.org/

Archives de l' État en Belgique. http://www.arch.be/

d'Ardenne, S.R.T.O, ed. 1961. *An Edition of þe Liflade ant te Passiun of Seinte Iuliene*, EETS o.s. 248. Oxford.

Arntz, Helmut & Hans Zeiss 1939. *Die einheimischen Runendenkmäler des Festlandes: Gesamtausgabe der älteren Runendenkmäler*. Leipzig.

Baer, Yitzhak & Lotte Levensohn. 1966. *A History of the Jews in Christian Spain, Vol. 2*. Philadelphia.

Bale, Anthony 2021. 'Towards an Un-edition of Sir John Mandeville'. DA21 (UnEdition) Presentation.
https://www.youtube.com/watch?v=I5Y3Y6Qyo64

Balde, Philipp. 1672. *Naauwkeurige beschryvinge van Malabar en Choromandel*. Amsterdam.

Banik, Gerhard. 'Ink Corrosion: chemistry'. 1998. *The Iron Gall Ink Website*.
https://irongallink.org/igi_index22a4.html
[Accessed 30 January 2020]

Barnes, Michael P. & Raymond I. Page. 2006. *The Scandinavian Runic Inscriptions of Britain*. Uppsala.

Barnes, Michael P. 1994. 'On Types of Argumentation in Runic Studies'. In *Proceedings of the Third International Conference on Runes & Runic Inscriptions, Grindaheim, Norway 8–12 August 1990*, ed. James E. Knirk. Uppsala. 11–29.

Barnes, Michael P. 2012, *Runes: A Handbook*. Woodbridge.

Barnes, Michael P. 2019, *The Runic Inscriptions of the Isle of Man*. London.

Barolini, Teodolinda ed. 2019. *Digital Dante*.
https://digitaldante.columbia.edu/dante/divine-comedy/
[Accessed 12 December 2019]

Barkova, Ekaterina E. 2013. 'Grafiko-Orfografičeskie Osobennosti Staršego Poluustava XIV–XV Vv'. *Vestnik Moskovskogo universiteta. Serija 9: Filologija* 6, 181–90.

Barrow, G.W.S. ed. 1960. *Regesta regum scottorum*, vol. i: *The Acts of Malcolm IV, King of Scots, 1153–1165*. Edinburgh.

Barrow, G.W.S., ed. 1999. *The Charters of King David I: King of Scots, 1124–53, and of his Son Henry Earl of Northumberland.* Woodbridge.

Barrow, G.W.S., ed. with W. W. Scott. 1971. *Regesta regum scottorum,* vol. ii: *The Acts of William I, King of Scots, 1165–1214.* Edinburgh.

Bataillon, Louis Jacques & Richard H. Rouse. 1988. *La Production du livre universitaire au moyen âge: exemplar et pecia.* Paris.

Bately, Janet ed. 1980. *The Old English Orosius.* EETS s.s. 6. London.

Bates, David ed. 1998. *Regesta regum anglo-normannorum: the Acta of William I (1066–1087).* Oxford.

Bates, David. 'Charters and Historians of Great Britain and Ireland: problems and possibilities'. In *Charters and Charter Scholarship in Britain and Ireland,* ed. Marie Therese Flanagan & Judith A. Green. Basingstoke.

Batten, E. C. ed. 1887. *The Charters of the Priory of Beauly.* London.

Baudin, Arnaud. 2011. *Collection de sceaux détachés. Catalogue analytique.* Troyes. https://www.academia.edu/21877752/Catalogue_analytique_de_la_collection_des_sceaux_détaché_des_Archives_départementales_de_lAube_sous_série_42_Fi_

Baugh, A.C., ed. 1956. *English Text of the Ancrene Riwle: BM MS Royal C.vi.* EETS o.s. 232. Oxford.

Beadle, Richard & A.J. Piper eds. 1995. *New Science out of Old Books: Studies in Manuscripts and Early Printed Books in Honour of A.I. Doyle.* Aldershot.

Bechetti, Luca 2006. 'Il degrado dei sigilli di cera: approcci metodologici ed etica di restauro'. In *Marques d'authenticité et sigillographie: recueil d'articles publiés en hommage à René Laurent,* ed. Claude de Moreau de Gerbehaye et André Vanrie. Brussels. 27-36.

Bechetti, Luca 2011. *I sigilli: orientamenti et metodologie di conservazione e restauro.* Padua.

Bede. 2006. *Beda Venerabilis: Historical Works*, ed. J.E. King. Cambridge MA.

Bédier, Joseph 1928. 'La Tradition manuscrite du *Lai d l'ombre*'. *Romania* 54, 161-96, 321-56.

Behr, Charlotte & Tim Pestell. 2014. 'The Bracteate Hoard from Binham – an early Anglo-Saxon central place?'. *Medieval Archaeology* 58, 44–77.

Belfour, A.O. ed. 1909. *Twelfth-Century Homilies in MS Bodley 343*. EETS o.s. 137. London.

Benedikt, Michael, ed. 1991. *Cyberspace: First Steps*. Cambridge MA.

Benevides, Francisco da Fonseca. 1878. *Rainhas de Portugal: estudo historico com muitos documentos*. Vol. 1. Lisbon.

Biblioteca Apostolica Vaticana. 1902-1988. *Codices vaticani latini: codices 2118–2192; 9734–9782*. Rome.

Biblioteca Apostolica Vaticana. *Digitvatlib*. https://digi.vatlib.it/

Biblioteca Apostolica Vaticana. *Opacvatlib*. https://opac.vatlib.it/

Biddick, Kathleen. 1998. *The Shock of Medievalism*. Durham NC.

Bischoff, Bernard. 1990. *Latin Palaeography: Antiquity & the Middle Ages*. New York.

Blackburn, Mark. 1991. 'A Survey of Anglo-Saxon & Frisian Coins with Runic Inscriptions'. In *Old English Runes & their Continental Background*, ed. Alfred Bammesberger. Heidelberg. 137–89.

Blake, Martin ed. 2009. *Ælfric's De temporibus anni*. Cambridge.

Blanc-Riehl, Clément 2011. 'La sigillographie: une science faite pour les historiens de l'art'. In *Pourquoi les sceaux? La sigillographie, nouvel enjeu de l'histoire de l'art*, ed. Jean-Luc Chassel & Marc Gil. Villeneuve d'Ascq. 127-36.

Blanc-Riehl, Clément 2012. 'Les prémices de la sigillographie française (1830-1880)'. *Bulletin de Liaison des Sociétés Savantes* 12, 6-8.

Bloche, Michel and Burette, Camille 2015. 'Un marqueur d'identité codifié'. In *Empreintes du passé: 6000 ans de sceaux*, ed. Archives départementales de la Seine-Maritime, Musée des Antiquités. Rouen. 75-88.

Bodleian Library Digital Manuscripts Toolkit.
http://dmt.bodleian.ox. ac.uk/manifest-editor/
[Accessed 9 December 2019]

Borges, Jorge Luis. 1940. 'Tlön, Uqbar, Orbis Tertius'. *Sur* 68, 36-46.

Borges, Jorge Luis. 1946. 'Del rigor en la ciencia'. *Los anales de Buenos Aires* 1.3, 53.

Bourcier, Georges. 1978. *L'orthographe de l'anglais: histoire et situation actuelle*. Vendôme.

Bradley, John, & Michele Pasin 2013. 'Structing That Which Cannot Be Structured: a role for formal models in representing aspects of Medieval Scotland'. In *New Perspectives on Medieval Scotland, 1093–1286*, ed. Matthew Hammond. Woodbridge. 203–214.

Brook, G.L. & R.F. Leslie, eds. 1963-78. *Laȝamon: Brut*. EETS o.s. 250, 277. London.

Brookes, Stewart, Dauvit Broun, John Reuben Davies, et al. 2019. *Models of Authority: Scottish Charters and the Emergence of Government, 1100–1250*.
http://www.modelsofauthority.ac.uk
[Accessed 20 February 2020]

Brookes, Stewart. 2020. 'The Book, the Whole Book, and Nothing But the... Digital Surrogate'. DA20 Presentation.
https://www.youtube.com/watch?v=nKQebeZ3PeU

Brooks, N. P. & S. E. Kelly eds. 2013. *Charters of Christ Church Canterbury*. 2 vols. Anglo-Saxon Charters 17 & 18. Oxford

Broun, Dauvit. 2001. 'The Changing Face of Charter Scholarship: a review article'. *The Innes Review* 52, 205–11.

Broun, Dauvit. 2005. 'The Adoption of Brieves in Scotland'. In *Charters and Charter Scholarship in Britain and Ireland*, ed. Marie Therese Flanagan & Judith A. Green. Basingstoke, 164–83.

Brown, C. ed. 1939. *Religious Lyrics of the XVth Century*. Oxford.

Brown, Michelle. 1990. *A Guide to Western Historical Scripts from Antiquity to 1600*. Toronto.

Browne, Clare, Glyn Davies & M.A. Michael. 2016. *English Medieval Embroidery: Opus Anglicanum*. Exhibition catalogue. London.

Bruce, Scott. 2020. 'The Lost Patriarchs Project: discovering Greek patristics in the medieval Latin tradition'. DA20 Presentation. https://www.youtube.com/watch?v=iRfybq64d2g&t

Brunner, Karl. 1965. *Altenglische Grammatik nach der Angelsächsichen Grammatik von Eduard Sievers*. 3rd edn. Tübingen.

Buringh, Eltjo & Jan Luiten van Zanden. 2009. 'Charting the "Rise of the West": manuscript & printed books in Europe. A long-term perspective from the sixth through eighteenth centuries'. *Journal of Economic History* 69.2, 409-45.

Buringh, Eltjo. 2011. *Medieval Manuscript Production in the Latin West: Explorations with a Global Database*. Leiden.

Buringh, Eltjo. 2014. 'The Role of Medieval Cities in Book Production: quantitative analyses'. In *Uses of the Written Word in Medieval Towns: Medieval Urban Literacy II*, ed. Marco Mostert & Anna Adamska. Turnhout. 119–77.

Burns, Anna. 2018. *Milkman*. London.

Burton, Janet, ed. 2004. *The Cartulary of Byland Abbey*. Woodbridge.

C11DB. See Scragg et al. 2004.

Cachey, Theodore & Louis Jordan. 1996. *Renaissance Dante in Print: 1472-1629*.
https://www3.nd.edu/~italnet/Dante/

Camden, W. 1633. *Remains concerning Britain*. London.

Cameron, Angus, Ashley Crandell Amos & Antonette diPaolo Healey et al., eds. 2018. *Dictionary of Old English: A to I online*. Toronto.
Cameron, Angus. 1973. 'A list of Old English Texts'. In *A Plan for the Dictionary of Old English*, ed. Roberta Frank & Angus Cameron. Toronto. 25-306.
Campbell, Alastair. 1959. *Old English Grammar*. Oxford.
Cantera Burgos, Francisco. 1952. *Alvar García de Santa María y su familia de conversos: historia de la Judería de Burgos y de sus conversos más egregios*. Madrid.
Care, Chris, Mike Edwards, Zoltán Farkas, Judson Herrman et al. 2008. 'Fragments of Hyperides' "Against Diondas" from the Archimedes Palimpsest'. *Zeitschrift Für Papyrologie Und Epigraphik* 165, 1-19.
Carley, James P. 2006. 'The Dispersal of Monastic Libraries and the Salvaging of the Spoils'. In *The Cambridge History of Libraries in Britain & Ireland: vol 1 to 1640*, ed. Elizabeth Leedham-Green & Teresa Webber. Cambridge. 69-90.
Carlson, David R. 2006. 'A Theory of the Early English Printing Firm: jobbing, book publishing, and the problem of productive capacity in Caxton's work'. In *Caxton's Trace: Studies in the History of English Printing*, ed. William Kuskin. Notre Dame.
Carmona de los Santos, María. 1994. 'Censo de colecciones españolas de matrices de sellos'. *Boletín de la ANABAD* 44.3, 29-42.
Carroll, Lewis. 1893. *Sylvie and Bruno Concluded*. London / New York.
Cartlidge, Neil. 1996. 'The Date of *The Owl & the Nightingale*'. *Medium Ævum* 65, 230-47.
CartulR: Répertoire des cartulaires médievaux et modernes.
http://www.cn-telma.fr/cartulR/index/
[Accessed 20 February 2020]
Cashion, Debra Taylor & Gregory Pass. 'METAscripta: the VFL Microfilm Metadata Project'.
https://metascripta.Omeka.net/exhibits/show/vflmicrofilm

Cashion, Debra Taylor. 2016. 'Cataloging Manuscripts, from Beasts to Bytes'. *Digital Philology: A Journal of Medieval Cultures* 5.2, 135-59.

A Catalogue of the Harleian Manuscripts in the British Museum. 1808.

Cerquiglini, Bernard. 1989. *Éloge de la variante: Histoire critique de la philologie*. Paris.

Cerquiglini, Bernard & B. Wing (trans). 1999. *In Praise of the Variant: A Critical History of Philology*. Baltimore.

Champion, Matthew, J. 2020. 'A Sea of Lost Words: the medieval graffiti inscriptions of England's parish churches'. DA20 Presentation. https://www.youtube.com/watch?v=WpX_GYURRu0&t=1s

CHATGPT. 2022.

https://chat.Openai.com/

Chardonnens, Lászlo Sándor. 2007. *Anglo-Saxon Prognostics, 900-1100*. Leiden.

Chassel, Jean-Luc. 1993. 'Dessins et mentions de sceaux dans les cartulaires médiévaux'. In *Les cartulaires*, ed. Olivier Guyotjeannin, Laurent Morelle & Michel Parisse. Paris. 153-170.

Clark, Cecily. 1983. 'On Dating "The Battle of Maldon": certain evidence reviewed'. *Nottingham Medieval Studies* 27, 1-22.

Clavero, Bartolomé. 1989. *Mayorazgo: propiedad feudal en Castilla 1369-1836*. Madrid.

Clemens, Raymond & Timothy Graham. 2007. *Introduction to Manuscript Studies*. Ithaca.

Clemoes, Peter, ed. 1997. *Ælfric's Catholic Homilies: The First Series. Text*. EETS s.s. 7. Oxford.

Clooney, George, Director. 2014. *The Monuments Men*. [Motion Picture].

Clough, Cecil H. 1984. 'The Library of Bernardo & of Pietro Bembo'. *Book Collector* 33, 305-31.

Cohn, Samuel K. 2007. 'The Black Death and the Burning of Jews'. *Past & Present* 196.1, 3-36.

Collins, Roger. 1994. *The Arab Conquest of Spain, 710-797*. Oxford.

Colson, Isabelle, Christian Degrigny & Michel Dubus. 2001. 'Les chartes scellées par des bulles de plomb et leur conservation aux Archives nationales'. *La Gazette des archives* 192, 221-238.

Connolly, Margaret, ed. 1993. *Contemplations of the Dread and Love of God*. 1993. EETS o.s. 303. Oxford.

Connolly, Margaret. 2018. 'The Edited Text and the Selected Text and the Problem of Critical Editions'. In *Editing and Interpretation of Middle English Texts: Essays in Honour of William Marx*, ed. Margaret Conolly and Raluca Raculescu. Brepols. 229–47.

Cook, A.S. 1891. 'The Evolution of the Lord's Prayer in English'. *The American Journal of Philology* 12.1, 59-66.

Coulon, Auguste. 1912. *Inventaire des sceaux de la Bourgogne... Départements de la Côte d'Or, de la Saône-et-Loire et de l'Yonne*. Paris.

Cowan, Ian B. & David E. Easson. 1976. *Medieval Religious Houses Scotland, with an Appendix on the Houses in the Isle of Man*. London.

Craig-McFeely, Julia. 2012. 'From Perfect to Preposterous: how digital restoration can both help and hinder our reading of damaged sources'. In *Cantus Scriptus: Technologies of Medieval Songs Proceedings of the 3rd Annual Lawrence J. Schoenberg Symposium on Manuscript Studies in the Digital Age, November 20–21, 2010*, ed. Lynn Ransom and Emma Dillon. Piscataway. 125–41

Craig-McFeely, Julia & Alan Lock. 2006. *DIAMM ... Digital Restoration Workbook*. Oxford.
https://www.diamm.ac.uk/publications/digital-restoration-workbook/
[accessed 30 January 2020]

Crane, Gregory, David Bamman & Alison Jones. 2013. 'ePhilology: when books talk to their readers'. In *A Companion to Digital Literary Studies* ed. Ray Siemens & Susan Schreibman. Oxford. 29-64.

Crick, Julia. 2001. 'Offa, Ælfric & the Refoundation of St Albans'. In *Alban & St Albans: Roman & Medieval Architecture, Art & Archaeology*, ed. Martin Henig & Philip Linley. [London]. 78-84.

Crick, Julia ed. 2007. *Charters of St Albans*. Anglo-Saxon Charters 12. Oxford.

Cubitt, Catherine. 1995. *Anglo-Saxon Church Councils, c. 650 – c. 850*. London.

Cunningham, Ian. 1989. 'The Manuscript Collections to 1925'. In *For the Encouragement of Learning: Scotland's National Library, 1689–1989*, ed. Patrick Cadell & Ann Matheson. Edinburgh. 119–38.

Cunningham, Ian. 1995. 'Syllabus of Scottish Cartularies'. *Monastic Research Bulletin* 1, 11.

Cunningham, Ian. 2001. *Syllabus of Scottish Cartularies: Holyrood*. https://scottishmedievalcharters.wordpress.com/scottish-cartularies/ [Accessed 20 February 2020]

DA19. 2019 (10-12 September). 'Dark Archives: A Conference on the Medieval Unread & Unreadable.' https://darkarchiv.es/19

DA20. 2020 (8-10 September). 'Dark Archives 20/20. A Voyage into the Medieval Unread & Unreadable' https://darkarchiv.es/20

DA21 (UnEdition). 2021 (18 March). 'Birth of the UnEdition'. https://darkarchiv.es/20/21

DALL E 2. 2022. https://openai.com/dall-e-2/

Dalton, J.N. 1917 ed. *The Collegiate Church of Ottery St. Mary: Being the Ordinacio et statute ecclesie Sancte Marie de Otery Exon. diocesis A.D. 1338, 1339* […]. Cambridge.

Dance, Richard. 2003. *Words derived from Old Norse in Early Middle English: Studies in the Vocabulary of the South-West Midland Texts*. Tempe.

Danmarks Runeindskrifter. Copenhagen University. www.runer.ku.dk

Dante Alighieri & Robin Kirkpatrick (trans.). 2007. *The Divine Comedy 3: Paradiso*. London.

Davies, Helen & Alexander J. Zawacki. 2020. 'Making Light Work: manuscripts and multispectral imaging'. *Journal of The Early English Book Society* 22, 179-98.

Davies, John Reuben. 2011. 'The Donor and the Duty of Warrandice: giving and granting in Scottish charters'. In *The Reality Behind Charter Diplomatic in Anglo-Norman Britain*, ed. Dauvit Broun. Glasgow. 120–65.

Davis, G.R.C. ed. 1958. *Medieval Cartularies of Great Britain: A Short Catalogue*. London.

Davis, G.R.C., ed. 2010. *Medieval Cartularies of Great Britain and Ireland*, rev. Claire Breay, Julian Harrison & David M. Smith. London.

Day, M., ed. 1952. *The English Text of the Ancrene Riwle: BM MS. Cotton Nero A.xiv*. EETS o.s. 225. Oxford.

De la Mare, Albinia C. 1973. *Handwriting of the Italian Humanists*. Oxford.

Debray, Régis & Eric Rauth (trans.). 1995. 'Three Ages of Looking'. Critical Inquiry 21.3, 529-55.

Deciphering Secrets: Unlocking the Manuscripts of Medieval Spain. https://grants.uccs.edu/deciphering-secrets/

Delmas, Marie-Claude. 1998. 'Quels instruments de recherche pour les sceaux? Tradition et perspectives d'avenir'. *Bibliothèque de l'École des Chartes*. 156, 573.

Deleuze, Gilles. 1968. *Différence et repetition*. Paris.

Deleuze, Gilles & Paul Patton (trans.). 1994. *Difference and Repetition*. New York.

Derolez, Albert. 2003. *The Palaeography of Gothic Manuscript Books*. New York.

Demay, Germain. 1873. *Inventaire des sceaux de la Flandre… Départements du Nord*. 2 vols. Paris.

Demay, Germain. 1877. *Inventaire des sceaux de l'Artois et de la Picardie… Départements de la Somme, de l'Oise et de l'Aisne*. Paris.

Demay, Germain. 1881. *Inventaire des sceaux de la Normandie... Départements de la Seine-Maritime, du Calvados, et la Manche et de l'Orne*. Paris.

Demay, Germain. 1885-86. *Inventaire des sceaux de la collection Clairambault à la Bibliothèque nationale*. 2 vols. Paris.

Derolez, René. 1954. *Runica Manuscripta: The English Tradition*. Bruges.

Derolez, René. 1998. 'The Origins of the Runes: an alternative approach'. *Academiae Analecta*, Klasse der Letteren, 60.1. Brussels.

Derrida, Jacques & Eric Prenowitz (trans.). 1995. *Archive Fever: A Freudian Impression*. Chicago.

Desmond, Karen. 2020. 'Fragments and Reconstructions: the written traces of polyphonic liturgical music in medieval Worcester and beyond'. DA20 Presentation. https://www.youtube.com/watch?v=6FvzKE0JYP4

DIAMM. See Digital Image Archive of Medieval Music.

DIMEV. 1995– . *Digital Index of Middle English Verse*, ed. L.R. Mooney, D.W. Mosser, E. Solopova, D. Thorpe, D. Radcliffe & L. Hatfield. http://www.dimev.net/

Dietz, Klaus. 2006. *Schreibung und Lautung im mittelalterlichen Englisch: Entwicklung und Funktion der englischen Schreibung ch, gh, sh, th, wh und ihrer kontinentalsen Entsprechungen*. Heidelberg.

DigiPalSlav. www.digipalslav.uni-freiburg.de

Digisig. http://www.digisig.org

Digital Image Archive of Medieval Music (DIAMM). www.diamm.ac.uk

The Digital Index of Middle English Verse. See DIMEV.

Digital Editions Live. 2021. https://historyofthebook.mml.ox.ac.uk/digital-editions-live/

diPaolo Healey, Antonette, with John Price Wilkin & Xin Ziangm eds. 2009. *Dictionary of Old English Web Corpus* https://tapor-library-utoronto-ca.elib.tcd.ie/ doecorpus/ [Accessed 7 January 2020]

Dobson, E.J. 1962. 'The Affiliations of the Manuscripts of Ancrene Wisse'. In *English and Medieval Studies Presented to J.R.R. Tolkien on the Occasion of his Seventieth Birthday*, ed. Norman Davis and C.L. Wren. London. 128-63.

Dobson E.J. & L.F. Harrison, eds. 1979. *Medieval English Songs*. London.

Dorofeeva, Anna. 2020. 'Book Ciphers and the Medieval Unreadable'. https://www.youtube.com/watch?v=H-gPzQlstQI

Douët D'arcq, Louis. 1863-1868. *Collections des sceaux [des Archives de l'Empire]*. 3 vols. Paris.

Dowden, J. ed. 1903. *The Chartulary of Lindores Abbey*. Edinburgh.

Drout, Michael D. C. & Scott Kleinmann. 2009. 'Philological Inquiries 1: method & Merovingians'. *The Heroic Age* 12 [no pagination].

Drout, Michael D. C. & Scott Kleinmann. 2010. 'Doing Philology 2: something "old", something "new". Material philology & the recovery of the past'. *The Heroic Age* 13 [no pagination].

Dspace. https://duraspace.org/dspace/

Dublin Core Metadata Initiative. https://dublincore.org

Dumville, David. 1992. *Wessex & England from Alfred to Edgar: Six Essays on Political, Cultural & Ecclesiastical Revival*. Woodbridge.

Duncan, A.A.M. ed. 1988. *Regesta regum scottorum*, vol. v: *the Acts of Robert I, King of Scots, 1306–1329*. Edinburgh.

Duncan, A. A. M. 1998. 'The Monk and the Medieval Archives of Glasgow Cathedral'. *The Innes Review* 49, 143–6.

Durkan, John. 1971. 'Missing Cartularies: the Thomas Innes evidence'. *The Innes Review* 22, 110–11.

Düwel, Klaus. 1992. 'Zur Auswertung der Brakteateninschriften: Runenkenttnis und Runeninschriften als Obserschichten-Merkmale'. In *Der historische Horizont der Götterbild-Amulette aus der Übergangsepoche von der Spätantike zum Frühmittelalter*, ed. Karl Hauck. Göttingen. 32–90.

Düwel, Klaus. 2007. 'Die Fibel von Meldorf: 25 Jahre und kein Ende — zugleich ein kleiner Beitrag zur Interpretationsproblematik und Forschungsgeschichte'. In *Zweiundvierzig: Festschrift für Michael Gebühr zum 65. Geburtstag*, ed. S. Burmeister, H. Derks & J. von Richthofen. Rahden. 167–74.

Düwel, Klaus 2008, *Runenkunde*. 4th edn. Stuttgart.

Duxfield, Polly. 2018. 'The Practicalities of Collaboratively Digitally Editing Medieval Prose: the *Estoria de Espanna* digital project as a case study'. Digital Philology 7.1, 78.

Earle, John. 1888. *A Hand-Book to the Land Charters & other Saxonic Documents*. Oxford.

Easson, D.E. ed. 1947. *Charters of the Abbey of Coupar Angus*, 2 vols. Edinburgh.

Easton, Roger L. & David Kelbe. 2014. 'Statistical Processing of Spectral Imagery to Recover Writings from Erased or Damaged Manuscripts'. *Manuscript Cultures* 7, 35–46.

Easton, Roger L., William A. Christens-Barry & Keith T. Knox. 2011. 'Ten Years of Lessons from Imaging of the Archimedes Palimpsest'. *Commentationes Humanarum Litterarum* 129, 5–34

Easton, Roger L. & William Noel. 2010. 'Infinite Possibilities: ten years of study of the Archimedes Palimpsest'. *Proceedings of the American Philosophical Society* 154.1, 50–76

Edsel, Robert M. 2009. *The Monuments Men: Allied Heroes, Nazi Thieves, & the Greatest Treasure Hunt in History*. New York.

Ellis, A.J. ed. 1867. *On Early English Pronunciation: with Especial Reference to Shakspere and Chaucer … Part IV*. EETS e.s. 2. London.

eScriptorium. https://escripta.hypotheses.org/

Eisenstein, Elizabeth L. 1979. *The Printing Press as an Agent of Change*. Cambridge.

Eisner, Martin. 2013. *Boccaccio & the Invention of Italian Literature: Dante, Petrarch, Cavalcanti, & the Authority of the Vernacular*. New York.

Elis-Nilsson, Sara. 2020. 'Using Manuscript Fragments to Map Lived Religion: the case of the cults of saints in medieval Sweden'. DA20 Presentation.
https://www.youtube.com/watch?v=9PwIVwSYQuI
ENVI. *Environment for Visualising Images.*
https://www.l3harrisgeospatial.com/Software-Technology/ENVI
Erbe, Theodor, ed. 1905. *Mirk's Festial: Collection of Homilies by Johannes Mirkus (John Mirk), Edited from Bodl. MS Gough Eccl. Top. 4, with Variant Reading from other MSS, Part 1.* EETS e.s. 96. London.
Ermatinger, C.J. 'Charles Joseph Ermatinger (1921-2002)'. *The Monuments Foundation for the Preservation of Art.*
https://www.monumentsmenfoundation.org/ermatinger-t-3-sgt-charles-j
[Accessed 6 December 2019]
d'Evelyn, C., ed. 1944. *The Latin Text of the Ancrene Riwle*, EETS o.s. 216. Oxford.
Everitt, Brian S. 2011. *Cluster Analysis.* 5th edn. Chichester.
'Exsultet'. 2019. Wikipedia: The Free Encyclopedia.
https://en.wikipedia.org/w/index.php?title=Exsultet&oldid=924431780
[Accessed 12 December 2019]
'Exsultet jam angelica turba caelorum'. Cantus: A Database for Latin Eccelsiastical Chant.
http://cantus.uwaterloo.ca/chant/664345
[Accessed December 12, 2019]
Fagin Davis, Lisa, chair. 2020. 'The Whole Book?'. DA20 Round-table debate.
https://www.youtube.com/watch?v=u2Cs6vVcZIA
Fontaine, Michael & Adele C. Scafuro, eds. 2014. *The Oxford Handbook of Greek and Roman Comedy.* Oxford.
Frankopan, Peter, chair. 2020. 'The Future of Scholarship'. DA20 Round-table debate.
https://www.youtube.com/watch?v=KrDqClTaINo

Franklin, Simon. 2019. *The Russian Graphosphere, 1450-1850*. Cambridge.

Faulkner, Mark & Lili Boorman. In preparation. 'A New Edition of the Old English Versions of King Offa's Grant of Cassio to St Albans. (Sawyer nos. 136, 136a)'.

Faulkner, Mark. 2017a. 'Dublin, Trinity College, MS 492: a new witness to the Old English Bede & its twelfth-century context'. *Anglia* 135, 274-90.

Faulkner, Mark. 2017b. 'Linguistic Evidence for the Compilation of Twelfth-Century Manuscripts Containing Old English: the case of Cotton Vespasian D. xiv'. *Neuphilologische Mitteilungen* 118, 279-316.

Faulkner, Mark. 2020. 'Quantifying the Consistency of "Standard" Old English Spelling'. *Transactions of the Philological Society* 118, 192-205.

Fiddyment, Sarah. 2020. 'Reading the Invisible: can biocodicology help interpret the history of a manuscript?'. DA20 Presentation. https://www.youtube.com/watch?v=EtG4k8pw6oE

Fisiak, Jacek. 1968. *A Short Grammar of Middle English*, pt 1: *Graphemics, Phonemics & Morphemics*. Warsaw.

Flammarion, Hubert. 2019. 'Les moulages de sceaux des Archives de la Haute-Marne'. *Les Cahiers haut-Marnais* 294.3, 107-38.

Floridi, Luciano. 2002. 'What Is the Philosophy of Information?'. *Metaphilosophy* 33, 1–2, 123–45.

Floridi, Luciano. 2007. 'A Look into the Future Impact of ICT on Our Lives'. *The Information Society* 23.1, 59–64.

Floridi, Luciano. 2010. 'The Philosophy of Information: ten years later'. In P. Allo ed., *Putting Information First*. Oxford.

Floridi, Luciano. 2014. *The Fourth Revolution: How the Infosphere is Reshaping Human Reality*. Oxford.

Floridi, Luciano. ed. 2015. *The Onlife Manifesto: Being Human in a Hyperconnected Era*. Cham.

Floridi, Luciano. 2018. 'Semantic Capital: its nature, value, and curation'. *Philosophy & Technology* 31, 481–97.

Floridi, Luciano. 2019. *The Logic of Information: A Theory of Philosophy as Conceptual Design*. Oxford.

Floridi, Luciano. 2020. *Il verde e il blu*. Milan.

Forrström, Gösta. 1948. *The Verb 'to Be' in Middle English: A Survey of the Forms*. Lund.

Förstemann, Ernst. 1900. *Altdeutsches Namenbuch*, 1: *Personennamen*. Bonn.

Foucault, Michel. 1966. *Les Mots et les choses*. Paris.

Foucault, Michel. 1971. *The Order of Things: An Archaeology of the Human Sciences*. New York.

Frank, Roberta. 1997. 'The Unbearable Lightness of Being a Philologist'. *Journal of English & Germanic Philology* 96, 486-513.

Fulk, R. D. 1992. *A History of Old English Meter*. Philadelphia.

Furnivall, Frederick J., ed. 1869-77. *A Six-Text Print of Chaucer's Canterbury Tales*. London.

Furnivall, Frederick J., ed. 1885. *The Harleian MS. 7334 of Chaucer's Canterbury Tales*. London.

Furnivall, Frederick J., ed. 1901-02. *The Cambridge MS. Dd.4.24 of Chaucer's Canterbury Tales, Completed by the Egerton MS. 2726 (the Haistwell MS.)*. 1901-02. London.

Geary, Patrick J. 1994. *Phantoms of Remembrance: Memory and Oblivion at the End of the First Millennium*. Princeton.

Gelling, Margaret. 1979. *The Early Charters of the Thames Valley*. Leicester.

Gerber, Jane S. 1994. *The Jews of Spain: a history of the Sephardic experience*. New York.

'Getty Manuscripts'. The J. Paul Getty Museum.
http://www.getty.edu/art/manuscripts/
[Accessed 12 December 2019]

Getty Vocabularies. 2019. 'Getty Vocabularies as Linked Open Data'. The Getty Research Institute. https://www.getty.edu/research/tools/vocabularies/lod/index.html [Accessed 6 December 2019]

Getty Vocabularies. 'Getty Vocabularies', *The Getty Research Institute.* https://www.getty.edu/research/tools/vocabularies/ [Accessed 6 December 2019]

Giacometti, Alejandro, Alberto Campagnolo, Lindsay Macdonald et al. 2017 (April). 'The Value of Critical Destruction: evaluating multispectral image processing methods for the analysis of primary historical texts'. *Digital Scholarship in the Humanities* 32.1, 101–22.

Gibson, William. 1984. *Neuromancer.* New York.

Gibson, William. 1987. *Count Zero.* New York.

Gibson, William. 1989. *Mona Lisa Overdrive.* New York.

Gillespie, Vincent. 2006. 'The Haunted Text: reflections in *A Mirror to Devout People*'. In *The Text in the Community: Essays on Medieval Works, Manuscripts, Authors, and Readers*, ed. Jill Mann & Maura Nolan. Notre Dame. 129-72.

Godden, Malcolm. 2011. 'The Old English Life of St Neot & Legends of King Alfred'. *Anglo-Saxon England* 39, 193-225.

Godden, Malcolm ed. 2000. *Ælfric's Catholic Homilies: Introduction, Commentary & Glossary.* EETS s. s. 18. Oxford.

Goering, J. & F.A.C. Mantello eds. 1984. *Templum Dei, Robert Grosseteste: edited from MS. 27 Emmanuel College, Cambridge.* Toronto.

Gomes, Saul António, António João Portugal & António Silva Araùjo. 2018. 'Uma matriz sigilar real portuguesa de ouro do século XV'. *Cultura, Espaço e Memória* 9, 367-86.

Gomes, Saul António. 2003. 'Percursos antigos e recentes da Sigilografia em Portugal'. In *Colecção esfragística da Faculdade de Letras da Universidade de Coimbra* [exhibition catalogue]. Coimbra. 39-59.

Gomes, Saul António. 2012. *Introdução à Sigilografia portuguesa: guia de estudo*. 2nd edn. Coimbra.

Gomes, Saul António. 2018. 'Sigilografia em Portugal: alguns desafios e problemas'. In *A investigação sobre Heráldica e Sigilografia na Península Ibérica: entre a tradição e a inovação*, ed. Maria do Rosário Barbosa Morujão & Manuel Joaquín Salamanca López. Coimbra. 525-38.

Gooding, Paul. 2012. 'Mass Digitization & The Garbage Dump: the conflicting needs of quantitative & qualitative Methods'. *Literary & Linguistic Computing* 28, 425-31.

Google. N-Gram Viewer.
https://books.google.com/ngrams
[Accessed 7 January 2020]

Green, A. A., M. Berman, P. Switzer & M. D. Craig. 1988. 'A Transformation for Ordering Multispectral Data in Terms of Images Quality with Implications for Noise Removal'. *IEEE Transactions on Geoscience and Remote Sensing* 26.1, 65-74.

Green, Judith. 1990. *English Sheriffs to 1154*. Public Record Office Handbooks 24. London.

Greetham, David. 1996. 'Phylum–Tree–Rhizome'. In *Reading from the Margins: Textual Studies, Chaucer, and Medieval Literature*, ed. Seth Lerer. San Marino. 99-126.

Gries, Stefan Th. & Martin Hilpert. 2008. 'The Identification of Stages in Diachronic Data: variability-based neighbor clustering'. *Corpora* 3. 59-81.

Gries, Stefan Th. & Martin Hilpert. 2012. 'Variability-Based Neighbor Clustering: a bottom-up approach to periodization in historical linguistics'. In *The Oxford Handbook of the History of English*, ed. Terttu Nevalainen & Elizabeth Closs Traugott. Oxford. 134-44.

Guéville, Estelle & David Joseph Wrisley. 2020. 'Rethinking the Abbreviation: questions and challenges of machine reading medieval scripta'. DA20 Presentation.
https://www.youtube.com/watch?v=p38lvPRRNmA

Guyotjeannin, Olivier, Laurent Morelle and Michel Parisse eds. 1993. *Les cartulaires: Actes de la table ronde organisée par l'école nationale des chartes et le G.D.R. 121 du C.N.R.S. (Paris, 5–7 décembre, 1991)*, Mémoires et documents de l'école nationale des chartes 39. Paris.

Haaf, Susanne & Christian Thomas. 2016. 'Enabling the Encoding of Manuscripts within the DTABf: Extension & Modularization of the Format'. *Journal of the Text Encoding Initiative* 10. https://journals.openedition.org/jtei/1650

Hablot, Laurent. 2017. 'Le programme «SIGILLA», base de donnée nationale des sceaux des archives françaises'. In *Le sceau dans les Pays Bas méridionaux, X^e-XVIe siècles. Entre contrainte sociale et affirmation de soi*, ed. Marc Libert & Jean-François Nieus. Brussels. 111-24.

Hablot, Laurent. 2019. 'SIGILLA. Un catalogue sigillographique numérique pour le XXIe siècle'. *Les Cahiers haut-Marnais* 294.3, 139-145.

Haddan, Arthur West & William Stubbs, eds. 1869-1878. *Councils & Ecclesiastical Documents Relating to Great Britain & Ireland*. 3 vols. Oxford.

Hamelius, P., ed. 1929-23 [1916]. *Mandeville's Travels, translated from the French of Jean d'Outremeuse: Edited from MS. Cotton Titus C.xvi, in the British Museum*, EETS o.s. 153-54. London.

Hammond, Matthew. 2013. 'Introduction: the paradox of medieval Scotland, 1093–1286'. In *New Perspectives on Medieval Scotland, 1093–1286*, ed. Matthew Hammond. Woodbridge. 1–52.

Hammond, Matthew. 2014. 'The Adoption and Routinization of Scottish Royal Charter Production for Lay Beneficiaries, 1124–1195'. In *Anglo-Norman Studies XXXVI: Proceedings of the Battle Conference 2013* ed. David Bates. Woodbridge. 91–115

Hammond, Matthew. [2020]. 'Robert I's Charters: Documents and Itinerary'. In *The Community of the Realm in Scotland, 1249–1424: History, Law and Charters in a Recreated Kingdom*. https://cotr.ac.uk/robert-charters/

Hanna, Ralph III. 1992. 'Producing Manuscripts and Editions'. In *Crux and Controversy in Middle English Textual Criticism*, ed. A.J. Minnis & Charlotte Brewer. Cambridge. 109-30.

Hanna, Ralph III. 2005. *London Literature, 1300-1380*. Cambridge.

Hanna, Ralph III. 2010. 'George Kane and the Invention of Textual Thought: Retrospect and Prospect'. *Yearbook of Langland Studies* 24. 1-20.

Hanna, Ralph III. 1996. Pursuing History: Middle English Manuscripts and Their Texts. Stanford.

Hanna, Ralph III. 'Editing Texts with Extensive Manuscript Traditions'. In Gillespie & Hudson, Probable Truth, 111-29.

Hanna, Ralph III & Sarah Wood, eds. 2013. *Richard Morris's Prick of Conscience: A Corrected and Amplified Reading Text*. Oxford.

Haraway, D. 1991. *Simians, Cyborgs and Women: The Reinvention of Nature*. New York.

Haraway, D. 2016. *Staying with the Trouble: Making Kin in the Chthulucene*. Durham.

Hardwick, Ch. & H.R. Luard, eds. 1856-1867. *A Catalogue of the Manuscripts Preserved in the Library of the University of Cambridge*. Cambridge.

Harsley, Fred. ed. 1889. *Eadwine's Canterbury Psalter, pt 2, Text & Notes*. EETS o.s. 92. London.

Harvard Medieval and Renaissance Manuscripts. 'Medieval & Renaissance Manuscripts'. *Harvard Digital Collections*. https://curiosity.lib.harvard.edu/medieval-renaissance-manuscripts?utm_source=library.harvard [Accessed 19 December 2019]

Hassabis, Demis. 2019. 'The Power of Self-Learning Systems'. https://www.youtube.com/watch?v=3N9phq_yZP0

Heath, Tom. *Linked Data-Connect Distributed Data Across the Web*. http://linkeddata.org/ [Accessed 9 December 2019]

Heizmann, Wilhelm & Morten Axboe, eds. 2011. *Die Goldbrakteaten der Völkerwanderungszeit — Auswertung & Neufunde*. Berlin.

Herbert, J.A., ed. 1944. *The French Text of the Ancrene Riwle: BM MS. Cotton Vitellius F.vii*. EETS o.s. 219. Oxford.

Higgins, Iain Macleod. 1997. *Writing East: The 'Travels' of Sir John Mandeville*. Philadelphia.

Hillgarth, J.N. 1978. *The Spanish Kingdoms, 1250-1516. Vol. 2.* Oxford.

Hilgarth, J.N. 1985. *Spanish Historiography and Iberian Reality*. Middletown.

Hills, Catherine 191, 'The Archaeological Context of Runic Finds'. In *Old English Runes & their Continental Background*, ed. A. Bammesberger. Heidelberg. 41–59.

Hilpert, Martin. 2013. *Constructional Change in English: Developments in Allomoprhy, Word Formation, & Syntax*. Cambridge.

Hines, John & Bengt Odenstedt. 1987. 'The Undley Bracteate & its Runic Inscription'. *Studien zur Sachsenforschung* 6, 73–94.

Hines, John. 1997. 'Functions of Literacy & the Use of Runes'. In *Runor och ABC*, ed. Stefan Nyström. Stockholm. 79–92.

Hines, John 2019a. 'Practical Runic Literacy in the Late Anglo-Saxon Period: inscriptions on lead sheet'. In *Anglo-Saxon Micro-Texts* ed. Ursula Lenker & Lucia Kornexl. Berlin. 29–59.

Hines, John. 2019b. 'Two Personal Names in Recently Found Anglo-Saxon Inscriptions: Sedgeford (Norfolk) & Elsted (West Sussex)'. *Anglia* 137, 278–302.

Hines, John. 2020, 'New Insights into Early Old English from Recent Anglo-Saxon Runic Finds'. *North-Western European Language Evolution* 73, 69–90.

Hilton, Walter. 2017 [2016]. *The Scale of Perfection, Book II: An Edition based on British Library MSS Harley 6573 and 6579*, ed. S.S. Hussey & Michael G. Sargent. EETS o.s. 348.

Hodgson, Phyllis, ed. 1944. *The Cloud of Unknowing and The Book of Privy Counselling*. EETS o.s. 218. Oxford.

Hogg, Richard M. 1992. *A Grammar of Old English*. Vol. 1: *Phonology*. Oxford.

Hogg, Richard M. & Robert W. Fulk. 2011. *A Grammar of Old English*. Vol. 2: *Morphology*. Oxford.

Holscher, Marenliese Jonah & Katharina Mähler. 2021 (17 May). 'Ready for the Big Show: how manuscripts are prepared for digitization'. *German Manuscripts-Deutsche Handschriften*, Blog post. https://hab.bodleian.ox.ac.uk/en/blog/blog-post-36/

Hoskin, Philippa M. & Elizabeth A. New. 2018. 'Imprint. A Forensic & Historical Investigation of Fingerprints on Medieval Seals'. *Medieval Prosopography* 32, 249-253.

Hotelling, H. 1933. 'Analysis of a Complex of Statistical Variables into Principal Components'. *Journal of Educational Psychology* 24, 417–441, 498–520.

Hotelling, H. 1936. 'Relations between Two Sets of Variates'. *Biometrika* 28.3/4, 321-77.

Hough, Carole, Simon Taylor, Eila Williamson, Brian Aitken & Dàibhidh Grannd. 2019. The Berwickshire Place-Name Resource. https://berwickshire-placenames.glasgow.ac.uk/ [Accessed 21 February 2020]

Hussey, Stan. 1992. 'Editing The Scale of Perfection: return to recension'. In *Crux and Controversy in Middle English Textual Criticism*, ed. Alastair Minnis & Charlotte Brewer. Woodbridge. 97–107

Hyvärinen, Aapo, Juha Karhunen, & Erkki Oja. 2001. *Independent Component Analysis*. New York.

IIIF. International Image Interoperability Framework. https://iiif.io/

IIIF. 'IIIF Presentation API 2.0'. International Image Interoperability Framework. https://iiif.io/api/presentation/2.0/#iiif-presentation-api-2-0 [Accessed 12 December 2019]

IIIF. 2019. 'IIIF Annual Conference & Showcase - Boston, MA - June 1-4, 2020'. *International Image Interoperability Framework.* https://iiif.io/event/2020/boston/#iiif-annual-conference-and-showcase-boston-ma-june-1-4-2020 [Accessed 9 December 2019]

ImageJ. https://imagej.nih.gov/

IMEV. 1943. *The Index of Middle English Verse.*, ed. C. Brown & R.H. Robbins. New York.

ImPRINT. https://www.imprintseals.org

The Index of Middle English Verse. See IMEV.

Ingham, Patricia Clare. 'Losing French: Vernacularity, Nation, and Caxton's English Statutes'. In *Caxton's Trace: Studies in the History of English Printing,* ed. William Kuskin. Notre Dame. 275-298.

Innes, C., ed. 1832. *Registrum Monasterii de Passelet.* Paisley.

Innes, C., ed. 1837. *Liber Sancte Marie de Melros.* Edinburgh.

Innes, C. ed. 1847a. *Carte Monialium de Northberwic.* Edinburgh.

Innes, C. ed. 1847b. *Liber Cartarum Sancte Crucis.* Edinburgh.

Innes, C. ed. 1849. *Registrum Sancte Marie de Neubotle.* Edinburgh.

Innes, C. & P. Chalmers eds. 1848–1856. *Liber Sancte Thome de Aberbrothoc,* 2 vols. Edinburgh.

International Image Interoperability Framework. See IIIF.

Irvine, Susan. ed. 1993. *Old English Homilies from MS Bodley 343.* EETS o. s. 302. Oxford.

Irvine, Susan. ed. 2004. *The Anglo-Saxon Chronicle: A Collaborative Edition,* vol. 7, *MS. E.* Cambridge.

Jacobsen, Lis & Erik Moltke 1941–2. *Danmarks Runeindskrifter.* 2 vols. Copenhagen.

Jacquet, Philippe. 2011. 'Radiographie, scanner et sigillographie'. In *Pourquoi les sceaux? La sigillographie, nouvel enjeu de l'histoire de l'art,* ed. Jean-Luc Chassel and Marc Gil. Villeneuve d'Ascq. 93-103.

Jacquet, Philippe. 2014. *Les sceaux des archevêques de Rouen: 1129-1229*. MA dissertation on History presented to the University of Caen Basse-Normandie.

Jacquet, Philippe. 2015. 'La tomographie du sceau pour redécouvrir le geste oublié'. In *Empreintes du passé: 6000 ans de sceaux*, ed. Archives départementales de la Seine-Maritime, Musée des Antiquités. Rouen. 282-283.

James, M. R. ed. 1904. *The Western Manuscripts in the Library of Emmanuel College: A Descriptive Catalogue*. Cambridge.

Jenkinson, Hilary. 1924. 'Some Notes on the Preservation, Moulding & Casting of Seals'. *The Antiquaries Journal* 4, 388-403.

Jenset, Gard B. & Barbara McGillivray. 2017. *Quantitative Historical Linguistics: A Corpus Framework*. Oxford.

Jolliffe, I.T. 2002. *Principal Component Analysis*. New York.

Jordan, Richard & Eugene Joseph Crook (trans.). 1974. *Handbook of Middle English Gammar: Phonology*. The Hague.

Kane, George, ed. 1960. *Piers Plowman: The A Version. Will's Visions of Piers Plowman and Do-Well. An Edition in the Form of Trinity College Cambridge MS R.3.14 Corrected from Other Manuscripts, with Variant Readings*. London.

Kane, George & E. Talbot Donaldson, eds. 1975. *Piers Plowman: The B Version. Will's Visions of Piers Plowman, Do-Well, Do-Better and Do-Best. An Edition in the form of Trinity College Cambridge MS B.15.17, Corrected and Restored from the Known Evidence, with Variant Readings*. London.

Kane, George. 1976. 'Conjectural Emendation'. In *Medieval Manuscripts and Textual Criticism*, ed. Christopher Kleinhenz. Chapel Hill NC: 211-26.

Kane, George. 1989. *Chaucer and Langland: Historical and Textual Approaches*. Berkeley.

Karasawa, Kazutomo. ed. 2015. *The Old English Metrical Calendar. Menologium*. Cambridge.

Kaufmann, Henning. 1968. *Ergänzungsband zu Ernst Förstemann Personennamen.* Munich.

Kelly, Thomas Forrest. 1996. *The Exultet in Southern Italy.* New York.

Kemble, John M. ed. 1839-48. *Codex diplomaticus aevi saxonici.* 6 vols. London.

Ker, Neil R. 1957. *Catalogue of Manuscripts Containing Anglo-Saxon.* Oxford.

Ker, Neil R. 1964. *Medieval Libraries of Great Britain: A List of Surviving Books.* 2nd edn. London.

Kestemont, Mike & Folgert Karsdorp. 2020a. 'Estimating the Loss of Medieval Literature with an Unseen Species Model from Ecodiversity'. DA20 Presentation. https://www.youtube.com/watch?v=53WdYlSk2pc

Kestemont, Mike & Folgert Karsdorp. 2020b. 'Estimating the Loss of Medieval Literature with an Unseen Species Model from Ecodiversity'. In *CHR 2020: workshop on computational humanities research, November 18-20, Amsterdam, The Netherlands.* http://ceur-ws.org/Vol-2723/short10.pdf

Kestemont, Mike & Wouter Haverals. 2021. 'UnEditing the Unspoken: hyperdiplomatic digital editions of the remarkable vernacular manuscript collection of the Herne Charterhouse (ca. 1350-1400)'. DA20 Event. https://www.youtube.com/watch?v=WKU1lfcSJUc

Keynes, Simon. 1993. 'A Lost Cartulary of St Albans Abbey'. *Anglo-Saxon England* 22, 253-79.

Kidwell, Carol. 2004. *Pietro Bembo: Lover, Linguist, Cardinal.* Montreal.

Kitson, Peter R. 'When did Middle English Begin? Later than you think!'. In *Studies in Middle English Linguistics*, ed. Jacek Fisiak. Berlin. 221-69.

Kleynhans, Tania and David Messenger. *R-CHIVE Spectral Analysis ToolKit.* http://www.cis.rit.edu/~tkpci/RCHIVE/

Knox, Keith. *Hoku.* www.cis.rit.edu/~ktkpci/Hoku_Software.pdf

Kolar, Jane, Andrej Štolfa, Matija Strlič et al. 2006. 'Historical Iron Gall Ink Containing Documents: properties affecting their condition'. *Analytica Chimica Acta* 555.1, 167-74.

Kraken. http://kraken.re/

Krause, Wolfgang. 1934, 'Die Runeninschrift von Sedschütz'. *Altschlesien* 5. 382–86.

Krawczuk, Wojciech. 2013, 'Runic inscriptions in Poland: do we need an Inventory?'. *Studia Historyczne* 56, 431–5.

Kristeller, Paul Oskar. 1967-92. *Iter Italicum [...] A Finding List of Uncatalogued or Incompletely Catalogued Humanistic Manuscripts of the Renaissance in Italian and other Libraries*. Leiden.

Kristeller, Paul Oskar. 2006. *Iter italicum*. Toronto. https://www.itergateway.org/resources/iter-italicum

Kubouchi, Tadao & Keiko Ikegami, eds. 2005. *The Ancrene Wisse: A Four-Manuscript Parallel Text: Parts 5-8, with Wordlists*. Frankfurt-am-Main.

Kurath, Hans, Sherman M. Kuhn & Robert E. Lewis eds. 2001. *Middle English Dictionary*. https://quod.lib.umich.edu/m/middle-englishdictionary/dictionary [Accessed 7 January 2020]

Kurzweil, R. 2005. *The Singularity is Near: When Humans Transcend Biology*. New York.

Kuskin, William. 2008. *Symbolic Caxton: Literary Culture and Print Capitalism*. Notre Dame.

Lähnemann, Henrike, et al. '#PolonskyGerman #BloggingMSS Presentations'. DA20 Event. https://www.youtube.com/watch?v=lF3WakdugSE

Lee, Haimin. 2019. '15 years of Google Books'. Blog post. https://www.blog.google /products/search/15-years-google-books/

LAEME. See Laing 2013-.

Laing, Margaret & Angus McIntosh. 1995. 'Cambridge, Trinity College, MS 335: its texts & their transmission'. In *New Science out of Old Books: Studies in Manuscripts & Early Printed Books in Honour of A. I. Doyle*, ed. Richard Beadle & A. J. Piper. Aldershot. 14-52.

Laing, Margaret, 2013–. *A Linguistic Atlas of Early Middle English, 1150–1325*. Version 3.2.

http://www.lel.ed.ac.uk/ihd/laeme2/laeme2.html

Land, N. 2011. *Fanged Noumena*. Cambridge MA.

Latour, Bruno. 2005. *Reassembling the Social: An Introduction to Actor-Network-Theory*. Oxford.

Laurent, René & Claude Roelandt. 1997. *Inventaires des collections de matrices de sceaux des Archives Générales du Royaume et de la Bibliothèque Royale*. Brussels.

Lawrie, A. C. ed. 1905. *Early Scottish Charters Prior to 1153*. Glasgow.

Lea, Henry Charles. 1896. 'Ferrand Martinez and the Massacres of 1391'. *The American Historical Review* 12, 209.

Lee, J. B., A. S. Woodyatt & M. Berman. 1990. 'Enhancement of High Spectral Resolution Remote Sensing Data by a Noise-Adjusted Principal Components Transform'. *IEEE Transactions on Geoscience and Remote Sensing* 28.3, 295-304.

Lee, Tim Berners. 2009 (12 March). 'The Next Web'. *TED: Ideas Worth Spreading*.

https://www.ted.com/talks/tim_berners_lee_the_next_web?language=en

[Accessed 9 December 2019]

Levada, Maxim & Tineke Looijenga. 2019. 'A Recently Found Belt Buckle with Rune-like Signs from Ukraine'. *Journal of Archaeology & Ancient History* 25, 2–18.

Lewis, Robert E. & Angus McIntosh. 1982. *A Descriptive Guide to the Manuscripts of the Prick of Conscience*, Medium Ævum Monographs, n.s. 12. Oxford.

Libert, Marc. 2011. 'La numérisation de la collection de moulages de sceaux des Archives générales du royaume de Belgique'. In *Pourquoi les sceaux? La sigillographie, nouvel enjeu de l'histoire de l'art*, ed. Jean-Luc Chassel & Marc Gil. Villeneuve d'Ascq. 117-26.

Libert, Marc. 2017. 'La numérisation en 3D de la collection de matrices de sceaux des Archives générales du Royaume'. In *Le sceau dans les Pays Bas méridionaux, X^e-XVIe siècles. Entre contrainte sociale et affirmation de soi*, ed. Marc Libert & Jean-François Nieus. Brussels. 91-109.

Lin, Yuri, Jean-Baptiste Michel, Erez Lieberman Aiden, Jon Orwant, Will Brockman & Slav Petrov. 2012. 'Syntactic annotations for the Google Books Ngram Corpus'. In *Proceedings of the ACL 2012 System Demonstrations*, ed. Min Zhang. Stroudsburg. 169-74.

Lindner, Thomas. 2016. *200 Jahre Indogermanistik*. Salzburg.

Lindsay, W. A., J. Dowden & J. M. Thomson, eds. 1908. *Charters, Bulls and Other Documents Relating to the Abbey of Inchaffray*. Edinburgh.

Lohr, Steve. 2020 (26 May). 'Remember the MOOCs? After Near-Death, They're Booming'. *New York Times*. https://www.nytimes.com/2020/05/26/technology/moocs-online-learning.html

Looijenga, Tineke 1996. 'Checklist Frisian Runic Inscriptions'. In *Frisian Runes & Neighbouring Traditions*, ed. Tineke Looijenga & Arend Quak, Amsterdamer Beiträge zur älteren Germanistik 45. Amsterdam.

Looijenga, Tineke 2003, *Texts & Contexts of the Oldest Runic Inscriptions*. Leiden.

Looijenga, Tineke. Forthcoming. 'Runic Literacy in North-West Europe, with a Focus on Frisia'. In *The Frisians of the Early Middle Ages*, ed. John Hines & Nelleke IJssennagger-van der Pluijm. Woodbridge.

López Villalba, José Miguel. 1998. 'Normas españolas para la transcripción y edición de collecciones diplomáticas'. *Espacio, Tiempo y Forma. Serie III, H.^{a} Medieval* 11, 285-306.

Love, Nicholas. 2005. *The Mirror of the Blessed Life of Jesus Christ: A Full Critical Edition, based on Cambridge University Library Additional MSS 6578 and 6686, with Introduction, Notes and Glossary*, ed. Michael G. Sargent. Exeter.

Luick, Karl. 1964. *Historische Grammatik der Englischen Sprache*. 2 vols. Oxford.

Lyotard, Jean-François. 1979. *La Condition postmoderne: rapport sur le savoir*. Paris.

Lyotard, Jean-François, Geoff Bennington (trans.) & Brian Massumi (trans.). 1984. *The Postmodern Condition: A Report on Knowledge*. Minneapolis.

M. Tullius Cicero. 1830. *Oratio pro Cn. Plancio*, ed. Eduard Wunder. Leipzig.

Maccoby, Hyam. 1998. 'The Tortosa Disputation, 1413–14, and Its Effects'. In *The Expulsion of the Jews and Their Emigration to the Southern Low Countries (15th–16th C.)*, ed. Luc Dequeker & Werner Verbeke. Leuven. 23-34.

Malone, Kemp. 1930. 'When did Middle English begin?'. *Language* 6, 110-117.

Manni, Domenico Maria. 1739. *Osservazioni istoriche sopra I sigilli antichi de' secoli bassi*. Florence.

Marsden, Richard. ed. 2008. *The Old English Heptateuch & Ælfric's Libellus de veteri testamento et novo*. EETS o.s. 330. Oxford.

Martínez-Dávila, Roger Louis. 2016a. *Deciphering Secrets: Burgos - A Tour of the Medieval City of Burgos (Spain)*.
https://youtu.be/SQDVIhhc8GY

Martínez-Dávila, Roger Louis. 2016b. *DS Burgos - Treasures of the Archive of the Cathedral of Burgos (Spain)*.
https://youtu.be/ZZQHu2WyvvI

Martínez-Dávila, Roger Louis. 2016c. *DS Burgos Muslim Artifacts Become Christian Museo de Burgos UC3M Standard*.
https://youtu.be/3z5s7PuiZEY

Martínez-Dávila, Roger Louis. 2016d. *Deciphering Secrets: Burgos - SILReST: Six Essential Strategies for Advanced Paleography.*
https://youtu.be/N4PgmILwaKw

Martínez-Dávila, Roger Louis. 2016e. *DS Burgos - Learning a Castilian Spanish Script from the 15th Century - Part 1.*
https://youtu.be/aI9nS98H1Is

Martínez-Dávila, Roger Louis. 2016f. *DS Burgos - Learning a Script from the 15th Century - Part 2.*
https://youtu.be/iy4wDa9oXX0

Martínez-Dávila, Roger Louis. 2018. *DS 6 - Burgos - AMP - Manuscript SJ-1-1.*
https://youtu.be/jV5AWmjBddg

Martínez-Dávila, Roger Louis, Séan Perrone, Francisco García Serrano-Nebras & María Martín de Vidales García. 2018. 'Deciphering Secrets of Medieval Cathedrals: Crowdsourced Manuscript Transcriptions and Modern Digital Editions'. *Bulletin for Spanish and Portuguese Historical Studies* 43, 1.2.

Martínez-Dávila, Roger Louis. 2018. *Creating Conversos: The Carvajal-Santa Maria Family in Early Modern Spain.* Notre Dame.

Martínez-Dávila, Roger Louis. 2018. *DS 1 Museo de Santa Cruz Islamic Art Architecture Part 3.*
https://youtu.be/U5xrchhjaQM

Martínez-Dávila, Roger Louis. *Deciphering Secrets: Unlocking the Manuscripts of Medieval Burgos MOOC.*
https://www.edx.org/course/deciphering-secrets-unlocking-the-manuscripts-of-3
https://www.coursera.org/learn/burgos-deciphering-secrets-medieval-spain

Masłej, D. 2016. *Modlitwa Pańska w polskim średniowieczu. Znad staropolskich rękopisów.* Poznań.

Matthews, P.M. 1965-6. *The Old English Life of Saint Pantaleon.* Unpublished University College London MA Dissertation.

Mattingly, W. 2021. 'Leveraging the UnEdition: medieval Latin data augmentation with manuscript reading'. DA21 (UnEdition) Presentation. https://www.youtube.com/watch?v=VxnYE8xkGY0

Mayer, L.S. 1906. *Music, Songs Etc. from an Early XVth cent. MS*. London.

McEwan, John A. 2015. 'The Challenge of the Visual: making medieval seals accessible in the digital age'. *Journal of Documentation*. 71.5, 999-1028.

McEwan, John A. 2017. 'The Past, Present & Future of Sigillography: towards a new structural standard for seal catalogues'. *Archives & Records*, 1-20.

McGann, Jerome J. 1997. 'The Rationale of Hypertext'. In *Electronic Text: Investigations in Method and Theory*, ed. Kathryn Sutherland. Oxford. 19-46.

McGann, Jerome J. 2014. *A New Republic of Letters: Memory and Scholarship in the Age of Digital Reproduction*. Cambridge MA.

McKinnell, John. 1975. 'The Date of *The Battle of Maldon*'. *Medium Ævum* 44, 121-36.

McKitterick, David. 2003. *Print, Manuscript and the Search for Order, 1450–1830*. Cambridge.

McNutt, Genevieve. 'Inaccessible and Inconvenient Archives at the Turn of the Century'. DA20 Presentation. https://www.youtube.com/watch?v=IftgircDu2E

McRoberts, David. 1977. 'The Scottish Catholic Archives, 1560–1978'. *The Innes Review* 28, 59–128.

McSparran, Frances, Paul Schaffner & John Price Wilkin eds. 2006. *Corpus of Middle English Prose & Verse*. https://quod.lib.umich.edu/c/cme/

'Mekel Mach 12'. *Crowley: Digital & Analog Document, Book & Film Scanning & Processing.* https://www.thecrowleycompany.com/scanners-software/product-brands/mekel-technology/microfilm-2/ [Accessed 12 December 2019]

Menéndez-Pidal, Juan. 1918. *Catálogo I: sellos españoles de la Edad Media.* Madrid.

Merritt, Herbert Dean ed. 1959. *The Old English Prudentius Glosses at Boulogne-sur-Mer.* Stanford Studies in Language & Literature 16. Stanford.

Milagros, Maria, ed. 1997. *Vocabulaire international de la diplomatique.* 2nd edn. Valencia.

Millett, Bella. 1994. 'Mouvance and the Medieval Author: re-wditing Ancrene Wisse'. In *Late-Medieval Religious Texts and Their Transmission: Essays in Honour of A.I. Doyle,* ed. A.J. Minnis. Cambridge. 9-20.

Millett, Bella. 2005. 'Editorial Aims and Principles'. In *Ancrene Wisse: A Corrected Edition of the Text in Cambridge, Corpus Christi College, MS 402, with Variants from Other Manuscripts,* ed. Bella Millett. I, xlv–lxi.

Millett, Bella. 2013. 'Whatever Happened to Electronic Editing?'. In *Probable Truth: Editing Medieval Texts from Britain in the Twenty-First Century,* ed. Vincent Gillespie & Anne Hudson. Turnout. 39-54.

Mirador. https://projectmirador.org/ [Accessed 9 December 2019]

Mitchell, Bruce. 1985. *Old English Syntax.* 2 vols. Oxford.

MLGB3. 2009-2014. Richard Sharp & James Willoughby, *Medieval Libraries of Great Britain.* Oxford. http://mlgb3.bodleian.ox.ac.uk/

'Modules'. *Omeka S* https://omeka.org/s/modules/ [accessed 18 December 2019]

Monnerie, Michel. 1994. 'Conserver et préserver les sceaux: dangers et remèdes'. *La Gazette des archives* 164, 44- 61.

'Monuments Men: "Lost Treasure" Featurette'. 2014 (8 January). https://www.youtube.com/watch?v=c9ZpyVJrMaQ [Accessed 9 December 2019]

Morawetz, Luise, Natascha Domeisen, Carolin Gluchowski & Lena Vosding. 2020. 'Blast from the Past and Back to the Future: manuscripts and digitisation'. DA20 Presentation. https://www.youtube.com/watch?v=kaAQ5_pLdRU

Moreno Cifuentes & María Antonia. 2008. 'Estudio de la conservación de la colección'. In *Historia y evolución del sello de plomo: la colección sigilográfica del Museo Cerralbo*, ed. José María de Francisco Olmos & Feliciano Novoa Portela. Madrid. 189-201.

Moretti, Franco. 2007. *Graphs, Maps, Trees: Abstract Models for a Literary History*. New York.

Morreale, Laura and Ben Albritton. 2020. 'Community, Collaboration, and the UnEdition'. DA21 (UnEdition) Presentation. https://www.youtube.com/watch?v=rpL2KY8Bk8E

Morris, Richard, ed. 1863. *The Pricke of Conscience (Stimulus Conscientiae): A Northern Poem by Richard Rolle de Hampole: Copied and Edited from MSS in the Library of the British Museum, with an Introduction, Notes, and Glossarial Index*. Berlin.

Morris, Richard. ed. 1867-8. *Old English Homilies & Homiletic Treatises: First Series*. EETS o.s. 29, 34. London.

Morris, Richard, ed. 1874-93. *Cursor Mundi: A Northumbrian Poem of the XIVth Century*. EETS o.s. 57, 59, 62, 66, 99 & 101. Oxford.

Mortimer, Richard. 1990. 'The charters of Henry II: What are the Criteria for Authenticity?'. In *Anglo-Norman Studies XII: Proceedings of the Battle Conference 1989*, ed. Marjorie Chibnall. Woodbridge.

Morujão, Maria do Rosário Barbosa & Anísio Miguel de Sousa Saraiva. 2002. 'Pergaminhos do Museu de Lamego. Séculos XV a XIX.

Características e conteúdos'. In *Museu de Lamego: pergaminhos*, ed. Agostinho Ribeiro & Alexandra Braga. Lamego. 29-46.

Morujão, Maria do Rosário Barbosa & Anísio Miguel de Sousa Saraiva. 2014. 'O selo: símbolo de representação e de poder no mundo das catedrais portuguesas'. In *O clero secular medieval e as suas catedrais: novas perspectivas e abordagens*, ed. Anísio Miguel de Sousa Saraiva & Maria do Rosário Barbosa Morujão. Lisbon. 205-264.

Morujão, Maria do Rosário Barbosa, Sérgio Lira, Anísio Miguel de Sousa Saraiva & Pedro Pinto. 2014. 'The Portuguese Sigillographic Heritage: SIGILLVM. A new research project on a remarkable & mostly neglected heritage'. In *Heritage 2014: Proceedings of the 4th International Conference on Heritage & Sustainable Development*, ed. R. Amoêda, S. Lira, & C. Pinheiro. Barcelos. 583-90.

Morujão, Maria do Rosário Barbosa. 2001. *Um mosteiro cisterciense feminino: Santa Maria de Celas, séculos XIII a XV*. Coimbra.

Morujão, Maria do Rosário Barbosa. 2012. 'Working with Medieval Manuscripts & Records: paleography, diplomatics, codicology & sigillography'. In *The Historiography of medieval Portugal. c. 1950-2010* ed. José Mattoso. Lisbon. 45-65.

Morujão, Maria do Rosário Barbosa. 2015. 'A imagem do poder no feminino: selos de rainhas portuguesas da Idade Média'. In *Reginae Iberiae: el poder regio femenino en los reinos medievales peninsulares*, ed. Miguel García-Fernández & Silvia Cernadas Martínez. Santiago de Compostela. 89-110.

Morujão, Maria do Rosário Barbosa. 2016a. 'Les pratiques de l'écrit dans les abbayes cisterciennes féminines du Portugal au Moyen Âge'. In *Les pratiques de l'écrit dans les abbayes cisterciennes. XIIe-milieu du XVIe siècle*, ed. A. Baudin & L. Morelle. Paris. 99-111.

Morujão, Maria do Rosário Barbosa. 2016b. 'The SIGILLVM project: the Portuguese sigillographic heritage in the light of a project's results'. In *Heritage 2016: Proceedings of the 5th International Conference on*

Heritage & Sustainable Development, ed. Rogério Amoêda, Sérgio Lira, & Cristina Pinheiro. Barcelos. I, 957-965.

Morujão, Maria do Rosário Barbosa. 2018. '"Esta carta lhe nom guardees se aseellada nom for": selos régios medievais do Arquivo Municipal de Lisboa'. *Cadernos do Arquivo Municipal de Lisboa*. 2ª série. 10, 25-45.

Mountain Scholar. https://mountainscholar.org

Muehlberger, Guenter, Louise Seaward, Melissa Terras, Sofia Ares Oliveira, Vicente Bosch, Maximilian Bryan, Sebastian Colutto et al. 2019. 'Transforming Scholarship in the Archives through Handwritten Text Recognition'. *Journal of Documentation* 75.5, 954–76.

Murchison, Krista A. 2020a. 'Righting and Rewriting History: recovering and analyzing manuscript archives destroyed during World War II'. NWO Project Database.
https://www.nwo.nl/en/projects/viveni191c021

Murchison, Krista A. 2020b.' (Re)collecting the Archive: Recovering Medieval Manuscripts Destroyed During WWII'. DA20 Presentation.
https://www.youtube.com/watch?v=tMpaLrTJQIE

Mustanoja, Tauno F. 1960. *A Middle English Syntax*, Part 1, *Parts of Speech*. Helsiniki.

Nance, Patricia Kay. 1991. *The Vatican Film Library at Saint Louis University, 1950-1990*. Unpublished MA thesis, University of Central Missouri.

Napier, Arthur S. ed. 1883. *Wulfstan*. Sammlung englischer Denkmäler 4. Berlin.

Neddermeyer, Uwe. 1998. *Von der Handschrift zum gedruckten Buch*. 2 vols. Wiesbaden.

Nedoma, Robert. 2003. *Personennamen in südgermanischen Runeninschriften*. Heidelberg.

Nedoma, Robert. 2016. 'The Personal Names on the Loveden Hill Urn & the Watchfield Case Fitting: possibilities & restrictions resulting from the sound system'. *North-Western European Language Evolution* 69, 3–37.

Neidorf, Leonard. ed. 2016. *The Dating of Beowulf: A Reassessment*. Cambridge.

Netanyahu, B. 2002. *The Origins of the Inquisition in Fifteenth Century Spain*. New York.

A New Index of Middle English Verse. See *NIMEV*.

Netz, Reviel, William Noel & Natalie Tehernetska. 2011. *The Archimedes Palimpsest*. New York.

Nielen, Marie-Adélaïde. 2007. 'L'inventaire des sceaux de la Champagne: un projet d'Auguste Coulon'. In *Les sceaux, sources de l'histoire médiévale en Champagne*, ed. Jean-Luc Chassel. Paris. 19-22.

Nielsen, Hans Frede. 1995. 'The Emergence of the *os* & *ac* Runes in the Runic Inscriptions of England & Frisia: a linguistic assessment'. In *Friesische Studien II*, ed. V. F. Faltings, A. G. H. Walker & O. Wilts. Odense. 19–34.

NIMEV. 2004. A *New Index of Middle English Verse*, ed. J. Boffey & A.S.G. Edwards. London.

Noel, William. 2019. 'Sanders Lectures 2018–2019'. Cambridge University Library. https://www.lib.cam.ac.uk/sandars/list-sandars-readers-and-lecture-subjects

Noel, William & Reviel Netz. 2007. *The Archimedes Codex: How a Medieval Prayer Book is Revealing the True Genius of Antiquity's Greatest Scientist*. Cambridge MA.

Nosova, Ekaterina. 2011. 'La collection de moulages de sceaux médiévaux de l'historien russe Nicolai Likhatchev (1862-1936): la provenance et l'usage'. In *Pourquoi les sceaux? La sigillographie, nouvel enjeu de l'histoire de l'art*, ed. Jean-Luc Chassel & Marc Gil Villeneuve d'Ascq. 65-72.

Odenstedt, Bengt. 1990. *On the Origin & History of the Runic Script*. Stockholm.

Okasha, Elisabeth. 2011. *Women's Names in Old English*. London.

Olea, Ricardo A. & George Christakos. 2005. 'Duration of Urban Mortality for the 14th-Century Black Death Epidemic'. *Human Biology* 77.3, 291-303.

Oliphant, Robert T. 1966. *The Harley Latin-Old English Glossary*. Janua linguarum series practica 20. The Hague.

Omeka S.
https://omeka.org/s/
[Accessed 9 December 2019]

Opalińska, M. Forthcoming. 'Continuity & Innovation in Medieval English Prayers'. In *What Words Remember, and Other Stories*, ed. L. Doležalová & J. Čermák. International Medieval Research Series. Turnhout.

Opalińska, M. 2020. 'Mnemonic Verses & Pastoral Care – the Case of MS Aldini 69 from Bibliotheca Universitaria in Pavia'. *Studia Neophilolgica*.

Oswaldi de Corda Opus Pacis. 2001. Corpus Christianorum Continuatio Mediaeualis 179. Turnhout.

Page, R.I. 1999. *An Introduction to English Runes*. 2nd edn. Woodbridge.

Page, Raymond I. 1984. 'On the Transliteration of English Runes'. *Medieval Archaeology* 28, 22–45.

Page, Raymond I. 1999. *An Introduction to English Runes*. 2nd edn. Woodbridge.

Pamuk, Şevket. 2007. 'The Black Death and the Origins of the "Great Divergence" Across Europe, 1300–1600'. *European Review of Economic History* 11.3, 289-317.

Parker on the Web. *Manuscripts in the Parker Library at Corpus Christi College, Cambridge.*
https://parker.stanford.edu/parker/
[Accessed 12 December 2019]

Parkes, M.B. 1983. 'On the Presumed Date & Possible Origin of the Manuscript of the *Ormulum*: Oxford, Bodleian Library, MS Junius 1'. In *Five Hundred Years of Words & Sounds: A Festschrift for Eric Dobson*. Cambridge. 115-27.

Parsons, David N. 1999. *Recasting the Runes: The Reform of the Anglo-Saxon Futhorc*. Uppsala.

Pastoureau, Michel. 1996. 'Les sceaux et la fonction sociale des images'. In *L'image: fonctions et usages des images dans l'Occident medieval*, ed. Jérôme Baschet and Jean-Claude Schmitt. Paris. 275-308.

Patterson, F.A. 1911. *The Middle English Penitential Lyric: A Study & Collection of Early Religious Verse*. New York.

Patterson, Lee. 1985. 'The Logic of Textual Criticism and the Way of Genius: The Kane-Donaldson *Piers Plowman* in Historical Perspective'. In *Textual Criticism and Literary Interpretation*, ed. Jerome McGann. Chicago. 55-91.

Paul, Suzanne (chair). 'The Future Archive'. DA20 Round-Table Debate. https://www.youtube.com/watch?v=GQgBEo4JAIc

Pearce-Moses, Richard. 2005. *A Glossary of Archival & Records Terminology*. Chicago.

Pearsall, Derek. 1985. 'Editing Medieval Texts: Some Developments and Some Problems'. In *Textual Criticism and Literary Interpretation*, ed. Jerome J. McGann. Chicago. 92–106.

Pearsall, Derek. 2013. 'Variants vs. Variance'. In *Probable Truth: Editing Medieval Texts from Britain in the Twenty-First Century*, ed. Vincent Gillespie & Anne Hudson. Turnhout. 197-205.

Pearson, K. 1901. 'On Lines and Planes of Closest Fit to Systems of Points in Space'. *Philosophical Magazine* 2.11, 559–72.

Pechenick, Eitan Adam, Christopher M. Danforth & Peter Sheridan Dobbs. 2015. 'Characterizing the Google Books Corpus: strong limits to inferences of sociocultural & linguistic evolution'. *PloS One* 10(10), e0137041.

Pelle, Stephen. 2015. 'The Date & Intellectual Milieu of the Early Middle English *Vices & Virtues*'. *Neophilologus* 99, 151-66.

Pelteret, David A.E. 1990. *Catalogue of English Post-Conquest Vernacular Documents*. Woodbridge.

People of Medieval Scotland. See PoMS.

Person, H. A. 1953. *Cambridge Middle English Lyrics*. Seattle.

Pettit, Michael. 2016. 'Historical Time in the Age of Big Data: cultural psychology, historical change & the Google Books n-gram viewer'. *History of Psychology* 19, 141-53.

Pfander, H.G. 1936. 'Some Medieval Manuals of Religious Instruction in England & Observations on Chaucer's Parson's Tale'. *Journal of English & Germanic Philology* 35.2, 243-258.

Phillips, Lee. 2016 (25 March), 'Meet the Largest Science Project in US Government History—the James Webb Telescope'. *Ars Technica*. https://arstechnica.com/science/2016/03/meet-the-largest-science-project-in-us-government-history-the-james-webb-telescope

Phillips, William D., & Carla Rahn Phillips. 2016. *A Concise History of Spain*. Cambridge.

Piers Plowman Electronic Archive. piers.chass.ncsu.edu

Polikarpov, Fëdor Polikarpovich. 1704. *Leksikon trejazyčnyj*. Moscow.

Pollock, Sheldon. 2009. 'Future Philology? The Fate of a Soft Science in a Hard World'. *Critical Inquiry* 35, 931-61.

PoMS. 2018. *People of Medieval Scotland: 1093–1371*. Amanda Beam, John Bradley, Dauvit Broun, John Reuben Davies, Matthew Hammond, Neil Jakeman, Michele Pasin & Alice Taylor (with others).
http://www.poms.ac.uk
[accessed 20 February 2020]

Pons-Sanz, Sara M. 2013. *The Lexical Effect of Anglo-Scandinavian Linguistic Contact on English*. Turnhout.

Pope, John C. ed. 1967-8. *Homilies of Ælfric: A Supplementary Collection*. 2 vols. EETS o.s. 259-60. London.

Popper, Karl. 1978. *Three Worlds: The Tanner Lecture on Human Values Delivered at the University of Michigan, April 7, 1978.* https://tannerlectures.utah.edu/_resources/documents/a-to-z/p/popper80.pdf

'Portable Antiquities Scheme'. https://finds.org.uk/

Powell, Susan, ed. 2009, 2011. *John Mirk's Festial, Edited from British Library MS Cotton Claudius A.ii.* 2 vols. EETS o.s. 334-35. Oxford.

Praat: Doing Phonetics by Computer. http://www.fon.hum.uva.nl/praat/

Praeconium. 2013. 'Praeconium Paschale: Exsultet. 2013, April 1'. https://youtu.be/E0lXz3NSmIMT [Accessed 12 December 2019]

Prévost, Agnès. 2008. 'La conservation des sceaux en cire aux Archives nationales'. *Support tracé* 8, 48-61.

Prévost, Agnès. 2011. *Cahier des clauses techniques particulières pour la conservation-restauration des sceaux et objets sigillographiques dans les services publics d'archives.* Paris.

PRO23: Public Record Office: Surrogate Copies of Records. Moulds or Impressions of Seals Deposited for Examination. https://discovery.nationalarchives.gov.uk/details/r/C11940

Pryce, Huw. 2005. 'Culture, Power and the Charters of Welsh Rulers'. In *Charters and Charter Scholarship in Britain and Ireland,* ed. Marie Therese Flanagan & Judith A. Green. Basingstoke. 184–202.

R-CHIVE Spectral Analysis ToolKit. https:// R-CHIVE.com

Rabus, Achim. 2019. 'Recognizing Handwritten Text in Slavic Manuscripts: a neural-network approach using Transkribus'. *Scripta & e-Scripta* 19, 9–32.

Raby, F.E.J. 1959. *A History of Secular Latin Poetry in the Middle Ages.* Oxford.

Rastall, R. 1973. *A Fifteenth-Century Song Book: Cambridge University Library Additional MS 5943.* Leeds.

Rastall, R. 1990. *Two Fifteenth-Century Song Books.* Aberystwyth.

RDF. 2014. 'Resource Description Framework. 25 February 2014'. *W3C Semantic Web*.
https://www.w3.org/RDF/
[Accessed 12 December 2019]

Redin, Mats. 1919. *Studies on Uncompounded Personal Names in Old English*. Uppsala.

Reeve, Michael D. 2011. 'Shared Innovations, Dichotomies, and Evolution'. In *Manuscripts and Methods: Essays on Editing and Transmission. Storia e letteratura. Raccolta di studi e testi 270*. Rome. 55-103.

Reid, R.C. ed. 1960. *Wigtownshire Charters*. Edinburgh.

Reissland, Birgit, Frank Ligterink, Claire Phan & Tan Luu. 'Ink Corrosion: slow changes over time'. 2020. *The Iron Gall Ink Website*.
https://irongallink.org/igi_indexfed1.html
[Accessed 30 January 2020]

Rêpas, Luís Miguel. 2003. *Quando a nobreza traja de branco: a comunidade cisterciense de Arouca durante o abadessado de D. Luca Rodrigues. 1286-1299*. Leiria.

Reynolds, L.D. & Wilson, N.G. 1991. *Scribes and Scholars: A Guide to the Transmission of Greek and Latin Literature*, 3rd edn. Oxford.

Rider, C. 2010. 'Lay Religion & Pastoral Care in Thirteenth-Century England: the evidence of a group of short confessional manuals'. *Journal of Medieval History* 36, 27-34.

Riksantikvarieämbetet. https://www.raa.se/hitta-information/runor

Ringe, Don & Ann Taylor. 2014. *The Development of Old English*. Oxford.

Ringrose, J.S. 2009. *Summary Catalogue of Additional Medieval Manuscripts in Cambridge University Library Acquired before 1940*. Woodbridge.

Ritz-Guilbert, Anne. 2011. 'Les sceaux médiévaux au XVIIe siècle: les dessins de sceaux dans la collection Gaignières, 1642-1715'. In *Pourquoi les sceaux? La sigillographie, nouvel enjeu de l'histoire de l'art*, ed. Jean-Luc Chassel & Marc Gil. Villeneuve d'Ascq. 45-60.

Robson, Glen. 'SimpleAnnotationServer'. Github.
https://github.com/glenrobson/SimpleAnnotationServer
[Accessed 12 December 2019]

Robinson, F. 1994. 'The Rewards of Piety: "Two" Old English poems in their manuscript context'. In *The Editing of Old English*, ed. F. Robinson. Oxford.

Robinson, P. N.d. *The Canterbury Tales Project*.
http://canterburytalesproject.com/CTPresources.html

Rogers, C. ed. 1879–80. *Rental Book of the Cistercian Abbey of Cupar Angus*, 2 vols. London.

Roman, Joseph. 1910. *Les dessins de sceaux de la collection de Gaignières à la Bibliothèque nationale*. Paris.

Romanov, Maxim, Matthew Thomas Miller, Sarah Bowen Savant & Benjamin Kiessling. 2017. 'Important New Developments in Arabographic Optical Character Recognition (OCR)'.
https://arxiv.org/pdf/1703.09550.

Ropa, Anastasija & Edgar Rops. 2020. 'The Elusive Archives of Medieval Livonia'. DA20 Presentation.
https://www.youtube.com/watch?v=pUJdxXiyR3U

Ross, Alasdair. 2006. 'The Bannatyne Club and the Publication of Scottish Ecclesiastical Cartularies'. *The Scottish Historical Review* 85, 202–33.

Roth, Norman. 2002. *Conversos, Inquisition and the Expulsion of the Jews from Spain*. Madison WI.

Rouse, M.A. & R.H. Rouse. 1991. *Authentic Witnesses: Approaches to Medieval Texts and Manuscripts*. Notre Dame.

Rouse, R.H., M.A. Rouse & R.A.B. Mynors. 1991. *Registrum Anglie de libris doctorum et auctorum veterum*. London.

Rousseau, Emmanuel. 2013. *Sceaux médiévaux d'Eure-et-Loir. Catalogue de la collection de sceaux détachés des Archives départementales d'Eure-et-Loir*. Chartres.

Ruiz, Teofilo F. 2011. *Spain's Centuries of Crisis: 1300-1474*. Oxford.

RuneS: Runische Schriftlichkeit. Union of German Academies. www.runesdb.eu

Russell, George & George Kane, eds. 1988. *Piers Plowman: The C Version. Will's Visions of Piers Plowman, Do-Well, Do-Better, and Do-Best. An Edition in the form of Huntington Library MS HM 143, corrected and restored from the known evidence, with variant readings*. Berkeley CA.

Samnordisk runtextdatabas. Uppsala University. www.nordiska.uu.se/forskn/samnord.htm/

Sánchez, Joan Andreu, Verónica Romero, Alejandro H. Toselli, Mauricio Villegas & Enrique Vidal. 2019. 'A Set of Benchmarks for Handwritten Text Recognition on Historical Documents'. *Pattern Recognition* 94, 122–34

Santos, Catarina I.A. & A. Rocha Gonsalves. 2011. 'The Conservation of Papal & Regal Lead Seals'. In *Care & Conservation of Manuscripts 12*, ed. Matthew James Driscoll. Copenhagen. 91-97

Santos, Catarina I. A. & Teresa M. V. D. Pinho e Melo. 2018. 'Haverá química na Sigilografia?'. In *A investigação sobre Heráldica e Sigilografia na Península Ibérica: entre a tradição e a inovação*, ed. Maria do Rosário Barbosa Morujão and Manuel Joaquín Salamanca López. Coimbra. 539-47.

Santos, Catarina. 2008. 'Estudo de selos de chumbo dos séculos XII-XVIII por técnicas de espectrometria de raios X'. Master dissertation on Chemistry applied to Cultural Heritage. Lisbon, Faculty of Sciences.

Sanz Fuentes, María Josefa. 1990. 'La recuperación de tipos sigilográficos y modos de aposición a traves de las formulas documentales'. In *Actas del primer Coloquio de Sigilografía. Madrid, 2 al 4 de abril de 1987*. Madrid. 145-53.

Sargent, Michael G. 2004. 'The Holland–Takamiya Manuscript of Nicholas Love's Mirror of the Blessed Life of Jesus Christ'. In *The Medieval Book and a Modern Collector: Essays in Honour of Toshiyuki Takamiya*, ed. Takami Matsuda, Richard A. Linenthal & John Scahill. Cambridge. 135–47.

Sargent, Michael G. 2013. 'Organic and Cybernetic Metaphors for Manuscript Relations: Stemma–Cladogram–Rhizome–Cloud'. In *The Pseudo-Bonaventuran Lives of Christ: Exploring the Middle English Tradition*, ed. Ian Johnson & Allan F. Westphall. Turnhout. 197-263.

Sargent, Michael G. 2014. 'Bishops, Patrons, Mystics and Manuscripts: Walter Hilton, Nicholas Love and the Arundel and Holland Connections'. In *Medieval English Texts in Transition: A Festschrift Dedicated to Toahiyuki Takamiya on his 70th Birthday*, ed. Simon Horobin & Linne Mooney. Woodbridge. 159–76.

Sargent, Michael G. 2019. 'Affective Reading and Walter Hilton's Scale of Perfection at Syon'. In *Reading and Writing in Medieval England: Essays in Honor of Mary C. Erler*, ed. Martin Chase & Maryanne Kowalski. Woodbridge. 130–49.

Sargent, Michael G. (chair). 2020. 'Inaccessibility and Bias'. DA20 Roundtable Debate.
https://www.youtube.com/watch?v=icfCXTbSiMo

Sawyer, P. H. 1968. *Anglo-Saxon Charters: An Annotated List & Bibliography*. Royal Historical Society Guides & Handbooks 8. London.

Scharer, Anton. 1982. *Die angelsächsische Königsurkunde im 7. und 8. Jahrhundert*. Vienna.

Schoenig, Steven. 2016. *Bonds of Wool: The Pallium & Papal Power in the Middle Ages*. Washington DC.

Schrijver, Peter. 2014. *Language Contact & the Origins of the Germanic Languages*. London.

Scott, W.W. & Matthew Hammond. *Syllabus of Scottish Cartularies: Raine's North Durham* (Coldingham).
https://scottishmedievalcharters.wordpress.com/scottish-cartularies/
'Scottish Medieval Charters: prosopography and digital humanities blog'.
https://scottishmedievalcharters.wordpress.com
[Accessed 20 February 2020]

Seymour, M.C., ed. 2002. *The Defective Version of Mandeville's Travels.* EETS o.s. 319. Oxford.

Scragg, D.G. 1974. *A History of English Spelling.* Manchester.

Scragg, D.G. ed. 1992. *The Vercelli Homilies & Related Texts.* EETS o.s. 300. Oxford.

Scragg, Donald, Alexander Rumble & Kathryn Powell, eds. 2004. *The Manchester Eleventh Century Spellings Database.* Manchester. https://mark-faulkner.com/c11db

Searle, W.G. 1897. *Onomasticon Anglo-Saxonicum.* Cambridge.

Seymour, M.C., ed. 1963. *The Bodley Version of Mandeville's Travels from Bodleian MS e Musæo 116 with Parallel Extracts from the Latin Text of British Museum MS. Royal 13 E.ix. 1963.* EETS o.s. 253. Oxford.

Seymour, M.C., ed. 1973. *The Metrical Version of Mandeville's Travels from the Unique Manuscript in the Coventry Corporation Record Office.* EETS o.s. 269. Oxford.

Seymour, M.C., ed. 2010. *The Egerton Version of Mandeville's Travels.* EETS o.s. 336. Oxford.

Sharpe, Richard, ed. with David X. Carpenter. *The Charters of William II and Henry I: History from the Writs and Charters of Two Norman Kings.* https://actswilliam2henry1.wordpress.com [Accessed 21 February 2020]

Sigilla: Base numérique des sceaux conservés en France. http://www.sigilla.org/

Sigillvm: Corpus dos selos portugueses. http://sigillvm.indexrerum.com/

SIGILLVM PORTVGALLIAE. http://portugal-sigillvm.net/

Sinai Palimpsests Project. 2015–20. www.sinaipalimpsests.org

Singer, Isidore, & Cyrus Adler. 1901. *The Jewish encyclopedia.* New York.

Singleton, Antony. 2005. 'The Early English Text Society in the Nineteenth Century: An Organizational History'. The Review of English Studies n.s. 56, 90-118.

Skeat, Walter, ed. 1867. *The Vision of William Concerning Piers Plowman: The 'Vernon' Text; or Text A.* EETS o.s. 28. London.

Skeat, Walter, ed. 1869. *The Vision of William Concerning Piers Plowman: The 'Crowley' Text; or Text B.* EETS o.s. 38. London.

Skeat, Walter, ed. 1873. *The Vision of William Concerning Piers Plowman: The 'Whitaker' Text; or Text C.* EETS o.s. 54. London.

Skeat, Walter, ed. 1894-1900. *The Complete Works of Geoffrey Chaucer, edited from numerous manuscripts.* 7 vols. Oxford.

Skeat, Walter, ed. 1886. *The Vision or William Concerning Piers Plowman in Three Parallel Texts.* Oxford.

Skeat, Walter, ed. 1885. *Parallel Extracts from Forty-Five Manuscripts of Piers Plowman.* London.

Skeat, Walter, ed. 1886. *Parallel Extracts from Twenty-Nine Manuscripts of Piers Plowman.* 2nd rev edn. EETS o.s. 17. Berlin.

Solopova, Elizabeth (chair). 2020. 'Loss and Dispersal'. *DA20* Round-table debate. https://www.youtube.com/watch?v=FZyhGsHAfkc

Sousa, António Caetano de. 1738. *História genealógica da casa real portuguesa....* Vol. 4. Lisbon.

Spearrit, Placid OSB. 1974. 'The Survival of English Spirituality among the Exiled English Black Monks'. *American Benedictine Review* 25, 287–316

Spencer, H.L. 2015. 'F.J. Furnivall's Last Fling: the Wyclif Society and Anglo-German scholarly relations, 1882–1922'. Review of English Studies n.s. 65, 791-811.

Spencer, H.L. 2015. 'F.J. Furnivall's Six of the Best: the six-text Canterbury Tales and the Chaucer Society'. *The Review of English* 66 (2015), 606–23.

Spurkland, Terje. 2005, *Norwegian Runes & Runic Inscriptions.* Woodbridge.

Spurkland, Terje. 2010. 'The Older *fuþark* & Roman Script Literacy'. *Futhark: International Journal of Runic Studies* 1, 65–84.

Stanford Literary Lab. https://litlab.stanford.edu/

St. Edmund Hall Choir & friends. 2020. 'Compline from the Crypt'. DA20 Event. https://www.youtube.com/watch?v=N5m7tAVGFaA

Stephenson, Neal. 1992. *Snow Crash*. New York.

Stevenson, W.H. 1914. 'Trinoda Necessitas'. *English Historical Review* 29, 689-703.

Stewart, Columba. 2020. 'Showing the Medieval and Early Modern World as it Actually Was: the expansion of the work of HMML (the Hill Museum & Library) beyond monastic libraries in Europe to global preservation of handwritten heritage'. DA20 Keynote Address. https://www.youtube.com/watch?v=YNWEfE8Nyfk

Stringer, Keith J. 2000. 'Acts of Lordship: the records of the lords of Galloway to 1234'. In *Freedom and Authority: Scotland c. 1050–c. 1650. Historical and Historiographical Essays Presented to Grant G. Simpson*, ed. Terry Brotherstone & David Ditchburn. East Linton. 203–34.

Suzuki, Seiichi. 2006. 'The Undley Bracteate Reconsidered: archaeological, linguistic & runological perspectives'. *Anglo-Saxon Studies in Archaeology & History* 13, 31–49.

Sweet, Henry. ed. 1871-2. *King Alfred's West-Saxon Version of Gregory's Pastoral Care*. 2 vols. EETS o.s. 45, 50. London.

Távora, Luís Gonzaga de Lancastre e. 1983. *O estudo da sigilografia medieval portuguesa*. Lisbon.

Taycher, Leonid. 2010. 'Books of the World, Stand up and be Counted! All 129,864,880 of you'. http://booksearch.blogspot.com/2010/08/books-of-world-stand-up-and-be-counted.html

Taylor, Alice. 2015. 'Auditing and Enrolment in Thirteenth-century Scotland'. In *The Growth of Royal Government in the Reign of Henry III*, ed. David Crook & Louise Wilkinson. Woodbridge. 85–103.

Taylor, Alice. 2016. *The Shape of the State in Medieval Scotland: 1124–1290*. Oxford.

Taylor, Pamela. 1995. 'The Early St Albans Endowment & its Chroniclers'. *Historical Research* 68, 119-42.

Taylor, Simon, with Gilbert Márkus. 2006–12. *Place-Names of Fife*, 5 vols. Donington.

Thomas, Gabor. 2000, 'A Survey of Late Anglo-Saxon & Viking-age Strap-ends from Britain'. Unpublished University of London PhD thesis.

Thomas, Sarah E. 2009. 'Rival Bishops, Rival Cathedrals: the election of Cormac, Archdeacon of Sodor, as bishop in 1331'. *The Innes Review* 60, 145–63.

Thomson, J.M., J.B. Paul, J.H. Stevenson & W.K. Dickson eds. 1882–1914. *Registrum magni sigilli regum scotorum: the Register of the Great Seal of Scotland*, 11 vols. Edinburgh.

Thomson, Samuel Harrison. 1934. 'A XIIIth century Oure Fader in a Pavia MS'. *Modern Language Notes* 49.4, 235-237.

Thomson, Samuel Harrison. 1969. *Latin Bookhands of the Later Middle Ages*. Londons.

Thomson, T., ed. 1840. *Liber Cartarum Prioratus Sancti Andree in Scotia*. Edinburgh.

Thomson, T. & C. N. Innes, eds. 1844. *The Acts of the Parliaments of Scotland, vol. 1: 1124–1423*. [Great Britain.]

Treharne, Elaine. 2020. 'Seeing and Been Seen. Digital Manuscripts and their Viewers'. DA20 Keynote Address.
https://www.youtube.com/watch?v=-lJgftAH0cg

Thrope, Samuel. 2020. 'The Curator in the Machine'. DA20 Presentation.
https://www.youtube.com/watch?v=GoBHyZ9Nhug

Timpanaro, Sebastiano. 2005. *The Genesis of Lachmann's Method*, ed. & trans. Glenn W. Most. Chicago.

Tock, Benoît-Michel. 2017. 'L'emprunt de sceau. nord de la France, XIIe et XIIIe siècles'. In *Le sceau dans les Pays Bas méridionaux, X^e-XVIe siècles*.

Entre contrainte sociale et affirmation de soi, ed Marc Libert & Jean-François Nieus. Brussels. 185-199.

Tolkien, J.R.R. & N.R. Ker, eds. 1962. *The English Text of the Ancrene Riwle: Ancrene Wisse [...] Corpus Christi College Cambridge 402*. EETS o.s. 249. Oxford.

Transkribus. www.transkribus.eu

Trovato, Paolo (chair). 2021. 'Birth of the UnEdition'. DA21 (UnEdition) Round-Table Debate.
https://www.youtube.com/watch?v=kIEv_3YP5SQ

Tucker, Joanna. 2019. 'Understanding Scotland's Medieval Cartularies'. *The Innes Review* 70, 135–170.

Tucker, Joanna. 2020. *Reading and Shaping Medieval Cartularies: Multi-scribe Manuscripts and their Patterns of Growth*. Woodbridge.

Turner, James. 2014. *Philology: The Forgotten Origins of the Modern Humanities*. Princeton.

Turner, S. 1840. *History of the Anglo-Saxons*. 6th edn. Vols. 1-3. London.

Upward, Christopher & George Davidson. 2011. *The History of English Spelling*. Chichester.

Verkörperung kommunaler Identität: eine forensische Analyse von Fingerabdrücken auf den Prägungen des mittelalterlichen Speyerer Stadtsiegels.
https://siegel.hypotheses.org/

VIAF: Virtual International Authority File.
https://viaf.org/ [Accessed 6 December 2019]

Vilain, Ambre. 2014. *Matrices de sceaux du Moyen Âge. Département des monnaies, médailles et antiques*. Paris.

Vincent, Nicholas. 2005. 'Regional Variations in the Charters of King Henry II (1154–89)'. In *Charters and Charter Scholarship in Britain and Ireland*, ed. Marie Therese Flanagan and Judith A. Green. Basingstoke. 70–106.

Vocabulaire international de la Sigillographie. 1990, ed. Conseil International des Archives, Comité de Sigillographie. Rome.

Vos, Stacie. 2020. 'The Dark Archive and the Silent Book: histories of access'. DA20 Presentation. https://www.youtube.com/watch?v=sKhRg8Y8BNo

Voynich MS: 17th Century Letters Related to the MS http://www.voynich.nu/letters.html

Warner, Rubie D-N. ed. 1917. *Early English Homilies from the Twelfth Century MS. Vesp D. xiv*. EETS o.s. 152. London.

Watson, Andrew G. 1987. *Medieval Libraries of Great Britain: A List of Surviving Books. Supplement to the Second Edition*. London.

Waxenberger. Gaby. 2006. 'The Representation of Vowels in Unstressed Syllables in the Old English Runic Corpus'. In *Das fuþark und seine einzelsprachlichen Weiterentwicklungen*, ed. Alfred Bammesberger & Gaby Waxenberger. Berlin. 272–314.

Waxenberger, Gaby. 2017. 'How "English" is the Early Frisian Runic Corpus? The evidence of sounds & forms'. In *Frisians & their North Sea Neighbours from the Fifth Century to the Viking Age*, ed. John Hines & Nelleke IJssennagger. Woodbridge. 93–124.

Weever, J. 1631. *Ancient Funerall Monuments within the United Monarchie of Great Britaine*. London.

Western Medieval Manuscripts. Digital Bodleian. https://digital.bodleian.ox.ac.uk/ [Accessed 12 December 2019]

Whitelock, D., M. Brett & C.N.L. Brooke eds. 1981. *Councils & Synods with Other Documents Relating to the English Church, vol. 1, A. D. 871-1204, pt 1, 871-1066*. Oxford.

Whitelock, Dorothy. ed. 1930. *Anglo-Saxon Wills*. Cambridge.

Wicker, Nancy L. & Henrik Williams. 2013, 'Bracteates & Runes'. *Futhark: International Journal of Runic Studies* 3, 151–213.

Wilson, R.M., ed. 1954. *The English Text of the Ancrene Riwle, Gonville and Caius College MS. 234/120*. EETS o.s. 229. Oxford.

Woodhouse, P. G. 2006 [1919]. *My man Jeeves*. London.
Woolf, R. 1968. *The English Religious Lyric in the Middle Ages*, Oxford.
Wree, Olivier de. 1641. *Les sceaux des comtes de Flandre et inscriptions des chartres par eux publiées*. Bruges.
Wright, T. & J. O. Halliwell, eds. 1845. *Reliquiae Antiquae: Scraps from Ancient Manuscripts Illustrating Chiefly Early English Literature & the English language. Vols. I-II*. London.
Younge, George Ruder. 2012. '"Those were good days": representations of the Anglo-Saxon past in the Old English homily on Saint Neot'. *Review of English Studies* 63, 349-69.
Zettersten, Arne & B. Diensberg, ed. 2000. *The 'Vernon' Text of the Ancrene Riwle*, EETS o.s. 310. Oxford.
Zettersen, Arne, ed. 1976. *The English Text of the Ancrene Riwle, Magdalene College Cambridge MS Pepys 2498*. EETS o.s. 274. Oxford.
Zhang, Yating. 2020. 'Digitalization and Practicalities of Medieval English Studies in China'. DA20 Presentation. https://www.youtube.com/watch?v=BEnNMSYF99g
Ziolkowski, Jan. 1990. 'What is Philology?'. *Comparative Literary Studies* 27, 1-12.
Zumthor, Paul. 1972. *Essai de poétique médiévale*. Paris.
Zumthor, Paul. 1992. 'Anonymity and Textual Instability'. In *Toward a Medieval Poetics*, trans. Philip Bennet. Minneapolis MN.
Z[upitza], J[ulius]. 1892. 'Kreuzzauber'. *Archiv für das Studium der neueren Sprachen und Literaturen* 88, 364-65.